World War II
A New History

This is a magisterial new global history of World War II.
Beginning in 1937 with the outbreak of the Sino–Japanese War,
Evan Mawdsley shows how the origins of World War II lay in a
conflict between the old international order and the new, and
then traces the globalisation of the conflict as it swept through
Asia, Europe and the Middle East. His primary focus is on the
war's military and strategic history, though he also examines the
political, economic, ideological and cultural factors which
influenced the course of events. The war's consequences are
examined too, in terms not only of the defeat of the Axis but also
of the break-up of colonial empires and the beginning of the
Cold War. Accessibly written and well-illustrated with maps and
photographs, this compelling new account also includes short
studies of the key figures, events and battles that shaped the war.

Evan Mawdsley is Professor of International History in the
Department of History, University of Glasgow. His previous
publications include *The Russian Civil War* (1983/2008), *The
Soviet Elite from Lenin to Gorbachev: The Central Committee and
its Members, 1917–1991* (with Stephen White, 2000), *The Stalin
Years: The Soviet Union, 1929–1953* (2003) and *Thunder in the
East: The Nazi–Soviet War, 1941–1945* (2005).

World

War II

A New History

EVAN MAWDSLEY

CAMBRIDGE
UNIVERSITY PRESS

CAMBRIDGE UNIVERSITY PRESS
Cambridge, New York, Melbourne, Madrid, Cape Town, Singapore, São Paulo, Delhi

Cambridge University Press
The Edinburgh Building, Cambridge CB2 8RU, UK

Published in the United States of America by Cambridge University Press, New York

www.cambridge.org
Information on this title: www.cambridge.org/9780521608435

First published 2009

Printed in the United Kingdom at the University Press, Cambridge

A catalogue record for this publication is available from the British Library

Library of Congress Cataloguing in Publication data
Mawdsley, Evan, 1945–
World War II : a new history / Evan Mawdsley
    p.   cm.
Includes bibliographical references and index.
ISBN 978-0-521-84592-2 (hbk.) – ISBN 978-0-521-60843-5 (pbk.)
1. World War, 1939–1945.   I. Title.
D743.M366   2009
940.53 – dc22   2009015410

ISBN 978-0-521-84592-2 hardback
ISBN 978-0-521-60843-5 paperback

Contents

Illustrations

Chapter frontispiece illustrations

Maps

Boxes

Acknowledgements

I would like to thank friends and colleagues who, despite being busy with their own research and teaching, took the time to read drafts of this book: Simon Ball, William Buckingham, Alex Marshall, Rana Mitter, Phillips O'Brien, Geoffrey Roberts, Ben Shepherd, and Alan Smith. Their expert advice usually came with the polite proviso that I was free to ignore it, but in almost all cases there was no further doubt in my mind. The anonymous reader for Cambridge University Press also provided encouragement and sensible counsel. Michael Watson, my editor, took special care to look at the book as it progressed and made many helpful suggestions on how to make the concept both digestible and attractive. Any errors, misjudgements, and infelicities remain my own responsibility.

Finally, this book is dedicated to my family – Gillian, Michael, and Robyn. Having put up with a decade of the Eastern Front, they endured yet another World War II book. Despite all this their interest in History has survived.

The heavy cruiser *Augusta*, flagship of the US Asiatic Fleet, anchored in the Huangpu River in August 1937. Shanghai burns in the background at the start of fighting there between the Chinese and the Japanese. After 1941 *Augusta* fought an action-filled war in European waters, escorting convoys to Russia and supporting with her heavy guns the Allied landings in North Africa and France. *Augusta* transported President Harry Truman to and from Europe for the Potsdam Conference in July and August 1945. While sailing home in *Augusta*, eight years after the Shanghai fighting, the President released the news about the atomic attack on Hiroshima.

Introduction

Hitler's war?

What was World War II about? This is a question which is related to – but not quite the same as – 'Why did World War II start?' For many people in Europe and America there is a standard narrative of the war. This is built around the rise and fall of Adolf Hitler or, in a rather broader version, around an extended German attempt to assert hegemony over Europe. This standard narrative begins with Hitler's and Germany's invasion of Poland in September 1939. 'Hitler's war' is certainly a thick strand of the story, and 'Germany's war' gives that strand more bulk, but there were other strands to the mid-century world crisis. World War II was also not simply a defence of liberal democracy (a cause exemplified by President Roosevelt's 'Four Freedoms' and the Allied Atlantic Charter). If the label 'totalitarian' means anything it can be applied as much to Stalin's USSR as to Hitler's Germany, and on the other hand the term hardly fits the Japanese case. The Nationalist China of Jiang Jieshi (Chiang Kai-shek) was hardly a democracy. Of course, the war *was* a struggle for 'freedom' against 'totalitarianism' for many of the participants, and in the end the happy outcome of the conflict (for some) strengthened a version of liberal democracy. But Allied victory did not make liberal democracy a global norm.

World War II was also not in essence only a war for decolonisation and national liberation, although that strand existed – paradoxically – in both Japanese and Chinese propaganda, and the end of formal imperialism was one indirect outcome of the global struggle. Nevertheless empires of a new type arose after 1945. Another strand was a 'race war' between (or against) ethnic groups, not only in the sense of the terrible and unique Nazi 'war against the Jews', but also of the struggle between 'Germanic' peoples and

Slavs, and in Asia between 'Europeans' and 'non-Europeans'. 'Racial' assumptions played a remarkably large part in top-level war planning for both sides.

The new order and the old

If we really want to look at the war from the broadest perspective then Axis war aims need to be taken at face value. The simplest but most fundamental expression of those aims was in the treaty that formally created the Axis 'alliance', the Tripartite Pact (the *Dreimächtepakt*). This was signed publicly in Berlin in September 1940 and included the following statement of aims:

The governments of Germany, Italy and Japan, consider it as a prerequisite of a lasting peace that each nation of the world receive the space [*Raum*] to which it is entitled. They have, therefore, decided to stand by and co-operate with one another in regard to their efforts in the greater East Asia space and in the European region respectively wherein it is their prime purpose to establish and maintain a new order of things [*eine neue Ordnung*] calculated to promote the mutual prosperity and welfare of the peoples concerned.[1]

The talk of 'lasting peace' was deeply hypocritical. The pressure for a global 'new order of things', however, was an essential concept for understanding the unstable global system before and during the war.

A new order presupposes an old order, an existing international system. I would locate this, not very originally, in the Paris Peace Treaties of 1919 and the Washington Treaties of 1921–2. (Both sets of treaties will be discussed at greater length in Chapter 1.) The Paris treaties (especially the Treaty of Versailles) blamed Germany for World War I, burdened it with financial reparations, and stripped it of territory and colonies. Hitler and many other Germans raged against the Versailles *Diktat*. But there was more to the 1919 Paris treaties than this. The treaties also reordered Central Europe after the collapse of Austria-Hungary and Ottoman Turkey (and, implicitly, after the crisis of the Russian Empire brought about by the Bolshevik Revolution); an international order was created based, however imperfectly, on the principles of ethnic self-determination. The Paris treaties also perpetuated the advantageous pre-1914 geopolitical and economic position of the British Empire and France, both in Europe and in the world as a whole. They provided a mechanism, the League of Nations, by which that status quo was to be maintained. Italy and Japan, as Allied powers in 1918, benefited from the Paris treaties: Italy won territory from Austria-Hungary and Turkey, and the Japanese received many of the German Pacific colonies. But Britain and France took much more.

What the Paris treaties were for Europe the Washington Treaties were for Asia. The agreements signed in Washington in 1921–2 guaranteed the post-1918 status quo in Asia and the balance of naval forces there. The Western countries (especially Britain) and Japan would keep their Asian colonies, but China would henceforth be guaranteed as a national state, and outside powers were not to seize any more of its territory. There was even more wishful thinking here than in the European treaties, as China was in a condition of great turmoil, especially following the abdication of the last child emperor in 1912.

Fifteen years later, in the 1930s, the future Axis powers envisaged the over-turn of this existing Paris/Washington global order. The leaders of these states had considerable public support for their challenge to the system. This was based in part on the broadly perceived unfairness of the actual treaties. It also came from a heightened sense of national priorities, with the rise of extreme and mass-based nationalist parties. Also important was the vulnerability of the international economic system, the apparent decadence of the 'old order' great powers (and the USA), and the peril of Soviet Communism. All these things were revealed or enhanced by the global economic Depression that began in the late 1920s.

World War II itself eventually lined up those states that wanted to defend the old order – a group which, surprisingly, eventually included Stalin's USSR – against those that wanted to completely challenge it, the 'haves' versus the 'have-nots'. In the end, in 1945, the term 'a new world order' was used by American commentators – fifty years before President George Bush Sr employed it – to describe a world quite different from what had been expected either by the 'Versailles powers' or by the advocates of the Axis 'new order'. This 'new world order' was not the cause for which various states went to war in 1937–41, nor was it an order of things which the chief beneficiaries, the United States and the USSR, had really expected in the late 1930s.

Context and perspective

Whichever strand is followed, and however the relationship between the old order and the new is interpreted, historical context is extremely important. The war cannot be understood without bearing in mind developments of the fifty years before it began, especially the completion of the European empires, the rise of mass politics in Europe and America, World War I, the Russian Revolution, and the Great Depression. These are outlined in Chapter 1. And this is also a book looking back seventy years. The Cold War has ended, the Soviet Union and its satellite system have broken up, Communism is finished as an international force, Germany has been reunified and Yugoslavia shattered. China and perhaps India have emerged as superpowers. The place of World War II in the history of the twentieth century is clearer. The final chapter (Chapter 14) will look at the extent to which the world after 1945 was 'made' by the war years, and the extent to which it was different from what had gone before. This is not just a new history of World War II for the 11 September 2001 / Gulf War II generation, although there are parallels for them. It may come as a surprise that terms like 'ethnic cleansing', 'regime change', 'clash of civilisations', 'weapons of mass destruction', 'new world order', 'shock and awe', even 'martyrdom', had a relevance for the 1930s and 1940s as much as for the century which followed.

Another current term which has great relevance now and then is 'globalisation'. As an historian, rather than a social scientist, this is not a concept with which I am wholly comfortable. A textbook definition is 'the process of increasing interconnectedness between societies such that events in one part of the world more and more have effects on peoples and societies far away'.[2] To historians, globalisation has been going on since the 1500s. We might argue that in World War II the 'new order' powers did not want (as a realistic medium-term goal) to establish global domination. What they wanted was an intermediate state of regional hegemony ('the space to which [each nation] is entitled', to quote the Tripartite Pact). They were, with hindsight, 'premature anti-globalists'. The 'old order' powers, too, were defending their own kind of regionalism.

Europe and Asia

But the larger point is that the challenge to the old order, and the war that followed that challenge, was global in scale. A basic argument of this book is that the war in Asia (and the Pacific) was as important as the war in Europe. The Asian war does not fit easily into the 'rise and fall of Hitler' narrative. The concept of the 'new order' was used by the Japanese Prime Minister Prince Konoe in an important statement of December 1938: 'Japan, China, and Manchukuo [a Japanese puppet state in northeastern China] will be united by the common aim of establishing a new order in East Asia and of realising a relationship of neighbourly amity, common defence against Communism, and economic co-operation'.[3] It is true that Nazi Germany's drive for hegemony in Europe was not *caused* by the (earlier) crisis in Asia – except that Hitler hoped that Britain's resistance would be weakened by Japanese threats to its Asian Empire. And it is also true that Japan would not have attacked Britain and America in December 1941 without the stunning events in Europe – German conquest of the Western European mainland and the Wehrmacht's early successes in the war against the USSR. But the Japanese also, and more fundamentally, would not have taken their decision to attack had they not been fighting a dragged-out, unwinnable, war in China since 1937.

The intention is not so much to privilege Asia as to see World War II as a global whole, both in its causes and in the way in which it was fought. Again, the September 1940 Tripartite Pact, signed between Germany, Italy, and Japan, provides an important perspective. Without mentioning the USA by name the Axis powers endeavoured to deter that country's entry into the war. Japan, Germany, and Italy undertook 'to assist one another with all political, economic, and military means' if one of them was 'attacked by a power at present not involved in the European war or in the Chinese–Japanese conflict'. President Franklin Roosevelt recognised the same holistic reality when he wrote to one of his diplomats in early 1941:

I believe that the fundamental proposition is that we must recognize that the hostilities in Europe, in Africa, and in Asia are all parts of a single world conflict. We must, consequently, recognize that our interests are menaced both in Europe and in the Far East. We are engaged in the task of defending our way of life and our vital national interests wherever they are seriously endangered. Our strategy of self-defense must be a global strategy.[4]

When did World War II begin?

Following on from the broad – global – geographical scope of this book is its chronological scope. If the war is taken to be as much Asian as European, and if it was in essence about the new order versus the old order, then it began in July 1937 and not in September 1939 (and not in June 1941 or December 1941). This is a history of what might be called the 'long' World War II (i.e. a war running from 1937 to 1945).

This early start requires a few words of justification. It is a fact that China and Japan were continuously at war from July 1937 until August 1945. While neither China nor Japan formally declared war in 1937 – Japan referred until 1941 to the China 'Incident' – in *real* terms one of the most bloody conflicts of the twentieth century was taking place and would continue until after Hiroshima. In contrast, September 1939 was just a way station in an existing global conflict. In that month 'only' Britain, France, Germany, and Poland entered a state of war, and their conflict was a regional war essentially confined to a small part of Europe. China and Japan had already been at war for two years, and Russia and America would not enter the war until 1941. As a more basic point, I start in 1937 because (as mentioned above) the war was about the all-out assault on a particular view of the world order, which applied to both Europe and Asia. The year 1937 saw the first full-scale armed challenge to that order (or – arguably – the first armed *response* to such a challenge), by the Chinese leader Jiang Jieshi.

If we are going back to 1937, why not go back to other armed struggles of the early and mid 1930s? Indeed why not see a thirty years war – for and against Germany hegemony – from 1914 to 1945? This becomes something of a historical parlour game, and we have to draw the line somewhere. The conflict in northeast China (Manchuria/Manchukuo) in 1931–2 and the Italian invasion of Ethiopia in 1935–6 were indeed challenges to the existing international order. My argument would be that these were events that had a beginning and an end, and that the end came before the continuous fighting of World War II. The course of the Spanish Civil War of 1936–9 does fall within the dates of my extended 1937–45 time span. That war involved advisors and fighting 'volunteers' from a number of European countries – and even a few Americans. It was portrayed (like the later struggle in Europe) as a struggle between Fascism and democracy. However, the war in Spain was essentially an internal struggle and it was resolved, for better or worse, six months before the outbreak of open international armed conflict in the rest of Europe. Thereafter Spain (unlike China and Japan) would play no major direct part in the global conflict. I would also, perhaps contrarily, argue that the Soviet–Japanese border incidents of 1938 and 1939 (Lake Khasan and Khalkhin Gol) and the Soviet–Finnish War of 1939–40 *do* fall within the scope of World War II, even though they came well before the German attack on the USSR in June 1941 and the beginning of the 'Great Patriotic War'.

Grand strategy

A short book on big events needs to know its limits. I am setting out to give an overview of the war and indeed, in geographical terms, a rather broader overview than some other general histories have attempted. Inevitably it is a bird's-eye view. Many themes are left out – World War II as a direct human experience, the historiography and various national perceptions of the war, war and culture, the home front and the domestic implications of war. It is not that I consider these things uninteresting, irrelevant, or unimportant. Rather they are too complex to be dealt with adequately in a short book. This is also not a history of the world in the late 1930s and the 1940s; it is a history of World War II.

The eminent Danish historian of the European Resistance, Jörgen Hæstrup, once took the British military pundit Basil Liddell Hart to task for his approach to history. Liddell Hart was the author of the *History of the Second World War*, published in 1970:

His description [Hæstrup complained] reminds one of an intellectual analysis of a game of chess, where white beats black because black omits to use his knight at a moment when this would have been possible, while white, however, gets the upper hand through a bishop-castle combination in the final movements . . . There is no room for imponderabilia in this logical analysis.[5]

Hæstrup's immediate complaint – a fair one – was that Liddell Hart's 750 pages almost completely ignored the Resistance. And yet Hæstrup was also criticising a way of looking at the war that was too abstract.

Even so, one valid approach to the history of World War II *is* to see it as something like a game of chess. World War II, however, was played not just by white and black but by a 'rainbow' of participants (to use an American war-planning term). The military and civilian leaders on either side did not know how many pieces the opponent had or where they were. The players of this game did not even know what their own pieces could do, let alone those of the enemy. Rather than beginning the game with the full set of sixteen pieces, they had to think many moves ahead (three or four years in the real world) when new pieces would become available, and they had to manage short-term and long-term advantages.

The mid-twentieth century world crisis was, in the end, a war, and this book is unapologetically about military operations. The emphasis is on what is sometimes called 'grand strategy', and the book is about the conduct of affairs by statesmen and generals. The book also takes World War II to have been at this level, for all sides, a rational activity (a 'game of chess'); no government entered the war with the aim of defeat. All the national elites involved had objectives – geopolitical, economic, ideological (including racial) – which they planned to achieve, or they had assets (and sometimes values) which they hoped to defend. Leaders made calculations about means and ends. These calculations were wise or unwise. The means utilised were often terrible and the ends desired sometimes ignoble or even inhuman. The decision-making process was much affected by flaws in national power structures, by misperception, by wildly differing cultural assumptions (of 'self' and 'other'), and by very different ideologies. But there was always a logic which the historian must attempt to recreate and assess.

The 'Tower of Empire' at the 1938 Empire Exhibition, held in the summer of the Munich crisis. The Exhibition was an important symbol of how other countries saw the Empire, and how Britain saw itself in the late 1930s, before the outbreak of the war with Germany. The event took place in Glasgow, and was a successor to the 1924 Empire Exhibition held at Wembley in London. Although now overshadowed by the Paris International Exposition of 1937 and the New York World's Fair of 1939–40, the 1938 Exhibition was a major event. The British colonies scattered across the globe were represented by pavilions; that of Canada was the largest. Other buildings showcased British economic achievements. The next great exhibition, in summer 1951, would be the Festival of Britain. Held on London's South Bank, it marked the end of post-war Austerity. By that time most of the great Empire would be gone, lost to Britain in the conflagration.

The world in 1937

Timeline

1919	Paris Peace Conference; Treaty of Versailles
1919	Creation of the Communist International (Comintern)
1921–2	Washington Conference on China and the Pacific
1927	Start of Soviet first Five-Year Plan
1929	Wall Street Crash (Great Depression begins)
1931	Mukden incident; Japan begins seizure of Manchuria
1933	NSDAP comes to power in Germany
1936	Anti-Comintern Pact between Germany and Japan
1937	Marco Polo Bridge incident; beginning of second Sino–Japanese War

The background to World War II

This chapter looks at three interrelated questions. What was the relative strength – real and perceived – of the major powers at the end of the 1930s? What factors – economic, political, diplomatic, historical – led the governments of those states to enter the war? And what were the expectations about the nature of a future war?

The two world wars developed very differently. World War I began with the 'big bang' of August 1914. Five great powers – Austria-Hungary, Germany, Russia, France, and the British Empire – all suddenly became involved in a general war. There is only one crisis for historians to consider. The assassination of Archduke Franz Ferdinand at Sarajevo can be seen as a causal event, or the way in which the five powers managed or mismanaged the happenings of one month. What we think of as World War II, in contrast, did not begin with one burst of conflict. Japan and China went to war in July 1937 after the Marco Polo Bridge incident. A second war began in Europe two years later, in September 1939; Germany invaded Poland, and Britain and France declared war on Germany. Italy entered the conflict in May 1940 and extended the fighting into the Mediterranean. A whole year passed before Germany invaded the USSR and opened what was to be the bloodiest theatre of European conflict. Then it was six more months before Japan attacked Britain and the United States. The last significant twist in World War II would not occur until eight years after the Marco Polo Bridge incident, when the USSR attacked Japan in August 1945. To understand the rolling development of the conflict, we need to look broadly at the international situation, and at the interests and attitudes of the individual states concerned.

The belligerents:
(1) Giants: the British Empire, China, and Russia

The next three sections aim to sketch the main belligerents in World War II, without considering the political or ideological dimensions (which will be covered later in the chapter). In 1939 – as in 1914 – the British Empire was the largest political entity on the planet. It had a population of some 530 million and an area of 13 million square miles. The concepts of 'empire' and 'imperialism' are now politically incorrect, but in the 1930s they were in common usage. An Empire Exhibition was held in 1938 (see chapter frontispiece); the main British overseas airline was 'Imperial Airways'; the head of the British Army throughout World War II was the 'Chief of the Imperial General Staff' (CIGS).

Britain commanded a huge empire, with the Dominions of Canada, Australia, South Africa, and New Zealand. Under more direct control of London was the huge asset of India, as well as most of sub-Saharan Africa, much of Southeast Asia, Hong Kong, and territories in the West Indies and the South Pacific. Victory in World War I had made the British Empire larger than ever. Territory was gained at the expense of the old German overseas territories in Africa and the Pacific, but especially from the defunct Ottoman Empire (Turkey). Britain now held a number of strategic 'mandated territories', including Transjordan and Palestine, which it ruled on behalf of the League of Nations. It also exercised close control over nominally independent countries such as Egypt and Iraq. The Royal Navy was the largest naval force in the world, with an extraordinary tradition. British possessions, and bases like Gibraltar, Malta, Alexandria, and Singapore, gave the Royal Navy a global strategic reach. Britain also possessed what was, by a considerable margin, the world's largest merchant navy.

The 'core' population, of metropolitan Britain, was, however, only 48 million, less than a tenth of the population of the Empire. The largest component of the Empire was India, with about 350 million people. The Indian Army would peak during the war at 3 million personnel, all volunteers, and it would play an essential part in the Middle East and Southeast Asia. Nevertheless the main part of the British Empire's fighting forces, especially in Europe and the Mediterranean, and much of the industrial labour, would have to come from 'European' troops and civilians. Before 1938 the British Army was very small, largely a colonial police force that was unsuitable for continental warfare in Europe.

The 'white' Commonwealth did significantly increase Britain's power. Canada had a population 10 million, Australia 7 million, and New Zealand 1.5 million. South Africa added a population of 2 million people of European descent – and 7.5 million non-Europeans. All four regions had enjoyed since the 1920s (legally since the Statue of Westminster of 1931) the status of self-governing 'Dominions'. The Dominions were undoubtedly a great asset to Britain when war came, both providing manpower in critical

Box 1 | The major powers: relative strength

A   Population in 1938 (millions)

	Home territory	Overseas colonies	Total
British Empire	47.5	483.8	531.3
China	411.7	0	411.7
USSR	168.9	0	168.9
USA	130.5	17.8	148.3
Japanese Empire	71.9	59.8	131.7
French Empire	42.0	70.9	112.9
Germany	75.4	0	75.4
Italian Empire	43.4	8.5	51.9

British overseas colonies includes self-governing 'dominions' [30.0 million].
Japanese overseas colonies includes Manchuria/Manchukuo. 'Germany' includes
Austria [6.8 million].)

B   Gross domestic product in 1938 ($ billion)

Gross domestic product (GDP) is the total market value of goods and
services produced (excluding income from abroad). The figures here
were compiled by the British economic historian Mark Harrison, using
international dollars and 1990 prices.

USA	$800.3	China	$320.5
British Empire	$683.3	French Empire	$234.1
USSR	$359.0	Japanese Empire	$232.3
Germany	$375.6	Italian Empire	$143.4

(From Mark Harrison, ed., *The Economics of World War II: Six Powers in
International Comparison* (Cambridge: Cambridge University Press, 1998),
pp. 3, 7. USSR population in A above is from the 1939 census.)

theatres and especially in extending Britain's power across the globe. Even
in numerical terms, however, the British population plus that of the 'white'
Commonwealth was still smaller than that of Germany. Furthermore, many
of their 'kith and kin' had settled in very distant lands, and the Dominions complicated the making of foreign and strategic policy. Despite the
undoubted bonding experience of World War I, they had their own security
priorities. As for Britain's other possessions, local nationalism was growing
in the 1920s and 1930s, but the British rulers were able to cultivate local

elites, and they were adept at playing one local ethnic group off against another.

The British Empire was economically very powerful, with a gross domestic product (GDP) twice that of Germany. British industrial production had, however, been overtaken by that of the United States at the turn of the century, and it was matched by that of Germany. The City of London was still a world financial centre, although it no longer occupied the dominant position it had held before 1914. Britain still had huge investments in Asia and Africa. The imperial system guaranteed British factories markets and raw materials. It helped Britain to survive the Great Depression of the late 1920s and the 1930s with less damage than that suffered by other countries.

The British Empire was what diplomatic historians describe as a 'satisfied power'. Its leaders did not want to expand their immense territory any further, and were content to defend the status quo. Nevertheless, the coming war was in large measure to be about this world Empire. Many foreign leaders believed Britain was too weak to defend its vast territory, certainly against multiple challenges. Japanese and Italian statesmen coveted strategic parts of the Empire, and China wished rid of British outposts and influence. German radical nationalists wanted to copy the British Empire, although Hitler looked to a continental version within Eurasia, rather than an overseas one. The Communist government in the USSR was committed to the overthrow of imperialism, and until 1933 Britain was its greatest enemy. The United States of America, which had broken away from British rule in 1776, wanted free access to the resources and markets of the Empire.

In contrast to our view from the early twenty-first century, very few Europeans in the 1920s and 1930s would have considered China to be a world power. And yet in population terms China was the second of the world's giants, after the British Empire. There were some 410 million people living in Chinese-ruled territory in 1937, more than a sixth of the world's inhabitants. Despite minorities and dialects the population was relatively homogeneous, compared to the British Empire. China had an area in 1937 of about 3.3 million square miles; the country was larger than the continental USA. It displayed the benefits and pitfalls of huge size, especially with its undeveloped railways and roads. It was too large for any foreign conqueror to assert full control over, but equally it was hard for any Chinese central

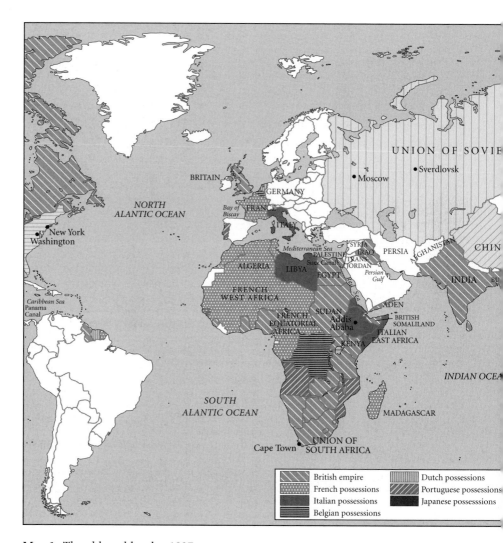

Map 1   The old world order, 1937

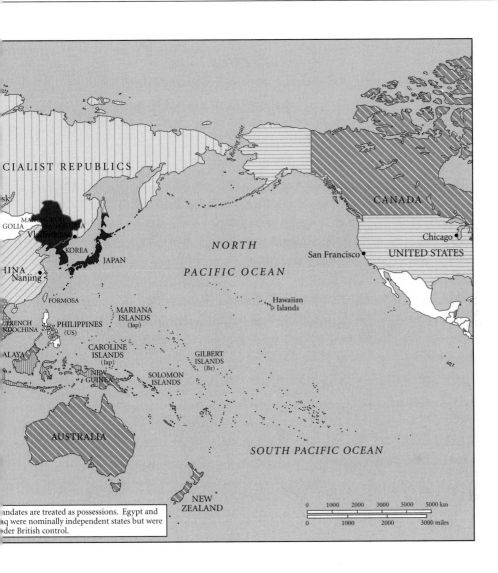

CIALIST REPUBLICS

sk

GOLIA

MANCHURIA

Vladivostok

KOREA

CHINA
Nanjing

JAPAN

FORMOSA

FRENCH
INDOCHINA

PHILIPPINES
(US)

MARIANA
ISLANDS
(Jap)

ALAYA

CAROLINE
ISLANDS
(Jap)

NEW
GUINEA

SOLOMON
ISLANDS

GILBERT
ISLANDS
(Br)

NORTH

PACIFIC OCEAN

San Francisco

UNITED STATES

Chicago

CANADA

Bering Strait

Hawaiian
Islands

AUSTRALIA

SOUTH PACIFIC OCEAN

NEW
ZEALAND

andates are treated as possessions. Egypt and
q were nominally independent states but were
der British control.

| 0 | 1000 | 2000 | 3000 | 5000 | 5000 km |
| 0 | | 1000 | | 2000 | 3000 miles |

government to administer or to defend. The total GDP was significant, but this national income was very low in per capita terms.

Taking a long-term perspective, China was in flux due to internal structural problems and the toxic external challenge of European imperialism. The central government was progressively weakened in the latter half of the nineteenth century, and it collapsed in 1912, when the Manchu dynasty was overthrown. The worst of outside exploitation seemed over in the 1920s, if only because the great powers could not agree among themselves about how to take advantage of China. By the early 1930s the Nationalist government in Nanjing (Nanking) was more powerful than any central authority in China had been for many decades. Nevertheless regional leaders ('warlords') still ran much of the country and a civil war was being fought between the Nationalist government and the Communists. The Chinese armed forces were weak and technologically backward. Foreign troops – European, Japanese, and American – were stationed in some numbers on Chinese soil.

About 8 million Chinese lived abroad, especially in Southeast Asia, but there was no pressure to incorporate them. China did not want to expand, and in the 1930s it was as much a satisfied power as Britain; the Nanjing government had trouble enough keeping control of distant provinces. The Nationalists did not, however, accept the status quo. They wanted to reduce the influence that foreigners, beginning with the British, had built up in China and in its borderlands over the past century.

The Union of Soviet Socialist Republics (USSR) came next in terms of population after the British Empire and China – there were nearly 170 million Soviet citizens according to the 1939 census. Remarkably, despite the great revolution of 1917 and the civil war and foreign intervention that followed it, 'Soviet' territory in 1922 was not much different from the Russian Empire of 1914. Some losses were suffered in the west, but the USSR took in a vast Eurasian space of 8.5 million square miles, twice that of China. An influential international school of 'geopolitics' (that of Halford Mackinder) saw the central part of the Soviet Union as the 'heartland', the new pivot of world power.

Only half the population of the USSR were ethnic Russians, and the country was formally a 'union' of independent 'soviet socialist republics', set up 1922. Ten republics existed in 1936. The vulnerability of the 'union' is clearer now, after the 1991 break-up of the USSR, than it was in the 1920s and 1930s. Even so, unlike in the British Empire, the dominant ethnic group of the USSR made up the largest proportion of the population, perhaps 65–70 per cent if the Slav Ukrainians and Belorussians are grouped with the ethnic Russians. There were also a considerable number of 'Russianised' non-Slavs – an outstanding example being the Georgian Iosif Dzhugashvili-Stalin.

Unlike China, the USSR had a strong central government; the country did not, after the early 1920s, suffer from warlordism or civil war. Before 1917 an increasingly centralised Tsarist system had been run from St Petersburg, and the Communist government – based from 1918 in the inland city of Moscow – largely copied that. As Stalin privately put it: 'The Russian tsars did a great deal that was bad . . . But they did one thing that was good – they amassed an enormous state, all the way to Kamchatka [in eastern Siberia]. We have inherited that state.'[1] Like the Japanese in Asia, the Russians were quick to pick up the key elements of technology and administrative structure that they needed for great-power status.

Economically, Russia was in a unique position. With a calculated GDP of some $360 billion it was the third-biggest economy, but this was low in per capita terms. Nevertheless the country had been developed rapidly since the 1890s, and from the later 1920s its new Communist rulers embarked on a full-scale industrialisation programme. The Soviet Five-Year plans for economic development, beginning in 1927, were with hindsight one of the most important background events to World War II.

The Soviet Union was in many senses a 'satisfied power'. The country had more in common with Britain and China (or the United States) than it did with Germany or Japan. Nearly all ethnic Russians lived in the USSR. The continental expanse of the country contained nearly all the resources required. The 'grievances' of the USSR were more abstract. On the one hand the Soviet leaders in Moscow felt – like the Chinese leaders in Nanjing – some claim to 'historic' and strategic territories that had been lost in previous decades. In the Russian case this meant losses in 1905 in Asia and, more importantly, losses in 1918 in Europe. There was also an interest in the parts of Poland that were inhabited by Belorussians and Ukrainians – Slavs but not ethnic Russians. Other motivations of Moscow's rulers were more abstract and ideological, and will be considered later – with the international Communist movement.

Like the British Empire and China, the extent, ethnic diversity, and resources of the USSR made it potentially vulnerable to 'internal' centrifugal forces and to predatory outsiders. Like the Chinese, the rulers of Russia suffered from understandable fears about 'capitalist' or 'imperialist' encirclement. Unlike the Chinese and British, the Soviet rulers had the means and ruthlessness to crush any internal opposition. As well, by the late 1930s, they possessed a military force able at least to screen the entire perimeter of their state.

The belligerents: (2) The United States and Japan

The United States and Japan were fourth and fifth in order of population. The United States would emerge as by far the most powerful country in the world in 1945. Compared with the traditional European 'powers' – like metropolitan Britain and France, or like Germany and Italy – the United States had a large population of 130 million (more than one and a half times that of Germany, three times the home population of Britain, France or Italy), and a much larger territory, 3.1 million square miles taking just the continental USA (excluding Alaska and other overseas territories).

Hitler would later belittle the 'mongrel' nature of the American population. Unlike the 'giants', however, the USA had a generally homogeneous, English-speaking, population – although 13 million African-Americans, mostly still living in the southern states, remained in a special, segregated. category. The federal political system was decentralised, with 48 'united' states. All the same, powerful national traditions existed, and the Civil War of 1861–5 had ensured a unique but robust political cohesion.

America had created its own overseas colonial empire at the end of the nineteenth century, largely as a result of the war with Spain. Like the empires of other imperial 'latecomers', this had a haphazard character. The Hawaiian Islands (annexed in 1898) and Alaska (purchased from Russia in 1867) allowed Washington to project its power into the central and northern Pacific Ocean. Other parts of the American empire were in military terms more of a liability, especially the Philippines.

The United States had much the highest GDP in the world, even in the Depression years, and the American wealth was even more remarkable in per capita terms. The country was largely self-sufficient in raw materials. At the turn of the century it had taken the lead in industrial production, and after 1914–18 Wall Street had become a centre of world finance.

It is often pointed out that in 1939 the army of the United States was smaller than that of Belgium. America also possessed no bases on the eastern side of the Atlantic, and had no way of militarily influencing events in Europe. However, the US Navy and the British Royal Navy were the two largest navies in the world, and, with its late 1930s warship construction programmes, America would soon outpace Britain. The American merchant fleet, the second largest, second in size only to Britain's, was also a considerable asset for projecting power.

America, like the 'giants', was essentially a status quo power. It did not want an increase in its formal empire, and in 1934 Congress even took the important decision to set its most populous – and exposed – colony, the Philippines, on the path to independence. As with the USSR, there was a degree of anti-colonial rhetoric in the United States, although in this case it was about the 'open door', gaining access for all states (and for American business) to the markets of the world. The government in Washington had the luxury of choosing when and where to fight. Distance from Europe and Asia gave the American population a plausible alternative of isolation, and the democratic tradition made it harder to commit the nation to war.

Japan was in historical terms the most remarkable of the 'powers', as it had only emerged as an international force at the turn of the century. Japan was the only part of Asia able to hold its own against the European imperialists. The Japanese home islands were small – compared to China or Russia – and relatively rugged. They were also largely lacking in key industrial resources like coal and oil, and had limited iron ore. Nevertheless the area of metropolitan Japan was half again as large as that of metropolitan Britain. Japan had a home population of over 70 million, which was considerably greater than the home population of Britain, France, or Italy. (World War II Japanese propaganda would claim an empire of 100 million – including Manchuria, Korea, and other colonies.) The home population was ethnically very homogeneous and well educated. The Japanese people possessed an extraordinary culture and a highly developed political system, centralised and modernised from the time of the so-called *Meiji* Restoration in 1868. (In this year centuries of 'military' rule by the *Shōgun* came to an end, and the Emperor was recognised as the centre of the political system; Mutsuhito, the *Meiji* Emperor, remained on the throne until 1912.) Unlike China, Japan adopted a European-style military system, and it developed a large navy as well as an army.

Like France (and unlike Britain), Japan had colonies near to home – Korea, Formosa, and – after 1931 – Manchuria. The Japanese economy had modernised rapidly, but Japan in the 1930s was not the world economic powerhouse it would become. The Japanese GDP was a third that of the United States at the end of the 1930s, and there was a large and poor agricultural sector. Japan was less affected by the Depression than Germany or the USA, but there was a strong sense that the current world system imposed unfair economic limits on the country.

The major difference with the United States, in terms of foreign policy, was that Japan was not a satisfied power. Unlike the other states discussed so far – the British Empire, China, the USSR, and the USA – Japan had an economic incentive to extend its control overseas, and to expand – rather than just maintain – its existing empire. Dangerous elements were at work here, and Japan's rulers were torn between two policies. They could take a leading role in the existing international system as 'responsible' participants. Or they could break out on their own.

The belligerents:
(3) Continental Europe: France, Germany, Italy

In a listing of the major powers by population, France would come after Japan and before Germany, based on the strength of its colonial empire. France was certainly a world power, and it is misleading to look at the history of the inter-war years from the hindsight of defeat by Germany in May and June 1940. France was not in a state of terminal decline; it lost a military battle that it could have won. The country had suffered great human and economic losses in World War I, but the absolute loss of life was less than that of Germany or Russia. The French Army, arguably more than any other single force, had won World War I. It should come as no surprise that the 1919 Paris Peace Conference worked in favour of French interests.

There was, however, a strongly sensed demographic problem. The population of metropolitan France was only 42 million, just over half that of

Germany, and slightly less than Italy. Like Britain and Japan, France in 1939 had a great many overseas subjects in North Africa, West and Central Africa, and Indochina. Altogether there were some 70 million of them, some of whom – especially from Algeria and Tunisia – contributed significantly to French Army manpower in Europe in 1939–40 and in 1943–5. The French Empire, like that of Britain, had expanded in 1919, gaining as mandates Syria and the Lebanon, and small amounts of former German colonial territory in Africa. France was relatively wealthy, in per capita terms. It had not developed industrially as much as Britain or Germany, and it was a smaller country in population terms to start with. The French overseas possessions were an important economic resource, but they were less valuable than those of Britain.

The essential strategic problem for France – unlike that for Britain – was that preparation for a ground war in Europe had to be the first call on national resources. France had to have a fairly large army, and it attempted to multiply its strength with a system of fortifications; the Air Force and the Navy were less well developed. Germany, before and after 1933, was the greatest danger. France had had to fight Germany on its eastern border in 1870 and 1914, and this vital frontier area would need to be defended again. In the 1930s this was also to some extent a 'new' border, created at Germany's expense when the provinces of Alsace and Lorraine were incorporated back into France (in 1918) – having previously been annexed by Germany (in 1871). Russia also had to prepare for a ground war, but it had the cushion of a great territorial space. And Russia had a much larger population than any single potential enemy, while France did not have the manpower, even with some help from its colonial empire, to fight Germany alone.

For twenty-five years before 1917 France had relied on an *entente* with Russia to balance Germany. After the Communist takeover in Russia, the French tried to create a replacement alliance system using the newly independent states of Poland, Czechoslovakia, Yugoslavia, and Romania, but those countries lacked the power and will that Tsarist Russia had provided before 1914. Britain was an obvious partner, but it could not directly help France against the threat of the German Army. Italy under Mussolini also emerged as a danger. The Fascists claimed the Mediterranean as an Italian sea; from time to time they questioned the French claims to Tunisia and even Corsica.

The second continental power was Germany. After 1933 Germany was often called the 'Third Reich'; the Nazis portrayed their regime as a successor to the German Empire (*Reich*), which had been created with the unification of Germany in 1871 and – as they saw it – was brought to an end in 1918. (For the Nazis the first Reich was the Holy Roman Empire, which existed for 900 years and was dissolved in 1806.) The Third Reich started World War II in Europe. Some historians see the years from 1914 to 1945 as essentially the time of a thirty-year 'German war'. Why was Germany such a world-class problem, given that the country came near the bottom of the population table of the world's major states?

Leaving aside, for the moment, political factors, an essential feature of the situation was that Germany was still the largest state in Western and Central Europe. It had a population nearly twice than of the home population of France or Britain. As was constantly stressed by Hitler and pre-war Nazi propaganda, this population had a relatively small 'living space' (*Lebensraum*) including Austria, of some 220,000 square miles. Of the major surviving European states, Germany was most changed territorially by World War I, losing lands to Poland, France, Belgium, Denmark, and Lithuania. (Germany also lost Austria-Hungary as a military partner.) East Prussia was divided from the rest of Germany by a region ceded to Poland and by the 'international' region of Danzig (now Gdansk). Most Germans, not just the extremists, felt aggrieved by this loss of territory on all sides of the old Reich.

Despite the radical nationalism (and racialism) evident in Germany in the 1920s and 1930s, the German population was remarkably homogeneous. Germany was considerably more centralised under the 1919 Weimar constitution than it would be in the post-1949 Federal Republic. The Nazis increased the centralist tendency. The Germans had an efficient bureaucracy. As an extension of this, they had an important military tradition, which had been one reason why a strong Prussia came into being in the eighteenth century. At Versailles Germany was restricted to an army of 100,000 men and a small navy; it was not permitted to possess an air force; the government of the Third Reich was able to make up for lost time relatively quickly, but it was not able, in five or six years, to carry out comprehensive rearmament.

The German economy was crucially important in a number of respects. Industry had taken off in the second half of the nineteenth century. The various German states had unified, first economically through a customs union and a new railway system and then – in 1871– politically. The new unified German Empire had – thanks to its basic resources and large, well-educated population – surpassed first France and then Britain in industrial production. One of the basic causes of the 1914 war was that the high state of German economic development was not matched by its territorial span of control. In the late 1930s the GDP was high, and German had great war-making potential, but some economic resources were limited, such as iron ore, oil, and rubber. World War I had shown the limits of the German economy, and military planners in Berlin were keenly aware of the potential problems (see Chapter 11). 'Reparation' payments ordered by the victorious Allies in 1919, and then the Depression of 1929, fatally destabilised first the German economy and then the democratic political system. The Nazis effected a remarkable economic turnabout after the 1933, partly through spending on rearmament, but this growth was not sustainable – at least not without a major European war and geographical changes.

The last major power was Italy. For all of its historical and cultural impor-tance, Italy in the 1930s was the poorest and weakest of the major states. Italy was ethnically homogeneous; indeed that was the point of unifying the new nation for the first time in the 1860s. The population was overwhelmingly Catholic. But the recent unification glossed over important regional divides, especially between the relatively developed north and the agrarian and back-ward south. Italy was lacking in most key resources of an industrial economy, especially coal and iron ore. It had the lowest GDP of any of the major states, barely half that of Japan, and average wealth was also low in per capita terms, especially compared to the other European states.

It may seem strange that Italy ended up among the revisionist powers in the 1930s, given that it had fought alongside the Allies in World War I and that its traditional enemy had been Austria. Part of the explanation is that Italy had made only minor gains at the Paris Peace Conference, taking coastal lands from Austria-Hungary in the Adriatic, and a small Alpine region in the north. Although the advent of the Fascist government accentuated feelings of dissatisfaction, many Italians already resented Britain's predominant position in the Mediterranean, controlling Gibraltar, Malta, and the Suez Canal. Mass emigration, to the United States and to South America, and mass employment of Italian workers in factories and construction work in Northern Europe, represented a lost asset. New colonies in North Africa, acquired from Turkey only in 1911, provided a momentum of expansion. Mussolini's colonial adventure in Ethiopia in 1935 would not be an unpopular one.

The international system

Most of these major powers originally fitted within an international 'system' of sorts. Although this system was global, it can be broken down into European and Asian components. The European system had pre-dated 1914. Indeed, broadly speaking, World War I was a defence of that system. The victory of Britain and France in World War I was a victory for the status quo of the late nineteenth century. Britain and France had been the dominant European powers, with global empires, and they kept that position. The war was a defeat for the main power – the German Empire – that challenged this status quo.

The Paris Peace Conference, opened by the victorious Allies in January 1919, confirmed all this, and it came to symbolise the international system in Europe. The conference confirmed the power of Britain and France, although Italy and Japan also played a role among the victorious Allies, and American ideas inspired much of the rhetoric. The Paris Conference accepted an independent Poland at the expense of Germany, Russia, and Austria-Hungary. It created an independent Czech and Slovak state (as one of the successors to Austria-Hungary). Romania and Serbia (the latter as Yugoslavia) were enlarged, gaining territory from Austria-Hungary. At the same time (although not as a direct result of the Paris Conference) Finland, Estonia, Latvia, and Lithuania gained their independence from the Russian Empire. While not destroying Germany and Russia as states, the Conference excluded them from its deliberations. The powerless German politicians had to sign the treaty thrust at them in May 1919, the famous *Diktat* of Versailles. (Austria, Hungary, Bulgaria, and Turkey were dealt with in four other treaties.)

At the Paris Conference, the victor powers formally based the European order on democracy and self-determination, principles that were identified with Woodrow Wilson. When, in the Atlantic Charter of August 1941, President Roosevelt and Prime Minister Churchill declared that 'they wish to see sovereign rights and self government restored to those who have been forcibly deprived of them' and 'a peace which will afford to all nations the means of dwelling in safety within their own boundaries', they were hark-ing back to 1919. The Paris Conference also created the League of Nations, based in Geneva, as a mechanism for maintaining the international order. The League had only limited powers. For complex reasons of its own internal politics the United States never joined, and the USSR did so only in 1934. The principles of the Paris Conference were confirmed by later meetings of the powers in the 1920s and early 1930s. In the Kellogg–Briand Pact, spon-sored by the USA and France in 1928 and signed, among others, by Germany and Japan, the powers renounced aggressive war. The pact would be used twenty years later, and after the terrible world conflict, to justify charges against the leaders of Germany and Japan in the Nuremberg and Tokyo war crimes trials.

This European international system would be challenged by states which felt themselves the victims of the Paris Conference, or who felt they had not benefited enough from it. They rejected a continent dominated by the 1918 victors. The Russians were the first to defy the Paris system (although they reversed course in the 1930s). The government in Berlin, even in the 1920s, wanted to reduce French influence and establish predominant German influ-ence in Central Europe, limiting or overturning the self-determination of the successor states. Berlin was prepared to collaborate with Moscow to achieve these aims. Soon after Hitler came to power in 1933 he pulled Germany out of the League of Nations, and out of the international system. The Italians, although they had benefited from the Paris Conference and were permanent members of the Council of the League, were also not satisfied. They left the League in 1937, after ignoring its protests about their invasion of Ethiopia. The Germans and the Italians came together in stages as an alternative Euro-pean bloc. The Anti-Comintern Pact of 1936 would be followed by the 1939 alliance, by the May 1940 Italian declaration of war, and by the signing – along with the Japanese – of the Tripartite Pact of September 1940.

The development of the international system in East Asia and the Pacific was quite different. World War I was not fought out here; there was only the quick seizure (in 1914) of scattered German colonies. The establishment of colonies here by the European powers, Japan, and the United States preceded 1914 by, at the very least, a decade. The Dutch, British, and French colonies were long established. Japan gained territory at the expense of China from 1895. America established Pacific colonies in the Philippines and Guam in

1898, after the war with Spain. The important check to Russian expansion came not in 1919 (as in Europe), but in 1905, when the Japanese blocked an attempt to get control of Manchuria.

The Washington Conference of 1921–2 was to Asia what the Paris Conference of 1919 was to Europe; the two meetings were the twin pillars of the international system. The conference which met in the American capital, from November 1921 to February 1922, set out the status quo in Asia. Unlike the Paris Conference, the Washington Conference was not a direct result of World War I, but it would not have taken the form that it did without the outcome of that war. Like Paris, Washington was a conference of the victors; Germany was not invited, and neither was Soviet Russia, despite its major Asian interests.

The Paris Conference disarmed Germany; the Washington Conference stopped a post-war naval construction race between the Allies. The Washington Naval Treaty provided for a fifteen-year 'holiday' in battleship construction. Britain and America would have naval parity, and the Japanese Navy would be 60 per cent of the size of the Royal Navy and the USA Navy. None of the powers would create new fortified naval bases in the Pacific area. The Washington Conference also produced the Four-Power Treaty by which Britain, France, Japan, and the USA guaranteed one another's Pacific island colonial holdings. With hindsight, the most important feature of the Washington Conference was the Nine-Power Treaty (see Box 2). In this document the signatories – most importantly Britain, Japan, and the United States – agreed to respect the independence and integrity of China.

The Washington Conference left the European and American colonial and economic presence in East Asia intact. The signatories agreed that none of them would take unilateral advantage of China. Japan accepted that its navy would be smaller than those its chief rivals. It was assumed, incorrectly, that Japan would perpetually play by these rules. As in Europe, there was an alternative to this international system. The extension of naval limitations at the 1930 London Conference ignited a blaze of protest in Japan. A year later would come the first great challenge to the whole international system (both in Europe and in Asia) when Japan seized Manchuria from China. Japan resigned from the League of Nations in 1933, when that body condemned the Manchurian action; in effect the Empire left the international system. In 1936 Japan refused to extend the naval treaties. It was a Japanese statesman, Prince

Box 2 | **The Treaty of Washington**

The nine-power treaty was signed by the British Empire, Belgium, China, France, Italy, Japan, the Netherlands, Portugal, and the United States in February 1922.

The Contracting Powers...agree:

(1) To respect the sovereignty, the independence, and the territorial and administrative integrity of China;

(2) To provide the fullest and most unembarrassed opportunity to China to develop and maintain for herself an effective and stable government;

(3) To use their influence for the purpose of effectually establishing and maintaining the principle of equal opportunity for the commerce and industry of all nations throughout the territory of China;

(4) To refrain from taking advantage of conditions in China in order to seek special rights or privileges which would abridge the rights of subjects or citizens of friendly States, and from countenancing action inimical to the security of such States.

(*The Avalon Project: Documents in Law, History and Diplomacy*, at http://avalon.law.yale.edu.)

Konoe Fumimaro, who would, in 1938, give wide currency to the concept of the 'new order', in this case a 'new order in East Asia' (see Figure 4). This would be restated, on a worldwide scale, in the Tripartite Pact of September 1940, which created the Axis.

The global economic system might be described as an integrated, inter-dependent, global capitalism, and a structure which seemed likely to be controlled, in perpetuity, by the richer powers. This system recovered reasonably well from World War I and functioned fitfully but adequately in the 1920s, although with important changes. Britain was not as powerful as it had been before 1914, and the central player became the United States. Post-war Germany suffered from a requirement to pay reparations. It went through an early inflation crisis, and the prosperity of the mid-1920s was supported by American loans.

World capitalism went into general crisis in the late 1920s. Economists still argue about the causes of the Depression, but it certainly had its roots in the American economy as much as the European one. The Depression is normally dated from the Wall Street Crash of October 1929. The integrated economy disintegrated. Individual states faced economic disaster, crises of their currencies, collapse of their stock markets and banking systems, and mass unemployment. They mostly attempted orthodox measures like reducing government spending or attempting to protect their own economies by putting up tariff barriers. Protectionism led to counter-measures by economic rivals, and international commerce was catastrophically reduced. A World Economic Conference which convened in London in June 1933 was unable to take the world economy out of depression. More dangerously, nationalist leaders of some major states, including the radical right in Germany and Italy, and militarists in Japan, also looked to an alternative economic model of autarcky, regional self-sufficiency. Each state would control a large regional economic zone – which the Germans called *Grossraum* – as part of the creation of an economic 'new order'.

Political ideologies: (1) Liberal democracy

World War II was, or course, not just about territory and resources. It was also about politics. It was depicted by the Allies, including the Stalinist USSR, as a struggle between democracy and Fascism, a battle for 'freedom'. Both in Europe and Asia, the post-World War I international order laid out norms of political democracy. This was not the issue Europe had gone to war over in 1914, but as the struggle continued it was more and more depicted in Allied propaganda as a war against Prussian militarism and tyranny – personified by Kaiser Wilhelm II. This 'democratic' orientation became easier in the third year of the war. Revolution had overthrown the Tsar, and with him the Russian autocracy; meanwhile the American republic entered the war. The Allies also used ethnic self-determination as a political weapon among the minorities of the Austro-Hungarian Empire. In his speech to Congress requesting a declaration of war, President Woodrow Wilson famously stressed the political dimension: 'The world must be made safe for democracy. Its peace must be planted upon the tested foundations of political liberty.'[2]

The eventual collapse of the traditional monarchies in Berlin, Vienna, and St Petersburg/Petrograd seemed to confirm the victory, on a European scale, of both parliamentary democracy and the principle of self-determination. Britain, France, and America were the political models, at least in the 1920s. Not only did they impose the terms of peace, but their victory seemed to prove their political superiority. Germany became a parliamentary republic, as did the new states of Central Europe. In Japan this was the era of *Taishō* democracy – named after the *Taishō* emperor (Yoshihito, 1912–26) – where something approaching multi-party government prevailed.

Sadly, the ideals of parliamentary democracy proved hard to live up to. Mussolini began moving Italy towards a Fascist dictatorship in 1922, and Marshal Piłsudski came to power after a coup in Poland in 1926. The Depression had a devastating effect on politics, and by the mid 1930s Fascist Italy and Nazi Germany had emerged as counter-models. But in Britain, France, and the United States the parliamentary structure worked, under strain but without serious challenge, through the 1930s, and even Japan was notionally a parliamentary monarchy at the end of the decade. (The National Diet building in Tokyo was completed in 1936.) In a basic statement of Allied war aims, the Declaration of the United Nations of 1 January 1942, the liberal agenda was clear. The signatories stated that for them 'complete victory over their enemies is essential to defend life, liberty, independence and religious freedom, and to preserve human rights and justice in their own lands as well as in other lands.'[3]

Political ideologies: (2) Communism

If, in the 1920s, there seemed to be a dark cloud on the political horizon of liberal democracy, it was not the radical right of Mussolini and Hitler, but rather 'Bolshevism' (Communism) and the Comintern. Communism was a by-product of World War I. The depth of the wartime crisis in Russia, and the weakness of urban liberal alternatives, enabled a radical Marxist group, Lenin's Bolsheviks, to seize power in 1917. In 1919 Moscow created an organisation – the Communist International or Comintern – to organise Communist parties in other states.

The spectre of *Bolschewismus* (as the Germans called it) remained a potent and permanent feature of the European (and American) political scene until 1991. Communist groups owing allegiance to the Comintern and Moscow developed as a greater or lesser political force in most countries, at varying stages of development, from Weimar Germany to China. Fear of Communism was an important background factor in the rise of Italian Fascism and the German NSDAP (Nazi party) in the early 1920s. In France, Poland, and other Catholic countries the militantly atheistic government in

Box 3 | The 'united front'

The Resolution of the 7th Congress of the Comintern, held in Moscow in August 1935, played an important part in determining the policy of the world Communist movement in the years before, during, and after World War II. The 'united front' policy was different from the dogmatic 'class against class' revolutionary policy which prevailed in the 1920s and after 1947.

The struggle for peace opens up before the communist parties the greatest opportunities for creating the broadest united front. All those interested in the preservation of peace should be drawn into this united front. The concentration of the forces against the chief instigators of war at any given moment (at the present time against Fascist Germany, and against Poland and Japan which are in league with it) constitutes a most important tactical task for the communist parties... The establishment of a united front with social-democratic and reformist organiza- tions (party, trade union, co-operative, sports, and cultural and educational organisations) and with the bulk of their members, also with mass national liberation, religious-democratic and pacifist organizations and their adherents, is of decisive importance for the struggle against war and its fascist instigators in all countries.

(From Jane Degras, ed., *The Communist International, 1919–1943: Documents* (Oxford: Oxford University Press, 1965), vol. III, p. 375.)

Russia was especially hated; the Papacy was strongly critical, notably in Pius XI's encyclical of March 1937. 'Godless Communism' also invoked a bitter reaction within much of the American electorate.

The ideological nature of the Soviet regime meant that it followed a dual policy. Even while the Soviet Foreign Commissariat was attempting to develop closer economic and even military co-operation with Germany in the early 1920s, the Communist International was working to bring about a socialist revolution there. The Comintern underestimated the potential of the NSDAP and thought – with the onset of the Depression – that Germany was in a near-revolutionary situation. Belatedly, in 1934–5, the Kremlin suddenly changed the 'line' of international Communism from a policy of 'class against class' – actually violent conflict with other socialist groups – to a policy of a 'united front' (see Box 3). The new line helped the rise of left-wing coalition governments in Europe, notably in France and Spain, and encouraged co-operation between Nationalists and Communists in China. The 'united front' would reach its ultimate form in the Grand Alliance of 1941–5, with the USSR fighting Fascism alongside Britain and the US. The road to that alliance, however, would be long, winding, and tragic, and the united front would not be long enduring.

Communism was also on the march in Asia in the 1920s. The Comintern leadership had come to the conclusion that the struggle with world capitalism would be fought more effectively in the colonies and in other areas subject to imperialism, rather than in the European 'metropolis' itself. The Communists were especially important in China. They were originally based in the coastal cities, where the small Chinese working class – and the westernised intelligentsia – were concentrated. Conflict with non-Communist Nationalists under Jiang Jieshi in 1927 (see below) led them to put down new roots inland in rural China. Anti-Communism was also a feature of Japanese policy. For Tokyo Russia combined the paradoxical twin evils of a European colonial power and a revolutionary force committed to overthrowing the social order in Japan. As it turned out, a major outcome of World War II would be the creation of Communist governments in China, and later in northern Korea and in Indochina.

The other side of the Soviet experience was the internal transformation of Russia. The country underwent a remarkable spurt of industrial development and Joseph Stalin emerged as unchallenged leader (see Figure 1). In the late 1920s Moscow's policy turned from egalitarianism and international revolution to forced-draught economic modernisation. Stalin's policy was 'socialism in one country', rapid development of the USSR regardless of revolutionary failures elsewhere. 'We are fifty to a hundred years behind the advanced countries,' Stalin told a meeting of managers in 1931. 'We must make up this distance in ten years. Either we do it, or we shall go under.'[4] The crash industrialisation projects of the first two Five-Year Plans (1927–32 and 1933–7) were accompanied by huge migrations and social changes. The standard of living did not rise, but output did. Russian steel mills produced 4 million tons of steel in 1927 (roughly the level before World War I), and nearly 18 millions tons in 1940. Soviet factories produced 800 motor vehicles in 1927, and 200,000 a decade later.

The 1930s were also a time of the consolidation of Stalin's personal power in what is often called (by outsiders) a 'totalitarian' system. He ensured his

Figure 1 | Joseph Stalin

Joseph Stalin (1879–1953) is shown here with Viacheslav Molotov (1890–1986), his closest comrade. Stalin (whose real name was Dzhugashvili) was a Georgian rather than a Russian, and he was a leader of a radical Marxist party with a doctrine of international revolution. Yet he became identified with Russian nationalism, and he used that sentiment with great effect after June 1941.

Churchill aside, Stalin was the most experienced executive of any of the World War II leaders. Contrary to many accounts (notably that of Trotsky), Stalin had an important military and political role in the Civil War of 1917–20. After Lenin died in 1924 a prolonged succession struggle began among his chief lieutenants; from this, Stalin emerged in first place by 1930. He identified himself with a policy known as 'Socialism in One Country', which argued that it would be possible to build a socialist economy in Russia even if the revolution did not develop rapidly elsewhere. Although some of Stalin's economic policies were cruel or even disastrous, they did increase the industrial potential of the country. It would be wrong to say that Stalin lacked an interest in external affairs, and his economic modernisation policies were intended in part to protect Russia against outside threats.

Stalin oversaw the creation of a totalitarian state in the 1930s. The Soviet propaganda machinery projected him as an all-knowing dictator. An extremely bloody purge was carried out in 1937–8. In June and July 1941 Stalin took over the war leadership, including the position of Supreme C-in-C of the Red Army. He made blunders, but he was generally – at least by the middle of 1942 – an able commander-in-chief. At the inter-Allied conferences he proved to be an effective advocate of Soviet interests.

Stalin ruled Russia for another eight years after the war, until he died from a stroke in 1953. In 1956 Nikita Khrushchev denounced Stalin in the famous 'secret speech' at the 20th Party Congress – for personal arrogance, for the purge of the party elite in 1937–8, and for wartime mistakes. Historians still labour to produce a balanced picture of Stalin.

position with a campaign of revolutionary 'terror'. This included the widely publicised political trials of former Communist rivals, and it spilled over in 1937–8 into a bloody 'purge' involving both the governing elite (including the leaders of the military) and the population as a whole. Something like 700,000 people were executed, and hundreds of thousands of other unfortunates were exiled to the labour camp system. The level of repression was worse than in Nazi Germany. Arguably this cauterisation removed a potential opposition to Stalin; it certainly brought up a new generation of leaders. The Terror did not create anti-Communism in other countries (that had existed since 1917). It did, however, reduce the standing of the USSR as a credible alliance partner (to the British and French), and it made Hitler think Stalin was vulnerable.

Political ideologies: (3) The radical right

The third political development, after liberal democracy and communism, was the 'radical right'. For many people it was the struggle with this last movement which was essence of World War II and which made it a 'just war'. The official ideology of the World War II Grand Alliance would be anti-fascism, a crusade to destroy an evil social movement.

Unlike liberal democracy and the Marxist revolutionary movement, the radical right appeared after the end of World War I. It sprang from the European social turmoil of 1919–20, from the vacuum left by the fall of the monarchies, and from fear of Bolshevism. It was fuelled by the presence of hundreds of thousands of disenchanted young men – soldiers and war-workers. Dragged from their peacetime lives, they had been unable to settle back into bourgeois normality.

It was in Italy that the radical right first took power. This was surprising, because Italy was one of the victor powers of World War I, and the country had had a pre-war constitutional monarchy. Many Italians, however, saw the liberal government as corrupt and ineffective, serving regional or class interests. They blamed it both for Italy's miserable performance in World War I, and for the lack of sufficient territorial gains after a huge national sacrifice (Italy lost almost as many soldiers in the war as did the British Empire). In 1919 the Fascist movement developed considerable popular support under Benito Mussolini (see Figure 2). Fascism was based on a programme that was self-described as 'totalitarian' and which stressed a movement focused

Figure 2 | **Benito Mussolini**

The Italian dictator Benito Mussolini (1883–1945), pictured above with Hitler in Munich in June 1940, was the first major Western European politician to challenge the post-1918 norms of parliamentary democracy.

Mussolini, like Hitler and Stalin, came from a humble background. He originally made his name, in the first decade of the twentieth century, as a journalist of the radical left. In World War I, he suddenly converted himself into a nationalist. He argued for

Italian entry into the conflict, and when war came in 1915 he volunteered for service. After the war, Mussolini developed the paramilitary Black Shirts of the Fascist movement to assert power by direct action, especially against the forces of the left. The common element in his actions was opposition of the 'liberal Italy' of the 1860s, which seemed so ineffective, and which had failed to achieve a satisfactory reward for Italian sacrifice in World War I.

After he came to power in 1922, Mussolini progressively consolidated his power. He made effective use of propaganda to build up the prestige of his government, and his own prestige as *Il Duce* (the Leader). A powerful and bellicose demagogue, he enjoyed considerable popularity in Italy. Although an extreme nationalist, he kept Italy out of serious foreign adventures until the middle of the 1930s. Even then, the democracies thought they might be able to use Mussolini and Italy as a counterweight to Hitler.

When he threw in his lot with Hitler he helped to destabilise Europe and to make domination by the Third Reich possible. In 1939 Mussolini signed a military alliance. In 1940 he brought Italy into another world war. He proved to have only a weak grasp of strategy, and when serious setbacks began he was challenged within his own party. With the invasion of Sicily in July 1943 Mussolini was deposed in an internal coup, but he was rescued from his mountain-top confinement by German commandos. Hitler still valued him as a personal comrade, although he expressed contempt for the Italian people. Mussolini created a new government in northern Italy; when that collapsed in April 1945 he attempted to escape to Switzerland. He was caught by Italian Partisans and shot; his body and that of his mistress Clara Petacci were hung upside down in the forecourt of a petrol station in Milan.

on the state rather than on the individual or on a particular social class. Its rhetoric was both anti-liberal and anti-Marxist. Mussolini was a charismatic figure, but by 1922 he had developed only a small following in parliament (22 seats out of 550). Under the pressure of a Fascist demonstration – the so-called 'March on Rome' – King Vittorio Emanuele III appointed Mussolini Prime Minister. Once in office Mussolini pushed through laws which kept the Fascists in power and neutralised their opponents. He gradually became a dictator, subverting the constitution and overshadowing the King.

Italy was a former ally, and the French and British took no steps to counter the rise of authoritarian rule. Mussolini would stay in power for twenty years, the longest-serving leader at the start of World War II. The Army supported Mussolini's nationalist foreign policy and his opposition to the left. Mussolini attracted widespread support from foreigners, both the radical right in Germany and East Central Europe, and also from conservatives in other countries, the latter as long as he did not upset the international status quo. The ideology of Fascism, unfortunately, increased the danger of conflict. As one of the movements key doctrinal documents put it, 'For Fascism, the growth of empire, that is to say the expansion of the nation, is an essential manifestation of vitality, and its opposite a sign of decadence.'[5]

The National Socialist (Nazi) movement in Germany was more important in the background to World War II than Italian Fascism, although Italy did serve as a model for developments north of the Alps. The 'Nazi' party (or NSDAP, National Socialist German Workers Party) was one of a number of small extreme nationalist groups that appeared in 1918–19. The NSDAP was based on nationalism, anti-Communism, anti-liberalism, and a kind of socialism. Antisemitism and a mystical attachment to the German (Aryan) *Volk* were not necessarily the core elements of its mass appeal, although the active members of the movement took them seriously enough. More practical causes than hatred of the Jews led ordinary Germans to support the Nazi movement. There had been strong authoritarian tendencies in the German Empire, and a yearning remained for the old certainties. The liberal political system was even weaker than in Italy. Liberals and the left were blamed for defeat in 1918. Liberal parliamentarism had failed to secure Germany's position in the world or, after the beginning of the Great Depression, to protect the German standard of living. The Nazis promised to fight Communism. In the Reichstag election of 1930 the NSDAP radically increased its representation, from 12 seats to 107 (out of 577). In the spring of 1931 the financial crisis in Central Europe worsened, and by the start of the following year more than 6 million Germans were out of work.

In the acute economic and political crisis of 1932–3 Hitler was allowed to form a government. He became prime minister (Chancellor, *Kanzler*) in January 1933, two months before Franklin Roosevelt became President. Successive elections had made the NSDAP the largest single party in the Reichstag, although without an overall majority. Once in control of the levers of power, the NSDAP set out to consolidate its grasp, creating a totalitarian state and making Hitler the Führer (Leader) of Germany. Opposition parties were closed down in the summer of 1933. From there Hitler would move rapidly towards rearmament and a radical revision of the Versailles Treaty.

Neither Fascism nor Nazism produced an international movement of the radical right, comparable to the Comintern. Nevertheless there were other right-wing movements and regimes in the 1930s, some of them inspired by the new regimes in Italy and Germany. Nearly all of these states might be called 'authoritarian' rather than totalitarian. They were based on traditional elites, they attached much weight to the church, and they explicitly argued for the preservation of the existing social order, rather than some radical new departure. Most of the states of Eastern and Southern Europe had fallen back on some form of authoritarian rule after the optimistic democratic beginnings of 1919, the exception being Czechoslovakia. Even France and the Low Countries had right-wing movements which, while not close to power in the 1930s, would flourish under the German military occupation after 1940.

Britain and France did not go to war in September 1939 because Germany was a right-wing dictatorship or because the Nazi state oppressed its ethnic and political enemies. Indeed they had some hopes that they might convince Fascist Italy to support them. Even when more was known about the oppression and aggression of the Axis powers the American Congress was unwilling to fight. With time, however, 'freedom' became the basis of British and American war aims. In the Atlantic Charter of August 1941 (remarkably before America entered the war) Churchill and Roosevelt spoke of a world 'after the final destruction of Nazi tyranny', in which 'all the men in all the lands may live out their lives in freedom from fear and want'. Stalin's famous radio address of July 1941 had made the same point: 'The war with

Figure 3 | **Adolf Hitler**

Adolf Hitler was dictator of Germany from January 1933 to April 1945, and a central figure in the history of World War II in Europe; the conflict is often called 'Hitler's War'.

Hitler had a limited education. By the standards of world leaders he was a relatively young man – he turned fifty in the year 'his' war broke out in 1939. He possessed remarkable powers of oratory. It is hard to imagine the war in Europe without Hitler, and he is probably the one individual whose physical removal would have changed the course of events. His existence in power made a conventional negotiated peace impossible; for the Allies, victory demanded 'regime change' in Germany.

Hitler achieved his greatest successes in 1935–40, establishing Germany's position by bluff and apparently easy military victories. Nevertheless, he made a fatal miscalculation in September 1939, when his invasion of Poland led to a general war with two European powers. Thereafter his strategy was a series of gambles to square the circle. Some gambles succeeded (France in 1940), or half-succeeded (Russia in 1941). As negotiation was never an option (for either side), Hitler had to keep rolling the dice. The 1942 Russian gamble was unsuccessful, and after Stalingrad Hitler's easy victories were over. As the war progressed, especially after 1942, the Führer (Leader) was less and less in the public eye. Yet the fate of the German people was tied to him and they feared revenge from Germany's victims. By July 1944 some of the elite could take a more realistic position, and a faction of the Army attempted to murder him. But most Germans in positions of power saw no alternative to following the Führer.

fascist Germany cannot be considered an ordinary war ... The aim of this national patriotic war is ... not only to eliminate the danger hanging over our country but also to aid all the European peoples groaning under the yoke of German fascism.'[6]

Political ideologies: (4) Japanese nationalism

World War II propaganda and post-war histories lumped Japan politically with Germany and Italy, as 'Fascist' or 'totalitarian'. Neither term is appropriate to Japan. Radical right elements – ultra-nationalists – did exist there, and they had much in common with the Fascist and Nazi hard core, but they never actually held power. More important was the rejection – by a wider strand of elite opinion – of parliamentary democracy. Like the USSR, some Japanese perceived that their country had an international mission, in this case a pan-Asian one of leading its region and expelling European influence.

The Japanese call the historical era from 1926 to 1989 the *Shōwa* period, after the emperor who reigned in those years. When he succeeded his father in 1926 the young Hirohito took the name *Shōwa* or 'Enlightened Peace'. The political situation in pre-1937 *Shōwa* Japan was very different from that in Italy or Germany. Germany's problems came largely from a lost war, and from a crisis of legitimacy of the republican government which replaced the Kaiser. Japan was largely unaffected by the outcome of the European war of 1914–18. Its last major conflict, the Russo-Japanese war of 1904–5, cannot be compared with Germany's *Weltkrieg* of 1914–18. Japan won a stunning victory on land and at sea; Germany had to endure a humiliating defeat. While the struggle against Russia was bitter, it lasted only twenty months, and Japan suffered 80,000 deaths (including victims of disease) – compared to 1,800,000 deaths for Germany in World War I.

Italy, rather than Germany, might seem to offer a better analogy with Japan. Italy, like Japan, was a World War I ally of Britain and France which fell out with its fellow victors. But in Italy there had been a substantial change of political structure in the early 1920s. The Fascist Party had taken a monopoly of power, and Mussolini became a new strongman. None of this applied to Japan, where the parliamentary system (the Imperial Diet), elected by universal male suffrage, remained formally intact. There was no one-party system, and certainly no Japanese dictator. Rather than a mono-lithic totalitarian structure, Japan's problem, before World War II, and during it, was a *lack* of central direction. Governments in Tokyo changed frequently – with fifteen cabinets between 1931 and 1945. The young Emperor (a man in his mid thirties during the crisis decade) was strongly influenced by the shadowy world of elder statesmen who had served under his grandfather.

The Japanese political system underwent unprecedented strain in the 1930s. At the governmental level this began with a crisis – already mentioned – over the London Naval Treaty negotiations of 1930. Although with hindsight the issues were of little practical importance, they acted as focus for extra-parliamentary action. The radical right, and factions within the armed forces, opposed the government's attempt to operate within the Washington Conference system. In late 1930 the Prime Minister was seriously injured by an assassin. The effective seizure of Manchuria in 1931–2, on the initiative of Japanese field commanders (see Chapter 2), put Japan at odds with the international system. This energised the forces of the radical right, and in May 1932 Prime Minister Inukai was assassinated in an attempted coup by junior officers (army and navy cadets). The most drastic event came in February 1936, when mid-level Army officers attempted another coup in Tokyo, bringing their units out onto the streets and attempting to establish a military dictatorship in the name of the Emperor (the so-called 'Shōwa restoration'). Several ministers were killed, but the coup was not supported by the senior generals.

More important than the young radicals, however, was the unchecked power of the Japanese military. Again, this was quite different from the situation in Germany and Italy. Far from the military being controlled by a central authority – a classic feature of totalitarianism – the Imperial Army and the Navy in the 1920s and 1930s behaved autonomously, regarding themselves as subordinate only to the Emperor. They could bring down governments by the resignation of the service ministers, and as a result they had a veto over policy. The accused in the Nuremberg War Crimes Trial were mostly leaders of the German Nazi Party; the accused at the Tokyo War Crimes Trial were mostly Japanese generals.

A primary goal of the World War II Allies with respect to Japan would be the removal of this military elite. The ultimatum issued at Potsdam in July 1945 stated the Allies' demand: 'The Japanese Government shall remove all obstacles to the revival and strengthening of democratic tendencies among the Japanese people. Freedom of speech, of religion and of thought, as well as respect for the fundamental human rights, shall be established.' But beyond these broad points there was an attack on the elite of generals and nationalistic civilians: 'Japan [was] to decide whether she will continue to be controlled by those self-willed militaristic advisers whose unintelligent calculations have brought the Empire of Japan to the threshold of annihilation.' 'There must be eliminated for all time', the ultimatum continued, 'the authority and influence of those who have deceived and misled the people of Japan into embarking on world conquest.'[7]

In the end, whatever the significant differences between Italy, Germany, and Japan, the stated war aims of the Allies became 'regime change'. This explained the insistence on 'unconditional surrender'. As President Roosevelt put it, in his famous statement at the Casablanca Conference in January 1943, 'The elimination of German, Japanese, and Italian war power means the unconditional surrender by Germany, Italy, and Japan . . . It does not mean the destruction of the population of Germany, Italy, or Japan, but it does mean the destruction of the philosophies in those countries which are based on conquest and the subjugation of other people.'[8]

Political ideologies: (5) Anti-colonialism

Anti-colonialism was a final strand of pre-war politics, and China was its most remarkable case. A revived Chinese state, organised on 'modern' lines, emerged in the big southern port city of Guangzhou (Canton) in the 1920s. This was based on the movement inspired by Sun Yat-sen, the *Guomindang* (*Kuomintang*) or Chinese 'Nationalist Party'. Dr Sun died in 1925, but his most effective general, Jiang Jieshi (Chiang Kai-shek) (see Figure 4), was able to use a newly formed army to extend Nationalist control. In 1927 Jiang marched his forces north to Nanjing (Nanking) and restored that city to its status as a capital, this time of a new republican China.

The political system of Nationalist China was certainly not an example of liberal democracy, although the 'Nanjing Decade' (1928–37) is sometimes looked on as a time of remarkable stability and progress – compared to what preceded it and what followed it. Jiang was a military dictator who ran a unique authoritarian state. The Nationalist leaders also took an early interest in the political and military efficiency of Bolshevism, and Jiang had been courted by Moscow in the mid 1920s. Once he had taken power, however, Jiang massacred the Communists in the coastal cities, and one of the enduring features of his long time in power would be militant anti-Communism. Jiang's 'New Life Movement' of the 1930s, arguably included Fascism among its other components. Although Japan had seized Manchuria in 1931–2 and made increasing demands in northern China, Jiang put defeat of the Communists first. 'The Japanese are a disease of the skin', he said, 'the Communists are a disease of the heart.'[9] In 1934–5 Jiang was able to drive the main Communist forces out of eastern China, making them undertake the 'Long March' to remote Shaanxi (Shensi) Province in the northwest.

What would later be called 'national liberation' was a general feature of the 1920s and 1930s that is often overlooked. It was, as we have seen, a major element in Comintern ideology, although this was played down during the second half of the 1930s. A considerable force advocating national independence existed in India in the form of Gandhi's Congress Party, and there were anti-colonialist groups in strategic regions such as Malaya, the Netherlands Indies, and French Indochina. Compared to the post-1945 years, this was a weak force, but it would be exploited by the Japanese. They would pay lip service to anti-imperialism and anti-Europeanism in their wartime ideology and propaganda.

Planning for the next war: (1) Armies

Although World War I was a terrible event, and was often described as a 'war to end all wars', in reality national leaders were soon thinking about what were the military 'lessons' of World War I, and how the next war would be fought. We will look at the rearmament and military policies of individual states in later chapters of this book, but some general points will be introduced here, and in particular the effect of the conflict of 1914–18.

World War I in Europe had been more costly than any war in recent history. Over 100 million soldiers and sailors were mobilised for war. Nearly 10 million died, mostly in combat, between 1914 and 1918. Germany lost 1.8 million men in battle, Russia lost 1.6 million, France lost 1.2 million, and the British Empire lost nearly 800,000. In contrast, the Russo-Japanese War of 1904–5 and the brief Franco-Prussian War of 1870–1 had each involved under 100,000 combat deaths, and about 140,000 soldiers had been killed in battle in the American Civil War. World War I was also remembered for the futile carnage of trench warfare. The front line in the West had become frozen in the autumn of 1914 and there had been little movement until the spring of 1918. War in Russia and in northern Italy was sometimes more fluid, but these campaigns also featured long periods of trench warfare, and none of the armies achieved war-winning victories. At sea, the huge fleets of battleships constructed before the war were never to fight a decisive battle.

One response to the tragedy of 1914–18 – especially in those countries that took a direct part in it – was a deep desire to avoid a repetition. The events and attitudes of the 1930s make little sense unless we remember that many national leaders and much of the population believed that another war had to be avoided at all costs. This helps us to understand British and French Appeasement, American Isolationism, and even the lack of enthusiasm felt among the German population when a European war began again in September 1939. An extensive popular anti-war movement developed in the 1920s, and a strong pacifist culture. At state level the whole Paris Conference system and the League of Nations can be seen – in part – as an attempt to provide an alternative to war. The Kellogg–Briand Pact of 1928 outlawed war, and the League sponsored a World Disarmament Conference in Geneva in 1932–4. Regrettably, none of these initiatives had the desired effect.

Another response to 1914–18, however, especially by military men, was to consider how to fight the war more effectively next time. Possible answers took in both broad and narrow forms. The broad form was greater national mobilisation, to allow states to withstand the political and economic pressures of modern warfare. The best-known inter-war exponent of this mobilization was General Erich Ludendorff, one of Germany's main World War I leaders, who used the concept of 'total war' (see Box 4). Ludendorff attempted, as well, to think through a situation where technology put civilians in the front line. National mobilisation was probably most thoroughly carried out by the government of the USSR in the 1930s. Total war was taken very seriously by

Box 4 | General Ludendorff and total war

General Erich Ludendorff (1865–1937) was Chief of Staff to General Hindenburg, in the 1914 defence of East Prussia. The Hindenburg–Ludendorff team took over the supreme command in 1916, overseeing both the armies and the war economy. Hindenburg served as President of Germany from 1925 to 1934; Ludendorff was on the fringes of politics and took part in Hitler's 1923 Munich *Putsch*. Ludendorff was one of the first to write about 'total war', and the term was widely used in Nazi propaganda.

During the World War the hostile armies fought in deep battle zones on a front many, many kilometres wide, so that the population of the countries were fully involved . . . and thus it may be said that today the theatre of war extends in every sense of the word over the whole territory of the countries involved. Not only the armies, but also the peoples [*Völker*] are directly exposed to military action . . .

* * *

As war is the highest challenge of a people for the preservation of its existence, a totalitarian policy [*die totale Politik*] must, for that very reason, elaborate in time of peace plans for the necessary preparations required for the struggle for survival of the people in war, and imbed the foundations for such a struggle for survival so deeply that they cannot be shaken in the critical time of war . . .

The nature of war has changed, the nature of politics has changed, and now the relationship between politics and the conduct of war must also change . . . Both war and politics serve the struggle for survival of the people [*Volk*], but war is the highest expression of the people's 'will to live'. Therefore politics is subservient to the conduct of war.

* * *

The *Feldherr* [supreme military leader or 'warlord'] must be appointed to his high office already in peace time, so that he can then take the responsibilities which he has to bear in time of total war.

He must have at his disposal, in time of war, the collective strength of the people, either directly, in the armed forces or indirectly, on the home front.

He must assure himself, in time of peace, that the resolution of the people is being brought about on accepted popular [*völkische*] foundations, that the youth are being educated in them, as well as the adult generation, and that the armed forces, and in particular the officers, are made firm in them. He has to see to it that the knowledge of the meaning of the readiness of a people for total war becomes the common knowledge of the government and of the state administration, indeed, of the people themselves . . .

The *Feldherr* has also to ensure that state finances and the economy will match the demands of total war, and that the necessary measures have been taken to secure the maintenance of living standards and of the economy, and the supply of the people and of the armed forces . . .

He looks . . . on the home front, after the maintenance of the people and after their spiritual and martial resolution.

He lays down guidelines for national policy [*Politik*], which must be fulfilled in the service of the conduct of war.

(From Erich Ludendorff, *Der totale Krieg* (Munich: Ludendorffs Verlag, 1937), pp. 5, 10, 114f.)

the German government and by some military leaders in Japan. Lip service, at least, was paid to it in Italy. Indeed, one could argue that the whole Axis project of regional conquest had to do with war preparations on a grand scale, securing resources for the next round of conflict. The British and French, in a rather different way, also saw the importance of what they called 'economic warfare', and they preferred it to a repetition of the bloody land campaigns of 1914–18.

As for the narrower military 'lessons' of World War I, the most significant area was ground warfare, where European army commanders looked at ways to restore mobility to the battlefield. Although 1914–18 seems the decisive moment in the history of warfare, a more important time for technical change had been the end of the nineteenth century. In those years firepower had become much more lethal and had developed the potential to transform the battlefield. The machine gun is the best-known new weapon, but more important were rapid-fire artillery pieces and magazine (multi-shot) rifles like the Mauser Model 1898. Railways developed as a crucial means of force concentration and supply. Since road mobility was much more limited, especially across ground broken up by battle, railway movement tended to favour the defender – who was generally able to rush in reinforcements to prevent a deep breakthrough.

Individual actions in the last years of World War I had shown that defensive firepower could be suppressed and trench lines overcome. These offensive successes had come from new infantry tactics, primitive armoured vehicles, and carefully planned artillery barrages. After the war a variety of conclusions was reached in different countries, as we will see in detail in later chapters.

The French placed reliance on the techniques that had won World War I in the offensive of 1918, especially co-ordinated artillery fire. The Germans, the size and equipment of their army limited to 100,000 by the Versailles Treaty, resorted to mobility, co-ordination, and training. The Russians eventually turned to mechanisation and 'deep' offensive, but innovation was easier for them because – having purged the old officer corps – they were starting from a blank slate. The British had an even more radical approach: although they had pioneered ground-troop mechanisation, they hoped to avoid ground war altogether, in favour of strategic bombing and naval power. All modern armies saw the value of motorisation, but all were aware of the costs involved in providing motor transport for mass armies.

Still, it is not clear that before May 1940 anyone, including the officers in command of the German Army, had realised the potential of tank warfare to win quick and decisive victories. There were some other omissions in military thought which, with hindsight, are surprising. None of the military establishments of the major countries seriously considered that guerrilla warfare would play an important role. This form of warfare had become more important in China in the civil war of the 1930s, and similar methods would soon be used to fight the Japanese. There was also, as we will see in the following section, little attention paid to the movement of armies across the sea.

Planning for the next war: (2) Navies and air forces

Naval war seemed to have changed less since 1900 than ground warfare, although ships and guns had become bigger. In the mid 1930s the super-heavy artillery of the armoured battleship was still regarded as the key to naval supremacy and naval combat. As already mentioned, the Washington Conference in 1922 had set limits on naval construction, in terms of both quantity and quality. Britain, the United States, and Japan agreed to a 5:5:3 ratio, and limits were set for displacement and armament. Meanwhile the Versailles Treaty forbade the German Navy from possessing any large battleships.

'Cruiser' war against commerce (the *guerre de course*) had for centuries been a major element in naval warfare, and the submarine provided a new technical means. Germany had built some 330 U-boats in World War I, and they sank 6,600 merchant ships – nearly 13 million tons of Allied shipping (over half the tonnage that they would sink in World War II). But the great sea powers had some hopes that this threat had been overcome. The U-boats had apparently been dealt with during the war by the introduction of the convoy system, and at the end of the war effective new sensors entered service (notably hydrophones and sonar). There were even some hopes that this indiscriminate means of warfare might be eliminated by international law.

Unlike submarines, aircraft had not played an especially important part in the war at sea in 1914–18. By the mid 1930s, however, attack aircraft could carry a torpedo, or a bomb bigger than a battleship's shell. Another new departure was availability of ship-borne aircraft, mainly on aircraft carriers. Only Britain, America, and Japan built a large carrier force in the inter-war years, and the admirals were still arguing about whether they had made the battleship obsolete. Another surprising omission, given that it would be such a crucial factor in World War II, was amphibious warfare. Armies and navies devoted little thought to 'combined operations', or to developing the special equipment required. It was, admittedly, hard to see before 1940 how sea invasions could apply to a European war, and amphibious operations had generally failed in World War I, notably the fiasco at Gallipoli. The Americans, however, had a requirement to seize Pacific islands as advanced naval bases for their ORANGE war plan against Japan, and they began to devise suitable tactics.

Aviation was a major factor in thinking about future war. World War I broke out less than eleven years after the first experimental heavier-than-air flight. Aircraft played a glamorous but secondary role in 1914–18, primarily in reconnaissance. Between 1918 and 1939 much more powerful all-metal aircraft were developed, with engines of up to 1,000 horsepower. Large aircraft now had an effective operational radius (to the target) of 400–500 miles, smaller aircraft (fighters) 200–300 miles. Everywhere in the 1920s and 1930s air power was regarded as a symptom of 'modernity'.

One important school of military thought argued that air power had become decisive in warfare. Although the concept was first developed by the Italian Douhet in the early 1920s, it was taken up by Lord Trenchard in Britain, who was the head of the world's first independent air force. From this point of view the sole purpose of air power ought to be strategic and 'independent' use. Any 'auxiliary' role, supporting the army or the navy, was a waste of precious resources. In the 1930s much was made of the strategic air threat and it was a big factor in deterring action. The British politician (and future Prime Minister) Stanley Baldwin famously summarised the accepted wisdom in 1932: 'I think it is well also for the man in the street to realize that there is no power on earth that can protect him from being bombed, whatever people may tell him. The bomber will always get through.'[10] When Hitler began rearmament he gave high priority (and high profile) to the German Air Force, and especially its bomber force. When the British, themselves, turned to rearmament, air defence was given priority over ground forces.

Critical to all the armed forces was the development of electronics. The 1920s saw the worldwide spread of radio. Aside from its role in popular entertainment, news dissemination – and propaganda in the totalitarian state – radio also had a profound effect on warfare. 'Real-time' communications were crucial for the command and control of mobile warfare, making possible air support of ground troops, amphibious operations, or the co-ordination of submarine attacks. By the 1930s radio sets were cheap and light enough to be installed in aircraft and individual vehicles. At the same time, and ultimately very important in the war to come, radio communication was vulnerable to interception; the nature of the intelligence war would be transformed. The other future military use of electronics, becoming evident only at the end of the 1930s, was in the form of sensors. Radar had the potential to bring about great changes, first of all in air defence systems. Even at the tactical level the electronic revolution would give the states with the most advanced technology a distinct advantage in battles at sea and in the air.

• • •

By the end of the 1930s all the major powers were rearming. The world was perched again on the edge of a precipice, despite a knowledge of what had happened between 1914 and 1918. World War II would not simply be a continuation of World War I, especially if it is seen on a global scale, but the 1914–18 conflict still had enormous importance. The basic international system, and in particular the domination of the world by Britain and France, was under challenge from the forces of a 'new order'. The first break in the system would come in Asia.

A devastated street in Chongqing (Chungking) in 1940 after a Japanese air raid.
Jiang Jieshi (Chiang Kai-shek) moved his capital from Nanjing to Wuhan, and then
from Wuhan to Chongqing, as the invaders advanced deeper into China.
Chongqing, on the upper Yangzi River and beyond the end of the Chinese railway
lines, was relatively secure from land attack, but the Japanese Army and Navy
mounted over 100 long-range terror air raids against the city in an attempt to break
Chinese morale. This was the first prolonged air campaign of World War II; it would
not be the last.

Japan and China 1937–1940

Timeline

1894–5		First Sino–Japanese War
1904–5		Russo–Japanese War
1921–2		Washington Conference
1931		Mukden incident; Japan begins seizure of Manchuria
1937	July	Marco Polo Bridge incident; beginning of Second Sino–Japanese War
1937	December	Nanjing massacre
1938	October	Japanese Army takes Wuhan and Guangzhou
1939	August	Soviet–Japanese Khalkhin Gol incident
1941	December	Japan attacks USA and Britain. Pearl Harbor

East Asia in the 1930s

World War II really began in China in the summer of 1937. It started with a skirmish between Japanese and Chinese forces near Beijing in northern China. The Tokyo War Crimes Trial of 1946–8 (see Box 5) blamed the outbreak of war on an unholy conspiracy of Japanese statesmen and generals. More fairly, it was the unintended but predictable outcome of Japanese policy over several decades.

Broadly speaking, both 'pull' and 'push' factors were at work. The most important – and unique – force pulling the Japanese was the 'dynamic' state of affairs in China. The resources of the huge country were tempting, the Japanese Army already had a presence, and the many Japanese civilians engaged in commerce in China genuinely needed protection. A stronger China might eventually be able to consolidate its border regions and even threaten Japan. This would, of course, actually happen in 1949 – if in a way hardly anyone had expected in the 1930s – with the creation of the Communist-led People's Republic. The 'push' factor was the Japanese political system, which has already been discussed (Chapter 1). Above all there was the unchecked role of the Japanese military and a sense in nationalist circles that Japan had to expand if it was to survive.

The Manchurian crisis of 1931–2 – two years before Hitler came to power – marked a turning point of international history. Japan took control of Manchuria (see Box 5) and challenged the global status quo that had existed since 1919. After Japan's victory over Russia in the war of 1904–5 – fought out in Manchuria – the region had remained part of China. The Japanese, however, gained a strong economic and military presence in the southern sector, holding short-term economic 'concessions' and key railways. There was a Japanese base on the strategic Kwantung (Liaodong) peninsula in southern Manchuria; the force stationed here and further north was the Kwantung Army (*Kantogun*). Manchuria was only loosely controlled by the 'official' Chinese government far away in Nanjing, and the real power in the region was the local Chinese warlord, Zhang Xueliang (Chang Hsueh-liang, the 'Young Marshal'). In late 1931 ultra-nationalist staff officers of the Japanese Kwantung Army organised a confrontation with Zhang. They acted outside the authority of the central Army command, let alone that of the Tokyo government. But, as the conspirators expected, Tokyo in the end

Box 5 | The Tokyo War Crimes Trial

Nearly a decade after the events described in this chapter the Tokyo War Crimes Trial convened to pass judgement on them. Officially known as the International Military Tribunal for the Far East (IMTFE), it had the task of establishing the victors' interpretation of the origins of the war in Asia and meting out punishment. The IMTFE convened in 1946 and completed its activities in 1948, two years after the Nuremberg trial. Many of the 24 men tried at Nuremberg – Hess, Göring, Ribbentrop, Speer – are still famous. The 28 Tokyo 'Class A' war criminals (accused of 'Crimes against Peace') are unknown in the West, with the possible exception of General Tōjō Hideki, the Prime Minister in 1941–4.

Only one civilian was hanged after the Trial: Baron Hirota Koki (1878–1948), who had been Prime Minister in 1936–7, when Japan signed the Anti-Comintern Pact, and Foreign Minister in 1933–6 and 1937–8. The other 6 executed men were senior Army generals (including Tōjō). Of the 20 condemned to life imprisonment, 11 were senior officers, including Field Marshal Hata, commander of the Chinese Expeditionary Army in 1938 and 1941–44; 2 of the 20 had been Prime Ministers, Hiranuma (1939) and General Koiso (1944–5). Only 4 of the 24 Nuremberg accused were career military officers, as opposed to 17 out of 28 at Tokyo.

Most of the accused in the IMTFE were charged and found guilty of being 'leaders, organizers, instigators, or accomplices in the formulation or execution of a common plan or conspiracy . . . to wage wars of aggression, and war or wars in violation of international law' (Charge 1), and of waging 'unprovoked war' against China or 'aggressive war' against the Allies (including the USSR). Those sentenced to life were paroled in 1954; Shigemitsu Mamoru, Foreign Minister in 1943–5 and sentenced to seven years' imprisonment, became Japanese Foreign Minister again in 1954. In the 1970s the names of 14 accused Class A war criminals – including Tōjō and Hirota – were listed at the Yasukuni Shrine to honoured war dead in Tokyo; this development still arouses great controversy, in both Japan and China.

supported them and allowed military occupation of the rest of Manchuria. For all practical purposes Japan had annexed the region. In early 1932 Tokyo masked this reality by creating the new state of 'Manchukuo', but the international community did not grant recognition. Indeed, Japan left the League of Nations in early 1933, after the organisation adopted a critical report and rejected the legitimacy of Manchukuo.

Box 6 | Manchuria

Few regions of the globe played a greater part than Manchuria in the geopolitics of World War II, although the actual fighting there lasted only a few days in 1945. It was the Japanese seizure of Manchuria in 1931–2 that made friendly relations between Japan and China impossible, and eventually spoiled any Japanese *modus vivendi* with wartime America and Britain.

Manchuria is a large region of China northeast of the 'Great Wall'. The total area is 600,000 square miles, compared to 140,000 for the four main islands of Japan. Manchuria was China's northern frontier, and it was relatively sparsely settled; some 30 million people lived there in the early 1930s. In 1932 the Japanese declared the independence of a new state called 'Manchukuo'. The Japanese installed Puyi, the last Qing dynasty emperor, as ruler. (Puyi was the subject of the 1987 film by director Bernardo Bertolucci, *The Last Emperor*.) The international community never recognised Manchukuo.

As a potential centre of heavy industry, Manchuria can be compared to the Ruhr or the Ukraine. It was also a source of foodstuffs (especially the soybean crop) and a planned place of settlement for Japan's excess millions. Manchukuo was at the heart of Japan's 'new order', but time was not available to fulfil Tokyo's hopes. The great majority of the population were Chinese, and more Koreans than Japanese settled in Manchukuo as farmers. The Japanese did devote much effort to industrialisation and infrastructure development, but coal and synthetic oil production never reached the targets hoped for. Ironically, the rustbelt of Manchuria is now one of the areas of China most in need of modernisation.

Manchuria was also at the heart of the Japanese confrontation with the USSR, and this was where the Kwantung Army, the cream of the Japanese Army until 1943, was stationed. In August 1945 Manchukuo was invaded by the Red Army in the middle of the Japanese surrender negotiations, and the Kwantung Army was quickly overrun. In modern China the term 'Manchuria' is little used; the provinces of Heilongjiang, Jilin, and Liaoning are known as the 'Northeast'.

The Japanese military occupation of Manchuria was not the beginning of World War II, nor even of the Sino–Japanese War. There had been no fighting between the troops of the Chinese central government and the Japanese Army. In the Tanggu (Tangku) Truce of May 1933 Nanjing accepted a humiliating ceasefire. The terms left outside Chinese control not only Manchuria but also

Jehol Province – between the Great Wall and Manchuria proper; China also had to agree to the demilitarisation of territory 70 miles south of the Great Wall.

Nevertheless the mid 1930s saw continuing pressure on northern China by hard-line elements of the Japanese Army, who hoped to detach from Nanjing's control a further strategic tier of three valuable provinces in northern China – Hebei (Hopei), Shandong (Shantung), and Shanxi (Shansi), as well as Chahar and Suiyuan in Inner Mongolia. A basic problem for Japanese grand strategy in the mid 1930s was that the Army and the Foreign Ministry pursued different policies. The former used physical force to encroach on Chinese territory, the latter hoped to win over Generalissimo Jiang Jieshi (Chiang Kai-shek), the leader of the central Chinese government in Nanjing since 1928, to a common anti-Communist cause (see Figure 4). Jiang, for his part, avoided reacting to the worst Japanese Army provocation. He was modernising his own military forces and preoccupied with 'pacification' of the Chinese Communists.

The small Chinese middle class and some of Jiang's warlord partners pressed for greater resistance to Japanese encroachments. The Chinese Communists – partly for reasons of self-preservation – increasingly emphasised the anti-Japanese struggle. In the Xi'an (Sian) incident of December 1936 Zhang Xueliang – thrown out of Manchuria – kidnapped Jiang, intending to force him to commit to a common struggle against the Japanese. Jiang had come to the western city of Xi'an to inspect preparations for a campaign against Communist-dominated Shaanxi province. He did not directly agree to the blackmail, but was freed nevertheless. This outcome of the Xi'an incident did in the end strengthen Jiang's position and orient him towards the anti-Japanese struggle. A so-called 'Second United Front' was formed – the *first* 'united front' between Nationalists and Communists having existed between 1923 and 1927.

Rearmament: China and Japan

Military and strategic factors lay behind the Japanese–Chinese confrontation of 1937. The new Chinese government of Jiang Jieshi in Nanjing had spent much effort on the expansion, consolidation, and modernisation of the so-called 'National Revolutionary Army'. With the hurried departure of a small Soviet training mission in 1927, the main advising role was taken by

Figure 4 | **Jiang Jieshi**

Jiang Jieshi (Chiang Kai-shek) (1887–1975) was the only supreme leader of any of the major fighting states in World War II who was a professional soldier. He had come to power through the army formed by Sun Yat-sen in the 1920s; his own military training had been in Japan in the first decade of the century. Jiang proved himself an able commander of military 'expeditions' that extended the authority of the Nationalist Party over much of China, and in 1928 he was awarded the rank of generalissimo. Despite his military background, Generalissimo Jiang's attempt to confront the better-organised Japanese Army in 1937–8 ended in defeat and retreat. The photograph above depicts him making a speech in Wuhan in central China in 1938, before the city was captured by the Japanese. By the end of 1938 he had been forced back to a remote new capital at Chongqing.

All the same, Jiang remained the personification of Chinese resistance, and the Japanese could neither destroy him militarily nor replace him politically. President Roosevelt chose to project him as a world leader. His moment as an international statesman came in late 1943, when he met President Roosevelt and Prime Minister Churchill as partners at the Cairo Conference. After 1945 China was plunged into a Civil War, which was lost to the Communists. Jiang fled to Formosa (Taiwan), where he would lead 'Free China' for another thirty years.

German experts, led in succession by two famous generals, Seekt and Falkenhausen. The German plan was to form a nucleus of better-quality Chinese divisions. When the Sino–Japanese War began in 1937 the Chinese Army on paper numbered 176 divisions (2 million personnel). Some 31 divisions (300,000) were directly controlled by Jiang Jieshi, and of these 10 (100,000) had undergone training by the German mission (the troops even wore the German 'coal-scuttle' helmet). The improvement of the Chinese ground and air forces in the decade after 1927 was one of the changes that persuaded Jiang that the time was now right to resist Japan. When the next crisis came in July 1937 – six months after the Xi'an incident – Jiang was prepared to attempt a more decisive policy.

Meanwhile, the Japanese forces were remarkably strong. Whatever the danger posed to the political system by the self-willed and overbearing leadership of the Japanese armed forces, those forces represented the most powerful military instrument in Asia. Unlike Germany, Japan had not suffered fifteen years of enforced disarmament. The Empire had arguably the most 'balanced' forces of any of the major world powers, both a powerful army and a modern navy. Military strength, however, made the Japanese too ready to resort to force in China, both in 1931 and in 1937.

The Navy was the third biggest in the world. Aside from shielding Japan from the British and American fleets, the ships and aircraft of the Imperial Navy would be extremely important in the early years of the Sino–Japanese War. China had a very long coastline and almost no navy. Japan also had a large state-supported aircraft industry, with most production going to the armed services; in 1939 its factories produced 4,500 aircraft. Japanese air superiority would have a remarkable effect both in China from 1937 and in the Pacific and Southeast Asia in 1941–2. It gave the Japanese Army and Navy flexibility and mobility, and it struck hard at the morale of enemy forces.

But much the most important branch of service in China was the Japanese Army. This had been centralised and reorganised on Prussian lines in the late nineteenth century, and it obtained valuable experience of modern 'high-firepower' war in the battles of 1904–5 against Russia. The Japanese Army had an active strength of 500,000 men at the end of 1937, and this had increased to about 2.1 million by the time of Pearl Harbor. However, the Japanese Army had not directly experienced the European 'total' war in 1914–18, an event which had such a profound influence on the German, Russian, British, and French armies. The Wehrmacht would win its battles in Europe and North Africa in 1939–42 through innovative technology and organisation, and a novel approach to war, especially the use of motorised forces. The Japanese Army, in contrast, was adequately provided with field artillery and light automatic weapons, but it was a conventional force built around the infantry.

Military reformers in Tokyo saw the larger problem of involvement in China. The Japanese Army was not actually *intended* to fight in China – the main enemy was supposed to be Russia (see below). The Japanese Army General Staff was, in 1937, very reluctant to be drawn into a large and extensive war in China. Such a commitment would divert resources which were badly needed for modernisation. The reformers would be proved right in 1943–5 by the Japanese Army's defeats in New Guinea, Burma, the Philippines, and Manchuria.

The Sino–Japanese War, 1937–1938

The immediate cause of the Sino–Japanese war was the incident at the Marco Polo Bridge (the Lugouqiao or Lukouchiao) on the night of 7–8 July 1937. The affair was relatively trifling. Since the Boxer Rebellion foreign powers had had the 'right' to station troops in the old capital of China, Beijing (officially named Beiping/Peiping in 1928–49). Japanese troops were on large-scale night manoeuvres at a training ground near the Marco Polo Bridge, southwest of the city (training for a war against the USSR, not against China). They believed they were being fired on, and one Japanese infantryman went missing – in fact he eventually returned to his unit. Skirmishing spread to other places in the vicinity of Beijing, with growing violence on either side. This was not like the 1931 Manchurian incident, which was manufactured by Kwantung Army hawks, nor was it like the 1939 Gleiwitz incident, even more cynically manufactured by the Nazis before the invasion of Poland. The events in China in 1937 had more in common with the uncontrolled spiral of crisis in Europe in July and August 1914. Attempts to negotiate a ceasefire failed. The Japanese shipped in reinforcements. Jiang Jieshi publicly committed himself to national resistance: 'All those who have blood and breath in them must feel that they wish to be broken as jade rather than remain whole as tile.'[1] Nanjing sent divisions from the central army to reinforce the regional troops of the current northern warlord Song Zheyuan (Sung Che-yuan). Meanwhile in Tokyo the government of Prince Konoe, in power since early June (see Figure 5), approved requests to send three divisions of reinforcements to northern China. The Japanese quickly consolidated their hold over the region, taking Beiping on the last day of July.

Jiang Jieshi made the fateful decision in August 1937 to extend the war to another front, in central China, by confronting the Japanese garrison at Shanghai. This seemed to make strategic sense: the main forces of the Nanjing government were in the lower Yangzi valley, and the Japanese were weak there. The distances were great; to take an analogy from European geography, Jiang's action was like escalating a crisis over Berlin by beginning another one at St Petersburg. A large foreign community lived in Shanghai's international settlements, and bombardments of the city by Chinese artillery and Japanese warships, and by aircraft of both sides, caught the world's attention. The Japanese were able to use their control of the sea rapidly to build up their forces. As the fighting around the city began to go badly, Jiang made no attempt to withdraw. The Japanese mounted a large naval landing at Hangzhou Bay southwest of Shanghai, which threatened the rear of the Chinese Army and finally set off a panicky retreat. Shanghai fell on 8 November 1937; the Chinese Army pulled back in confusion, but the invaders were unable to effect a battle of encirclement and annihilation.

Now it was the turn of the Japanese to escalate the fight and to attempt to pursue it to a quick and decisive end. The Japanese Army plan for war against China – seen beforehand in Tokyo as an unlikely event – had been to seize a few strategic coastal cities. That was no longer enough. In mid November 1937, for the third time in Japanese history, an Imperial General Headquarters (Imperial GHQ) was set up to co-ordinate the war effort. The Japanese Army's approach owed much to what it had learned from its Prussian mentors: 'Sokk-sen, sokk-katsu' – 'quick war, quick settlement'. The Japanese attempted to achieve a rapid and decisive victory by pushing on to take Nanjing – 175 miles up the Yangzi from Shanghai – and forcing Jiang to the peace table. Nanjing had symbolic importance as both the modern national capital and the burial place of Sun Yat-sen, the father of the republic.

Figure 5 | **Prince Konoe**

Prince Konoe Fumimaro (1891–1945) was the most important Japanese politician in the period of World War II. The photograph shows him (on the left) with industrialist Asano Ryozo shortly after the war. A leading member of the aristocratic Fujiwara clan, personally close to the Emperor, Prince Konoe first served as Prime Minister from June 1937 to January 1939, at the time of the outbreak of the Sino–Japanese War and the Japanese occupation of much of western China. Although he did not instigate the war he supported it, and in November 1938 he put forward the concept of the 'new order' under which Japan would dominate Asia. In July 1940 Konoe became Prime Minister again and led the country as it drifted into direct confrontation with Britain and the United States. Although he resigned in October 1941, unwilling to actually unleash war against Britain and America (he was replaced by General Tōjō), Konoe had pursued hard-line policies that in late 1941 meant that Japan had to choose between war and capitulation.

In 1944–5 Prince Konoe worked to convince the Emperor to bring the war to an end, partly on grounds of preventing revolution and saving the monarchy. He poisoned himself in December 1945 when he discovered he was liable to be tried as a war criminal; he was as responsible for the war as any of those generals and politicians who were actually hanged by the Allies. A nationalist and pragmatic conservative, he might be compared to Theobold von Bethmann-Hollweg, Chancellor of Germany before and during World War I, whose role and responsibility were masked by the more obvious German military leaders and by the Kaiser.

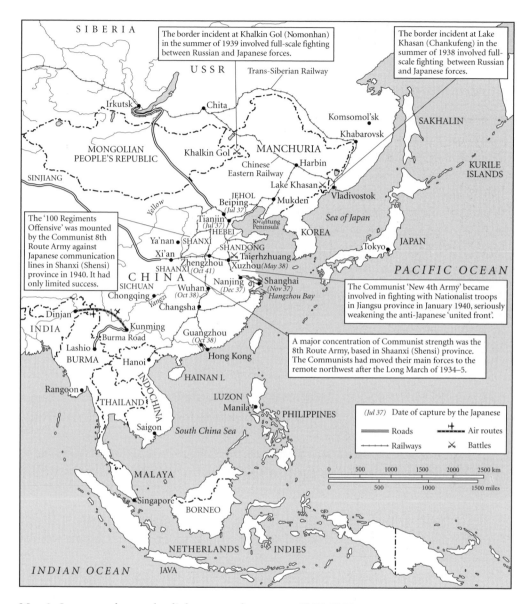

The border incident at Khalkin Gol (Nomonhan) in the summer of 1939 involved full-scale fighting between Russian and Japanese forces.

The border incident at Lake Khasan (Chankufeng) in the summer of 1938 involved full-scale fighting between Russian and Japanese forces.

The '100 Regiments Offensive' was mounted by the Communist 8th Route Army against Japanese communication lines in Shanxi (Shensi) province in 1940. It had only limited success.

The Communist 'New 4th Army' became involved in fighting with Nationalist troops in Jiangsu province in January 1940, seriously weakening the anti-Japanese 'united front'.

A major concentration of Communist strength was the 8th Route Army, based in Shaanxi (Shensi) province. The Communists had moved their main forces to the remote northwest after the Long March of 1934–5.

(Jul 37) Date of capture by the Japanese

—— Roads   ╪╪╪ Air routes

↔↔↔ Railways   ✕ Battles

0   500   1000   1500   2000   2500 km
0   500   1000   1500 miles

Map 2 Japanese advances by diplomacy and conquest, 1937–1941

Box 7 | The Nanjing massacre

Report from the Nanjing Office of the German Embassy, 15 January 1938:

On 9 January [1938], after an interruption of one month, the Nanking [Nanjing] office was reopened... According to reports of my German and American informants, when it became known that foreign representatives were intent on returning to Nanking, feverish operations were begun to remove corpses lying about the streets – in some places 'like herrings' – of civilians, including women and children, slain in a campaign of pointless mass murder.

In a reign of terror lasting several weeks, including massive looting, the Japanese have turned the business section of the city... into a heap of rubble, in the midst of which a few buildings whose exteriors appear somewhat less damaged are still standing. This arson, organized by the Japanese military, is still going on to this day... as are the abduction and rape of women and girls. In this respect, the Japanese army had erected a monument to its own shameful conduct...

There is no evidence that any action has been taken... by higher authorities against individual perpetrators, since the Japanese are silent about these matters and refuse to understand that a ruthless cauterizing of these offences would accomplish more than all attempts to cover them up.

It is considered a self-evident matter of honour for the Japanese army to murder without further ado (indeed there are thousands of such cases) every enemy soldier no longer actively engaged in combat, as well as any man judged to be such by some non-commissioned officer, whose decision cannot be appealed.

(From John Rabe, *The Good Man of Nanking: The Diaries of John Rabe* (London: Little, Brown, 1999), pp. 120–2.)

Nanjing itself fell without a fight, and badly disciplined Japanese troops massacred prisoners and civilians, and raped thousands of Chinese women (see Box 7).

The Japanese and Chinese governments had discussed terms to end the conflict, through the intermediary of the German ambassador. But the victories of Shanghai and Nanjing and the refusal of the Nationalists to accept defeat made the Konoe government extend its demands. For the moment Tokyo even ruled out Jiang as a negotiating partner. The Japanese did not formally declare war on China, and they officially called the conflict the 'China Incident' (*Shina Jihen*). Japan still paid lip service to the Kellogg–Briand Pact of 1928 (the 'Paris Treaty'), whose signatories (including Japan) agreed

that they 'condemn recourse to war for the solution of international controversies, and renounce it, as an instrument of national policy in their relations with one another'.[2] More practically, both China and Japan wanted to
avoid triggering the US Neutrality Acts, which would have blocked American
imports.

The international community was alarmed by the outbreak of full-scale
war in China, but the tormented country was far away. In October 1937
President Roosevelt made a famous speech in Chicago in which – by impli-
cation – he proposed the 'quarantine' of aggressive and warlike countries. But
this was followed by contradictory statements, and little action was taken.
In early 1941 the President permitted the formation of a small American-
manned air detachment – the famous 'Flying Tigers' – but they were not
ready for action until after Pearl Harbor. The British, with bigger interests in Asia and lower regard for the Nationalist Chinese government, were
even more reluctant to become involved. Europeans were concerned with
other events, especially in 1938 with the German–Austrian *Anschluss* and
the Czechoslovak/Sudeten crisis. Only the USSR took concrete steps, signing
a Non-Aggression Treaty with Jiang in August 1937 and providing military
help; this was all the more remarkable as it coincided with the height of
Stalin's purges of 1937–8. It is now known that from 1938 the USSR sent
1,300 aircraft and 1,600 field guns to the Nationalists; 5,000 Russian 'advisers'
served in China, a considerable number taking part in air combat against the
Japanese.

In the spring of 1938 the main fighting was for the more easterly of the
trunk railways connecting the valleys of Yellow River and the Yangzi. The key
point was the town of Xuzhou (Hsuchow), which was also the junction with
an east–west railway. The Chinese Army won a local victory at nearby Taier-
zhuang in April 1938, but the following month it had to give up Xuzhou. By
capturing this junction the Japanese had linked up their northern (Beiping)
and central (Shanghai) armies. Battles also raged in Henan Province around
the strategic city of Zhengzhou (Chengchow), another point where north–
south and east–west railways crossed. The Nationalists took the desperate
step in June 1938 of breaching the Yellow River dikes, changing the course
of the great river and flooding the plains to the southeast of Zhengzhou.
This prevented the Japanese gaining control of the vital railway, but at an
enormous cost for the civilian populations downstream in Henan, Anhui,

and Jiangsu provinces. The loss of life evidently numbered in the millions. Zhengzhou was eventually taken by the Japanese in October 1941.

In the summer and autumn of 1938 the centre of the fighting turned to Hubei Province and the conurbation of Wuhan, which is formed from the three towns of Hankou (Hankow), Wuchang, and Hanyang. Wuhan was the strategic central point where a north–south trunk railway crossed the Yangzi. The city had become the Nationalist capital after the fall of Nanjing. This campaign involved fighting on a very large scale, and the Japanese Army may have used poison gas. Wuhan fell in October 1938; Jiang Jieshi left the town just before the end. In the same month the Japanese Navy landed an expeditionary force on the south coast, near Hong Kong, and took Guangzhou (Canton). This was China's last big port; with it the Nationalists lost a major route for bringing in supplies from the outside world. After capturing Wuhan and Guangzhou the Japanese Army had effective control of most of the vital economic regions of western China, and most of the railway system. There, at the end of 1938, the fronts became locked into place. Bitter fighting would continue, but the overall position remained unchanged until 1944.

China: the war drags on, 1939–1941

The Japanese Army had spread across a vast area of north and central China, as well as some ports in the south. The extent of this area (excluding Manchukuo) was roughly what the Germans occupied in Russia in 1941–4. Within the Japanese perimeter, the occupiers' immediate control was limited to the main cities and transport corridors, especially the railways. The Nationalist armies also still held most of the country south of the Yangzi, and the highlands west of the Beijing–Wuhan railway. The ten months between the fall of Nanjing and the fall of Wuhan gave the Chinese some time for evacuation to the west and south. Jiang Jieshi established a new capital at Chongqing (Chungking) in the mountainous western province of Sichuan (Szechwan); this was on the upper Yangzi beyond the famous gorges. Sichuan was not Jiang's political base, and the province was largely cut off from outside help. The new capital was, however, beyond the Chinese railway network, and the Japanese Army could not break through the mountains. On the negative side the Chinese had little basis for a modern war industry. Their only supply routes were the railway to Hanoi/Haiphong in French Indochina, the Burma Road, and the long road to Soviet Central Asia. Even these tenuous links would be interrupted and effectively cut following unexpected events in Europe.

Japanese attempts to break south from the Yangzi were halted by the Nationalists at Changsha (200 miles south of Wuhan) in Hunan Province in September 1939, and again in September 1941; the city fell only in June 1944. In the winter of 1939–40 Jiang attempted a co-ordinated series of counter-offensives using all his nine 'war areas' (theatre commands), but little was achieved, and many lives were lost. As for the Chinese Communists, with their smaller forces, they had been organised into the 8th 'Route' Army (in Shaanxi Province) and the 'New 4th' Army in Jiangsu Province (north of Shanghai). To some extent goaded by Nationalist charges that they were not pulling their weight, the 8th Route Army under the Communist generals Peng Dehuai (P'eng Te-huai) and Zhu De (Chu Teh) mounted the '100 Regiments Offensive', in the late summer and autumn of 1940. As many as 400,000 personnel, organised in 115 regiments, took part. The objective was to shake the Japanese position in the northern Shanxi Province. Mao Zedong, who by this time had emerged as primary (but not yet all-powerful) leader of the Chinese Communist Party, argued against an over-hurried escalation from guerrilla warfare to more conventional tactics, but he was overruled. The Communist forces temporarily blocked some of the main Japanese-held railway lines, but the occupiers were able to secure their position by the end of the year. The new commander of the (Japanese) North China Area Army, General Okamura, launched a savage counter-insurgency drive to destroy villages supporting the guerrillas, under the slogan of the 'Three Alls': 'Kill all, burn all, destroy all.' The start of 1941 saw a reopening of open hostility between the Communists and the Nationalists. Fighting broke out between the Communist New 4th Army and its Nationalist neighbours in Chinese-held areas on the lower Yangzi. The 'united front' was now in tatters.

The Japanese armed forces had achieved a spectacular military success. The Empire fielded a million soldiers (25 divisions) in China. At an operational and tactical level the Japanese military system had shown itself to be formidable. Fighting against a much larger enemy the Japanese armed forces had achieved victory after victory. There was no sign that the Chinese armies of the Nationalists or the Communists were going to be able

Box 8 | The Japanese 'new order'

Statement of Prime Minister Prince Konoe Fumimaro, 22 December 1938:

The Japanese Government are resolved . . . to carry on military operations for the complete extermination of the anti-Japanese [Nationalist] Guomindang Government, and at the same time to proceed with the work of establishing a new order in East Asia together with those far-sighted Chinese who share in our ideals and aspirations. A spirit of renaissance is now sweeping over all parts of China and enthusiasm for reconstruction is mounting ever higher . . .

Japan, China and Manchukuo will be united by the common aim of establishing a new order in East Asia and of realising a relationship of neighbourly amity, common defence against Communism, and economic co-operation . . .

If the true object of Japan in conducting the present vast military campaign be fully understood, it will be plain that what she seeks is neither territory nor indemnity . . . Japan not only respects the sovereignty of China, but she is prepared to give positive consideration to the questions of the abolition of extra-territoriality [i.e. special status of foreigners in China] and the rendition [ending] of Concessions and Settlements – matters which are necessary for the full independence of China.

(From *Documents on British Foreign Policy* (London: HMSO, 1955), Third Series, vol. VIII, p. 343.)

to counter-attack effectively or even that guerrilla warfare was going to seriously threaten the invaders' position. The war had been fought on a massive scale, and was costly for both sides. One estimate is that the Japanese lost (in deaths) 220,000 personnel in China in 1937–9, and 100,000 in 1940–1. (Reflecting the more static situation of later years, the Japanese would lose only 157,000 men in China in 1942–5.) Chinese military losses in 1937–41 have been estimated as 1.03 million. By contrast, in the Battle of France in 1940 – the costliest German campaign before June 1941 – German losses were 45,000, and French losses 90,000.

In December 1938 Prince Konoe declared a 'new order' in Asia (see Box 8). All the same, the Japanese government could not bring the war in China to final victory. Unlike Hitler in Russia after 1941, the Japanese invaders did at least attempt a 'political' solution. But the puppet government they installed in occupied Nanjing under Wang Jingwei (Wang Ching-wei) had little real effect. Wang was a remarkable figure. Jailed in 1910 for attempting to assassinate the Qing regent, a close comrade of Sun Yat-sen, he had been a rival with Jiang Jieshi for the succession to Dr Sun. Wang went over to the Japanese after the fall of Wuhan, in the expectation that China's war was unwinnable. But the Japanese Army and the government of Prince Konoe could not agree on a consistent policy towards Wang. They wanted to create a puppet state which they could dominate, but they also wanted to keep open the option of coming to terms with Jiang. Wang had left Chongqing at the end of 1938; his government was recognised by the Japanese, after a long delay, only in March 1940.

Both the Chinese and the Japanese were damaged by the war. Jiang's attempt at resistance seemed futile. Nationalist China had lost the most valuable parts of its territory, and it had been physically cut off from the outside world. But the Japanese, too, had put themselves in a difficult position. This was not the war the Japanese General Staff had wanted to fight. As would later be said about the American involvement in Korea in 1950, it was 'the wrong war, in the wrong place, at the wrong time'. Modernisation of the Japanese Army had to be forgone to pay for a low-technology colonial war in China. Access to the resources of China, especially in the north, was offset by the cost of maintaining a big army there. A few far-sighted officials in Tokyo compared the China expedition to the campaign of the French Empire in Spain, the bloody 'ulcer' which fatally weakened Napoleon. A more subtle danger was that the easy Japanese victories bred overconfidence and arrogance, apparently confirming the view that morale and offensive spirit were more important than modern equipment.

The Sino–Japanese War also increased the influence of the military leaders and conservative nationalists in Japan, which would have devastating consequences when the Western powers were confronted in 1940–1. Already estranged from the Western powers by the Manchurian crisis of 1931–3, Tokyo was pushed towards direct confrontation by the Sino–Japanese War. There was one significant positive gain for the Japanese: their Army and Navy were at war strength, and both services obtained great operational experience. Victorious campaigns in China heightened the confidence and morale of both the officer corps and the rank and file. When war began with Britain and America in late 1941 the Japanese forces would fight it with significant advantages.

Japan and the USSR

It might seem unnecessary to waste words here on Soviet–Japanese strategic relations in 1937–41; after all, the two countries went to war only in August 1945. Nevertheless Japanese policy from 1937 to 1941 makes little sense without the Russian factor. The main danger for the government and Army leadership in Tokyo in the mid 1930s was neither China, nor Britain, nor the United States; it was the Soviet Union. As Prime Minister Hirota put it in a top-level strategic planning document in mid 1936, this was the first national objective: 'The repletion of Army forces will aim at a strength to resist the forces the Soviet Union can employ in the Far East. The garrisons in Manchukuo and Korea will be replenished in order that they can deliver the initial blow to Soviet forces in the Far East at the outbreak of hostilities.'[3] For the Russians, too, a war in the Far East against Japan became a central element of military planning.

The expanding Russian state had claimed territory on the Pacific coast since the 1600s. It had extended and consolidated this in confrontations with China in the 1850s; the Russians founded the port of Vladivostok on the Sea of Japan. Conflicting interests between Russia and Japan over Manchuria and even Korea in the 1890s led the two states to war in 1904. In the peace terms Russia was obliged to give up its lease to the Kwantung Peninsula and connecting railways, and it ceded to Japan the southern part of Sakhalin Island. (All this would be 'returned' to Russia by the USA and Britain at Yalta in 1945 – without consulting the Chinese – in exchange for Stalin's promise to attack Japan.) After the 1917 Bolshevik Revolution the Japanese – along with the Allied powers – sent warships and troops to occupy the Russian Far East. The British and Americans withdrew their small expeditionary forces in 1919 but Japan kept a garrison in coastal Siberia until 1922.

Russia had seemed greatly weakened by world war and revolution, but from about 1928–9 the Japanese Army began to consider the possibility of war with a reviving USSR. Tokyo was alarmed by a Soviet Red Army punitive incursion into Manchuria against the local warlord Zhang Xueliang in late 1929. There were bigger dangers from Tokyo's point of view. Russia was still a vast continental state with a population twice that of Japan; it was the European power with the strongest interest in Northeast Asia. Second, the Moscow-based Communist International (Comintern) was feared as a direct threat to the Japanese internal status quo, and there were real ideological fears behind the agreement Japan signed with Germany in 1936, the Anti-Comintern Pact: 'The High Contracting States agree that they will mutually keep each other informed concerning the activities of the Communist International, will confer upon the necessary measure of defence, and will carry out such measures in close co-operation.'[4] Finally, the USSR was changing very rapidly from the late 1920s, with the industrialisation projects of the Five-Year Plans (including the development of Siberia), and the revival and motorisation of the Red Army.

Rearmament: the USSR

Soviet rearmament, in turn, was speeded up partly by a fear of Japan. Tokyo had, after all, occupied exposed Russian territory in 1918–22, and was seen by Moscow as a partner in the 'capitalist encirclement'. The Japanese occupation of all of Manchuria in 1931–2 was extremely threatening. Rather than Chinese warlords like Zhang Xueliang, the Russians now faced a large and effective Japanese Kwantung Army (which had previously been concentrated in distant southern Manchuria). The Japanese could now even launch an attack east out of Manchuria to the Pacific, taking or cutting off Vladivostok. The Soviet Far East was very sparsely settled; the population of eastern Siberia was just 4.5 million in 1937. There was only one practical line of communications, the vulnerable Trans-Siberian Railway which ran around the edge of Manchukuo.

When it came to rearmament the Communist government, like the Nazi government in Germany a few years later, was not bound by fiscal orthodoxy. Indeed, unlike in Germany the totality of industry was already under direct state control. Stalin's planned industrialisation of the Five-Year Plans (beginning in 1927–32) was linked to armaments production and mobilisation capability. In the mid and late 1930s this investment paid off with the massive expansion and re-equipment of the Red Army (including the air force), a development that would have a profound effect on the outcome of World War II. Russia not only built up its own armed forces, it also provided military aid to the Czechoslovaks, the Spanish Republic, and China.

Stalin took steps to appease Japan; in 1935 the USSR sold to Manchukuo (i.e. to Japan) the interests in the Chinese Eastern Railway (across Manchuria) which it had inherited from Tsarist Russia. (Again, Stalin would get back this concession at Yalta in 1945.) The main thrust of Soviet policy, however, was the massive build-up of Soviet strength in the eastern USSR. Submarines and heavy bombers appeared on the Pacific coast. Most important was the growing ground force; in 1931 the Red Army had 6 divisions in the Far East, by 1939 it had 30. The USSR, as we have seen, was the only effective supporter of Nationalist China after the war began in 1937. In another, more sinister development, Stalin's secret police carried out in the autumn of 1937 the forced deportation of the entire Korean minority living in the Soviet Far East. These unfortunates – men, women, and children – were identified by Moscow as potential Japanese 'fifth-columnists' and were shipped off in railway goods wagons to Central Asia.

One of the costs for Tokyo of the unexpectedly long campaign against Jiang Jieshi was that the Japanese had to bring in troops earmarked for Manchuria. This seriously weakened the Japanese position with respect to the Russians. Two bloody incidents were fought out with the Red Army on the borders of Manchuria, and in both the Japanese Kwantung Army came off worse. The first, in 1938, was at Lake Khasan (Changkufeng), near a strategic hill on the borders of Korea, Manchuria, and the USSR, about 100 miles from Vladivostok. The second, in the summer of 1939, was fought out 600 miles to the west, on the far (Mongolian) side of Manchuria at Khalkhin Gol (Nomonhan). Neither incident is regarded as formally part of World War II, but they were important tests of power. Soviet losses at Khalkhin Gol (killed and missing) were nearly 10,000, and Japanese losses about 25,000; these can be compared to the 16,000 men the Germans lost during the 'real' war in Poland a month or so later. Both the Soviet–Japanese border battles – and especially Khalkhin Gol – showed the Japanese that the Red Army was a dangerous opponent. The Japanese were impressed by the strength of the Soviet forces, their armour and artillery, and especially their ability to mount powerful operations with such forces at a distance of 350 miles from the nearest railhead. Khalkhin Gol, with the brilliant encirclement and destruction of a whole Japanese division, was also the making of the officer in command; Georgii Zhukov would be Stalin's outstanding leader in the Great Patriotic War of 1941–5.

Soviet–Japanese relations changed after Khalkhin Gol. Another part of the global war broke out – in Europe – in September 1939. Stalin adopted a more cautious policy. The USSR was also now, after the August 1939

Nazi–Soviet Pact, operating in apparent partnership with Germany. In April 1941 the USSR and the Japanese signed a Treaty of Neutrality, in which they pledged not to attack each other. The USSR even recognised Manchukuo – in exchange for Japanese recognition of the Soviet-dominated Mongolian People's Republic. Soviet aid to the Nationalist Chinese, already tailing off, was halted. The next diplomatic revolution was occasioned by the outbreak of war between Germany and Russia in June 1941. This might have led to a Kwantung Army assault on Siberia, but by that time a Japanese movement against Southeast Asia was already looming (see Chapter 5).

German artillery moves into Poland in September 1939. This imposing SdKfz 7 was a half-track, designed to pull a medium artillery piece through difficult terrain; it entered service on the eve of the war. Germany had, however, begun serious rearmament only in 1933, and its military forces were a mix of the old and the new. The military campaign of September 1939 would be fought in a traditional Prussian manner. The invasion of Poland led Britain and France to declare war on Germany. Hitler's underestimation of their resolve turned a border war against a despised neighbour into a premature and much more dangerous conflict with two European great powers.

Hitler's border wars 1938–1939

Timeline

1919		Paris Peace Conference; Versailles Treaty
1933	January	Nazis take power in Germany
1938	September	Munich Crisis
1939	August	Nazi–Soviet pact
	September	Germany invades Poland; Britain and France declare war

Tearing up the Versailles *Diktat*

The outbreak of the war in Europe in 1939 is one of the most familiar themes of twentieth-century history. It raises the question of how Germany, isolated and largely unarmed in the early 1930s, flanked by three wary great powers – Britain, France, and the USSR – was able to shatter the status quo and achieve early victories.

The installation of a German government led by Adolf Hitler in January 1933 did not immediately set off international conflict, nor did the violent consolidation of dictatorial power by the NSDAP in the year or two that followed. The momentous first step towards war came in March 1935, when Hitler denounced the disarmament clauses of the Versailles Treaty. Germany would now have a proper army of thirty-six divisions, formed from short-service conscripts, and with the full range of weaponry. Perhaps most significant for the immediate confrontation with the Versailles powers, Germany would also have an air force, the Luftwaffe. Covert arms violations had been taking place under the Weimar government (in collaboration with the Soviets). Further steps were taken from the moment the NSDAP came to power, in 1933. But it was open German rearmament in early 1935 that began the period of 'active revision' in Europe.

The immediate response was the Franco–Soviet Treaty of Mutual Assistance, a five-year pact under which France and Russia promised to aid each other in the event of unprovoked aggression by another state. Hitler in turn used the ratification of this treaty by the French Chamber of Deputies in February 1936 to justify sending elements of his army into the Rhineland, the region of western Germany (either side of the Rhine) which had been demilitarised under Versailles. The Rhineland was strategically crucial. Unless German troops garrisoned the Rhineland, Germany, and especially the vital Ruhr industrial region, was defenceless against attack. The Reich now devoted considerable resources to laying out a stout defensive zone here, known as the *Westwall* or 'Siegfried Line'. In 1944–5, Hitler would deploy the last scraps of his forces for a defence of the *Westwall* and the Rhineland, this time against American armies. Meanwhile, looking at the situation from the perspective of Germany's 1936 opponents, military forces based on territory west of the Rhine posed a direct threat to the Netherlands, Belgium, and northern France (as they had in 1914 and would again in May 1940 and December 1944).

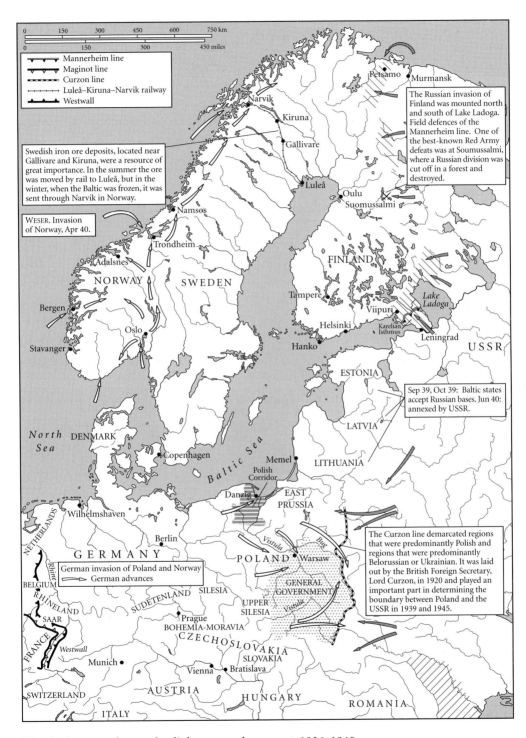

Map 3 German advances by diplomacy and conquest, 1936–1940

The following text appears within the map:

Scale bars:
0 150 300 450 600 750 km
0 150 300 450 miles

Legend:
- Mannerheim line
- Maginot line
- Curzon line
- Luleå–Kiruna–Narvik railway
- Westwall

Swedish iron ore deposits, located near Gällivare and Kiruna, were a resource of great importance. In the summer the ore was moved by rail to Luleå, but in the winter, when the Baltic was frozen, it was sent through Narvik in Norway.

WESER. Invasion of Norway, Apr 40.

The Russian invasion of Finland was mounted north and south of Lake Ladoga. Field defences of the Mannerheim line. One of the best-known Red Army defeats was at Soumussalmi, where a Russian division was cut off in a forest and destroyed.

Sep 39, Oct 39: Baltic states accept Russian bases. Jun 40: annexed by USSR.

The Curzon line demarcated regions that were predominantly Polish and regions that were predominantly Belorussian or Ukrainian. It was laid out by the British Foreign Secretary, Lord Curzon, in 1920 and played an important part in determining the boundary between Poland and the USSR in 1939 and 1945.

German invasion of Poland and Norway
German advances

Place names and labels on map:
Petsamo, Murmansk, Narvik, Kiruna, Gällivare, Luleå, Oulu, Suomussalmi, Namsos, Trondheim, Adalsnes, NORWAY, SWEDEN, FINLAND, Lake Ladoga, Bergen, Tampere, Viipuri, Oslo, Helsinki, Karelian Isthmus, Leningrad, Stavanger, Hanko, USSR, ESTONIA, North Sea, DENMARK, LATVIA, Copenhagen, Baltic Sea, Memel, LITHUANIA, Polish Corridor, Danzig, EAST PRUSSIA, Wilhelmshaven, Berlin, Vistula, Bug, NETHERLANDS, GERMANY, POLAND, Warsaw, BELGIUM, Rhine, GENERAL GOVERNMENT, SILESIA, RHINELAND, SAAR, UPPER SILESIA, Vistula, FRANCE, Westwall, Prague, BOHEMIA-MORAVIA, CZECHOSLOVAKIA, Munich, SLOVAKIA, Vienna, Bratislava, SWITZERLAND, AUSTRIA, HUNGARY, ROMANIA, ITALY

The Rhineland crisis is sometimes portrayed as the great missed opportunity to stop what Winston Churchill later called the 'unnecessary war'. Germany was indeed militarily weaker in 1936 than it would be in future. But a number of factors worked against a vigorous response by the states that feared Germany. The NSDAP had been in power for three years, and the new Wehrmacht was already strong enough to make outside military intervention much more than a walkover. Only the French Army could take direct action, and the London government refused to support Paris. Britain's diplomatic response to Hitler's rearmament announcement had been the Anglo–German Naval Agreement of June 1935, which allowed Hitler to tear up the Versailles naval limitations – including the ban on U-boat construction – as long as the *Kriegsmarine* stayed under 35 per cent of British strength in each ship type. At the time of the Rhineland crisis Britain was embroiled in a Mediterranean crisis over Mussolini's invasion of Ethiopia (begun in October 1935). America and Russia, for their part, took no direct interest in the Rhineland crisis. As a final inhibiting factor, the remilitarisation of the Rhineland could not be considered international aggression. Full sovereignty of all German territory – and the right to arm to the same level as other states – were not in themselves unreasonable demands. Hitler's requirements, for all many statesmen knew, might be confined to this.

Rearmament: Germany

The most extraordinary feature of the Wehrmacht victories of 1938–42 was how recently Germany had rearmed. Before the NSDAP came to power, in 1933, Germany had an army of only 100,000 men. Officially, even in 1935, Germany had no tanks, military aircraft, or heavy artillery. Two rather different things need to be borne in mind when discussing the German build-up. The first is how Hitler used the new German Army and Luftwaffe to bluff stronger opponents into allowing the consolidation and initial expansion of the Third Reich. And the second is how these early military decisions impacted on the *actual* war-fighting capabilities of the Wehrmacht from September 1939, and especially from May 1940 onwards.

What made the German military so potent, both as a diplomatic threat and as a war-fighting instrument? We have seen that Germany started with a larger manpower base than any individual European rival except Russia, and this was combined with a modern economy. The armed forces of Prussia/Germany had a remarkable history dating back to the early 1600s. The equipment and technology of ground and air war were now changing so fast that latecomers – at least those with advanced economies – suffered no real disadvantage; indeed, they were the ones who were not left with a scrapheap of obsolete equipment. Rapid rearmament was embarked upon with very little thought for financial orthodoxy or the long-term health of the economy. Under Hitler the German government set out on an expensive and rash grand strategy that eventually necessitated the achievement of national objectives by military means.

The development of German ground forces would be crucial when the real fighting began. Ground force equipment was not, however, the fundamental thing. The panzer divisions (see Box 13) were even as late as 1939 equipped mainly with Panzer II light tanks, with only a small number of (medium) Panzer IIIs, and with an even smaller number of (heavy) Panzer IVs. What were shown to be more important in 1939–40, were doctrine, organisation, and communications. Unlike their enemies in 1939–40, the Germans concentrated what tanks they had in large formations. Armour was also an independent branch of service, freed from the influence of the infantry and cavalry.

In September 1939, the month of the invasion of Poland, the American news magazine *Time* described for its readers 'a war of quick penetration and obliteration – Blitzkrieg, lightning war'.[1] This brought 'Blitzkrieg' into popular usage, but the term was not one the German military themselves generally used, nor was it a wholly accurate statement of how their high command hoped to fight great-power enemies. What did exist in the German military was a doctrinal stress on the war of movement and on flexibility. In part this was the traditional Prussian approach to war, but it also drew on the lessons from World War I and – by necessity – on what had been required by the German Army's weak position in the 1920s.

On the other hand, features which would be important in the real war in 1939–40 were less obvious in the pre-war period of tension. Rivals and victims in the late 1930s did not cave in because they knew the Germans had transformed the nature of ground warfare; even the Wehrmacht did not know that. It was enough that Germany now had a large modern army, and to recall that Prussian and German armies had fought very effectively in 1866, 1870, and 1914–18.

In the fraught diplomacy of the late 1930s the spectre of the Luftwaffe counted for more than the panzer force. This came about partly from contemporary international beliefs about the potency of 'air power' and partly from Nazi propaganda that exaggerated the pace of the Luftwaffe build-up. German aircraft played a notorious (and overblown) role in the Civil War in Spain. Hermann Göring, one of the top NSDAP leaders, was patron of the Luftwaffe. When its existence was officially admitted in 1935, the Luftwaffe's strength already totalled nearly 1,900 machines and production was 200–300 a month. By August 1938 there were 2,900 first-line aircraft, many of them advanced types. The Luftwaffe 'strategic' bomber force carried great diplomatic weight in the 1930s war of bluff. In terms of future actual war-fighting the Germans also did the right thing and built multi-purpose aircraft. Battlefield support ('strike') aircraft were part of the Wehrmacht's combined-arms concept; most senior officers of the new Luftwaffe came from the Army anyway.

In aircraft, unlike tanks or artillery, German equipment had a significant qualitative edge over most potential enemies. For the first three years of the European war Germany would seem to dominate the sky, at least over the continent. Aircraft design and procurement were and are risky businesses. The Luftwaffe's pre-war generation – the Messerschmitt fighters, the Junkers Ju 87 ('Stuka') dive bomber, the Heinkel, Dornier, and Junkers medium bombers – were successful designs, technically superior to most foreign types. The patronage of Hitler and Göring coincided with an international leap into new technologies: monoplanes rather than biplanes, powerful supercharged motors, all-metal construction. Germany was on the cutting edge; the air rearmament programme was well managed, and the Germans were lucky to suffer few production hiccups. The Luftwaffe would not be so fortunate with their next generation of aircraft in 1940–3 (with the exception of the Focke-Wulf fighter); the service would then have to soldier on in 1943–5 with modified versions of the planes with which it began the conflict.

The Germans could not have everything their own way in the 1930s. Even with the go-ahead of the Anglo–German Naval Agreement, expansion of the *Kriegsmarine* was difficult. Major investments needed to be made in German shipyards and specialised engineering plants (some of the first big

Figure 6 | **Heinkel 111 bomber**

A German Heinkel He 111 medium bomber in the process of being 'bombed up' during the Spanish Civil War. The Luftwaffe (Air Force) was the most striking achievement of Hitler's mid-1930s rearmament programme. The He 111 was the most important aircraft in Luftwaffe service in 1939, by which time nearly 1,000 examples were available.

The development of the He 111 began in early 1934, a year before Germany rejected the arms limitations of the Versailles Treaty; the machine was initially described as a commercial transport. Designed to carry a bomb load of 1,000 kg (2,200 lb) at high speed, the He 111 was a potent threat in the late 1930s and an effective medium-range bomber throughout much of World War II; it made up the backbone of the air armada that attacked Britain in 1940. The He 111 was surpassed by later German designs like the Junkers Ju 88 and dwarfed by Allied heavy bombers, but it remained in production until 1944.

Box 9 | Reflections of Admiral Raeder, 3 September 1939

Admiral Erich Raeder was C-in-C of the German Navy from 1928 to 1943. This personal memorandum expressed his pessimistic appraisal of the situation at the beginning of the war.

Today the war against France and England broke out, the war which, according to the Führer's previous assertions, we had no need to fear before about 1944 . . . As far as the Navy is concerned, obviously it is in no way very adequately equipped for the great struggle with Great Britain by autumn 1939. It is true that in the short period since 1935 . . . it has built up a well-trained, suitably organised submarine arm . . . the submarine arm is still much too weak, however, to have any decisive effect on the war. The surface forces, moreover, are so inferior in number and strength to those of the British Fleet that, even at full strength, they can do no more than show that they know how to die gallantly.

(From 'Fuehrer Conferences on Naval Affairs', *Brassey's Naval Annual*, 1948, pp. 37f.)

ships had Swiss machinery). Major warships required long building times. Hitler did in January 1939 approve a long-term programme, the 'Z' plan, for a battleship navy to be ready in the mid 1940s, but this came to nothing. Germany's eventual enemies were also fortunate that the political strength of the independent Luftwaffe and the conservative outlook of Hitler and senior naval officers led to a neglect of naval aviation.

Rearmament: France and Britain

The World War I victors began the decade of confrontation with much stronger armed forces than those of the Third Reich. In the early 1930s Britain and France already had big military establishments; the German military had since 1919 been severely restricted. But other factors held back the responses of the democracies. Although Germany had lost half again as many soldiers in 1914–18 as France, and more than twice as many as Britain, the awful memory of the war affected the will of the democracies more than that of totalitarian Germany. Leaders and electorate sought alternatives. The British and French governments also felt more bound by financial constraints – the need for balanced budgets – than did the Nazi government in Berlin.

All the same, France had the largest army in Europe. The fiasco of 1940 makes us overlook the considerable investment the French government made; indeed, over the whole inter-war period France spent more on armaments per capita than did any other European state. Much of this funding went on equipment for the Army. The Air Force (the *Armée de l'Air*) was weaker, partly because of French industrial backwardness, partly because less funds were available than in Germany, and partly because – unlike Britain – France did not have the luxury of forgoing high expenditure on the Army. France had to face the threat of fighting a land war on its own, against a state with a larger manpower pool, with advanced technology, and with a strong military tradition. For France Britain had limited potential as a partner, because of its diplomatic caution, its different geopolitical priorities, and the extreme weakness of its army. French attempts to develop friendships with new states in Eastern Europe might have had some value as a deterrent to Germany. In the event of actual war, however, there was little France could do to help those states, and vice versa.

French strategic doctrine in the 1930s envisaged a prolonged war. This was in sharp contrast to the doctrine of 1914, which had stressed early offensive action. In the 1930s the French military assumed that a well-prepared defence could hold off an attacker and that in the long term economic factors would count. Such a conflict would wear down Germany; it would allow the best use of the economic and (overall) demographic advantages of the anti-German camp and exploit the possibilities of blockade. The ability to fight this kind of war would, it was hoped, also deter German aggression.

The British, too, increased their spending on armaments in the later 1930s. The special features for Britain were imperial commitments and a great reluctance to repeat the 'continental' strategy of 1914–18 by sending ground forces to the European 'mainland'. The self-governing Dominions – Canada, Australia, New Zealand, and South Africa – were even more unwilling to despatch forces to another major war in mainland Europe. Also, even more than the French, the British saw their rearmament options as limited by the need to balance the budget and maintain the flow of exports; a healthy economy was regarded as one of Britain's strongest long-term weapons.

When the Treasury allocated more funds to armaments after 1935, they went to the Royal Navy and to the Royal Air Force, as a deterrent and as a defensive shield for the homeland; the British Army had the lowest priority.

These choices are understandable, but without ground forces to deploy there was little that Britain could do physically to block German actions or even to stiffen French resistance. It was only in the winter of 1938–9 that the extent of Hitler's demands became clear enough to government, to voters, and to the Dominions. The strategy rapidly shifted gear, with plans for the British Empire to provide a total of fifty-five divisions. But this was very late in the day.

Italy chooses sides

Germany was not the only major European state openly dissatisfied with the status quo in the middle of the 1930s. The other one was Fascist Italy. The background to Mussolini and Fascism has already been outlined (see Chapter 1). Two further aspects need to be considered here: Italian foreign policy in the mid 1930s – after Hitler and the NSDAP came to power – and the development of Italian military power.

It is hard to imagine that Italy on its own, even under Mussolini, could have set off a general European war. On the other hand Fascist Italy bears much responsibility for Hitler's successes. Historians continue to debate whether Mussolini had a long-term plan of aggression, or whether he was just an opportunist, ready to side with whichever power bloc could give him more. Certainly a central plank of Fascist ideology was international struggle, and the regime made much of the legacy of the Roman Empire, which had controlled the Mediterranean. But as a relatively weak power in terms of population, resources, and military assets, Italy was not in a position to achieve this programme on its own. Mussolini's 'March on Rome' was in 1922, and he had consolidated his internal power by 1925. There followed a decade of bombastic statements but no serious international initiatives.

Things were different once Britain and France became preoccupied with a rearming and more assertive Germany. The Italian invasion of Ethiopia (Abyssinia) came in October 1935 – a few months after Hitler announced rearmament. The ineffectual response of the British and French – they had their own African colonies – showed indecision and disunity. The British took a firmer line than the French, but to no effect. Ethiopia, which had been a member of the League of Nations, was annexed by Italy, and merged with earlier colonies as Italian East Africa (*Africa Orientale Italiana*, AOI); Ethiopia was not even given Manchukuo's fig leaf of quasi-independence. Italian East Africa was different from Manchukuo in two other respects: it had little economic value, and it was strategically indefensible once the British closed the Suez Canal (as the East African campaign of 1940–1 would show). Mussolini followed his diplomatic and military triumph in East Africa by sending Italian military forces to fight as 'volunteers' in the Civil War that began in Spain in July 1936. At the end of 1936 he joined Germany and Japan in the Anti-Comintern Pact.

Despite Mussolini's stirring of the pot, in the late 1930s the British and French still made an effort to appease him as a lesser and weaker evil, and even as a southern prop against Nazi Germany. Italy had been the ally of Britain and France in World War I. It had gained some Austrian territory in 1919, and had reason to fear Germany. Despite this, Fascist Italy made claims to territory in French Tunisia and Corsica, and even southeast France, with noisy sabre-rattling in late 1938. Mussolini pressed on, occupying Albania in April 1939 and finally throwing his lot in with Hitler in the military alliance (the 'Pact of Steel') of May 1939.

Italy did represent a considerable military factor. As one of the victors of World War I, the country had not been subject to disarmament. The Army was kept large, at least on paper, and comprised about seventy divisions in 1940 – if not the '8 million bayonets' that Mussolini boasted about. While Germany had been banned from military aviation for about fifteen years after 1918, the Fascist regime from the start placed emphasis on the Air Force. The most important force in the great-power calculations of the 1930s was probably the Italian Navy. Italy had engaged in a busy naval construction race with France in the 1920s. The Navy, aided by the Air Force, could endanger the British position in the Mediterranean, especially as part of a global challenge alongside the Japanese and the Germans.

On the other hand Mussolini and the Italian military leaders were aware of the discrepancy between their forward policy and the resources of their relatively poor country. Like Japan's war in China, Italy's expeditionary campaigns in Ethiopia (1935–6) and Spain (1936–9) diverted funds from military modernisation and led to losses of equipment. Comprehensive modernisation of the forces in the 1930s was slow.

Distant titans: the USSR and the United States

An armed and unco-operative Italy (like an armed and unco-operative Japan) was a significant background factor in British and French diplomatic caution in the 1930s. The really remarkable thing about the pre-war crisis, however – with hindsight – was how little attention was paid in London and Paris (and indeed in Berlin and Rome) to the 'superpowers' that would swamp them all half a dozen years later – the USA and the USSR. (The Japanese, in their own way, had a more realistic assessment of the situation.)

Of all the European states it was the Russians who first began serious rearmament, with the Five-Year Plans in 1927. The 1931 Japanese annexation of Manchuria then developed as a direct threat to Soviet territory (see Chapter 2). The victory of an overtly anti-Communist and anti-Slav movement in Germany in 1933 increased Russian fears, especially after Germany signed a non-aggression pact (in early 1934) with Russia's hostile neighbour Poland. The strength of Soviet armed forces rose from 610,000 in 1927 to 930,000 in 1935, and 1.5 million in 1938; between 1930 and 1939 Soviet factories produced some 15,000 tanks. Alongside this extraordinary military build-up came a change in Moscow's diplomatic posture – from blustering hostility against the West to attempted co-operation with the 'peace-loving' capitalist states against Germany and Japan (see Chapter 1). When, in 1935, Germany began open rearmament, the USSR made defensive agreements, first with France and then with Czechoslovakia.

Various factors masked the Kremlin's rapid rearmament and reduced the impact of its diplomatic reorientation. The details of Soviet military expansion were kept secret. The Baltic states and Poland blocked the Red Army from practical access to the cockpit of Central Europe. Diplomatically, Soviet Russia had been rigidly hostile to Britain and France – and to the whole Versailles system – in the 1920s, so it was hard to take Moscow's change of heart seriously. Politically the atheistic Bolshevik bogeymen still inspired as much dread as the Nazis. Russia was in strategic terms the natural partner of France against Germany – more so than Britain – but the French Catholic right was viscerally anti-Communist, and most of France's Eastern European allies were terrified of the Kremlin and Bolshevism. Britain, for its part, was angered by Comintern propaganda directed against its colonies. The terrible Soviet trials and purges that began on a mass scale in mid 1937 made the perception of the USSR even worse. Just as the Red Army embarked on a genuinely impressive expansion and re-equipment programme, its most senior commanders were arrested and shot. (See Chapter 5 for further details.)

The United States was very different from the USSR, yet there were important similarities. The differences were clear enough. Stalin, in the totalitarian USSR, could reverse Soviet policy single-handedly and overnight; President Roosevelt had to move step by step behind the American electorate and Congress. The military forces and armament industries of the Soviet Union expanded rapidly in the 1930s; those of the USA changed little until the end of the decade. On the other hand the USA and the USSR were both states of almost continental span. They had much larger populations than individual European 'powers', even Greater Germany, and they had abundant raw materials. Neither state had belonged to the League of Nations in the 1920s or early 1930s. Like Moscow, Washington was not one of the 'players' in the 1930s; both countries were mistrusted or discounted by the Western Europeans. The USA, like the USSR, seemed far too distant to project military power into Central Europe. Like Russia (and more so than Britain and France), the United States was preoccupied with an internal crisis, in America's case the Great Depression, in Russia's the Great Terror. Both the USA and the USSR were reluctant to get involved in another war in Western Europe. America had lost 115,000 men in World War I, and Russia had lost 1,700,000, but both countries felt they had taken up a heavy load against Germany and received little in return.

Just as Hitler was trying to undo defeat in World War I, so American policy seemed to centre on not repeating the 'mistake' of entry into the war in 1917. This misfortune had supposedly been provoked by special interests (the arms manufacturers) and by the placing of US merchant ships in harm's way. The main overt US political response to growing tension in Europe in the second half of the 1930s was Congressional legislation to keep America *out* of future wars – the Neutrality Acts (see Box 10). A few pious statements by President Roosevelt, and even the recall of the US ambassador to Berlin in late 1938 after anti-Jewish riots, had little impact. Not only did America not intervene in European affairs in the late 1930s, it also took only limited steps to build up its armaments. America had a very small army and no conscription. However, two developments – both beginning in 1938 – would be significant in the long term. One was a major renewal of the US Navy, partly in response to events in

Box 10 | The American Neutrality Acts

The Neutrality Acts summed up Washington's diplomatic weakness in the late 1930s. A 'plague on both your houses' policy, the legislation put America into a position where the future 'Arsenal of Democracy' could not sell weapons to states that were victims of aggression, or even advance them loans. In August 1935, after the beginnings of German rearmament, Congress passed the first Neutrality Act. It empowered President Roosevelt to identify war situations and make illegal the sale and shipment of arms to either side. The second major Neutrality Act, signed into law by Roosevelt early in his second term (May 1937), blocked both the sale of arms and the granting of financial credits. In the crisis summer of 1939, over the President's objection, Congress left the arms embargo in place; Britain and France could not even rely on being able to purchase American equipment if they went to war with Germany. In November 1939 – too late to deter Hitler – a revised Neutrality Act allowed export of armaments, provided they were paid for in cash and were not carried in American ships to Europe.

America's Neutrality legislation was influenced by a national tradition of non-intervention in external (especially European) affairs that dated back to the Founding Fathers. This tradition was reinforced by the widespread belief that Americans had been lured on false pretences into World War I. The United States political system was highly sensitive to public opinion. President Roosevelt – a Democrat – knew that he would have to stand for re-election in 1936, and would have to fight to keep control of Congress in the 1938 election. The Democrats had a healthy majority in both the Senate and the House of Representatives. On the other hand separation of powers and conflicts within the Democratic Party limited Roosevelt's control, and inherent political caution weakened his initiative.

the Far East. The other was the beginning – despite the Neutrality legislation – of large-scale American military production and supply to France, Britain, and China. Especially important here was the US aircraft industry.

Overall, in confronting a revisionist Germany, British and French statesmen – notably Prime Minister Chamberlain and Premier Daladier – took a blinkered Western European view. They exaggerated the influence that Fascist Italy could have as an intermediary, and they failed to take possible new partners into their calculations. France and Britain should not have worried, to the extent that they did, about engaging Hitler on their own. After all, the hostility of Communist and Slav Russia to Nazi and Aryan Germany could be assumed, and there was a large and growing Red Army. At the same time Britain's 'worst-case' scenario – having to prepare for simultaneous wars against Germany, Italy, and Japan – should have been mitigated by a realisation that Japan also faced a larger US Navy and a substantial contingent of the Red Army. The Americans and Russians, for their part, were not blameless. They were less directly threatened by Nazi Germany and less prepared to get involved. Only the Russians gave evidence of a larger view, and they were affected by their own bizarre and terrible internal Marxist power struggle, especially in 1937–8. So it was that the camp of those who wanted to contain Germany, Italy, and Japan was afflicted, nearly fatally, by myopia and distrust.

The Czechoslovak crisis, 1938

Hitler's real aims went beyond tearing up the Versailles *Diktat*, beyond the achievement of full sovereignty, and beyond the restoration of lost border territories. These real aims were to be achieved by war rather than diplomacy, and not even 'just' by re-fighting World War I. Hitler made this clear in November 1937 to a handful of top state and military leaders, at a secret meeting made notorious a decade later at Nuremberg (see Box 11). The aim of the Third Reich, he said, was 'to preserve the racial community [*Volksmasse*] and to enlarge it'. Although the scenarios he chillingly outlined differed in detail from what would actually happen from 1938 to 1941, Hitler was clear that they would involve war: 'Germany's problem could only be solved by means of force, and this was never without attendant risk.' Austria and Czechoslovakia were laid out as early targets, should the opportunity present itself.[2] The German dictator made the same grandiose statements to another secret conference, of Wehrmacht leaders, in May 1939, after he had decided on war with Poland. He stressed the geopolitical goal and economic aims of 'living space' (*Lebensraum*) and the impossibility of achieving such aims without military action.

Germany had dropped from the circle of great powers. The balance of power had been effected without Germany's participation. This equilibrium is disturbed when Germany's demands for the necessities of life make themselves felt, and Germany re-emerges as a great power. All demands are regarded as 'encroachments' . . .

Box 11 | The Nuremberg Judgment, 30 September 1946

That plans were made to wage wars, as early as 5th November, 1937, and probably before that, is apparent . . . That Germany was rapidly moving to complete dictatorship from the moment that the Nazis seized power, and progressively in the direction of war, has been overwhelmingly shown in the ordered sequence of aggressive acts and wars already set out in this Judgment . . .

In the opinion of the Tribunal, the evidence establishes the common planning to prepare and wage war by certain of the defendants. Continued planning, with aggressive war as the objective, has been established beyond doubt . . .

The argument that such common planning cannot exist where there is complete dictatorship is unsound. A plan in the execution of which a number of persons participate is still a plan, even though conceived by only one of them; and those who execute the plan do not avoid responsibility by showing that they acted under the direction of the man who conceived it. Hitler could not make aggressive war by himself. He had to have the co-operation of statesmen, military leaders, diplomats, and business men.

(From The Law as to the Common Plan or Conspiracy, Judgment of the International Military Tribunal, *The Avalon Project: Documents in Law, History and Diplomacy*, at http://avalon.law.yale.edu.)

A mass of 80 million people [in Germany] has solved the ideological problems. So, too, must the economic problems be solved. No German can evade the creation of the necessary economic conditions for this. The solution of these problems demands courage . . . [A]dapting oneself to circumstances is unacceptable. Circumstances must rather be adapted to aims. This is impossible without invasion of foreign states or attacks upon foreign property.

Living space [*Lebensraum*] proportionate to the size of the state is the basis of all power . . . The choice remains between ascent or decline.[3]

The alteration of Germany's eastern borders – partly in the interest of 'revisionism' (concerning the Versailles Treaty), partly to obtain *Lebensraum* – was the immediate cause of war in Europe. Although Axis rhetoric envisaged a conflict between a new order and an old order, in fact the order that Nazi Germany now challenged in East Central Europe was 'new', dating back to the end of World War I and the creation of new 'nation states' (most notably Poland and Czechoslovakia). The German annexation of Austria in March 1938 – the *Anschluss* ('the coming together') – was a special case, as this was not against the wishes of much of the local population. (Hitler, of course, was an Austrian.) Although the union of Austria and Germany had been specifically prohibited at Versailles, it could not be opposed on grounds of ethnic self-determination, nor did the French or British do much to oppose Hitler's bold initiative. Nevertheless the *Anschluss* meant that Hitler's state now shared a common border with Italy, Hungary, and Yugoslavia, and it surrounded the western part of Czechoslovakia on three sides.

The Czechoslovak crisis of 1938, six months later, was different from the *Anschluss* and more dangerous for Europe. Nazi Germany was now claiming territories from a state that certainly did not wish to give them up, and which had the military wherewithal to resist such claims. Ostensibly at issue were the rights of the ethnic Germany minority within Czechoslovakia (the 'Sudeten' Germans). Aside from the question of the sanctity of the 'historic' borders of western Czechoslovakia, however, was the fact that the military defences of the Czechoslovak state had been erected in these hilly borderlands. (This intractable strategic-ethnic dilemma could finally be resolved only by the forced expulsion of 2.5 million Sudeten Germans in 1945–6.)

The case of the Sudeten Germans met with some sympathy outside the Reich in the 1930s, and in any event the other powers were afraid of accidentally slipping into a general war with Germany. Attempts at international compromise were central to the British concept of Appeasement, personified by Neville Chamberlain, prime minister since May 1937. It is often argued that concessions made by Chamberlain at the September 1938 Munich Conference won Britain and France time to rearm, but the same was true for Germany. Hitler was not bluffing about the use of force against Czechoslovakia, and he was prepared to take the risk that the British and French would intervene in a German–Czechoslovak war. Some of his military leaders were less confident that general war could be avoided, and they were unsure of Germany's readiness to fight such a war. The Chief of the German Army General Staff, General Beck, secretly resigned.

The Czechoslovak crisis was followed by a six-year European tragedy, and there are many 'might have beens'. Would sterner resistance by Britain and France have forced Hitler to back down? Might a firm stand have led to the collapse of the Nazi regime? Could the Soviets have been relied on more? Would it have been better to fight in 1938 with Germany only partially rearmed and the considerable Czechoslovak Army available? Should the Czechoslovaks have fought, as the Poles did in 1939? But outsiders (including Western public opinion) did not appreciate how extreme and inflexible Hitler's geopolitical programme actually was. The Czechoslovaks, for their part, decided that the military position was hopeless. The result was the Munich agreement of September 1938, by which the British and French (and Italians) accepted the immediate cession of the Sudeten territory to Germany. The Hungarians and Poles also took regions of Czechoslovakia to which they had ethnic or historic claims. The Russians, who had had good relations with the Prague government, were not invited to take part in the Munich negotiations. America, again, had no direct involvement in the crisis, and the British did not encourage US participation.

Immediately after the Munich meeting, in the late autumn of 1938, governments on both sides took a much harder view. Armaments programmes accelerated. The state-sponsored race riots of *Kristallnacht* in November, in which Jewish shops were attacked, synagogues burned down, and a hundred Jews killed, had less impact on diplomacy. For the general public, however, the next dramatic steps came five months after Munich, in March 1939, with Hitler's sudden occupation of the rest of Czechoslovakia. The western part of the country was now directly incorporated into the Reich as the 'Protectorate of Bohemia-Moravia', and the eastern part became the puppet state of Slovakia. The British and French responded by providing guarantees to a number of Eastern European states (first to Poland and then to Romania and Greece) in the event of further German encroachments. With this they finally drew a line in the sand which Germany could cross only at its peril.

One immediate result of the Czechoslovak crisis of 1938–9 was that the Third Reich again became stronger. Germany lost a significant military danger to the south, and it gained the sizeable benefit of the Czech arms industry. The fate of Czechoslovakia also dealt a blow to French attempts to build a system of friendly (and anti-German) states in Eastern Europe. The September 1938 crisis led Hitler to underestimate future British and French resolve. 'Our enemies are little worms,' he told his generals in August 1939. 'I saw them at Munich.'[4] Stalin came to a similar conclusion; after Munich he was less prepared to make common cause with the British and French. This led him to search for another solution to Russia's security problem – accommodation or even collaboration with Germany.

There was a positive outcome of the Czechoslovak crisis for the British and French, but it was less tangible. Hitler had overturned the attempted Munich compromise. His obvious bad faith strengthened the political hand of the British and French governments with respect to their own electorates – and in the British case with respect to the Dominions. When another crisis arose, around Danzig and Poland, a firmer policy could and would be taken up.

Poland and the Nazi–Soviet Pact

Poland was for the Germans an especially bitter part of the Versailles settlement. The newly re-created Polish state of 1918–20 was formed partly from eastern Germany. It took in both 'historic' German/Prussian lands and many ethnic German inhabitants. Many Germans would have been glad to redraw the border and settle scores with Catholic and Slav Poland, but the Nazi leadership aimed for the extinction of Poland as a state and the exploitation of its territory as German *Lebensraum*. Hitler's tactics were to focus on an immediate and limited issue, the city of Danzig (now Gdansk). Danzig was a port city near the mouth of the Vistula River; most of Danzig's inhabitants were Germans, but the city and its environs were administered by the League of Nations. Berlin now demanded cession of Danzig to Germany and provision by the Poles of transport routes across the neck of the narrow Polish 'corridor' which separated Danzig, and East Prussia as a whole, from the rest of Germany.

As we have seen, in March 1939 the British and French had promised support to a number of Eastern European states – including Poland – in the event of further German aggression. London and Paris were worried less about Hitler's acquisition of *Lebensraum* than about the attitude of the ring of smaller states surrounding Germany – especially in southeastern Europe. Later on – in the 1941 Atlantic Charter and elsewhere – the Allied struggle would be portrayed as a war for democracy and against dictatorship. Such a rationale did not apply to 1930s Poland – or indeed to most other Eastern European states. Poland was a dictatorship; in 1926 the Polish Army overthrew the parliamentary system set up on independence and installed as dictator Jozef Piłsudski, a hero of the national revolution. The authoritarian regime, devoted to a national 'cleansing' (*sanacja*), continued after Piłsudski's death in 1935, although without a central leader of his stature. The regime of Piłsudski and later of the so-called 'colonels' was not viciously repressive, but it reflected a country divided on class and ethnic lines, and overseen by irresponsible and inflexible leaders.

Diplomatically, the Poles in 1939 were victims of their own success in 1919–20. The leaders in Warsaw who carved out a 'big Poland' had been short-sighted and foolish. Poland had gained extensive mixed-population territories in both the west and the east, at the expense of Germany (Upper Silesia and the Baltic/Danzig corridor) and of Russia (western Belorussia, western Ukraine). Warsaw could as a result count on neither big neighbour as an ally. It was no fault of the Poles that both neighbours by the 1930s were totalitarian regimes, committed in the one case to 'Aryan' racial superiority and expansionism and in the other to international revolution. But the Polish colonels' concept of a 'Third Europe', bringing in their partners of choice, Hungary and Romania, was a fanciful delusion. Meanwhile they refused to co-operate with the Prague government because of trivial border issues, and in 1938 they actually joined with Hungary and Germany in the dismemberment of Czechoslovakia.

Although European statesmen had seen the Danzig crisis coming at least since the spring of 1939, the German–Soviet Non-Aggression Pact (usually known as the 'Nazi–Soviet Pact') came out of the blue. It was signed on 23 August 1939, after German Foreign Minister Ribbentrop's sudden flight to Moscow. Despite preliminary conversations, the German–Soviet Pact came together finally only in the last week of August. Historians still debate the origins of the Pact, with some putting forward the extreme interpretation that it was Stalin's way of luring Hitler (and Europe) into a destructive war. The Soviet dictator is on record as saying – a week after the war began – that he saw 'nothing wrong' in the 'two groups of capitalist countries . . . having a good hard fight and weakening each other'.[5] But in reality the initiative for the Pact seems to have come from the German side rather than the Soviet one. There was little sign that the alternative configuration, a British–French–Soviet military alliance, was going to develop, despite slow-motion talks between military delegations in Moscow. Nevertheless, such an East–West pact would have been Europe's last best chance to deter Hitler.

Here was another episode where a state self-consciously reprised the experience of World War I. For Stalin the reorientation in August 1939 echoed the earlier world conflict. In 1917–18 Lenin had laid down a new policy, under which Bolshevik Russia would manoeuvre between two blocs of warring and predatory Imperialist powers. In the 1918 Peace of Brest-Litovsk Lenin's government suddenly aligned with the German-led Central Powers, turning its back on Russia's allies of 1914–17. Stalin repeated this in 1939.

On another level, the point of the Non-Aggression Pact was aggression. It was an extreme victory of the 'revisionist' powers, who made common cause to tear up the terms of Versailles or – more broadly – to undo the unfavourable outcome for them of World War I. Germany and Russia agreed, in a secret protocol, to a division of the northern part of Eastern Europe. The German claim to Danzig and the Soviet claim to 'western Belorussia' and 'western Ukraine' were essentially based on the principle of ethnic self-determination. But the greater 'carve-up' was based on geopolitics and history. (The 'deal' had elements in common with a later informal agreement struck between Churchill and Stalin in Moscow in October 1944.) In 1939 Germany and the USSR agreed that Polish territory, whatever happened to the Polish state, would be divided into two spheres of influence. Territorially the Russians got more than the Germans. In the final version of the pact they were given a free hand in both the Baltic States and Finland, and also in Bessarabia (the Romanian region that had been a pre-1918 Russian province).

The Nazi–Soviet Pact was both more and less than a diplomatic revolution. It was probably not crucial to the outbreak of war. Hitler's Operation WHITE (*Fall Weiss*), the invasion of Poland, was set up without foreknowledge that the pact with Moscow could be concluded, but on the assumption that the Russians would not intervene. On the other hand the Pact was extremely important in the overall strategic picture of the developing European war, a point Hitler stressed to his wavering generals. Historians differ about how seriously the French and British in 1938–9 took the part the USSR could play in an 'eastern front' against Germany. But in any event the Nazi–Soviet Pact now ruled out British–French military co-operation with Moscow. And those statesmen and military leaders who looked one step ahead could see that the economic pressure which a British–French blockade could apply was now much reduced. A 'friendly' Eurasian giant to the east – on top of a friendly Italy in the Mediterranean – meant Germany at war would have sufficient access to foodstuffs, minerals, and oil.

Two other aspects of the Nazi–Soviet Pact need to be mentioned. Clever and dramatic as it was from Hitler's short-term point of view, the Pact antagonised his older partners, Japan and Italy. For them Communist Russia was still the ideological and geopolitical enemy. The Japanese cabinet resigned in dismay and confusion when the Pact was announced. Global co-operation with Germany by Japan and Italy – against Britain and France – was now less likely than before. The second aspect was more important: '*Lebensraum*-by-partnership' was a nonsense for Hitler. The Pact guaranteed neither 'living space' nor raw materials for Greater Germany, and so it was inherently unstable.

Hitler crushes Poland

The first shots of World War II in Europe were fired early on 1 September 1939. The old German battleship *Schleswig-Holstein* bombarded Danzig's Westerplatte, a Polish military enclave at the mouth of the Vistula River. In the hours that followed, the Wehrmacht launched a broad attack along Poland's borders. Britain and France issued ultimatums demanding the cessation of hostilities. Germany ignored these demands, and on 3 September Britain and France declared war (see Box 12).

Under Operation WHITE, the invasion of Poland, two German army groups carried out a rapid converging advance; one drove south from Pomerania and East Prussia (northeastern Germany), the other east from Silesia (eastern Germany). The overall commander was the German Army C-in-C (Commander-in-Chief), General Walther von Brauchitsch. This was the first of six great offensives that Hitler and his Wehrmacht would launch between September 1939 and June 1942. The attacks had many common characteristics: all (except the invasion of Norway) employed large tank forces, all displayed very high mobility, in all the Luftwaffe played a vital supporting role, and all exploited the element of surprise. In most cases operations were mounted against disorganised or weak enemies; the defenders' high command had usually been isolated. Individual enemy units might put up local resistance, but they were rendered incapable of effective movement.

Operation WHITE was the original version of this offensive template, and the first real test of German arms since 1918. The Wehrmacht fought the

Box 12 | Prime Minister Chamberlain announces war

Neville Chamberlain (1869–1940), the British Prime Minister, spoke over the BBC on 3 September 1939 to announce the beginning of war with Germany.

I am speaking to you from the Cabinet Room at 10, Downing Street.

This morning the British Ambassador in Berlin handed the German Government a final note stating that unless we heard from them by 11.00 a.m. that they were prepared at once to withdraw their troops from Poland, a state of war would exist between us.

I have to tell you that no such undertaking has been received, and that consequently this country is at war with Germany.

You can imagine what a bitter blow it is to me that all my long struggle to win peace has failed. Yet I cannot believe that there is anything more or anything different I could have done and that would have been more successful.

Up to the very last it would have been quite possible to have arranged a peaceful and honourable settlement between Germany and Poland, but Hitler would not have it.

He had evidently made up his mind to attack Poland whatever happened; and although he now says he has put forward reasonable proposals which were rejected by the Poles, that is not a true statement . . .

His actions show convincingly that there is no chance of expecting that this man will ever give up his practice of using force to gain his will. He can only be stopped by force.

We and France are today, in fulfilment of our obligations, going to the aid of Poland, who is so bravely resisting this wicked and unprovoked attack on her people. We have a clear conscience. We have done all that any country could do to establish peace. The situation in which no word given to Germany's ruler could be trusted and no people or country could feel themselves safe has become intolerable.

> (From Radio Address, 3 September 1939, *The Avalon Project: Documents in Law, History and Diplomacy*, at http://avalon.law.yale.edu.)

campaign much as they planned it. Unlike the nibbling advance in Czechoslovakia, Hitler aimed here for the rapid and complete overthrow of the Polish state; this was not just a limited land-grab for Danzig or the Polish Corridor. Speed was essential to present the international community with a *fait accompli* and to free up troops in case Britain, France, or Russia should come to Poland's aid. The campaign would have been perfectly understandable to a Prussian field marshal of the nineteenth century. The Germans did not use massed armour. The planners spread the individual panzer divisions (six

Box 13 | The panzer division

The German panzer division was the most significant military organisation of 1940, the instrument of Hitler's domination of Europe. It combined hitting power with very high cross-country mobility. Unlike the tank units of World War I, the panzer divisions could break through the enemy's front line and drive deep into rear areas. Prior to the late 1930s, infantry divisions and – in much smaller numbers – cavalry divisions were the standard elements of armies. The British and Russians experimented with tank formations in the early 1930s. The 1st Panzer Division (converted from an existing cavalry division) was formed in late 1935; *Panzer* is the German word for 'armour'. At the outbreak of war in 1939 the German Army had six panzer divisions. Panzer divisions were by 1940 concentrated into panzer corps (two panzer divisions) and even a 'panzer group' (two panzer corps). Against an unprepared or demoralised enemy these large panzer formations could achieve decisive results.

A panzer division of May 1940 comprised four tank battalions (*Panzer-Abteilungen*) – with a total of about 175 tanks – plus an infantry regiment, and an artillery regiment. After the French campaign the number of panzer divisions was doubled; the original formations were split in half and left with fewer tanks but more 'motorised' infantry. By 1942 there were 26 numbered panzer divisions (1st to 26th), although a few more were added later in the Wehrmacht and in the *Waffen SS*. They made up only a small proportion of the German ground forces. Other armies began to set up similar formations (armoured divisons, mechanised corps) on the eve of the war, and the panzer victory in May–June 1940 led to imitation on an even wider scale.

in all) among infantry corps, but their infantry could move rapidly, especially the motorised formations (see Box 13). The German artillery, also, was witheringly effective.

The divisions of the Polish field army, deployed close to the western and northern frontier, were unable to disengage and were enveloped, paralysed, and then destroyed. Meanwhile, spearhead German troops raced through gaps in the Polish line, and by 7 September a panzer division rolled up to the outskirts of Warsaw (although a real siege of the city began only three weeks later). The Luftwaffe quickly gained air superiority over the smaller, obsolete, and dispersed Polish Air Force; in consequence the ability of the Poles to move troops or bring up supplies, especially via the rail-way network, was greatly reduced. The Polish government did not give up, even with the paralysis of its field army. Nevertheless, Warsaw was encir-cled. The government and the high command had already fled, but the city was the ultimate symbol of Polish independence. Massed artillery and air attacks were mounted on 25 September – what the Poles called 'Black Mon-day' – and two days later Warsaw capitulated. The last Polish field units gave up a week later. There was no national surrender; the Polish govern-ment and tens of thousands of soldiers crossed over the southern border into exile to continue the war abroad. The road back would be long and tortuous.

Even if the attackers had been less skilful, and even if the defenders had been better deployed and better led, Poland's defeat was inevitable. A country of 80 million had gone to war against one of 34 million (of which only 22 million were ethnic Poles). The Polish Army was on paper the fourth biggest in Europe, but in the 1939 campaign the Germans had twice as many troops, three times as much field artillery, four times as many aircraft, and five times as many tanks. Poland was a large country by Central European standards, but western and central Poland – where the Polish high command chose to fight – was a relatively small theatre of operations, 300 by 400 miles in extent – comparable to Belgium and the Netherlands. Unlike the Chinese in 1937, the Poles could not outrun the invaders, and they had no inaccessible hinterland to run to. A week or so after the start of the campaign, General Rydz-Smygly, the Polish C-in-C, considered a withdrawal to the southeast and to a 'Romanian bridgehead' with Poland's erstwhile Balkan ally. That was, however, a strategic whimsy.

The speed of the defeat had much to do with Polish mistakes. Rydz-Smygly had deployed what forces he had in a long thin line close to the western border. (From the mid 1930s Polish war plans did not deploy regular forces in the east against Russia; until August 1939 joint German–Soviet action had seemed unlikely.) The forward defence made sense in a limited conflict. It covered the territorial gains of Versailles from a German 'smash and grab'; what Poland faced in 1939, however, was full-scale war. Forward deployment also covered the ethnically Polish region, between the western border and the Vistula River, where reservists required for the expansion of the Army lived. Western Poland was also the country's (limited) industrial base. With hindsight, however, it is clear that the Poles would have been wiser to deploy their forces further east, and this was what the French high command had recommended.

There are myths, big and small, about this first tragic campaign of the European war. The Polish Air Force was not destroyed on the ground. Polish lancers on horseback did not charge German tanks. The Poles themselves later blamed the French for urging them to delay mobilisation during the Danzig crisis, but that was a minor factor. Anglo-French 'betrayal' of Poland is another myth. In 1914 Russia and France (and even Britain) had supported one another militarily in a way that had prevented the German Empire from winning a quick decisive victory in either east or west. In 1939 there was little joint planning, or even much knowledge of the potential ally's plans. The March 1939 guarantee by London and Paris aimed to deter the Germans, not physically to block their attack; the British and French could not – it would turn out – defend even Belgium. The Polish government did expect a French offensive in the West, and in mid September the French mounted a small attack into the Saar, taking a few villages outside the *Westwall* which had been abandoned by the Germans. However, the underlying reality was that the Germans, as the initiators of war, had achieved surprise in Poland (more so than in August 1914) with their hidden mobilisation, initial deployment, and attack. The *Westwall* and the limited German garrison in the west provided enough short-term cover for the Reich. There was no way the French (much less the British) could have mounted even quixotic ground or air operations before the Polish Army disintegrated.

The fourth partition of Poland

Stalin had little time for the Poles. He privately remarked in September 1939 that the 'annihilation' of Poland meant 'one fewer bourgeois fascist state to contend with'.[6] The importance of the Russian invasion of eastern Poland on 17 September is, however, often exaggerated. It was reprehensible diplomatically (and ultimately was to prove very costly for Moscow). But contrary to what is sometimes alleged, the cynical Soviet action played no part in the final outcome or the speed of the Polish collapse.

Germany initiated the demise of Poland, and Hitler would have attacked that country with or without Soviet declared neutrality. The Polish Army had effectively collapsed over a week before the Red Army unexpectedly crossed the border.

There was also some strategic logic in the Soviet action. The German–Soviet protocols signed on 23 August – hidden behind the public Non-Aggression Pact – had made the Vistula River the main demarcation line between the two 'spheres of influence'. By the second week of September, however, German troops engaged in a deep encirclement of the Polish Army were operating well east of that river line. There was no guarantee that Stalin's new friend would keep his side of the bargain. From the Kremlin's perspective, Soviet inaction might have ended with Germans in occupation of the whole of Poland, and with the Wehrmacht stationed 35 miles from Minsk. In the event, in the second German–Soviet treaty – signed on 28 September 1939 – Hitler's zone was extended to take in the ethnically Polish territory immediately east of the Vistula, with the demarcation line becoming the Bug River – the so-called 'Curzon line'. (This was the supposed ethnographic boundary between territory inhabited by Poles and territory inhabited by Ukrainians and Belorussians; it had been laid out in 1920 by a British Foreign Secretary, Lord Curzon.) In exchange the Baltic state of Lithuania was transferred from the German 'sphere of influence' to the Soviet one.

Poland played a high price for defeat. There was no attempt to create a rump 'Polish' puppet government. Even Mussolini complained (privately) about the complete extinction of the Polish state. Half the Polish territory allotted to the Reich in the German–Soviet agreements was incorporated directly into eastern Germany; the other half became a semi-colonial appendage of the Reich known as the 'General-Government'. Poland's 1939 eastern territories were incorporated directly into the Ukrainian and Belorussian 'republics' of the USSR. Against Germany the Poles would get their revenge in 1945, when they were given their western territories back, plus much of East Prussia, Pomerania, and Silesia; the German population had fled the Red Army or was deported by the Poles. Against the USSR, however, there would be no Polish appeal. The Soviets kept the territory gained in 1939, under agreements made with Britain and America at the Teheran and

Yalta conferences in 1943 and 1945. Indeed, what was annexed in 1939 is still part of today's Belarus and Ukraine.

Soviet occupation was cruel, with arrests and deportation of the Polish intelligentsia and of active nationalists. The mass execution of several tens of thousands of Polish POWs at Katyn and elsewhere in the USSR in the spring of 1940 was an extreme crime even by Stalin's standards. The German occupation was even worse. The events of the September 1939 campaign foreshadowed the 1941 BARBAROSSA campaign and the full-scale Holocaust. The German Army treated civilians with brutality. There was no Nanjing massacre; German troops were too well disciplined and German terror too sophisticated. During the September campaign, however, the SS deployed for the first time the *Einsatzgruppen*, special task forces intended to terrorise and physically destroy ideological and racial enemies. Although the ultimate victims would be the Polish Jews, the first were among the Polish intelligentsia. By December 1939 some 50,000 civilians had been murdered, among them 7,000 Jews. The region annexed directly into the Reich was subjected to radical Germanisation. The General-Government, even worse off, was starved and stripped of people for forced labour. Ultimately German-occupied Poland became the main setting for the Holocaust.

Poland resisted more fiercely than other states facing Nazi aggression. Its government did not sue for peace. Its army fought ineffectively, but fiercely. About 16,000 Wehrmacht personnel were killed in Poland in 1939. In contrast, the Czechoslovaks capitulated without firing a shot. Denmark hardly resisted in 1940, and in Norway the Germans lost only 1,300 men. During the invasion of the Balkans in April–May 1941 the Germans lost 150 men in Yugoslavia (a country about the same size as Poland) and about 1,000 in Greece (excluding Crete). Only about half again as many German servicemen (27,000) were killed in the first phase of the French campaign (up to Dunkirk) as were killed in Poland. The Poles, for their part, lost 60,000 soldiers. Compared to what would come later in the east, however, German losses were tolerable. (And the human cost on both sides in Poland in 1939 was much lower than in the two – still unknown – Japanese campaigns already fought in China.) The main thing for the Wehrmacht, however, was that the aims of Operation WHITE were achieved very rapidly and without any effective intervention by the French or British. Unlike in World War I,

Germany had not had to fight on two fronts, and it looked as though it might not have to do so in the future.

· · ·

Each of the major powers approached the outbreak of a new war in Europe with the course and results of the 1914–18 conflict in mind. For Germany the aim was to undo the 1919 settlement while building up military strength in depth, and meanwhile to avoid a war on two fronts. For Britain and France the aim was to subdue Germany, but at less terrible human cost to themselves than in World War I. For Italy the aim was, again, to stay out at least until the tipping point. For many Americans the main thing was to avoid being dragged by vested interests into another pointless European conflict. For the leaders of Soviet Russia this was the second round of the great imperialist war, in which they did not favour one group of capitalists over the other.

One of the main arguments of the present book is that the origins of the war in Asia and of the war in Europe have much more in common than is often acknowledged. On the other hand there were features on each continent that were quite distinct. Japanese statesmen stumbled into war with China in 1937 – albeit following on from their overbearing behaviour and from a lack of centralised control over their military field commanders. By comparison, Germany's initial moves in 1935–9 were opportunistic but carefully controlled at the highest level, sometimes ignoring the advice of cautious military men. Later on, in 1941, politicians in Tokyo carefully calculated the initiation of a general war with Britain and America (as we will see in Chapter 7). In contrast, in 1939 Hitler stumbled blindly and prematurely into a general war with Britain and France.

German artillerymen parade near the Arc de Triomphe in Paris, June 1940. Hitler's seven-week victory in France followed striking offensive successes in Poland and Scandinavia. Although German tanks and aircraft played a spectacular part in the French campaign, much of the fighting was done by more traditional forces like those shown above; the German Army on the outbreak of war had nearly 600,000 horses. The guns of the artillery were often pulled by horses rather than motor tractors; the supply wagons of the infantry were also horse-drawn.

Germany re-fights World War I, 1939–1940

Timeline

1939	September	Germany invades Poland; Britain and France declare war; USSR occupies eastern Poland
	November	USSR invades Finland
1940	April	Germany invades Norway
	May	Germany invades Belgium, the Netherlands, and France
	June	France surrenders
	September	Battle of Britain

The grand strategy of 1939–1940

War had broken out in Europe. One of the more heartening early events, for the Allies, had occurred off distant South America in December 1939, with the scuttling of the *Graf Spee* after a naval battle; the 'pocket battleship' had been raiding Allied shipping. But the conflict was really neither a 'global' nor a 'world' war. So far it was not even a European war, rather a regional conflict – something like the Crimean War of 1854–6. Britain, France, and Poland were arrayed on one side, and Germany on the other. Other big European states – notably Italy and Russia – had declared their neutrality. Moreover, after the fall of Poland the shooting mostly stopped. An American Senator dubbed the situation the 'Phoney War', and the term stuck. Germany was about to achieve an astonishing military victory, knocking France out of the war in the six-week Blitzkrieg. In the winter of 1939–40, however, almost no one anticipated this – and certainly not the Wehrmacht high command.

In October 1939 the two sides had to decide what to do next. Hitler had not expected that his attack on Poland would lead to British and French declarations of war. Germany was in a vulnerable position. The best option for Hitler would have been a temporary return to peace, with the strategic position of the Third Reich considerably strengthened. His new Soviet partner evidently took a similar view. On the day of the supplementary German–Soviet Treaty (28 September) foreign ministers Ribbentrop and Molotov issued a joint statement: 'The German government and the government of the USSR . . . in mutual agreement express the opinion that the liquidation of the present war between Germany on the one hand and England and France on the other would be in the interests of all nations.' Continuation of the war, the statement continued ominously, would be the fault of the Allies, and would lead to further 'consultation' between Moscow and Berlin.[1] London and Paris, however, showed no sign of coming to terms. Battle rather than diplomacy would be required to bring a resolution of the European crisis.

If the war was to continue, then the military planners on the two sides had to devise strategies. For both the Allies and the Germans a direct attack to overthrow the main enemy was still only a distant possibility. Local gains and 'economic' warfare – including blockade and limited bombing campaigns – were a more likely short- and medium-term prospect. Control and denial of raw materials were seen as vital (see Chapter 9).

Most of Europe was not yet involved in the war, so neutral states figured importantly in the strategic calculations of the two sides. The large European neutrals – Italy and USSR – had great potential. They were geopolitically powerful, they controlled access to vital resources, their entry into the war could tip the military balance, and they were themselves 'players' in the competition for control of the smaller states. Of the nineteen smaller European neutrals Slovakia and – arguably – Hungary were already in the German orbit. On the other side of Germany and at the core of Europe, Switzerland, Belgium, and the Netherlands were clearly important, and Belgium at least was central to the war plans of both sides. In the Balkans, Romania, Bulgaria, Yugoslavia, and Greece represented potential assets in terms of population, geographical position, and raw materials. Northern Europe was also a zone of interest; here were Denmark, Norway, Sweden, Finland, Estonia, Latvia, and Lithuania. Turkey had shown its strategic value in World War I, but in 1939 – with Russia neutral – it was far removed from the centre of the conflict. Spain and Portugal took their places in the same outer circle, and a final neutral there was Eire.

Hitler, rightly or wrongly, regarded Britain rather than France as his main enemy. The Germans had to advance to the European coastline if they were seriously to threaten British oceanic trade or to attack British territory with the Luftwaffe. (The Germans, to repeat, had no advance knowledge that the overthrow of France would give them – by June 1940 – bomber airfields on the Channel coast and U-boat bases on the Bay of Biscay.) From this point of view Belgium, the Netherlands, and Norway were especially important. Hitler's main initiative – in October 1939 after diplomacy failed – was to order an attack on the Low Countries and northern France. This operation was given the codename YELLOW (*Fall Gelb*), but it would not be mounted for seven months.

For the Allies the neutral periphery held avenues of threat to themselves, but also points of German economic vulnerability. Unlike Britain and France, the Third Reich had only indirect and difficult links to the world's resources. A major German source of high-grade iron ore was located in Arctic Sweden, accessible for four months of the year (when the northern Baltic was frozen) only through the Norwegian Atlantic port of Narvik. The most important German source of petroleum was in Romania; also seemingly vulnerable were the oil wells and refineries in the Soviet Caucasus.

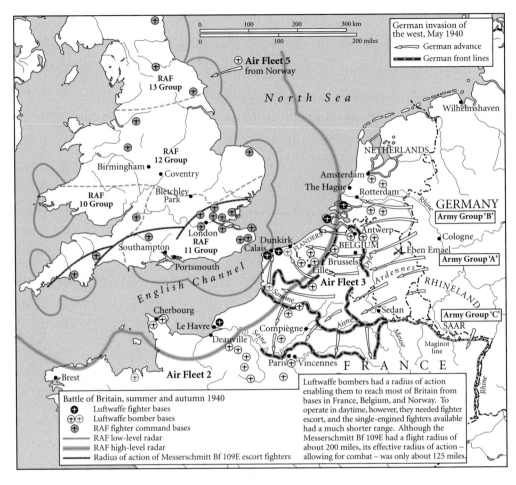

Map 4 Germany defeats France, 1940

There were fewer disagreements about general European strategy between the British and the French in 1939 and 1940 than there would be between the British and the Americans in 1942 and 1943. The French high command under General Maurice Gamelin were sensibly focused – at least at the strategic level – on the defence of northeastern France and a possible pre-emptive advance into Belgium. Neither French nor British leaders wanted – in 1939–40 – to launch a direct ground attack on German territory. World War I had been far too bloody an experience, and access to global resources seemed to give the Allies an inherent advantage over the long haul. Neither Ally was keen on an immediate strategic bombing campaign against Germany, partly due to a lack of suitable aircraft and partly from fear of provoking Luftwaffe reprisals. As far as either Paris or London thought offensively, they both looked – at least in the short and middle term – to a peripheral strategy, making use of sea power and smaller European allies.

This peripheral strategy led the governments of Daladier and Chamberlain to make strategic decisions that with hindsight seem incomprehensible and even ridiculous. In mitigation, the Germans had not yet demonstrated an ability to rapidly project power. The Polish case might have suggested that little reliance could be put on the medium-sized and smaller states, but Poland had been directly adjacent to Germany; it had been threatened from three sides by the Wehrmacht and on the fourth by the Red Army. There was also a not unreasonable political concern that if the Allies did not support the smaller neutrals against Germany (or Russia), those states would drift under German 'protection' without resistance.

The first strategic option – at least for the French – was to construct a position in the Balkans. A number of the medium-sized states in southeastern Europe had good relations with France and bad relations with countries that were now friendly to Germany. In particular, Yugoslavia was fearful of Italy, and Romania was fearful of Russia and Hungary. France and Britain, meanwhile, had forces and bases in the eastern Mediterranean. There was an attractive historical precedent: the collapse of the German coalition in 1918 had begun in the Balkans, with the surrender of Bulgaria. But 1939–40 was not 1918, and French plans to put together a Balkan bloc came to nothing. The British, in particular, feared that Allied action in the Balkans would push neutral Italy towards Germany.

The Winter War

In the end the Allies made more progress in schemes for involvement in Scandinavia. A complicating factor here was the surprise Soviet invasion of Finland at the end of November 1939. The Finns put up an unexpectedly stout resistance. The Allies – with French Premier Daladier providing the impetus – took steps to come to their aid. The general idea was to send a small expeditionary force to Finland via Narvik in northern Norway, moving through the electric railway line in northern Sweden to the Baltic, and seizing control of the northern Swedish iron-ore fields as they passed through them. The Allied plans were admirable in the abstract – the defence of gallant (and democratic) little Finland – but they made little strategic sense. This would have been true even if Norway and Sweden had been ready to throw their lot in with the Allies, which was certainly not the case.

Allied planning can be – hazily – understood if several further factors, beyond economics and rallying the neutrals, are taken into account. First, Daladier was under increasing political pressure at home to do *something*. Second, there were the anti-Communist attitudes of important leaders in London and Paris – especially Daladier and other French conservatives – fuelled by Moscow's anti-Allied rhetoric and the opposition of the French Communist Party to the war against Germany. The third factor was a false sense of Russian weakness and a belief that there was little to fear from the Red Army; unlike Germany, the USSR had no easy way to retaliate against Allied actions.

Fortunately – with hindsight – it took some time for the Allies to decide what to do. In the meantime Finland requested an armistice with the Russians in early March 1940. The Russian terms were mild enough to diffuse the worst fears of the Swedes and the Norwegians. The end of the war scuppered plans to send the Allied expeditionary force. (It also scuppered proposals for air raids against Soviet oil installations in the Caucasus. These had reached the stage of aerial reconnaissance, as British planes violated Soviet airspace to inspect Baku.) The Allies were left with much more limited options in Scandinavia, and these were played out in April.

The Soviet–Finnish Winter War (December 1939 through February 1940), and the Soviet advance into the Baltic states (Estonia, Latvia, and Lithuania), seems a back channel in the course of 'World War II'. The USSR was, after all, neutral, even if the Allies might have used Finland as a pretext for going to war with it. The Baltic, however, had common features with wartime events elsewhere. On the one hand developments there were part of the same overall pattern of the undoing of the 1918–20 peace settlement. Finland and the Baltic states (and most of Poland) had been part of the Russian Empire in 1914, just as Czechoslovakia had been part of Austria-Hungary, and Danzig had been part of Germany. On the day war began with Poland, and in the early honeymoon of the Nazi–Soviet Pact, Hitler put the position directly: 'Russia and Germany fought each other in the World War only to suffer its consequences equally in the end. This shall not happen a second time!'[2]

Developments in the eastern Baltic were a direct consequence of the German–Soviet secret agreements of August and September 1939, which gave Moscow a sphere of influence there. But another common feature was that the USSR feared an aggressive Germany, and it faced the same military challenge in this neutral region that France and Britain faced with respect to neutral Belgium or Norway. Left empty, the Baltic states were a vulnerable gap in the Soviet defences; whichever side occupied the neutral territory first would gain a great advantage.

Stalin had immediately annexed eastern Poland into the USSR, but this did not happen in Estonia, Latvia, and Lithuania. In October 1939, however, Moscow forced the Baltic governments to sign agreements to allow Soviet troops, ships, and aircraft to be based on their territory – while keeping their independence. (Annexation of the three Baltic states would come in the summer of 1940, in the different diplomatic environment after the fall of France.) At the same time the USSR asked Finland to hand over a belt of territory west of Leningrad. It also requested use of a naval base in southwest Finland at Hanko, covering the entrance to the Gulf of Finland; the Tsarist Russian fleet had been based here in World War I. Moscow originally proposed a trade, exchanging Soviet territory further north (although this was mostly empty forest). These were much better terms than Helsinki would have to accept after the Winter War, although Finnish concessions in October 1939 might have led to greater Soviet demands. In any event the Finns refused even the initial bargain.

On 30 November 1939 Stalin suddenly launched a full-scale invasion of Finland. The Red Army's campaign was not to be like the Wehrmacht's in Poland two months before, let alone the future rapid-fire operations in

Denmark and southern Norway. The overconfident Red Army had attacked without sufficient preparation. The battlefield was a wild land of forest and lakes, covered by heavy winter snow. The Soviets could not break through the narrow Finnish position in the Karelian Isthmus and the field fortifications of the Mannerheim Line. North of Lake Ladoga whole Soviet divisional columns were wiped out. When the war with Finland began the Soviets also set up a puppet government just inside their territory, under the Finnish Communist Otto Kuusinen. This suggested – rightly or wrongly – that Stalin's real aim was the complete overthrow of bourgeois Finland, a peril which unified the Finnish population against the invaders.

The Winter War was the most bloody single episode in European warfare from September 1939 through June 1941. The Finns lost nearly 50,000 men, a very high figure in a population of 3.6 million. As for the Russians, they lost no fewer than 110,000 men (killed and missing), 50 per cent more than the Wehrmacht lost in Poland, Norway, the Low Countries, and France combined. Finland is generally seen as a fiasco for the Red Army. It is not to the credit of the Red Army high command that it mounted an attack in winter and in difficult terrain. All the same, the Russians won the war, getting the territory and bases that they wanted after three months's fighting, and learning some valuable lessons. Commanders who distinguished themselves in the Finnish war – and some did – were given the most senior posts in the Red Army. Finland lost a wide belt of territory to the west of its old frontier with the USSR (a deal not unlike the Munich agreement of 1938), and it had to accept the Soviet naval base at Hanko. But Finnish resistance, international pressure, and Stalin's eventual caution meant that Finland – unlike Czechoslovakia, Poland, or the Baltic states – survived as an independent state. Finland certainly did not cease to be a danger to the USSR, as would become clear with the 'continuation war' against the Red Army in June 1941.

The invasion of Norway

The Allied plan to send an expeditionary corps to Finland had been abandoned. The only option was now the laying of mines in Norwegian waters south of Narvik to block the iron-ore route from Sweden. As it happened, British mine-laying and German landings came simultaneously. Norway and

Denmark had seized Hitler's restless attention back in October 1939. Control over Scandinavia made even more sense from a German point of view than an Allied one. Norway, in particular, would protect vital natural resources (especially Swedish iron ore) and provide open-sea bases for the commerce war against Britain. Hitler was also thinking of a long conflict, and like Daladier he wanted action. The German Navy, whose battle fleet had been bottled up in the North Sea in World War I, was enthusiastic about a breakout in the north. In January and February 1940 the Wehrmacht put together a very daring plan, called Operation WESER (*Weserübung*). The first remarkable feature of the plan was close co-operation of German ground, sea, and air forces; the second was the maximum use of surprise.

The German invasion came almost exactly a month before the great offensive against the Low Countries and France. Norway was the second of Hitler's six offensives, and the only one in which the German Navy played a major role. A number of widely scattered strategic points in Denmark and Norway were attacked simultaneously at dawn on 9 April. Denmark was easy; German ground forces crossed the border and met no resistance. The invasion of Norway was much more difficult. The German Navy put battalion-sized Army detachments ashore, landing them at dawn from cargo ships and warships. In the south of Norway there were five separate points of attack. In the centre of the Norwegian coastline the objective was Trondheim. In the north – 1,200 miles away from the main German naval base of Wilhelmshaven – a daring strike was made at Narvik. Small parachute drops and air-landed reinforcements – a new element in warfare – gave the Luftwaffe possession of vital airfields in Norway (and Denmark) and immediate control of the coastal airspace in the Danish straits and off southern Norway. Altogether the Luftwaffe had assembled no fewer than 500 transport aircraft to support the main attack; the Allies had no comparable airlift capability.

The Norwegian defences were weak and unready. The Allies, too, were caught by surprise, although there had been some warnings through diplomatic channels and they had anticipated counter-moves to their planned mine-laying campaign. The invaders used stormy weather to mask their movement. For the Allies Trondheim was a missed opportunity; they failed to mount a direct counter-attack there to dislodge the Germans before they could be supported from the south. For the Wehrmacht Narvik was almost 'a port too far'. The Royal Navy quickly counter-attacked the small northern port and sank a flotilla of new German destroyers there. British, French, and Polish forces landed and hemmed in the German mountain troops that now held only Narvik itself and the head of the short railway line leading to Sweden. In the end the military crisis in France (in late May) led to the Allied decision to abandon Narvik. This in turn saved the trapped Germans from having to retreat into neutral internment.

The name of Vidkund Quisling will always be linked with the 1940 invasion. Admiral Raeder had introduced the Norwegian Fascist leader to Hitler in late 1939, and Quisling – in a parallel with Kuusinen and the Communists in Finland – declared a rival government as soon as the Germans landed. But Quisling's movement was tiny, and he had no effective 'fifth column'. Quisling's unpopularity among Norwegians meant that the occupiers kept him at arm's length. (Later, in 1942, Quisling was made puppet head of state, and he would be executed as a traitor after the liberation.) King Haakon escaped from Oslo on the day of the first landings. The Germans had not used commandos to trap him; with experience they would later become better at this particular exercise. The King organised a more prolonged Norwegian resistance to the invasion, and he eventually went into exile in Britain.

Once the fighting in Norway began, the British – who with their stronger fleet were running the Allied effort – demonstrated poor co-ordination of sea, land, and air elements. Lessons were learned and 'combined operations' could only get better in terms of doctrine and specialised equipment (there were only a handful of Allied landing craft in April 1940). The mediocre quality of much of the British Army was made clear (the best-equipped troops were in France), and the Royal Air Force (RAF) had to make do in Norway with a few squadrons of biplanes. The shortcomings of the Royal Navy were particularly striking, especially the weakness of carrier air power. All things considered, the Japanese Navy put up a better performance off the coast of central China in the autumn of 1937.

The Germans took quick control over a large northern territory that was very valuable to them (and which would have been even more valuable had they not completed a quick victory in France at the same time). The Germans, fortunately, did not have everything their own way; risk-taking has a price. The German Army took minor losses in Norway, and the Luftwaffe suffered considerable wear and tear, but the Navy was temporarily crippled. The Royal Navy did not use its great surface-ship advantage, but there were some gallant destroyer actions, and British submarines and land-based aircraft achieved good successes. Norwegian coastal defences sank a brand new German heavy cruiser. Most of Admiral Raeder's small surface fleet was sunk or under repair until the late autumn of 1940; he was left in June with three cruisers and four destroyers ready for action. This would contribute to the impracticality of an invasion of Britain in the autumn of 1940. The Allies, for their part, were extremely fortunate that U-boat torpedoes had been faulty.

In Hitler's grand scheme Trondheim was to have been made into the main Atlantic naval base, with a new *Autobahn* running south to the Reich. During the war Norway would in fact be a major base for German naval and air forces. The irony for the Allies was that they originally became entangled in Scandinavia partly to help Finland fight the USSR. In the real world the strategic importance of Norway was that German forces based there could interdict – remarkably successfully – Arctic convoys carrying supplies to Murmansk and Arkhangelsk for Britain's great Eastern ally.

For the Allies, setbacks in Scandinavia had remarkably weighty political consequences, given the limited scope of the campaign compared with what would come later in France. The mishandling of the proposed Finland expedition was the immediate cause of the resignation of Premier Daladier, late in March, and his replacement by Paul Reynaud – although the development was as much explained by the snake pit of French party politics as by strategic debates. On the British side the elderly Neville Chamberlain – he was nearly seventy – had demonstrated that he was an uninspiring and narrow-minded war leader, and that his heart was not in it. Having announced 'peace in our time' after Munich in 1938, Chamberlain claimed on 4 April 1940 that Hitler had 'missed the bus' – that he had not attacked when the Allies were at their weakest. Five days later began the spectacular German assault on Norway. By early May the Allies had lost all of southern and central Norway and had still not rooted the besieged Germans out of Narvik. In the House of Commons 'Norwegian' debate of 7–8 May a large number of MPs abstained in a vote of confidence, and the Prime Minister felt compelled to resign. Chamberlain was to be replaced on the 10th by Winston Churchill, although as First Lord of the Admiralty (i.e. Minister of the Navy) Churchill had made unhelpful interventions in the Norwegian campaign (and he was only four years younger than Chamberlain). Nevertheless neither the Norwegian defeat nor the state of Britain's armed forces were Churchill's fault. The new Prime Minister would possess vital qualities as a national leader (see Figure 7).

Figure 7 | **Winston Churchill**

Of World War II leaders only Hitler and Stalin bear comparison with Winston Churchill (1874–1965) in terms of power and influence over events. He is shown in the dramatic picture above in 1941 with his wife Clementine and with General Władysław Sikorski (centre right), Prime Minister of the Polish government-in-exile and Commander-in-Chief of Polish forces. Churchill was a charismatic leader, able to bridge class distinctions and national boundaries. The son of a British aristocrat and an American heiress, he had both an entrée into the British Establishment and a unique ability to grasp the vital 'special relationship' with the USA. He cultivated close links with President Roosevelt from October 1939 onwards, and as an orator and writer he won over public opinion across the Atlantic. First elected to Parliament in 1900, Churchill was fluid politically. He moved from the Conservatives to the Liberals and back again; he was distrusted by the more narrow-minded Conservatives but able to work well in wartime with Labour.

Churchill led intervention against Bolshevik Russia in 1919–20. Nevertheless Stalin saw him as a pragmatic imperialist – rather like himself in his later years. Like Hitler, Churchill had a global vision, although of a very different kind. He was an Imperialist, and it was his opposition to Indian home rule at the end of the 1920s that led to his temporary departure from active politics. During these 'wilderness years' Churchill became an outspoken critic of the attempts to reach an accommodation with Nazi Germany. This stance, Churchill's rhetorical powers, and his military experience made him a logical candidate to replace Neville Chamberlain as Prime Minister in May 1940.

For a civilian, Churchill had exceptional military knowledge. He had seen front-line service in colonial wars and in the First World War – like Hitler – and he had been a high-level administrator of the armed forces (1st Lord of the Admiralty, 1911–15, Secretary of State for War, 1919–22) – like Roosevelt. As a war leader Churchill had – like Stalin – a tendency to micromanagement. General Brooke commented in his diary: 'God knows where we would be without him, but God knows where we shall go with him!'[a] On the other hand Churchill never lost sight of the 'big picture', and he did much to energise his commanders. Only Hitler matched his visits to the battlefronts. Churchill's military leadership, as we now know, made much use of ULTRA intelligence. His 'peripheral' strategy was compatible with the resources of the Empire, and matched Britain's overall national objectives. He combined all this with extraordinary powers of oratory and prose. Unlike the other wartime supreme leaders, Churchill also left his mark on the historiography of his times, with a multi-volume account, *The Second World War*.

[a] Viscount Alanbrooke, *War Diaries 1939–1945*, ed. Alex Danchev and Daniel Todman (London: Weidenfeld & Nicolson, 2001), p. 207.

Planning for the Western Front

The Wehrmacht launched its main attack in the West on 10 May 1940, while the fighting in Norway was still going on. The German campaign in France and the Low Countries was one of the most important turning points of the whole European war. Before the campaign Germany's long-term prospects were questionable; after it Hitler dominated Western and Central Europe and to many people seemed invincible. Historians still heatedly debate what happened in these momentous weeks. At the very least the popular contemporary conception of an inert, unprepared, and obsolete French Army – hunkered down behind the Maginot Line and then overwhelmed by a pre-planned Hitler Blitzkrieg – has been effectively challenged.

The strength of the armed forces of France has already been outlined (see Chapter 3). The French Army had won World War I, and it served as a model for many other foreign militaries (including, to some extent, the Red Army). It was certainly in a better state than the British or American ground forces of 1940. The French had trained many conscripts during the 1920s and early 1930s. The construction of the defensive system in the east known as the Maginot Line maximised available manpower. The French ground forces were well equipped. Their artillery outnumbered that of the Germans, and they had many anti-tank guns. They had as many tanks as the Wehrmacht, and these tanks were not inferior in firepower or protection. The level of motorisation was at least as high as on the German side. The French commanders did not see themselves as hopelessly outclassed. They had been shocked by the speed of Germany's victory in September 1939, but they assumed this was a special case caused by Polish incompetence.

Doctrine and organisation were vitally important factors. It would be oversimplifying things to say that the main shortcoming of the French Army was that it had a defensive strategy rather than an offensive one. The French approach in the 1930s was modelled on the war-winning methods of 1918. While mobility and flexibility were the heart of the German system, the French put a premium on firepower and centralised control. The Germans stressed the *Bewegungskrieg* (war of movement). The central French concept was the *bataille conduite*, usually translated as the 'methodical battle'; this was a phased, centrally controlled offensive involving infantry, massed artillery, and armour. The French did not anticipate the independent role of armoured forces. They allocated most of their tanks not to tank divisions but to battalions co-operating with individual infantry divisions. The first two heavy armoured divisions were formed only in the winter of 1939–40, after the Polish campaign.

The *Armée de l'Air* had a weak bomber force and a fighter force generally inferior to that of the Luftwaffe. Even the last-minute purchase of large numbers of American-built fighters and bombers – a foretaste of what would come later in the war – could not make good the shortfall. Unlike the British the French did not have radar. The *Armée de l'Air* had become an independent branch of service at the start of the 1930s, but it had not worked out a clear relationship with the Army.

Both sides recognised the extreme importance of Belgium and the Netherlands. This was not because the Low Countries were seen as the unprotected route into northern France (around the Maginot Line), through which Germany could deliver a knockout blow. The perspective before 10 May 1940 – as we have already seen – was different: whichever side gained control of the Low Countries would have an advantage in a subsequent prolonged war. Belgium and the Netherlands were neutral – Belgium only since 1936 – but neither the Allies nor the Germans could depend on this. From the German point of view, if the British and French were to occupy Belgium the likelihood would be that the Brussels government would not resist, and the Allied armies would pose a deadly threat to the industrial region of the Ruhr. The territory of Belgium and the Netherlands was also invaluable to Germany for mounting sea and air attacks against Britain. From the Allied point of view a successful German occupation of Belgium would immediately threaten the industrial region of northern France. Meanwhile the Belgian Army of twenty-two divisions seemed a significant potential addition to the Allied forces. Each side knew in general terms what the other was thinking: France had planned since 1920 to move forces into Belgium in the event of another war with Germany, and German attack plans were compromised when a Luftwaffe courier plane crashed at Mechelen in Belgium in January 1940.

Although the French would later be accused of blind commitment to a defensive strategy, the fact is that their best forces were committed to a rapid *advance* into Belgium to pre-empt the enemy, as soon as Brussels gave the go-ahead or the Wehrmacht precipitated action. There was debate within the Allied high command about how far to go – perhaps even far enough north to support the Dutch. The main hope, however, was to reach the Dyle River in Belgium and establish a secure defensive line there. It was this tactical French offensive, the 'Dyle Plan', rather than the passive defence of the Maginot Line, that would lead to the fatal undoing of the Allied cause.

Meanwhile the Germans were making their own grand preparations. As already noted, as soon as the fighting stopped in Poland Hitler had ordered (on 9 October 1939) preparation for an attack in the West, to be called Operation YELLOW (*Fall Gelb*). The Wehrmacht did not have a force superiority, it had suffered losses in Poland, and the time of year was late. This offensive fitted in with Hitler's reckless approach, but it was not as rash as it sounded, since the objective was relatively limited: the Low Countries and perhaps part of northeastern France. The aim was to achieve the position which Germany had held after the first campaign of World War I. The initial military plan was also an unoriginal one, following in broad outline the strategic concept of 1914 (the so-called Schlieffen Plan). The right wing of the invading force would pivot through the Netherlands and Belgium; the forces on the western frontier were divided into three army groups, with Army Group 'B' – in the north – being the point of concentration.

This German offensive could not be put into effect in the autumn or winter of 1939 because of unsatisfactory weather conditions. Air support was a vital element of the plan and there was too much cloud cover for effective or safe air operations. Meanwhile an alternative offensive concept had been taking shape within the German officer corps. This was the brainchild of General Erich von Manstein (see Figure 8), who was the Chief of Staff of the – central – Army Group 'A' (under General von Rundstedt). Army Group 'A' had been tasked with a secondary role in the original scheme. Now Manstein argued that the main concentration of the whole offensive should be with his army group in the centre of the front. It should not be with Army Group 'B', which was moving into the Netherlands and Belgium on the northern/right wing. Army Group 'A' would thrust directly from east to west, across northern France, with a potentially war-winning objective on the French coast. Above all, it would be hitting the vulnerable flank of French and British forces as

Figure 8 | General Erich von Manstein

General Erich von Manstein (1887–1973), shown here (centre), was a brilliant planner and commander. He had a crucial impact on the conduct of German operations in 1940. Manstein won acceptance from Hitler for the 'Sickle Cut' plan – a rapid drive across northern France – and this led to the decisive defeat of the Allied armies in May 1940. Manstein personified one of the greatest assets Nazi Germany inherited: the skill, self-confidence, and cohesion of the Prussian officer corps. His natural father and uncle were generals, and he was adopted by (and took his surname from) a third general. His uncle was Field Marshal Paul von Hindenburg, hero of World War I and President of Weimar Germany. Under Kaiser Wilhelm II, Manstein was commissioned into the elite 3rd Foot Guards and trained for the General Staff. He served as a planner in World War I, and by the later 1930s his abilities and connections had raised him to senior Army posts.

After the 1940 victory Manstein served in Russia, where Hitler promoted him to Field Marshal for the capture of Sevastopol'. He was able to restore order to the German southern front in early 1943 after Stalingrad but eventually fell out with Hitler over the organisation of the Army. Retired in early 1944, he refused to take part in the Army conspiracy against Hitler. Manstein was imprisoned by the British for war crimes committed by his forces in Russia. On his release he produced an influential memoir, *Lost Victories*.

they moved into Belgium and Holland. The daring concept was known as the 'Sickle Cut' (*Sichelschnitt*).

Manstein's plan also had the advantage of doing the unexpected, not simply repeating the Schlieffen concept. The divisions from Army Group 'A' would move through a region the French Army could be expected to cover lightly. The rough wooded territory of the Ardennes region in Luxembourg and southern Belgium did not seem a passable approach route for large motorised forces, and to the west of the Ardennes the steep Meuse River valley (in France) appeared an easily defended line that could be covered by second-class French troops. In the end Manstein was able, in February 1940, to put his case for 'Sickle Cut' directly to Hitler – although not before the Army high command had posted him away from the Western Front for being insubordinate. Operation YELLOW was altered to concentrate German armour in Army Group 'A'. It was Hitler's great moment of strategic intuition. The Allies, for their part, had no inkling of the revised German deployment. Later in the war the British would learn much from intercepted Wehrmacht radio communications; in April and May 1940 the code-breaking system was still in its infancy. In France and the Low Countries, as in Norway, the Allies were still operating in the dark.

The invasion of France and the Low Countries

'It was hard to believe on a most glorious spring day with all nature looking quite its best, that we were taking the first step towards what must become one of the greatest battles in history!'[3] Such was the diary entry of one of the British corps commanders, General Brooke, as German operations began on 10 May. The northern advance of German Army Group 'B' saw some sensational events including a glider assault on the Belgian fortress of Eben-Emael (10 May) and a heavy Luftwaffe attack on the Dutch city of Rotterdam (13 May). On 14 May the Netherlands surrendered. The attention of the Allies was fixed on the river crossings into northern Belgium, and to some extent on the Netherlands. The French, with the support of the British Expeditionary Force (BEF), implemented their own plan and pushed north towards the Dyle River in Belgium.

But the significant action – thanks to Manstein and 'Sickle Cut' – was in the centre. The situation was a strategic vortex: the French and British

Box 14 | The Stuka attack on Sedan

An account of the dive-bomber (Stuka) attack on Sedan, by Sergeant Prümers of 1st Panzer Division. The Luftwaffe air strike helped achieve one of the critical break-throughs of the 1940 campaign, and the Stuka became a dreaded symbol of the Blitzkrieg. *Stuka* was the abbreviation of *Sturzkampfflugzeug*, the generic term for 'strike aircraft', although the name is usually linked with one particular aircraft, the Junkers Ju 87.

Three, six, nine, oh, behind them still more, and to the right aircraft, and further to the right aircraft, and still more aircraft, a quick look in the binoculars – Stukas! And what we are about to see during the next twenty minutes is one of the most powerful impressions of this war. Squadron upon squadron rise to a great height, break into line ahead and there, there the first machines hurtle perpendicularly down, followed by the second, third – ten, twelve aeroplanes are there. Simultaneously, like some bird of prey, they fall upon their victim and then release their load of bombs on the target. We can see the bombs very clearly. It becomes a regular rain of bombs, that whistle down on Sedan and the bunker positions. Each time the explosion is overwhelming, the noise deafening. Everything becomes blended together; along with the howling sirens of the Stukas in their dives, the bombs whistle and crack and burst. A huge blow of annihilation strikes the enemy, and still more squadrons arrive, rise to a great height and come down on the same target. We stand and watch what is happening as if hypnotized; down below all hell is let loose! At the same time we are full of confidence ... and suddenly we notice that the enemy artillery no longer shoots ... while the last squadron of Stukas is still attacking we receive our marching orders.

(From Alistair Horne, *To Lose a Battle: France 1940* (London: Macmillan, 1969), p. 247.)

were advancing northeast into Belgium, the German main force was advancing southwest and west into northern France. The German panzer and motorised divisions were able to pass rapidly through the Ardennes; the Allied air forces missed the chance to attack the congested roads. Supported by the Luftwaffe, and taking advantage of the collapse of a pair of weak French reserve divisions, infantry elements of one of the German spearheads managed to make a rapid crossing over the Meuse at Sedan (on 13–14 May), supported by massed waves of Stuka dive bombers (see Box 14). The local commander, General Heinz Guderian, on his own initiative – and rather than waiting for the arrival and build-up of German infantry – ordered a rapid advance by his tanks west beyond the Meuse. Erwin Rommel, another German soldier who would distinguish himself later in the war, effected a quick Meuse crossing further north.

With their tanks across the Meuse, counting on their speed to put off any flank attack – and to some extent ignoring the reservations of the professional soldiers of the German high command – the concentrated panzer force (Panzer Group Kleist) headed for the coast to complete the encirclement of the Allied forces in northern France and Belgium. By 15 May the French high command was aware that the position at the front was unravelling. The French had no ready operational reserves; General Gamelin, the French C-in-C, had positioned his spare mobile divisions on the extreme left flank for the deep advance into Belgium. On 20 May – after an advance of 150 miles beyond the Meuse – the German spearheads reached their objective, the Somme estuary on the coast. They had cut off a large number of French and British divisions. The same day Gamelin was replaced by General Maxime Weygand.

France surrenders

The French and British troops were unable to assemble a co-ordinated counter-attack against the rapidly moving German spearheads. The divisions trapped in Belgium could not to fight their way out to the south. A large Allied force, including most of the British Expeditionary Force, was trapped at the end of May in a large pocket on the coast around Dunkirk, between the new line of German Army Group 'A' and the advancing Army Group 'B'. The successful evacuation of much of the BEF through Dunkirk and other coastal ports was an event of the greatest importance (see Box 15).

The second phase of the German attack, south from the Somme, was given the codename Operation RED (*Fall Rot*). It began on 5 June. This phase of the battle, as the Germans moved south into France, involved heavy fighting. French resistance was more stubborn than in the first weeks, but the Germans had brought up their infantry and by weight of numbers were able to break through. On 10 June the French government left Paris, first for the Loire region, and then for Bordeaux. The same day Italy declared war and began limited operations in the mountainous border region of southeast France.

Box 15 | Dunkirk

The evacuation of Allied forces at Dunkirk began on 26 May and ended on 4 June; the British called the affair Operation DYNAMO. Nearly 340,000 personnel, two-thirds British, one-third French, were embarked. The British Expeditionary Force (BEF) had to leave most of its heavy equipment and stores behind. Dunkirk was potentially a turning point of the war as a whole. The French had already suffered a mortal blow, but the complete loss of the BEF would have left Britain vulnerable to invasion and might have led the government in London to make peace on Hitler's terms. As Winston Churchill put it a few days later, 'The whole root and core and brain of the British Army, on which and around which we . . . are to build the great British Armies in the later years of the war, seemed about to perish on the field.'[a]

The rapidly advancing Wehrmacht had cut off the Allied forces in Belgium and northern France and pushed them back into a coastal enclave around Dunkirk. It seemed that the unstoppable panzer advance would wipe out the enclave. On 24 May Hitler issued the famous 'halt order' (*Halte-Befehl*) instructing German armoured troops to halt and refit. In their memoirs the German generals blamed Hitler for allowing the British to escape through fatal indecision. Some historians maintain that the Führer wanted to avoid a bloody defeat that would hamper an expected accommodation with Britain. Others have blamed Göring for promising Hitler that the Luftwaffe alone could deal with the Dunkirk pocket. Most likely Hitler, and his senior generals, thought it necessary to refit the armoured forces before beginning the second stage of the campaign in France, south of the Somme. It is also the case that the region around the port city had some natural defences; after D-Day the German Army held Dunkirk as a 'fortified place' for seven months, from September 1944 to May 1945, bypassed by the Allied armies. From the British perspective the Dunkirk evacuation in 1940 was the end of the war on the continent, but in fact the French fought on for another three weeks; many of the French troops brought out of Dunkirk disembarked in western France.

The British, remarkably, were able to turn a humiliating defeat into a moral turning point. Part of the myth of the 'miracle of Dunkirk' was the 'little ships' – pleasure boats and fishing craft – that crossed the Channel in large numbers, an expression of popular involvement in the saving of the army. In reality most of the embarkation was accomplished by the Royal Navy, and from the harbour of Dunkirk rather than over the beaches. Later in the war the Germans had to mount similar – and successful – evacuations, from Sicily in 1943 and the Crimea in 1944, although these involved a smaller number of troops.

[a] Speech of 4 June 1940, Churchill Centre (Washington DC): at www.winstonchurchill.org.

The French government collapsed in crisis. Premier Reynaud resigned on 16 June and was replaced by Marshal Pétain, the eighty-four-year-old hero of the 1916 Battle of Verdun. The following day Pétain made a radio address in which he declared that France had lost and would have to sign an armistice. The logic of this decision was that the defeat of France was inevitable, and there was no chance the British could hold out on their own. The French wanted to get the best terms they could while their forces were still intact. Hitler was glad to oblige, and an armistice was signed on 22 June 1940.

The French government had decided not to continue the campaign south and west of the Seine. It also did not take the struggle abroad, as the Poles did, although the French colonies, especially in North Africa, might have served as a bolt hole. Not all Frenchmen agreed with this decision to capitulate. As the armistice was being signed General de Gaulle in London had declared that he would continue the struggle, but at the time his gesture seemed quixotic. The great majority of the armed forces of France followed their government. This was to lead to direct fighting between the erstwhile Allies, as the British sank ships of the French fleet in harbour at Mers-el-Kébir in Algeria to prevent any chance of their falling into German hands. Churchill was also making the point here that there could be no doubting the resolve of the British Empire to continue the war, and that its forces would henceforth act ruthlessly.

The cost of the six-week Battle of France was relatively low, given its momentous impact. This also says something about the extent of effective French resistance, especially in the early critical phase of the battle. Some 1.8 million French soldiers were made POWs, and most of them were sent to camps in Germany later in the summer. Total Wehrmacht losses were 45,000 personnel killed, while the French lost 90,000 and the British Army 11,000 (plus 41,000 POWs and missing). These figures were considerably higher than for the Franco–Prussian War of 1870 (which lasted longer and involved smaller armies). But the casualties were much less than at the start of World War I; in 1914 alone the French lost 380,000 men killed, and the Germans almost as many. The casualties were also much less than would be suffered in subsequent German campaigns in World War II.

> ## Box 16 | **Their finest hour**
>
> This famous quotation is from a speech made by Prime Minister Winston Churchill on 18 June 1940.
>
> ---
>
> What General Weygand called the Battle of France is over. I expect that the Battle of Britain is about to begin. Upon this battle depends the survival of Christian civilization. Upon it depends our own British life, and the long continuity of our institutions and our Empire. The whole fury and might of the enemy must very soon be turned on us. Hitler knows that he will have to break us in this Island or lose the war. If we can stand up to him, all Europe may be free and the life of the world may move forward into broad, sunlit uplands. But if we fail, then the whole world, including the United States, including all that we have known and cared for, will sink into the abyss of a new Dark Age made more sinister, and perhaps more protracted, by the lights of perverted science. Let us therefore brace ourselves to our duties, and so bear ourselves that, if the British Empire and its Commonwealth last for a thousand years, men will still say, 'This was their finest hour.'
>
> (From Churchill Centre (Washington DC): at www.winstonchurchill.org.)

The Battle of Britain

With the fall of France an emboldened German high command turned to Britain. In mid July Hitler issued a directive for a hastily planned invasion (Operation SEA LION). 'Since England, in spite of its hopeless military situation, shows no sign of being ready to come to an understanding, I have decided to prepare a landing operation against England, and, if necessary, to carry it out.'[4] Hitler's generals and admirals could never have completed preparations in the stipulated six weeks, and by the time of the proposed mid August readiness date a serious Luftwaffe attack had scarcely started.

Both sides had been reluctant to get involved in a 'strategic' air bombing campaign, although German inhibitions were reduced with the conquest of the Low Countries and the elimination of northern France as an enemy air base; the Ruhr industrial region now seemed much less threatened. The Luftwaffe, however, needed time to develop forward bases (usually French airfields). Stukas and bombers attacked British coastal shipping in July. Göring's

Figure 9 | Supermarine Spitfire

The Spitfire remains one of the best-known aircraft of World War II. First flown in 1936, this fighter kept Britain at the forefront of aviation technology. The aircraft had a powerful new engine, the Rolls Royce Merlin. Its performance at high altitude and its heavy armament – initially eight machine guns – made it an outstanding bomber interceptor. (The Mk VB pictured opposite is armed with even more lethal 20 mm cannon.)

With its streamlined fuselage and unique elliptical wings, the Spitfire was a truly beautiful aircraft. It was identified in the popular mind with British technical genius and with the victory in the 1940 Battle of Britain. A full-length wartime propaganda film was produced, 'The First of the Few' (1942), with Lesley Howard playing R. J. Mitchell (1895–1937), the Spitfire's chief designer. Mitchell developed his design concepts through the Supermarine racing seaplanes of the 1920s and 1930s. The Supermarine company was taken over by the arms conglomerate Vickers-Armstrong in 1928, which facilitated the eventual mass production of the aircraft. In reality the Spitfire was outnumbered in the 1940 RAF Fighter Command by the Hawker Hurricane. The Hurricane was also Merlin-powered and heavily armed, but it had a less advanced airframe, and had much less development potential.

The main shortcomings of the Spitfire were its small size and limited range, making it less effective than later fighters as a fighter bomber or a bomber escort. The Spitfire was, however, the backbone of the RAF's fighter force throughout the war. It was uprated to take on new versions of the German Messerschmitt Bf 109 and the Focke-Wulf Fw 190, notably in the Mk IX version of 1942. It operated on nearly all fronts of the war. A version of the Spitfire (the Seafire) flew from British carriers off Japan in 1945. A total of 22,000 Spitfires were built.

pompously named 'Eagle Day' (*Adlertag*, 13 August 1940) started a more serious air campaign. The Luftwaffe targeted RAF airfields and aircraft factories in the southeast of England. In early September the focus shifted to London. Now the long-feared tit-for-tat reprisals of total war had set it. The London 'Blitz' (as the British called it) was in part Hitler's angry response to a British night raid on Berlin in late August; that raid had been Churchill's answer to a small – and a possibly accidental – Luftwaffe attack on London's outskirts.

The scale of the air campaign which became known as the 'Battle of Britain' was limited, compared to what had been feared beforehand by the British authorities and to what would be inflicted on Axis cities. Total British civilian deaths between June and December 1940 were 23,000 (compared to 50,000 in Hamburg over just four nights in the summer of 1943, or 410,000 in Japan between March and August 1945). The notorious night raid on the city of Coventry (a centre of the British motor industry) in November 1940 killed 'only' 568 people – about a hundredth part of the 1943 Hamburg losses. (Strategic bombing is discussed more fully in Chapter 9.)

The RAF victory in the Battle of Britain was also not a 'miracle'. The Luftwaffe had suffered significant losses (in combat and accidents) in Norway, the Low Countries, and France. Britain's aircraft production had already caught up with and surpassed that of the Third Reich. German intelligence about the damage effects of Luftwaffe attacks was poor. The British integrated air defence system, with effective Spitfire and Hurricane fighters (see Figure 9), radar, ground-based fighter control and an aircraft repair system, was a remarkable asset. Historians tend to see the August 'airfields' strategy – striking at RAF bases – as the most dangerous phase of the German air campaign, but even these attacks were hitting only a small part of the total British force. As for the attacks on London, the great metropolis was just on the edge of the maximum range of the Messerschmitt Bf 109 fighter, the main Luftwaffe bomber escort, and so German losses in daytime attacks became unacceptably high. In October the Luftwaffe turned to night raids, which the RAF was unable to intercept. Such raids could not cause the precise damage to an economic or military 'target system' that was required. The British night bombing campaign against Germany would take years to achieve much effect – arguably not a war-winning effect even then – and that was with many more and much larger aircraft.

The main point, however, is that by the beginning of August – several weeks before 'Eagle Day' – it was clear to Hitler that invasion in the 1940 campaigning season was not a practical option. The RAF and the Royal Navy were too strong, and the Germany Army lacked the specialised shipping required to carry out and sustain a large cross-Channel landing. In July 1940 the Führer had already turned his thoughts to an invasion of Russia. This was well before the official postponement date of SEA LION on 17 September. The air campaign had no clear focus, partly because of Hitler's initial caution, partly because of rival tactics within the Luftwaffe command, and above all because – with invasion ruled out – there was no achievable military objective.

The Battle of Britain had political goals as much as military ones. No one knew in advance whether concentrated bombing of civilians would cause chaos and panic, whether it would lead to a fatal fall in national morale that would force the politicians to the peace table. The British government had since 1937 helped organise a substantial Air Raid Precautions (ARP) system, and this popular mobilisation sustained morale throughout the Blitz. Improvised shelters and the London Underground system provided some protection. Children were evacuated from major cities in September 1939 (although some returned when there was no immediate German threat). Slogans like 'London can take it!' (the title of a 1940 propaganda film) genuinely did sustain morale and won popular support for Britain in the United States and elsewhere. We now know that it is hard to make civilian morale crack under this kind of bombing, and this was true both in Britain and later in Germany. It is understandable, however, that Hitler would try to see if the air weapon worked; it did not.

With hindsight, the outcome of the Luftwaffe's air offensive of August and September 1940 re-emphasised German weaknesses that had been visible before May. Germany was a mid-strength power that had begun comprehensive rearmament only in 1935. Although the Luftwaffe medium bomber force had been given one of the highest priorities in Hitler's pre-war armaments programme, its machines had nothing like the range or bomb load required for an effective strategic campaign. Germany also had no navy to mount an invasion in the late summer of 1940. Even without taking into account the German ships lost or damaged in Norway, the Royal Navy had begun the war with an unbeatable lead. At the same time, however, the Battle of Britain was an event of extreme political importance. The great air battle revived British

Box 17 | Air combat

From RAF Flight Lieutenant Richard Hillary's account of the Battle of Britain:

I saw ... the pilot put his machine into a half roll, and knew that he was mine. Automatically, I kicked the rudder to the left to get him at right angles, turned the gun-button to 'Fire', and let go in a four-second burst with full deflection. He came right through my sights and I saw the tracer from all eight guns thud home. For a second he seemed to hang motionless; then a jet of red flame shot upwards and he spun out of sight.

For the next few minutes I was too busy looking after myself to think of anything, but ... after a short while ... my mind began to work again.

It had happened.

My first emotion was one of satisfaction, satisfaction at a job adequately done, at the final logical conclusion of months of specialised training. And then I had a feeling of the essential rightness of it all. He was dead and I was alive; it could so easily have been the other way round; and that would somehow have been right too.

(From Richard Hillary, *The Last Enemy* (London: Macmillan, 1942), p. 121.)

spirits after Dunkirk, and it consolidated the popularity of Churchill. It also increased American popular support for the resilient British.

• • •

In 1918 the German Army was defeated by the French and British Armies. In 1940 the Wehrmacht defeated the French Army, and drove the British Expeditionary Force from the continent. On 21 June the French agreed to sign an armistice. As the German press bulletin put it:

In the Forest of Compiègne, the Führer conducted the state act of the presentation of [armistice] conditions in the same railway coach in which, on November 11, 1918, Marshal Foch dictated the terms of the armistice to the German delegates, under the most dishonourable circumstances. Today's act in the Forest of Compiègne has erased the injustice perpetrated against German military honour.[5]

In this rewriting of history the Führer left nothing to the imagination. Adolf Hitler truly seemed to have re-fought World War I and this time won it. Germany was no longer in the perilous position of April 1940; Hitler had not – in Chamberlain's memorable words – 'missed the bus'. The correlation of forces in Europe had changed profoundly. Britain had lost

France; Germany had gained Italy; Russia was still friendly to Germany. Nazi Germany had won over, conquered, or cowed most of the smaller European neutrals. Hitler had largely won the struggle for economic resources that had seemed so important in 1939 and early 1940.

The outcome of the Battle of France and the Battle of Britain put both Hitler and Churchill in a peculiar situation. Britain was Germany's only remaining enemy. Churchill had been left without allies on the continent. Enemy forward bases threatened the British Isles with air attack, blockade, and invasion. The Empire was now challenged by the Italians in the Mediterranean as well. The British government faced the hard choice between coming to an accommodation with Germany or continuing the war alone. Pétain and the politicians had made the former choice for France. But it had also become clear that the British government under Churchill was not going to accept any peace terms, and that Hitler had no quick military route to knock Britain out of the war.

Meanwhile Hitler had different strategic choices. One was to offer generous peace terms which mainstream British politicians – if not Churchill and his supporters – could accept. This was, however, inherently impossible. Re-fighting and winning World War I might have been enough for the German population and even for most of the generals. It was not enough for Hitler and the NSDAP. Hitler's requirement for *Lebensraum* and world domination went far beyond the mainstream German aims in World War I. The second – relatively slow – solution was to mount a war of attrition against Britain, against its trade and its overseas colonies in collaboration with Italian (and perhaps Japanese) allies. This Axis peripheral strategy, and the British (and American) response to it, is discussed in Chapter 8. The final alternative for Hitler was to eliminate the British hope of gaining Stalin's USSR as a new continental partner to replace France. An attack on Russia would allow Germany to use its main asset, land power. Victory in the East would finally guarantee the resource base of the Third Reich. Hitler made his decision in July 1940, when he began planning for the Russian option (see Chapter 5).

What had taken place between September 1939 and October 1940 was also the 'limited' part of the European war. The German victories had been much easier than those of 1914–18, and the casualty toll had been much less than anyone could have expected. The conflict was now about to enter a new and much more terrible phase.

German troops search a captured Red Army soldier in June 1941. An extreme feature of Hitler's war of ideology was the death of millions of Soviet prisoners of war in German captivity. There is no serious book about this subject in English, despite the fact that the death toll among the POWs – 2.5 to 3 million – took in half those captured, and was between a quarter and a third of the Soviet Union's 10 million 'military' deaths.

The visible mistreatment of their sons and brothers in uniform was a significant factor in turning the local Russian civilian population against the German occupiers. In the longer term, after the German defeat, those POWs who survived to be repatriated were treated badly by the Soviet regime, almost as 'traitors to the motherland'. Legal 'rehabilitation' came only under President Yeltsin in 1994.

Wars of ideology 1941–1942

Timeline

1939	October	Nazi terror in Poland begins
1940	July	Hitler decides to invade USSR
1941	April	Invasion of Yugoslavia and Greece
	June	Invasion of USSR: Operation BARBAROSSA
	July	Mass murder of Jews by SS *Einsatzgruppen* begins on captured Soviet territory
	September	Germans take Kiev
	October	Construction of Auschwitz II (Birkenau) death camp begins
	October	Battle of Viaz'ma–Briansk: Operation TYPHOON
	December	Battle of Moscow
1942	January	Wannsee Conference on the European Jews

Hitler's choices

Hitler decided to attack Russia in July 1940. He made this fateful choice very soon after the fall of France, and before the difficulties of the air attack on Britain had became clear.

The Führer had stunned the world, both friends and foes, by his sudden reversal of policy towards Stalin's USSR in August 1939. The German–Soviet Non-Aggression Pact (see Chapter 3) was followed by important territorial and economic agreements. Geopolitically a German–Soviet 'alliance' made a great deal of sense. It divided much of Eastern Europe into German and Soviet spheres of influence. The Pact meant that the Wehrmacht did not have to fight a war on two fronts. The Germans received important supplies of food and minerals from the USSR, plus a transit route across the Eurasian 'heartland' to the outside world. Now, just eleven months later, the German dictator turned his back on this arrangement.

The causes of Hitler's fateful change of course were complex. There had been some problems agreeing on territorial terms with the Russians in the Balkans – Stalin drove a hard bargain – but this was not an insurmountable obstacle to 'correct' relations. There was an ideological dimension, something that is stressed in this chapter's title. Hitler had been an avowed anti-Communist (and anti-Slav) throughout his political life. But he could probably have co-existed with the Russian communists for some time, in order to defeat other enemies. There was the struggle for a new geopolitical order which would give Nazi Germany the *Grossraum* of Russia, with the grain of the Ukraine and the oil of the Caucasus. But this also was something for the long run. There was the Red Army, a menace which Hitler himself would publically refer to on 22 June 1941 as a reason for the invasion. In 1942–3, once they realised how strong the Russians were, the German leaders did have second thoughts. Propaganda Minister Goebbels said – after Stalingrad – that in June 1941 'it was two minutes before twelve!'[1] But before 22 June 1941 Hitler and the German military leadership did not actually fear an attack by the Russians.

More important as a factor behind the decision to attack Russia was the easy victory over France; this convinced Hitler and his generals that the same thing could be accomplished in the East. The Wehrmacht had stumbled upon Blitzkrieg, as the means to a rapid 'operational' solution of a strategic problem. The Blitzkrieg had much in common with the traditional Prussian approach to war – rapid and violent movement and an early and decisive 'battle of annihilation' (*Vernichtungsschlacht*). It was now assumed that this could be applied on a continental scale. Foolhardy optimism was increased by flawed assessments of Russian strength, which were based on political and racial assumptions: that the Red Army and the Jewish-Bolshevik government of Stalin would collapse before a vigorous German assault.

The immediate cause of Hitler's July 1940 decision for an attack against the USSR came from the existing war situation. The conflict that had begun in 1939 could not be concluded, as long as the forces of the British Empire remained in the field. Germany lacked the naval forces to invade Britain or even to threaten its colonies. In the summer of 1940 there seemed to be no way that the British government would be forced to the peace table. Churchill's position was far from hopeless, especially as he could look forward – even if only in the medium term – to an eventual co-belligerent in the form of the USSR. As Hitler said in his 1945 *Testament*: 'The only way to force the English to make peace was to take away, through the annihilation of the Red Army, their hopes of confronting us on the Continent with a comparable opponent.'[2] Here, too, was a theatre of war in which the existing ground forces of the Wehrmacht could be used immediately and to good effect.

In December 1940 the directive for Operation BARBAROSSA was issued: 'The German Wehrmacht must be prepared, even before the conclusion of the war against England, *to overthrow Soviet Russia in a rapid campaign*.'[3] The overall strategic concept was to destroy the Red Army in the 'borderlands' west of the Dvina and Dnepr rivers before it could be withdrawn into the Russian hinterland; the unstated model was the victory in France, where the Wehrmacht quickly knocked out the main Allied armies north of the Somme. The USSR would then be occupied, after a rapid pursuit, to a line on the far side of European Russia, stretching from Arkhangelsk (on the White Sea) to Astrakhan (on the Caspian Sea), and demarcated by the middle and lower Volga River.

Hitler's decision was a foolish one. Germany did not have a high-level planning structure to evaluate potential enemies and to calculate a rational grand strategy, although it must also be said that the senior generals went along with the decision to attack Russia. With hindsight, we might also say

Box 18 | Rudolf Hess flies to Britain

Rudolf Hess (1894–1987) was the Deputy Führer and one of Hitler's oldest and closest comrades. Hitler had dictated most of *Mein Kampf* to him, and Hess had introduced the future Führer to geopolitics. On the night of 10–11 May Hess piloted a high-performance Messerschmitt fighter on a long-distance flight solo from Munich to a location just outside Glasgow, where he took to his parachute. Much remains inexplicable about this event, but given the planned timing of the BARBAROSSA attack (the final date of 22 June was set only on 30 April), it is hard to believe that the flight and Hitler's planned polar shift of German strategic policy were not somehow connected.

The official Russian view was that the Hess flight was a German peace feeler which the British disavowed. Others have argued that the British secret service (SIS) had been playing a secret 'game' to convince the Germans that there was a right-wing peace faction in Britain. Some historians suggest that prominent figures in the British Establishment believed that Churchill's inflexible anti-Hitler policy was bankrupting the Empire, and were quite prepared to join a common struggle against Bolshevism. Hess's mental state is debatable; nevertheless he may well have wanted to undertake an heroic personal act which would raise his gradually declining status with Hitler. He may also have believed that an envoy of his high status would be required to convince the British peace faction of German *bona fides*. Hess did not necessarily assume that his flight would be a one-way mission, or an event which the world would immediately learn about. Hitler, for his part, may have seen the Hess mission as a gamble on a diplomatic coup of the greatest importance (like Ribbentrop's August 1939 flight to Moscow). Perhaps Hitler regarded it as an initiative he could plausibly deny.

Churchill and the British authorities announced Hess's arrival and imprisonment, but provided little other information. Hess was interviewed by some senior officials, apparently to little effect. After the war, whatever doubts now existed about Hess's mental state, he was treated as fit to stand trial, although he made no coherent testimony at the Nuremberg trial. Hess was indeed complicit in all the early crimes of the NSDAP, including the wars of aggression, but he was condemned to life imprisonment rather than to hanging. The Allies kept him in Berlin's Spandau Prison, guarded in turn by the four occupying powers. Hess's suicide while under British guard at Spandau in 1987 (aged 93) did not put off the conspiracy theorists. One argument was that the improved relations the new Soviet leader, Gorbachev, sought with the West might have led to Soviet permission for Hess's release. This in turn would have led to the exposure of embarrassing facts.

that the German high command did not have a better route out of its strategic impasse. Britain had not surrendered, and its forces were recovering from the disaster in Flanders. However negatively the Germans assessed the USSR, the Red Army could be expected to grow stronger over time. Although for the moment Russia willingly provided the Reich with necessary resources, Stalin could cut the flow at any time. Not attacking the USSR was in reality as dangerous an option as Operation BARBAROSSA.

The Axis invasion of the Balkans, April 1941

Before the attack on the USSR Hitler launched the fourth of his six major wartime offensives (fourth, after the campaigns in Poland in 1939, and in Norway and France in 1940). Mussolini had unexpectedly set upon Greece in October 1940. The Greek Army and the mountainous terrain stopped the Italian Army, and then the Greeks drove Mussolini's troops back. The British – also fighting Italy – provided some air and naval support, but the Greek government was wary of provoking the still neutral Germans. Despite this, and about the same time that the BARBAROSSA directive was drafted (December 1940), Hitler ordered preparations for a future attack on Greece, Operation MARITA. This blow would knock out Britain's last active partner in southeastern Europe, solidify German influence in the Balkans and the eastern Mediterranean, and provide a protective cushion around the oil fields of Romania.

Hitler's Balkan campaign did not unfold entirely according to plan. After the fall of France most of the Central European states had made haste to reorient themselves towards the Third Reich. Hungary and Bulgaria had already been friendly towards Germany (partly because they also wished to regain territory lost in 1918). As for Romania, it was pushed into close co-operation with Germany by the Soviet annexation of its northeastern territory (Bessarabia); in November 1940 Bucharest signed the Tripartite (Axis) Pact. The remaining piece of the Balkan jigsaw puzzle was Yugoslavia, but even here the government seemed prepared to come to terms with Hitler. In March 1941 the Yugoslavs also signed the Tripartite Pact. This act was, however, followed at the end of the month by a military coup led by (Serbian) nationalist air force officers. Hitler immediately ordered preparations to fold an attack on Yugoslavia into the attack on Greece.

The German invasion in early April 1941 – now of both Yugoslavia and Greece – was carried out with some Italian and Bulgarian support. It was a military triumph, fought at the pace of the French campaign and against a much weaker enemy. Belgrade was subjected to a massive Luftwaffe attack. The Yugoslav Army, ethnically divided, ineptly led, and badly equipped, collapsed with hardly a fight. (This was a remarkable event, given the fierce three-year guerrilla war that was to follow in parts of the country.) The Greek conventional forces fought rather better, with some British help, but the six-month war with Italy had weakened Greece. The country was politically divided, and the Greek Army tried unrealistically to hang on to all its pre-war territory. The Greek Army lasted only two weeks, and by mid May the British had even been thrown out of their toehold on Crete (see also Chapter 10).

In the last months of his life Hitler claimed that the Balkan campaign fatally delayed his invasion of Russia. Historians still debate this question. Operation BARBAROSSA was originally set for 15 May 1941, and it was actually launched five weeks later, on 22 June. There were other factors, aside from the Balkan campaign, that delayed the attack on Russia. But the 600,000 Germans troops that operated in the Balkans, especially the motorised spearhead units, had to be refitted. The final air assault against the British on Crete in May cost the Germans a large number of transport aircraft and the irreplaceable asset of their airborne forces; the latter would never again be used on any scale in their intended role.

The USSR: weakness in strength

When Hitler threw his forces against Russia he did so with a number of advantages. The first was the invaluable experience – operational and tactical – gained in the French campaign. The second was the ability to concentrate all the best divisions of the German Army and the mass of the Luftwaffe against Russia – also thanks to the French victory. The third was the element of surprise, which Hitler emphasised in the BARBAROSSA directive.

Soviet Russia, too, had strengths. Nikita Khrushchev made many valid criticisms in his 'de-Stalinisation' campaign of the 1950s and 1960s. It was unfair, however, to charge Stalin and his government with not preparing the USSR for war. As discussed earlier in this book (Chapter 2), the USSR had undertaken a military build-up in the late 1930s, and we tend to ignore this because of the military purge of 1937–8 (see Box 19). The Red Army was

Box 19 | The purge of the Red Army

Stalin's military purge of 1937–8 is often cited as a major cause of the military catastrophe which engulfed that Soviet forces three years later. The best-known victim of Stalin's military purge was Marshal Mikhail Tukhachevskii (1893–1937); the Deputy Commissar of Defence was the main sponsor of the rapid modernisation of the Red Army in the 1930s and the advocate of the 'deep battle' offensive strategy. With Tukhachevskii died a cohort of other modernisers.

In the past, historians have often exaggerated the impact of the purge, to the point where it was hard to understand how the Soviet forces could also have won great victories in 1943–5. Soviet officer losses were not the frequently cited number of 35,000, and the victims did not make up – as is sometimes asserted – half the Soviet officer corps. To start with, the number of commanders and commissars who were arrested (most of whom were indeed shot) was something like 20,000, out of a total of 142,000. (For the sake of comparison, Soviet losses in the first three months of the war included 142,000 'command staff', out of 440,000 in service on 22 June.) In the 1937–8 purge, losses were extremely high among very senior ranks, down to the level of division commander. But at the middle level the death rate was lower. For example, some 276 commanders with a rank equivalent to colonel died in the purges in 1937–41, but 1,713 men (including the future Marshals Zhukov, Vasilevskii, Konev, and Rokossovskii) had held that rank in 1936.

Why did Stalin, who was building up the military potential of the USSR, allow the NKVD (secret police) to massacre so many Red Army command staff? First of all, the Army was a relatively small component of the 'Great Terror'; the NKVD executed no fewer than 680,000 people in 1937–8. Second, this was a time of extreme, even hysterical, distrust, when political trials suggested that 'enemies of the people' were everywhere. As far as the Soviet military are concerned, it is not impossible that Franco's attempted army revolt in Spain in July 1936 was an alarm signal for Stalin and his closest comrades. In any event, the very thing that an army needed to function effectively, a cohesive officer corps, was what was most politically dangerous to Stalin and the Communist elite. Finally, Stalin saw the purge – both in civilian life and in the Red Army – as a renewal, opening up jobs to a cohort of younger, better-trained officers, and moreover a cohort whose loyalty to himself would be more single-minded than that of their predecessors.

expanded from 1.6 million personnel in January 1938 to over 5 million in 1941. The third Five-Year Plan (1937–41) saw the pay-off for earlier industrial investments. Stalin's Russia had developed a huge military-industrial complex, and it now achieved 'wartime' scales of arms production, especially of tanks (averaging 2,500 a year in 1937–41), artillery pieces (10,000 a year), and aircraft (8,000 a year). Molotov was correct in his memoirs: 'The growth of our military industry in the years before the war could not possibly have been greater!'[4] The USSR had also developed the potential to expand its armaments production even further, thanks to the drafting of industrial mobilisation plans and the construction of dual-purpose factories. The problem with the early 'freezing' of mass production was that Soviet fighters and bombers, of a high standard in the mid 1930s, were obsolete in 1941. For a variety of reasons, including the Red Army purge, new aircraft types had not been developed. This was less of a problem with small arms, tanks, and artillery systems, where the cycle of innovation was longer.

The Soviet forces were not inexperienced. Stalin's Russia was already in effect a participant in World War II, as has been mentioned earlier in this book. The Soviets sent advisors, equipment, and even fighting personnel to Nationalist China from 1937 onwards. The Red Army itself had fought large battles on the borders of Manchuria in 1938 and 1939. The USSR carried out a military occupation of eastern Poland in 1939. It invaded Finland. It took over the Baltic states and Bessarabia after the fall of France in 1940. The setbacks suffered in the Soviet–Finnish War led Stalin to shake up the Soviet command structure. In May 1940 the newly minted Marshal Timoshenko was made People's Commissar of Defence; he replaced Stalin's old crony Voroshilov, who had led the Red Army for fifteen years. Timoshenko set in train an ambitious programme of training and reorganisation.

The USSR also suffered from a number of disadvantages. One was the after-effects of the Red Army purge of 1937–8. This not only weakened the Soviet forces, but led potential enemies and potential allies to underestimate them. Another disadvantage was, paradoxically, the mushroom growth of the Red Army in the late 1930s, which meant that the overall level of training declined. The USSR had also in 1940 annexed a belt of territory to the west (the Baltic states, eastern Poland, and eastern Romania), but it had not had time to integrate this into its defensive system.

One further Soviet disadvantage – Red Army war plans – has been the subject of historical controversy. Hitler announced on 22 June that Germany had attacked because Russia itself was about to strike, and the notion of a pre-emptive Operation BARBAROSSA has been repeated by a number of revisionist historians in Germany and in Russia itself. (See Box 20.) While these claims, in their baldest form, do not stand up to scrutiny, it is the case that the Red Army was geared towards offensive warfare. As Stalin famously put it in a speech in May 1941: 'The Red Army is a modern army, and a modern army is an offensive army.'[5] After the May 1940 Blitzkrieg in France this sentiment was found in all of the world's leading armies, but the Red Army had, since the cavalry battles of the Civil War of 1917–20, favoured offensive mobile warfare. The essence of the 'deep battle' doctrine sponsored by Tukhachevskii was offensive, and this also explains the masses of tanks built in the 1930s. Soviet war plans in 1940–1 assumed offensive action. Stalin installed one of his the most energetic and offensively minded young generals, Georgii Zhukov, as Chief of the General Staff in January 1941.

There were three major – indeed near-fatal – difficulties connected with this offensive doctrine. First, the slow pace of re-equipment and reorganisation, and the weak levels of Red Army training, meant that the doctrine was militarily naïve; the Red Army was not capable of mounting massive co-ordinated offensive operations in 1941. Second, this strategy involved 'forward deployment' of tanks and aircraft to achieve maximum offensive effect, but such deployment exposed Soviet forces to an enemy first strike. And thirdly, the specific offensive (or counter-offensive) plan drafted by the high command envisaged a Red Army thrust into southern Poland and the concentration of armoured forces in the Ukraine, facing this part of Poland; in reality the heaviest fighting would come further north, in Belorussia.

Achieving surprise

The Red Army was neither fully mobilised nor at a state of readiness when the Wehrmacht struck. There was no comparable surprise in May 1940 in France. Even the attack on America by Japan was more limited. Washington expected an attack in the near future; it just did not anticipate one particular local attack, on Hawaii. The success of the surprise attack on Russia also had much worse consequences.

Box 20 | The Suvorov controversy

'Viktor Suvorov' is the pen name of a former Soviet Army intelligence officer named V. B. Rezun', who came over to the West in 1978; Aleksandr Suvorov (1730–1800) had been one of Tsarist Russia's greatest generals. Deeply anti-Soviet, Rezun' worked anonymously in the UK as an intelligence analyst, and a number of books and articles appeared under the name of Suvorov. Although his earliest books were exposés of the modern Soviet military, Suvorov turned later to history, and in particular to the theme of Stalin's pre-1941 intentions. In *Icebreaker* (1990) Suvorov depicted a Machiavellian Stalin who persistently wanted conflict with the West. Capitalism might have 'frozen over' after the revolutions of 1917–19, but Hitler could set off a new world war and act as an 'icebreaker' for Communism. Suvorov argued that, having lured Hitler into World War II, Stalin then planned to deliver the *coup de grâce* with a surprise attack on the Third Reich. This attack was scheduled for the late summer of 1941 and was put off only by the Wehrmacht's pre-emptive strike.

Suvorov's argument aroused a lively response in post-Communist Russia, West Germany, and elsewhere. In Russia conventional 'patriotic' military writers were scandalised, but the public were fascinated and enjoyed Suvorov's ironic style. *Icebreaker* (*Ledokol*) and a number of Russian-published sequels (not available in English) became best-sellers. In Germany the Suvorov controversy became an element of the 1990s *Historikerstreit*, a right–left, post-Cold War debate about Germany's place in World War II (see Chapter 14, below). Joachim Hoffmann and others made an argument similar to Suvorov's. Elsewhere in the West there were two heavyweight responses to Suvorov, both of which rejected his argument about Stalin's offensive preparations. *The Grand Delusion* (1999), by the Israeli historian Gabriel Gorodetsky, was both a masterly discussion of pre-war Soviet policy and an extended reply to Suvorov. Gorodetsky dismissed all talk of offensive Soviet war plans, arguing instead that Stalin operated from a position of weakness and did not believe that Hitler planned to attack him in 1941. Stalin's 'delusion' was that Hitler was open to negotiation. David Glantz, the most prolific author on the USSR in World War II, produced *Stumbling Colossus* (1998), in which he argued that the Red Army was too weak to attack, that Stalin was very aware of its weaknesses, and that he cast Soviet strategy in a defensive mould. The certainties of Gorodetsky and Glantz were shaken by Russian documents that became available after the fall of Communism and which showed that the Red Army (if not Stalin) did have offensive war plans. Arguments continue about whether these projects were for a surprise attack on Germany or for a rapid counter-attack.

Suvorov's mission was to expose a wicked and devious Stalin. He made little attempt to demonstrate that Hitler knew about Stalin's supposed plans. In fact, whatever Stalin may have intended, the Germans did not know about the preparations of the Red Army, and Hitler had other reasons for attacking Russia. Suvorov also spent little time considering the consequences of the Soviet offensive posture and how the Red Army's plans led to its being caught by surprise.

Foreign states – Britain and America – sent well-grounded warnings to Moscow. Soviet agents in Germany and Japan provided accurate intelligence. How could Germany have prepared an army of hundreds of divisions and millions of men to attack Russia, based partly in occupied or neutral countries (Poland and Romania), without the Russians noticing? Until Soviet intelligence reports were made available in the 1990s, historians did not realise that the Soviet high command in fact had a correct overview of the scale of the German build-up in the East. At the end of May 1941, General Golikov, the head of Soviet military intelligence, reported to Stalin that the Germans had '120–2' divisions facing the USSR. The actual figure on 22 June was 121; a further 14 German divisions were held in reserve. There were, however, serious qualifications with this Soviet estimate. First of all, the Russians greatly exaggerated the *total* size of the Wehrmacht (assuming about 290 divisions when there were actually 209). This meant that the build-up in the east seemed to be only 40 per cent of German divisions, and the main German effort thus still seemed to be directed against Britain and its Empire. In reality 60 per cent of German divisions were stationed in the east. Second, for a number of months, Soviet intelligence had been over-reporting the scale of the German threat. It informed Stalin at the end of 1940 that German strength in the east was already about 100 divisions when the correct number was 36. So the May 1941 estimate did not pick up the great surge of German strength in the spring. Third, the May 1941 Soviet estimate was accurate for the overall eastern build-up, but wrong about detailed locations. Golikov placed the main concentration of '120–2' enemy divisions in the south facing the Ukraine, while in fact the largest build-up was in the centre, facing Belorussia.

Accurately assessing the global *scale* of Hitler's threat was not enough. In the more intangible area of *intention* much was left to Stalin's intuition. The German forces were there, but were they there to attack or to intimidate? The Soviet dictator indulged in some wishful thinking, based on the notion that the longer Russia could avoid entry into war the further its force build-up would have progressed. He also assumed that the Red Army – whatever the limitations of its training and re-equipment programme – was fundamentally strong. Stalin's assessment was that Hitler did not plan to attack the USSR in the summer of 1941. This judgement was certainly not based on blind trust in the German leader; Stalin was not a trusting person. At the core of Stalin's judgement was the belief that the Germans would be very foolish to attack a powerful Russia before they had knocked Britain out of the war. Hitler's rational decision – based on World War I – would be to avoid a war on two fronts. We know with hindsight that Stalin was right – the two-front war would be suicidal for the Third Reich.

Stalin did receive accurate warnings of Hitler's intention to attack, but these were hidden among other inaccurate and contradictory information, some of it planted as 'disinformation' by the Germans. Winnowing out the 'true' information is easy with hindsight; not so beforehand. Churchill's warnings might have been a provocation designed to lure Russia into war. Stalin may also have thought that the end of June was too far into the summer for an attack; had the Germans wanted the longest possible campaigning season, they would have moved in mid May. Stalin appears to have thought that the continuing German build-up was bluff, designed to force Soviet concessions. And there was evidently another factor for Stalin to consider. As with Japan, there might be differences between politicians and generals; it was important for Russia not to undertake acts that would allow German 'hotheads' to tip their country into war.

Finally, beyond the issues of scale and intentions there was *timing*. When would the Germans strike? How far could the Red Army respond to provocation? Practical problems forced Hitler to postpone the start of BARBAROSSA several times, which muddied the intelligence picture. Stalin's main military advisors – Generals Timoshenko and Zhukov – urged him to begin mobilisation, and indeed in the late spring of 1941 800,000 reservists were secretly mobilised and several reserve armies were ordered to begin movement into the so-called 'second strategic echelon'. But full-scale mobilisation of reservists was not carried out, nor were front-line formations brought up to war readiness. Neither of these measures could have been kept secret from the Germans, and in Stalin's mind they might precipitate the very attack he was attempting to avoid. Premature Russian mobilisation in 1914 had, after all, contributed to the outbreak of a general war. Stalin wrongly assumed that he would have enough of an intelligence warning to bring his troops to readiness when required. However, the Germans skilfully concealed their final deployments. It was only last-minute warnings by politically motivated deserters that gave Moscow any warning, and this came only a few hours before the start of the attack – far too late.

Blitzkrieg in Russia, 1941

Hitler's fifth and grandest offensive of World War II, Operation BAR-BAROSSA, began before dawn on Sunday, 22 June 1941. The Germans achieved near complete tactical surprise. In the first hours the Luftwaffe mounted mass air strikes against the forward-based Red Army Air Force. In contrast to what happened in Poland and France, the Germans were able to destroy many enemy aircraft on the ground at the start of the campaign. Other Soviet air regiments were overrun at their exposed bases. The total Soviet losses in the first few days were 2,000 planes. For the next year the Germans would have air superiority. As the three army groups of the German *Ostheer* (Eastern Army) rolled ahead, forward-based Soviet ground formations were encircled and overrun before they could make any serious response.

The Soviet central command system was not on a war footing, and its communication links with forward army groups were quickly disrupted. Moscow could neither give orders nor obtain accurate information. The military situation was worst in the middle of the Soviet front, in Belorussia. Here Hitler had deployed his largest formation, Army Group Centre, spearheaded by two 'panzer groups', each with half a dozen panzer or motorised divisions. The Soviet Western Army Group was surrounded around Belostok and Minsk in Belorussia, and destroyed as a fighting force in a matter of days. Three whole Soviet field armies were lost. This disaster (and not the initial attack on 22 June) apparently drove Stalin to a brief nervous collapse at the end of June. General Pavlov, commander of Western Army Group and a hero of the Finnish war, was recalled to Moscow and shot. Pavlov was a scapegoat; the forward deployment of his forces and the low state of alert were the responsibility of Stalin and the central military leadership.

Map 5 The German invasion of Russia, 1941–1942

Figure 10 | Marshal Georgii Zhukov

Marshal Georgii Zhukov (1896–1974), pictured here early in the war, was the greatest of Stalin's commanders. Arguably he was the finest soldier of World War II; certainly he had the most remarkable career. Zhukov won important victories even in the first six months of the war, notably at Moscow in December 1941. In August 1942 Zhukov was made Deputy C-in-C under Stalin. After playing an important role as a 'Stavka representative' in organising the Battles of Stalingrad (1942–43), Leningrad (1943), Kursk (1943), the Ukraine (1943–44), and Belorussia (1944), he directly led the final assault on Berlin by the 1st Belorussian Army Group.

Six years younger than Eisenhower, nine years younger than Montgomery and Manstein, Zhukov was the son of poor peasants and received very little formal schooling. He fought in World War I as an enlisted cavalry trooper. He was a protégé of the cavalry leaders Budennyi and Timoshenko, and he was untouched by the military purge of 1937. His name was made by command of the Soviet forces at the Khalkhin Gol border incident in 1939, when he encircled and destroyed a Japanese division. From that time on he was identified as the Red Army's specialist in offensive warfare. He was promoted to senior posts in the army in Europe, first as commander of the spearhead forces in the Ukraine and from early 1941 as head of the General Staff. He avoided punishment for the catastrophe of 22 June, but fell out with Stalin over strategy after the war started, and was dismissed from the General Staff at the end of July. In early October 1941 Stalin recalled him from the front to take over the defence of Moscow. A talented commander, and forceful personality, he was able to put together a powerful counter-attack. In January 1943, after victories at Moscow, Stalingrad, and Leningrad, Stalin made Zhukov a Marshal of the Soviet Union; he was the first commander to receive this rank during the war.

Zhukov received Field Marshal Keitel's surrender at Karlshorst (Berlin) in May 1945. After the war he slipped from Stalin's favour and was removed from the most senior posts. He was made Minister of Defence by the de-Stalinising Khrushchev in 1955, but was suddenly sacked two years later; he spent some years in enforced and secluded retirement. Zhukov received limited 'rehabilitation' after Khrushchev's ouster in 1964, and was allowed to write memoirs. In 1995 the post-Communist government erected an equestrian statue of Zhukov in Red Square.

In the northern part of the front, the former Baltic states, fewer Soviet forces were encircled, but the defenders were pushed back very rapidly. The German spearheads took bridges across the Dvina River within days of the war's outbreak. German Army Group North was very soon on the approaches to Leningrad. Soviet resistance was most effective in the south, in the Ukraine. Here Timoshenko had concentrated the largest element of the Red Army (partly, as we have seen, to mount the planned counter-offensive into Poland). General Kirponos had 960,000 men and 4,800 tanks, compared to 680,000 men and 2,200 tanks under Pavlov in Western Army Group, Rundstedt's Army Group South was weaker than Army Group Centre. The heaviest tank battles of World War II so far were fought out in the western Ukraine, but the Russians were gradually forced back. Two full armies of Southwestern Army Group were rolled up west of the Dnepr in early August, and their commanders made prisoner. This prompted a fierce order from Stalin. He called on his troops to fight to the end; officers and soldiers who surrendered were condemned, and their families threatened with punishment.

The Soviet command system was gradually consolidated, after an inexcusably late start. Stalin (unlike Hitler or Roosevelt) had not been formally in charge of the pre-war armed forces, and he had not delegated full powers to anyone else. There was no pre-war command centre, and the GHQ or Stavka was set up only on 22 June, initially under Marshal Timoshenko, and using the apparatus of the General Staff. Stalin, who had finally taken over from Timoshenko as Supreme C-in-C at the Stavka on 10 July, ordered that the main reserves of the Red Army should be deployed around Smolensk. They would fill up the huge hole created on the main route to Moscow by the destruction of Western Army Group. Still wedded to their offensive doctrine, the Red Army's 'Western Theatre', now under the overall command of Timoshenko himself, mounted a series of counter-attacks around Smolensk in July and August. These were very costly to the Red Army, but some historians have seen them as a turning point of the war; the German onslaught was temporarily halted.

It was indeed at this point that the fundamental weakness of the German Army's BARBAROSSA concept became clear. Unlike what had happened in Poland and France, the destruction of the enemy army on the frontiers proved impossible in Russia. The Wehrmacht could not smash the bulk of effective Soviet forces in a planned-for six-week 'battle of annihilation' west of the Dvina–Dnepr Line. The destruction of the Soviet Western Army Group was operationally as devastating as the entrapment of the French and British armies north of the Somme in 1940. The distances, however, were much vaster than those in France and the roads were worse. The breadth of the active front in France and the Low Countries was 150 miles; the breadth of the main front in Russia was 750 miles. The depth of the attack in the West, measured by the distance of the *Sichelschnitt* drive from German territory to the English Channel, was about 250 miles; the Dvina–Dnepr Line was 200–350 miles back from the frontiers. The distance of the pursuit from the Somme-Aisne Line to Paris, the critical area in the second phase of the French campaign, was only 75 miles; the distance from the Dvina–Dnepr Line to Moscow was 350 miles. And German forces were no more numerous in 1941 than in 1940.

Secondly, the Germans – like intelligence services in other countries – had miscalculated the strength of the Red Army. German intelligence somewhat underestimated Soviet forces on the western border, but it was very wrong about the mobilisation potential of the Red Army as a whole. General Halder, the Chief of the Army General Staff, complained in mid August about the situation: 'At the start of the war we had counted on about 200 enemy divisions. We have now counted 360. These divisions are not as well armed or equipped as ours, they are often poorly led. But they are there. And if we knock out a dozen of them, then the Russian puts up another dozen.'[6] German intelligence was even less accurate in its estimate of the scale of equipment. It expected 10,000 Soviet tanks when the total number was 23,000, and 6,000 aircraft when the total was 20,000. Unlike the Poles and the French, the Russians had reserves which they could throw in; they could replace losses and equip hastily mobilised reserve units.

Most important, Hitler's invasion had been based on political and racial assumptions that the Stalinist system would collapse 'like a house of cards'. In fact the Communist Party had held power ruthlessly for nearly twenty-five years, aided by the massive secret police apparatus of, successively, the Cheka, the GPU, and the NKVD. The purges of 1937–8 helped ensure Stalin would not suffer the fate of Mussolini in 1943, overthrown from within for his military failures. Stalin also made effective appeals to the population, especially in his radio speech of 3 July 1941, when he addressed his 'brothers and sisters' and emphasised Russian patriotism (and the crucial value of Russia's new friends in Britain and the United States). The slogan on the masthead of *Pravda* changed from 'Proletarians of all lands, unite!' to 'Death to the German occupiers!' This was the 'Fatherland war', and the fatherland was Russia. Moscow's propaganda cited heroes of the Russian military past. Stalin was, of course, an ethnic Georgian, but he identified himself effectively with the Russian cause. Russian national cohesion should not be exaggerated – the mass surrenders of Soviet troops testify to that. But there was going to be no political capitulation.

Hitler and his generals realised that they had not succeeded in wiping out the Red Army west of the Dvina–Dnepr Line. They began to argue about what to do next. General Halder, the original architect of the German campaign, now urged an advance beyond the Dvina and Dnepr to Moscow; the Red Army would be destroyed by forcing it to defend the approaches to the capital. Hitler favoured a more indirect approach. He may have wanted to avoid Napoleon's 'Moscow' mistake of 1812. He was also aware by August 1941 that the war was going to be more protracted than originally expected, and he now wanted to go for 'economic' objectives in Leningrad and in the Ukraine. Leningrad seemed almost in his grasp, and the eastward advance of Army Group Centre presented the opportunity of a huge flanking movement from the north behind Kiev and Dnepr to trap the Soviet forces in the Ukraine. He also realised that an advance towards Moscow would be possible only once Army Group Centre's flanks had been made secure. There was also a need to allow marching infantry to catch up with the motorised spearheads, to build up supply lines, and to deal with vast numbers of encircled Russian soldiers.

German Army Group Centre was ordered to go over to the defensive, and its main mobile forces (panzer groups and air corps) were committed to the flanks. Hitler succeeded in carrying out the great Kiev encirclement. The Dnepr Line in the Ukraine was breached. The Red Army, more rigidly controlled than ever, had been forbidden to fall back. The Ukrainian capital fell in mid September, and most of the remaining forces of Southwestern Army Group – four field armies – were lost; General Kirponos died with his troops. It was probably Hitler's greatest single victory of the war; he took Kiev, destroyed an entire Soviet army group, and captured 665,000 prisoners. Leningrad, meanwhile, did not surrender, but it had been encircled and neutralised. Hitler pulled out his troops when they were near to success, neither taking the city nor making the blockade so tight that the city would certainly starve. Leningrad remained in Soviet hands through a 900-day siege that cost a million civilian lives.

The first months of the war in the USSR had been fought at huge cost for both sides. Russian losses were immense, up to 2.05 million men by the end of September 1941, perhaps 70–80 per cent of them captured rather than killed. German losses from 22 June to the end of September 1941 were 185,000, greatly exceeding the 102,000 men lost in the 21 months of the war up to 22 June. The Luftwaffe also lost 2,180 aircraft to ground fire and Soviet fighters over Russia in 1941, compared to 1,290 in the $3\frac{1}{2}$ months of the Battle of Britain.

The Battle of Moscow, 1941

Now the end of the campaigning season approached. Apparently successful on the flanks and eager for success in 1941, Hitler was now prepared to follow the advice that General Halder had given in the high summer. Army Group Centre would bring the Red Army to battle in front of Moscow. Operation TYPHOON, mounted at the very end of September, was a final attempt at a 'battle of annihilation'. The Red Army was holding a line 30 miles east of Smolensk and 200 miles west of Moscow. For the first time in the war three German panzer groups were concentrated in one sector of the front, that of Field Marshal von Bock's Army Group Centre. Air strength had also been concentrated here.

TYPHOON began with an extraordinary German victory in the so-called 'twin' Battle of Viaz'ma-Briansk. The Germans fought exhausted or inexperienced Soviet units which were caught by surprise and overrun or encircled near the towns of Viaz'ma and Briansk. The Russians had not expected another German surge in the centre. The Stavka was mesmerised by the collapse in the Ukraine and the crisis at Leningrad, but it assumed that German strength must be getting worn down. In the Battle of Viaz'ma-Briansk the Germans took another 760,000 POWs; the equivalent of another 70 Soviet divisions had disappeared. Hitler's intention had been to destroy the Red Army rather than to take Moscow, but the road to Stalin's capital now seemed well and truly open. The Stavka tried to throw together a new defensive line 75 miles west of Moscow, but at first they had only military scraps to work with.

Stalin recalled General Zhukov, his best commander, from Leningrad to command the Western Army Group. The Stavka, ominously, began to set up a new emergency defensive line *east* of Moscow, on the Volga River. There was rapid evacuation of some of the ministries and factories in Moscow to Kuibyshev, and a short-lived panic in the city in mid October. But Stalin decided to stay in Moscow, and Zhukov convinced him that the city was not in imminent danger. The onset of the *rasputitsa* (see Figure 11) turned the roads to mud and slowed the German advance. On 7 November Stalin staged the annual 'Revolution Day' military parade in Red Square. (7 November was the date of the 1917 Bolshevik Revolution.)

Once the ground hardened in mid November, Army Group Centre was able to drive east again, but the weather was now getting very cold. Hitler cannot be blamed for imposing a foolhardy and blind offensive on his professional advisors; they agreed with his orders. General Halder and Field Marshal von Bock urged Hitler to continue the drive on Moscow, arguing that the Red Army was exhausted. As Halder put it, 'although [we are] weak in the knees...the enemy is worse off than we are: he is on the verge of collapse.'[7] He used the example of the Battle of the Marne, when an earlier German Army had fatally paused in front of Paris in 1914.

Stalin, however, had been able to build up reserves. These, including some full-strength divisions, moved from the Far East when it became likely that the Japanese were going to move south against Britain and America rather than north against Siberia. Zhukov, crucially, convinced Stalin that the moment had come to throw his armies into a counter-attack in front of Moscow, rather than keeping them in reserve in case the city fell. Timing was all important. The enemy's momentum was spent, and he had not begun to dig himself in. Zhukov's counter-offensive, initially with four armies, was launched on 6 December (a day before the Japanese attack on Pearl Harbor). German advance troops that had been working their way around the Moscow suburbs from the north were thrown back. Zhukov's attack coincided with the onset of winter. The Germans were not encircled – as they would be at Stalingrad the following winter – but they were forced back 50–150 miles through the snow-covered countryside. There were no German reserves. It was a very close-run thing; the deep snow meant that artillery and transport

Figure 11 | **The *rasputitsa***

The *rasputitsa* was a particular feature of the climate in Russia: the spring and autumn rain and mud seasons turned dirt roads to mush and quiet rivers into swollen and unfordable torrents. The spring *rasputitisa* followed the thaw of winter snows. The autumn one was brought on by rain. In contrast, the winter freeze, except when the snow was very deep and the weather extremely cold, was better for military movement; troops and motor vehicles could more easily traverse hard ground surfaces and frozen lakes and rivers.

The autumn *rasputitsa* played an especially important role in 1941, slowing down German Army Group Centre in October, when the Soviet defensive line had been shattered at the start of Operation TYPHOON. The climate hurt not only the Germans; the spring *rasputitsa* of 1942 helped stop the Soviet counter-offensive. The photograph above shows German troops evacuating their wounded in March 1942; a Demag D7 artillery tractor ploughs slowly through the mud of the spring *rasputitsa*. The little D7 half-track was quite unsuitable for the wild conditions of the Russian front.

could no longer move. Army Group Centre faced the prospect of abandoning them and attempting a further retreat on foot.

The Battle of Moscow, more than the Battle of Stalingrad, marked the turning point of the war. On 8 December Hitler secretly admitted that the offensive was – for the moment – over. The German high command was radically shaken up, the three German army-group commanders were removed, and Hitler put himself in the place of General Brauchitsch as C-in-C of the German Army (Hitler was already commander of the armed forces – the Wehrmacht – as a whole). Hitler publicly blamed the setback on the winter weather, but winters are always hard in Russia and the Germans knew about them. They also knew about the *rasputitsa*. It was not that the Germans failed to get to Moscow because the weather broke; rather, they were caught by the freeze because they had failed to reach Moscow. Also, it was not that they lost the Battle of Moscow because they had a chaotic command structure; rather, they had a chaotic command structure because they lost the Battle of Moscow.

Germany had began World War II as an inferior power. It could win the war only if it could pick its enemies off one at a time, when they were isolated. But the British Empire had survived, and the British forces were holding their own. Now Russia, too, had held out – albeit at much greater human cost – against the best that Nazi Germany could throw at it. Meanwhile in December 1941 the United States actively joined the war. The Third Reich was doomed.

War of annihilation

Hitler's campaign in Russia had an immediate and rational diplomatic-strategic goal – the isolation of Britain. There was a logic, too, in the desire of generals and industrialists to broaden the resource base of the Third Reich. But beyond these there was the deeply irrational factor of ideology, without which developments on the Russian front are incomprehensible. 'This is a fight of annihilation,' Hitler told a planning conference of his senior commanders in March 1941.[8] Operation BARBAROSSA was something new in warfare, even for Germany. It was different from the desultory fighting with the British Empire, different from the 1940 campaign in France, different even from the war in Poland and its brutal aftermath. It was also unlike Japan's war in China. The objective of the Third Reich was not minor gains at Russia's expense, but rather the destruction of the Russian state. It also had a pronounced racial dimension. The later Allied terms of 'unconditional surrender' were mild compared to what Germany's leaders had in mind for the USSR.

Hitler made it clear to his senior generals that the normal laws of war would not apply to the war in Soviet Russia. Before June 1941 the German Army willingly prepared what are now called the 'illegal orders', by which the harshest measures were to be taken against resistors and political opponents. The most notorious document was the 'commissar order', which instructed that Red Army political commissars and other Communist officials be shot out of hand. Other decrees drafted before the invasion gave the German Army very harsh powers to deal with civilians who opposed its control.

More broadly, Hitler's plans assumed ruthless exploitation of the population and resources of the USSR. The model was the exploitation and suppression of Poland after 1939. The occupied territory of the USSR (unlike occupied territory in the West) was put under the long-term control of Heinrich Himmler's SS (*Schutzstaffel*), the vast and sinister organisation which was the backbone of the Nazi regime. The Germans intended that over time the population structure of the former Soviet territory would be changed. The SS prepared an infamous long-range scheme, '*Generalplan Ost*', for the wholesale displacement of millions of Slavs and for the introduction of Germanic settlers. In the short term the SS envisaged mass starvation on Russian territory as a means of guaranteeing food supplies for the Reich. On ideological grounds Hitler refused – as with Slavic Poland – to countenance the creation of collaborator regimes in the east, led either by anti-Soviet Russians or by members of anti-Russian minority peoples – like the Balts, Belorussians, and Ukrainians. In this, the policy was very different from that of the Japanese in China, or even of the Germans in Russia in 1917–18.

The implications of this occupation regime – in terms of collaboration and resistance – will be discussed more broadly in Chapter 10. For the moment, however, it is enough to say that it caused enormous harm to the western and southern regions of the European USSR and made impossible collaboration above the individual level. In all, some 17 million Soviet civilians would die during the war, many of them the victims of direct enemy action or of conditions created by the occupiers. Historians will continue to argue about whether a different German policy might have won 'hearts and minds'. It is true that German troops were sometimes regarded as 'liberators' in the regions they entered, but this was mainly in the border regions that had just been brutally occupied by the Red Army and NKVD in 1939 and 1940. The reception of the Wehrmacht became more hostile as the Germans moved deeper into Russia and after the population experienced Hitler's strategy of exploitation and repression. Above all, a counter-factual argument (e.g. 'what if' the Germans occupiers had treated the conquered Soviet peoples better) makes little sense if it does not take into account Nazi ideology or the prejudices of many Germans about the 'culturally inferior' Slavs.

A crime without a name

The Nazi mass murder of European Jews, which we now know as the Holocaust or the *Shoah*, was inter-cut with the battles of World War II. For many people this genocide was the central event, and defined the essence of the conflict. Most historians would now argue that as an implemented policy the Nazi mass murder of Jews dates from the second half of 1941, after the start of the war in Russia.

Racism, especially hatred of the Jews, had been a central feature of Hitler's ideology for many years. After 1933 the Nazis segregated Jewish Germans from the rest of the population, and stripped them of their civil rights and property. Radical racial laws were passed and, in the autumn of 1938, the Nazis encouraged widespread violence again Jewish property and synagogues (the so-called *Kristallnacht*). Hitler, if not his generals, also saw in the Jewish 'plutocracy' the source of Germany's woes as a great power. The European Jews, he believed, had whipped up hostility to the 'New Germany' and to its legitimate aspirations. The Jews in the USA influenced Roosevelt, and the 'Jewish-Bolsheviks' controlled Russia.

Hitler made a public warning in the Reichstag on 30 January 1939: 'Should the international Jewry of finance [*Finanzjudentum*] succeed, both within and beyond Europe, in plunging mankind into yet another world war, then the result will not be a Bolshevization of the earth and the victory of Jewry, but the annihilation of the Jewish race in Europe!'[9] War did indeed lead to an incremental brutalisation and radicalisation. The obvious point is that most of the eventual victims of Hitler's racial policy lived in countries which he did not control until the Wehrmacht's successful wars of conquest. The Jewish population of Germany in 1933 was only about 500,000. The Nazis could not have implemented a policy of racial mass murder in peacetime within the borders of the 1939 Reich. They did institute a large 'medical' euthanasia (T4) programme (mainly killing the mentally disabled). Even that, however, came only after the outbreak of war in 1939, and it was kept secret.

International public opinion was no longer a serious factor after September 1939. As we have seen, the population of defeated Poland – Poles and Jews – was treated savagely. The beginning of the war with Russia in 1941 reduced even further the inhibitions on Nazi activities. Mass murder, involving hundreds of thousands of men, women, and children, really began in the autumn of 1941 in the western regions of the USSR. *Einsatzgruppen*, small mobile SS police killing units (see Box 21), followed directly behind the front-line Wehrmacht, with oral instructions to kill Jews. The massacre of the Jews on a large scale in Russia began before the German advance there had been checked. Western Russia provided 'opportunities' to the murderers, both a large and helpless Jewish population and an extensive territory hidden from foreign observers.

The British were aware through ULTRA intercepts of German radio messages that mass 'police' killings of civilians were taking place. They correctly identified this as something new. Churchill publicly condemned these actions in August 1941: 'As his armies advance, whole districts [of Russia] are being exterminated. Scores of thousands – literally scores of thousands – of executions in cold blood are being perpetrated by the German police-troops upon the Russian patriots who defend their native soil.' 'We are in the presence', Churchill concluded, 'of a crime without a name.'[10] But Churchill did not publicly say at this time that the Jews were the main victims; he was talking about something even larger – anti-Slav rather than anti-Jewish.

Churchill was right about this being a crime without a name. The Nazi leaders sometimes used among themselves the ambiguous term 'Final Solution' (*Endlösung*) of the Jewish Question. Other names date from after the war. The term 'genocide' was a neologism that came into wide use only in 1948, when the UN produced a convention on the crime. The term 'Holocaust' came into general use only in the 1960s, and it normally refers to the

Box 21 | The *Einsatzgruppen*

The four *Einsatzgruppen* (literally 'task forces') were mobile SS killing units which followed closely behind the advancing Wehrmacht. They were first used in the 1939 Polish campaign. Despite their infamous record in occupied Russia, the personnel of the *Einsatzgruppen* were very few, initially about 3,000 police officials.

In the first rush after 22 June, advance squads from the *Einsatzgruppen* shot groups of Jews, initially younger men (itself an unprecedented crime), but the violence rapidly escalated to include women and children. In September 1941, *Einsatzgruppe* C, helped by the Wehrmacht, organised the infamous Babii Iar (Babii Yar) massacre of 30,000 Jews in Kiev. A major target for these 'security' units was supposed to be the surviving Communist leadership after the early collapse of the USSR, and it was only when this was delayed that the *Einsatzgruppen* were turned back on the remaining Jews in the western borderlands of the USSR. Police units from Germany and locally conscripted militias reinforced them.

The operations of the *Einsatzgruppen* are arguably the beginning of the Holocaust as an implemented policy. It is generally accepted that about 500,000 Jews were killed outright by the *Einsatzkommandos* and other Nazi police units in the 'first sweep' of killing in the USSR in 1941. At least as many Jews were killed in occupied Russia during the more systematic massacres of 1942 and later.

The Allies had some knowledge of the scale of the killing, as they intercepted and decrypted *Einsatzgruppen* wireless reports. In 1947–8 the *Einsatzgruppen* leaders were the object of sub-trial at Nuremberg, Case No. 9; only a handful of the accused were executed.

killing of the Jews. The Hebrew word *Shoah* ('calamity') is also used. More recently – with the Civil War in the former Yugoslavia – the term 'ethnic cleansing' began to be used, although that term would better fit pre-1941 German policy (forced expulsion and pogroms), rather than the full-blown extermination campaign.

The policy of mass murder developed at about the same time in Western and Central Europe, in regions that the Germans had controlled for the past two years. To some extent this followed the precedent of the mass killings in Russia. Another factor was that the authority and resources of the SS had been increased with the outbreak of war, and the restrictions on its actions reduced. The change came at a time when the initial Nazi policy of concentrating European Jews in Polish ghettos had caused their persecutors 'practical' problems, not least of which was food supply. The entry of the United States into the war in December 1941 meant that the Jews would not be needed as hostages to ensure American non-intervention. As Goebbels noted in his diary the day after the German declaration of war on the USA, 'Now the world war has come. The destruction of the Jews must be its necessary consequence.'[11]

The policy was different in Western and Central Europe from that in the borderlands of the USSR. Rather than the killers – the *Einsatzgruppen* – hunting down and shooting racial enemies – the victims were moved by rail to 'extermination' centres and subjected to industrialised murder. The mass deportation of Jews and gypsies (Roma) was laid down by the SS leader Reinhard Heydrich at the Wannsee Conference in Berlin in January 1942. The methods were perfected in the course of 1942. The definitive instrument of mass extermination, with which the Third Reich will be forever identified, was the vast death camp at Auschwitz (see Figure 12). The process continued until the supply of victims – across Europe – had been exhausted.

World War II made the Holocaust possible, but Hitler did not go to war with Poland in 1939 with the killing of the Polish Jews as one of his primary objectives, nor did he go to war with Russia to kill the Jews of the USSR, or even 'just' to subdue and enslave the Slavs. Even less was the German Army driven solely by imperatives of racial ideology. The Allies did not fight Hitler primarily to defend the Jews (and indeed they did not at the time make public all they knew about the scale of the mass murder). Antisemitism was a central part of the ideology of National Socialism, but so were extreme nationalism, imperialism, and violent anti-Communism.

The mass murder of the European Jews and other racial 'undesirables' had no crucial impact on the conduct or immediate course of the war. It did not divert German resources or tie up the transport system. It probably did not greatly complicate the Nazi maintenance of internal security. It may have made a negotiated peace with the Allies impossible, but the Nazi elite had burned their boats already in other ways. In the long term, however, the Holocaust utterly discredited the Nazi government and the cause of the Third Reich in the war of 1939–45, even in the eyes of most Germans.

Figure 12 | **Auschwitz**

Elderly Jewish men from Hungary await 'selection' on the railway platform at Auschwitz-Birkenau, in May 1944. Jews and others were brought here from all over Western and Southern Europe; the SS immediately killed the weak in the gas chambers and worked the fitter ones to death. The total number of Jewish victims at Auschwitz has been estimated as about a million, plus over 100,000 ethnic Poles and 25,000 gypsies.

The Polish town of Oswiecim is known in German as Auschwitz. It lies in the region of Upper Silesia, which was annexed to the Reich in 1939 and subjected to 'Germanisation'. The original concentration camp (Auschwitz I) was a converted Polish Army barracks; it began to function in 1940. Construction of the nearby and much larger Auschwitz II (Birkenau) started in October 1941. It was both a camp for housing 80,000 forced labourers in very primitive conditions, and a centre for mass murder. The SS conducted toxic gas experiments at Auschwitz I in the autumn of 1941, and Birkenau began to function as a full-scale murder centre in 1942. When fully developed, Auschwitz II had four big gas chambers and crematoriums. After a climax of mass killing involving hundreds or thousands of Jews from Hungary, the SS destroyed the gas chambers in November 1944. In the following months the camp guards compelled the surviving forced labourers to march west under terrible winter conditions.

The Auschwitz complex relates more broadly to the history of World War II. In late 1940 the German industrial giant IG Farben developed plans for a giant new chemical complex here, and the Reich government provided lavish investment funds. Auschwitz was close to central Germany, and had good rail communications and access to large coalfields required for energy and for chemical processes. By the middle of the war it was also important that Upper Silesia was remote from enemy bomber bases. And, of course, it had unlimited supplies of forced labour to construct and to work the industrial complex. The main product of the Auschwitz complex was supposed to be synthetic rubber (*Buna*), but this never even achieved production. IG Farben had more success with the production of methanol, used in explosives and aviation fuel. Some of the industrial facilities of greater Auschwitz are still functioning.

Auschwitz is now a UNESCO World Heritage site, and Auschwitz I and II are museums.

CHAPTER

6

A victorious Soviet soldier waves the red flag over the central square in Stalingrad. Most of the city had been reduced to ruin after the six-month battle. The entire German 6th Army, under Field Marshal Paulus, surrendered. Hitler's offensive plans in Russia were over. The Germans, like the Allies and the peoples of occupied Europe, realised that a turning point had been reached. The long German retreat began. Hitler and his propaganda minister Joseph Goebbels declared that the Reich must now mobilise all its resources for 'total war'.

The Red Army versus the Wehrmacht, 1941–1944

Timeline

1941	December	Soviet winter offensive begins
1942	May	Red Army defeated in Battles of Khar'kov and the Crimea
	June	German Operation BLUE in south Russia begins
	November	Soviet counter-offensive at Stalingrad begins
1943	February	Surrender of German 6th Army at Stalingrad
	July	German CITADEL offensive (Battle of Kursk)
	August	Beginning of liberation of Ukraine
1944	April	Red Army reaches 1941 border in the Ukraine

Stalin's winter offensive

We often see the early months of 1942 as a dark time for the Allies. The British and Americans suffered disasters in the Battle of the Atlantic, in North Africa, and especially in Southeast Asia and in the Pacific. In Russia, however, the picture seemed much better. For five months after the December 1941 Moscow counter-offensive the Red Army still held the initiative. General Zhukov's attack not only stopped the Blitzkrieg, it seemed to threaten the very survival of the Germany Army in Russia. In the depth of winter a continued German retreat could have degenerated into a precipitate rout. Hitler in December ordered a 'stand-fast': commanders were 'to intervene in person to compel the troops to fanatical resistance in their positions without regard to the enemy broken through on the flanks or in the rear'.[1]

In early January Stalin, who seemed to think he was seeing a repetition of Napoleon and 1812, ordered a general offensive on all sectors of the front. It was he rather than Hitler who now assumed that the enemy's strength was spent. Soviet propaganda for six months switched over to a slogan urging 'complete defeat of the Hitlerite forces in the year 1942'. It was significant that in his important Red Army Day message of 1942 Stalin made no reference to the Allies. The Red Army's leaders, including Marshal Shaposhnikov – Chief of the General Staff since July 1941 and now Stalin's main adviser – were evidently much less enthusiastic than Stalin about mounting new attacks. They knew that time was needed to train and equip new Red Army formations. They especially did not want to disperse their efforts all along the 800-mile front from the Black Sea to Leningrad. General Zhukov, in particular, wanted scarce resources concentrated on his Western Army Group, in front of Moscow.

Stalin did not take the advice of Shaposhnikov and Zhukov. This was not simply megalomania or naïveté. The centre was indeed the main concentration of German forces, but it also seemed essential to relieve blockaded Leningrad in the north, and to prevent the fall of Sevastopol' (the naval fortress in the Crimea) in the south, where the Germans managed to continue offensive operations. Retaking Khar'kov, between Sevastopol' and Moscow, also seemed an essential first step to liberating the Ukraine, and protecting the approaches to the Caucasus.

Nine Soviet army groups, spearheaded by new 'shock armies', lurched forward. The most important fighting zone, in front of Moscow, ended up as a crazy jigsaw of opposing forces. The Germans were dug into all-round defensive positions – 'hedgehogs' – with Soviet cavalry, ski troops, and even airborne forces operating on their flanks and behind them. Junkers tri-motors dropped supplies into isolated outposts like Demiansk. Hitler's insistence on 'stand-fast' worked, helped by the limited offensive potential of the Red Army. The region was thickly forested, first covered by snow and then affected by the spring *rasputitsa*. The Germans kept hold of the spine of the railway and road system. Soviet winter offensives around Leningrad and in the Crimea gained little ground and cost a huge number of lives.

In mid February 1942 Hitler could tell his commanders that the 'danger of a panic in the 1812 sense' had been 'eliminated'.[2] Zhukov later recalled bitterly that the Soviet winter advance was a 'Pyrrhic victory'. The tragedy was that even at great human cost the Soviets were not able to relieve Leningrad nor to save Sevastopol'. A great offensive in May 1942 to liberate Khar'kov also broke up in the face of German manoeuvre. The Germans shattered what fresh tank forces the Red Army had been able to assemble (for the first time with British and American help). The Red Army lost some 1.4 million men in these terrible battles of the first half of 1942. German losses were only a fraction of this, something under 200,000. Stalin's strategy of wearing down the German reserves had been counter-productive. It was the Russians who were worn down.

Hitler's second campaign in Russia

Hitler's Russian drive of 1942, which climaxed in the Battle of Stalingrad, was actually the sixth and last of his World War II offensives. It is sometimes called his 'second (Russian) campaign' (i.e. after BARBAROSSA), but it was far from being a simple repetition. The situation had changed. The German Army was weaker, and its supply lines were longer. The United States was in the war. The preliminary directive for Operation BLUE (*Fall Blau*), drafted in April 1942 – two months before the start of operations – was much less ambitious than the BARBAROSSA directive of December 1940. The object was not (as in BARBAROSSA) 'to overthrow Soviet Russia in a

Figure 13 | **T-34 tank**

The Soviet T-34 was the most important tank of World War II. It was considerably superior to the standard German tank of 1940–1, the Panzer III. Although the T-34 had entered service in the autumn of 1940 and was available in some numbers by 22 June 1941, it was only after the winter of 1941–2 that it became the main tank of the Red Army.

The qualities of the T-34 included an ingenious design (sloped armour which increased its resistance), a heavy gun (76 mm bore compared to 50 mm for the Panzer III), a powerful diesel motor, and a suspension which allowed high speed. Many of the other tanks of the twentieth century were inspired by the T-34, the first of these being the 1943 German Panther. In the summer of 1943, German tanks appeared with heavier guns and stronger armour, and these were superior to the T-34-76; the vehicle pictured opposite was knocked out by the Germans in southern Russia at that time. The original T-34-76 was successfully updated, in a way that the American M4 Sherman was not. The T-34-85, in service in early 1944, had a number of detailed improvements, but the main change was that it mounted a high-velocity 85 mm gun in a new turret.

The lead T-34 factory, at Khar'kov in the Ukraine, was successfully evacuated to the Urals in 1941, where its capacity was hugely expanded. Another early plant was developed at Stalingrad, and was for a time caught up in the fighting in the city. Production was also carried out at Gor'kii in central Russia, at Cheliabinsk and Sverdlovsk in the Urals, and at Omsk in Siberia. The T-34 was built in larger numbers than any other tank, 35,000 of the 76 mm model and 23,000 of the T-34-85. In contrast, 'only' 50,000 M4 Shermans were built. In the Red Army the T-34 became a 'universal' or all-purpose tank; other Russian tanks, the heavy KV and IS (Stalin) series and the light T-60, were built in much smaller quantities.

Box 22 | **Not one step backwards!**

The city of Rostov fell without a fight on 23 July 1942. Stalin now drastically changed the Soviet propaganda line, which since January had stressed that 1942 was to be 'the year of our final victory'. He issued his most famous wartime directive, Order No. 227 of 29 July:

It is necessary to completely end any talk to the effect that we can keep on retreating indefinitely, that we have much territory, our country is vast and rich, our population is large, grain will always be abundant. Such talk is false and harmful, it weakens us and strengthens the enemy, for unless we stop retreating we will be without grain, without fuel, without metal, without raw materials, without factories, without railways.

This means it is time to stop retreating.

Not one step backwards! This must now be our main slogan.

It is necessary steadfastly, to the last drop of blood, to defend each position, each metre of Soviet territory, to hold every patch of Soviet soil, and to hold it as long as possible.

(From Evan Mawdsley, *The Stalin Years: The Soviet Union 1929–1953* (Manchester: Manchester University Press, 2003), p. 134.)

rapid campaign', but rather to deny key raw materials to Russia's war effort, to gain them for the Third Reich, and to do so in the estimated year before American forces could make a significant contribution to the war in the West. The 1941 campaign had had three huge army groups – North, Centre, and South – each driving into Russia. In 1942 the main effort was planned to be in the south, with a drive to the Caucasus. German Army Group Centre was to remain where it stood, threatening Moscow, but drained of mobile forces. An attack on Leningrad by Army Group North was planned to come only after success had been achieved in the south.

Operation BLUE began on 28 June 1942, although in the previous month successful German battles at Khar'kov and in the Crimea had already weakened the Red Army and blown gaps in its defences. A huge campaign was fought in the great arc of the Don River, across a front 350 miles wide. The Battle of the Don Bend, like the 1941 Battle of Viaz'ma-Briansk, is a major forgotten event of World War II; like Viaz'ma-Briansk it was overshadowed by a later Soviet victory. The Russians lost 2,500 tanks and 370,000 men. The Germans quickly overran the important coal-mining region of the Donbass

(Donets River basin) and then the city of Rostov, which fell without a battle in late July. Rostov, at the mouth of the Don River, was the gateway to the Caucasus.

BLUE was a very complicated operation, even for the Germans, and was intended to pass through a number of phases. The general objective was the Caucasus region, but first the invading German Army was to secure its northern flank along the Don River and at the Volga city of Stalingrad. In what historians generally regard as a critical strategic blunder, on 23 July Hitler issued a new directive in which two arms of the German Army would advance *simultaneously*, one arm (Army Group 'B') on Stalingrad, and the other arm (Army Group 'A') through Rostov towards the Caucasus. Hitler's decision was partly based on the early successes at Khar'kov and in the Crimea, and he put great faith in flexible Luftwaffe support. Although each of the arms of the German advance had a number of striking successes and each made rapid progress towards its objectives, Hitler's directive violated the strategic principle of the concentration of effort. The two arms moved further and further apart as they advanced rapidly to the east and the southeast.

The southeast direction of the German advance, across the North Caucasus region towards the oil wells of the Caspian Sea, originally seemed the most important sector. Russian resistance here was weak – the region now had no land-route connection to central Russia. But there was a vast area to move through. The North Caucasus was sparsely inhabited, and German supply lines were stretched taut. Hitler was so frustrated by the slowing progress that in September 1942 he took over direct command of Army Group 'A' (on top of being C-in-C of the Army and C-in-C of the Wehrmacht). This micromanagement could not get the panzers even to the oil city of Groznyi, and the real prizes of Baku and the Caspian still lay 350 miles further away.

Stalingrad

Meanwhile the heaviest fighting had developed further north, around Stalingrad, involving General Paulus's 6th Army from German Army Group 'B'. In late August a panzer corps from 6th Army drove through to the Volga River just north of the city.

The city of Stalingrad, stretching along the west bank of the Volga, was the administrative centre of a large agricultural region. With a population of

Map 6 The Soviet–German front, 1943–1944

only half a million it was not one of the largest towns in Russia (it was smaller than Rostov). The Soviet government, however, had regarded Stalingrad as a 'safe' city, deep in the Russian hinterland, and had sited a number of important arms plants here. Control of the city, moreover, was essential for the Germans if they wanted to anchor the northern flank of their salient (or bulge). Stalingrad controlled movement up and down the lower Volga, an important route for barges bringing oil and Lend-Lease war material from the south. The city also had a symbolic name. Formerly Tsaritsyn, it had been named after Stalin in 1925 because of his role in the defence of the city against the Whites in the Civil War. Khrushchev would rename the place Volgograd in 1961, as part of his campaign against Stalin.

Accounts of the battle tend to focus on the close-up fighting in the ruins of Stalingrad, as the two armies fought each other, hand to hand and building by building. This was the first major urban fighting on the Eastern Front. As in World War I, the pace of the advance within the city was glacially slow, as the Russians were slowly pushed back towards the Volga. They were able to bring reinforcements across the river and from the south, and they had artillery emplaced on the east side of the river. And the Germans, too, were pinned down in Stalingrad.

The most decisive developments of the Battle of 'Stalingrad' were actually taking place outside the ruins of the city. Of the seven Soviet armies involved in the battle, only one – General Chuikov's famous 62nd – was actually fighting in the city itself. The others were behind the line of the Don or to the south of Stalingrad. And the Stavka had begun in mid September 1942 to develop a plan for a comprehensive counter-attack, not just to push the Germans out of Stalingrad but to effect a really deep encirclement. The Soviet high command had tried to bring this off on a number of earlier occasions, but had always failed. Now the Red Army was stronger and better led, and the Germans were weaker and badly exposed. The open steppe of southern Russia allowed freer movement than the forests of central Russia.

Stalin listened to the advice of General Aleksandr Vasilevskii (a brilliant planner who replaced Shaposhnikov as Chief of the Red Army General Staff in July 1942) and General Zhukov (appointed Deputy Supreme C-in-C in August). Vasilevskii and Zhukov urged him to delay the counter-offensive until stronger Soviet forces had been assembled. The plan was called Operation URANUS. The Stavka began secretly to deploy north-west of Stalingrad a new army group under General Vatutin, with a 'tank army' and two infantry armies. Meanwhile a smaller striking group took shape south of Stalingrad. Both forces went undetected by German intelligence. The Russians calculated that the 'quiet' distant flanks of the Axis salient, which were covered by second-line, Romanian, forces, were especially vulnerable. The Germans, for their part, assumed that the Russians were too weak to mount an offensive. The Red Army had already launched big counter-attacks around Moscow, which Army Group Centre had successfully repelled.

Operation URANUS was launched, after months of preparation, on 19 November 1942. Many historians argue that URANUS was the turning point of World War II. The Red Army achieved surprise, cleverly camouflaging the movement of their troops to the start line. The Romanian formations crumbled in front of them. Soviet troops wheeled around, 100 miles to the west of Stalingrad. Within five days the two spearheads of the Soviet offensive had joined hands at Kalach on the Don. The Russians rapidly built up the thick ring around Stalingrad, making it strong enough to prevent Paulus breaking out and German relief troops from breaking in. Paulus and 6th Army were trapped in Stalingrad in a huge pocket (what the Russians call a *kotel'* or kettle), 75 miles from the nearest friendly troops. Hitler, repeating the orders of the previous winter, ordered Paulus to stand fast. He believed he had to gamble everything on Stalingrad, because withdrawal was tantamount to defeat. It would be a fatal decision.

Field Marshal Manstein – architect of the 1940 'Sickle Cut' offensive in France – arrived from Leningrad to take command of a relief force. Göring promised that the Luftwaffe could supply Stalingrad by air, as it had supported Demiansk and other encircled pockets in 1941–2. Manstein's Operation WINTER STORM was seen off by the Russians, and their victory in the mobile battle on the snowy steppe was a remarkable achievement. As for Göring's air bridge, it soon became clear that it would fail, given the size of the encircled force and the difficult weather conditions. The Luftwaffe lost no fewer than 500 transport aircraft in the Stalingrad airlift. The Red Army was also able to overrun the supply airfields nearest to the city. The Stavka launched more offensives further west along the flanks of the bulge, and Hungarian and Italian positions there caved in. By the middle of January the Stalingrad pocket was 200 miles deep in Soviet-held territory. Operation RING wore down the resistance of the Stalingrad defenders, who were now starving and out of ammunition. On 31 January Paulus climbed out of his basement headquarters and surrendered his forces. It was almost exactly ten years since Hitler took power in January 1933.

The blame for the Stalingrad debacle lay partly with Hitler as theatre commander. He had foolishly expanded a great bulge in southern Russia, and then tried to defend a long perimeter with second-rate troops. Later on he was attracted to the tactics of 'stand-fast', because they had worked in the winter of 1941–2. Stalingrad was also, however, the fault of the Army. Paulus was more a planner than a field commander. A more experienced and decisive officer might have avoided the mire of the early street battles, might have left a mobile reserve, or might have insisted on immediate withdrawal after 19 November. General von Weichs, the commander of Army Group 'B' – the immediate superior of Paulus – was not a man to challenge the Führer. General Halder of the Army General Staff had been an enthusiastic supported of the original BLUE concept – although he had been dropped in the autumn from his post. Hitler's professional advisors in the Wehrmacht high command (especially Generals Keitel and Jodl) did not contradict him.

Hitler had been distracted by events elsewhere, by Rommel's battle for survival at Alamein in October 1942, by Operation TORCH on 7 November, and by the subsequent occupation of Vichy France (see Chapter 10). Hitler had also publicly committed himself to holding Stalingrad. In September he told a huge audience in the Berlin *Sportpalast* that Germany would never be driven from the city, and at Munich in November he claimed that Stalingrad was already Germany's: 'We have it. There are only a few tiny places [left in enemy hands] there.'[3]

Stalingrad is also explained by the strategic gambles that Hitler had to make to have any hope of winning the war. He did indeed take chances, at longer and longer odds, but if he accepted the 'safe' option he was certain

Box 23 | Alexander Werth at Stalingrad

Probably the best Western journalist to report from Russia was Alexander Werth (1901–69). Born in Russia, Werth emigrated with his family to Britain after 1917. During the war he worked for the BBC and for the *Times*, broadcasting from Russia and producing books and articles. He later wrote a book that is still essential reading for a balanced grasp, *Russia at War*. The volume combines political and military analysis with sympathetic description. Alexander Werth was among the first foreign journalists to visit to Stalingrad, in February 1943, just after the German surrender.

The nearer we got to Stalingrad, the more bewildering was the traffic on the snow-bound road. This area, in which the battle had raged only so very recently, was now hundreds of miles from the front, and all the forces in Stalingrad were now being moved – towards Rostov and the Donets. About midnight we got stuck in a traffic jam! . . . Weird-looking figures were regulating the traffic – soldiers in long white camouflage cloaks and pointed white hoods; horses, horses, and still more horses, blowing steam and ice round their nostrils, were wading through the deep snow, pulling guns and gun-carriages and large covered wagons; and hundreds of lorries with their headlights full on. To the side of the road an enormous bonfire was burning, filling the air with clouds of black smoke that ate into your eyes, and shadow-like figures danced around the bonfire warming themselves . . .

Such was the endless procession coming out of Stalingrad: lorries, and horse sleighs and guns, and covered wagons, and even camels pulling sleighs – several of them stepping sedately through the deep snow as though it were sand. Every conceivable means of transport was being used. Thousands of soldiers were marching, or rather walking in large irregular crowds, to the west, through this cold deadly night. But they were cheerful and strangely happy, and they kept shouting about Stalingrad and the job they had done . . . In their *valenki* [felt boots], and padded jackets, and fur caps with the earflaps hanging down, carrying tommy-guns, with watering eyes, and hoarfrost on their lips, they were going west.

(From Alexander Werth, *Russia at War, 1941–1945* (London: Barrie & Rockliff, 1964), pp. 552f.)

to lose in the long run. As he told the new Chief of the Army General Staff, Zeitzler, in December 1942: 'To think that I will come back here again next time is madness . . . We won't come back here, so we can't leave. There has been too much bloodshed to do this.'[4]

In the last analysis, however, Hitler did not lose the Battle of Stalingrad; the Red Army won it. Above all the result at Stalingrad reflected the growing effectiveness of the Soviet forces. The Russians had had eighteen months to overcome the crisis caused by the destruction of much of the pre-war army in the summer of 1941 and the evacuation of the most exposed industrial plants. The Red Army received 5,600 tanks and 3,400 guns in the second half of 1941, and 14,800 tanks and 6,800 guns in 1942. Many new 'rifle' (infantry) divisions and tank 'corps' (comparable to armoured divisions) entered service. Stalin could declare early in 1943 that the Red Army was again a 'cadre' army. Lend-Lease from the West was not yet a crucial factor, but thanks to pre-war investment and successful mobilisation, coupled in some cases with evacuation, the flow of munitions was sufficient. Stalin was more prepared to listen to military advice, and he had better advisors. The Red Army had developed the unique system of 'Stavka plenipoteniaries', senior officers (most notably Zhukov and Vasilevskii), who were flown out from Moscow and delegated *ad hoc* to co-ordinate the activities of several army groups on specific operations. Stalin kept in close contact. Vasilevskii eventually took the main share of co-ordinating the Stalingrad counter-offensive, as Zhukov was preoccupied with an unsuccessful Soviet offensive in front of Moscow, Operation MARS. After Stalingrad both Zhukov and Vasilevskii were promoted to the rank of Marshal of the Soviet Union; Stalin himself was awarded the same rank a few weeks later.

The only consolation for the Germans was that their enemy could not pull off an even deeper encirclement. The ten-week agony of 6th Army had at least provided an essential distraction. Army Group 'A' in the Caucasus was pulled back through Rostov (which the Red Army took in mid February 1943). But the capitulation of 6th Army was something really new. At Moscow in 1941 Army Group Centre had been pushed back only 50–150 miles, and no German formations had surrendered. At Stalingrad an entire Axis field army was trapped, with 5 corps headquarters, 22 German divisions, and many non-German Axis troops. Equally devastating was the psychological blow to German prestige; the Wehrmacht no longer seemed invincible. Many more Axis troops were lost in the winter battles on the Don and elsewhere in southern Russia – something like 325,000 over the winter of 1942–3. Stalingrad coincided with the success of the Allied operations in North Africa and with the Japanese evacuation of Guadalcanal in the Pacific. The winter of 1942–3 was the time that the Allies finally gained the initiative on all fronts except in China.

Anticlimax at Kursk, 1943

Operation BARBAROSSA was Hitler's 1941 offensive campaign in Russia. Operation BLUE, on a smaller scale, was his 1942 campaign. There was nothing comparable in 1943. Hitler's strategy was no longer to conquer to Russia or even to take the oil. The 'war of annihilation' was now a thing of the past. The propagandists of the Nazi regime now feted the Wehrmacht not as conquerors but as 'defenders of European civilisation'. As Stalingrad fell, Hitler warned publicly that 'the Asiatic-Bolshevik wave will break into our continent'. Goebbels called for 'total war' mobilisation and warned of an 'assault from the steppe'.

The front-line Red Army had reached its full strength of well over 6 million troops in the middle of 1943, up from 2.8 million at the end of 1941, although there was now a shortage of men of prime military age. Quality continued to improve, and it was evolving into a two-tier force. Guards troops and armoured forces became an elite, better equipped and better supplied than much of the infantry. At the beginning of 1943 Stalin instituted wholesale changes to improve the training of the command staff, and to raise their status; they were given orderlies and new uniforms with epaulettes. For the first time since the 1917 Revolution the term *ofitser* was reinstated.

The Soviet government increasingly used appeals to Russian patriotism rather than to an abstract USSR identity or to Marxist internationalism. The Germans occupied the Ukraine and Belorussia, with the second- and third-largest ethnic groups in the USSR, until late in 1943; ethnic Russians were left as the dominant population of the area still controlled by Moscow. The Russian Orthodox Church had been persecuted in the 1920s and 1930s; now Stalin reinstated the Patriarch and reopened some churches, although this was partly a device to help 'Russify' the mixed-religion western borderlands as they were recaptured. In 1943 an inspiring new Soviet national anthem replaced the 'Internationale'. The Communist Party broadened its popular base by easing entry; it more than doubled in size during the war.

In the late winter of 1942–3 the Stavka had ambitious plans to crush Army Group North and Army Group Centre in the same way that they had crushed the German southern forces at Stalingrad. Stalin and his leading generals were still prone to exaggerate their strength and disperse their efforts. The Germans prevented disaster in the centre by an orderly withdrawal in March 1943 from the big strategic zone (the Rzhev-Viaz'ma salient) directly in front of Moscow; Army Group Centre's defensive line was much shortened, and troops were released for operations elsewhere. Zhukov's Operation SPARK did reopen a narrow land corridor into Leningrad in January 1943, but follow-up operations to trap Army Group North were unsuccessful. In the south Field Marshal Manstein's mobile defence was able to stop the Russians' post-Stalingrad race to the Dnepr River, and in mid March Manstein even recaptured Khar'kov.

Now it was the Red Army which seemed to be in an exposed position. The Russian advance early in 1943 had create a large salient in the centre of the front, south of Moscow, around the town of Kursk. Hitler's plan was to paralyse the Red Army for the rest of 1943 by snipping off the Kursk bulge in another great battle of encirclement. He also needed a military victory for psychological and prestige reasons, to bolster the confidence of his allies after massive defeats at Stalingrad and in North Africa. In his directive Hitler declared that 'the victory at Kursk must have the effect of a beacon seen around the world'.[5]

The offensive, codenamed CITADEL, was to take advantage of the shortening of the German line (after the retreat), and the arrival of reinforcements from Germany. Hitler expected high-quality reinforcements from the West, especially panzer divisions with the new Tiger, Ferdinand, and Panther tanks. For the first time these vehicles would give a technical edge over the Soviet T-34. But the preparations were long drawn out. The German high command first conceived CITADEL in mid March 1943, but the attack did not begin until three and a half months later, on 5 July.

Unlike in 1942, Stalin took the advice of his generals to let the Germans strike the first blow. The Russians used the waiting time to bring up reinforcements and prepare field defences in depth inside the Kursk salient. Soviet intelligence was better than it had been in the first two years of the war; from Britain came both official information and – apparently – help from Soviet spies working within British intelligence. It was not difficult, in any event, to work out the likely routes of the German attack. CITADEL, when it came, was a fierce attack into the northern and southern sides of the bulge. During the summers of 1941 and 1942 the panzers had seemed unstoppable, overrunning defences or turning their flanks. Now, despite the open steppe and fine summer weather, German armour made only slow progress. Soviet minefields, anti-tank guns, dug-in infantry and tanks, all wore down the attack. Soviet mobile forces were poised to counter-attack at the critical point. A week after the offensive began Hitler called a halt, partly because of the British-American invasion of Sicily (10 July 1943). The fearful logic for the Third Reich of war on two fronts became now fully evident.

The importance of the Battle of Kursk can be exaggerated. There were moments of high drama like the drive of II SS Panzer Corps (see Box 24) and the resulting fight at Prokhorovka on the south side of the Kursk bulge – the biggest tank battle of World War II. Although Hitler eventually concentrated armoured forces on a scale never seen before or later – 15 panzer divisions, 2,500 tanks – and the Soviets did the same – the overall German effort was less than in 1941 or 1942, and its aims were more limited. The Red Army took heavier losses at Kursk than the Wehrmacht. The battle was, however, certainly a German defeat. The *Ostheer* did not achieve its geographical, strategic, or political objectives, and it was soon to be in precipitate retreat. At best a greater German success at Kursk would simply have delayed the Soviet offensive. The Battles of Moscow and Stalingrad were much more significant turning points.

The Ukraine, 1943–1944

Histories of World War II exaggerate the Battle of Kursk; on the other hand they make too little of the rapid Soviet march across the Ukraine that followed it, from August 1943 to May 1944 (see Figure 14). The Stavka had massed great forces for the 1943 summer campaign: 22 infantry armies and 5 tank armies. Massive Soviet attacks erupted north and south of Kursk in July and August – the Orel operation (Operation KUTUZOV) and the Belgorod-Khar'kov operation (Operation RUMIANTSEV). These battles were on a bigger scale than Kursk, and it was now the Red Army that held the initiative.

Box 24 | The *Waffen-SS*

The *Waffen-SS* was the armed force of the Nazi SS. Although by the end of the war it had become something of a rival to the conventional German Army, the *Waffen-SS* developed slowly as a military force. It played only a small role as elite motorised infantry in the campaigns in Poland and France. Even at the time of Operation BARBAROSSA there were only a handful of *Waffen-SS* formations. After the set-back of the BARBAROSSA offensive, however, the *Waffen-SS* began to change in a number of respects. It grew in size, recruiting first Germans living outside the Reich, then appropriate 'Nordic' types from Lorraine, the Netherlands, and Scandinavia, and finally members of almost every ethnic group of occupied Europe except the Jews, Poles, and Russians.

The *Waffen-SS* was organised on conventional military lines, in brigades, divisions, corps, and even armies. A few *Waffen-SS* formations were equipped and trained to a high standard and developed into an elite shock force for the whole German military. The best-known, equipped as panzer divisions from 1943, were 1st, 2nd, 3rd, 5th, and 12th SS Panzer Divisions (respectively '*Leibstandarte Adolf Hitler*', '*Das Reich*', '*Totenkopf*', '*Wiking*', and '*Hitlerjugend*').The first three of these, as I SS Panzer Corps, were thrown into battle after the Battle of Stalingrad in the spring of 1943 and achieved the remarkable success of recapturing Khar'kov. The peak of *Waffen-SS* operations was at the Battle of Kursk, where the tanks of these three divisions made up a third of the panzer force in the southern wing of the abortive German advance. *Waffen-SS* divisions also served in Normandy in 1944; *en route* to the area the 2nd SS Panzer Division '*Das Reich*' perpetrated the notorious massacre at the French village of Ouradour-sur-Glane. The Waffen-SS were thrown into the attack, now at army-level strength, in Hitler's last offensives in the Ardennes (December 1944) and in Hungary (March 1945). Ethnic-French Waffen-SS units were among the last defenders of Berlin.

The German position was shattered. No large forces were trapped, but Hitler's armies in the south were now driven rapidly back. Khar'kov changed hands for the fourth and last time in August. At the end of September 1943 the Red Army finally reached the Dnepr River, which it had been striving towards since May 1942.

Hitler thought more and more in defensive terms. In August 1943 he began the creation of a belt of defences known as the *Ostwall* (East Wall), stretching 1,000 miles from Narva on the Baltic south to the Black Sea, and incorporating the line of the middle Dnepr River. Later, in March 1944, he ordered the establishment of 'fortified places' as key features of German deployment. In reality the Wehrmacht had neither the time nor the resources to develop effective fortifications. In any event Hitler now placed priority on the Western Front and the repulse of the expected Allied landing in France. He reckoned that once the Americans and British had been driven into the sea he would have time to consolidate his position in the East.

The Red Army was able to keep moving across the Ukraine through the late autumn *rasputitsa* and the winter of 1943–4. This was one of the most extraordinary features of the campaign, and it was caused by German weakness and growing Soviet strength, including hundreds of thousands of Lend-Lease Studebaker trucks. Soviet progress contrasted favourably with the situation in Italy; there the American and British armies were stalled south of Rome, after their initial landings in September 1943. Stalin had committed no fewer than six 'tank armies' to different sectors of the front. Although German Army Group South was led by one of Hitler's most able commanders, Field Marshal Manstein, in October and November 1943 the Soviets cracked the line of the middle Dnepr and liberated Kiev. Bridgeheads on the western shore were rapidly expanded, and the Red Army effected a big encirclement at Korsun' in January and February 1944. Large Soviet formations commanded by Marshals Zhukov and Konev then drove across the western Ukraine, meeting little effective resistance. Hitler's desperate attempt to hold the Dnepr bend (further downstream), with its important mineral resources, proved impossible. The area fell in February 1944. In the south the Red Army cut off the Crimea, and advanced onwards to Odessa and the edge of Bessarabia; the Crimea itself fell in April 1944. The Red Army overran nearly all Hitler's 'fortified places' in the Ukraine, and by the end of March 1944 Stalin's tanks had reached the Carpathian Mountains and the natural western border of the Ukraine and of the USSR.

The *Ostwall* held firm between Belorussia and Russia proper – stout defences could be improvised in the wooded zone – and in the north the

Figure 14 | **The German retreat across the Ukraine**

In the bleak frozen steppe of the Ukraine, German troops from Army Group South – oddly enough mountain troops (*Gebirgs-jäger*) – take cover from Soviet fire. The vehicle was one of the mainstays of German armour in the second half of the war, *a Sturm-geschütz* or *StuG* (assault gun). The *StuG III* was based on the chassis of the Panzer III, but did not have a turret; note the 'skirt' of armour on the sides of the vehicle to increase protection.

Hitler's *Ostheer* was rolled back across the Ukraine during the winter of 1943–4 in an important but forgotten campaign. The Red Army had now fully gained the initiative, and it could sustain its offensive even during the winter months. By May 1944 nearly all of the Ukraine was in Soviet hands.

Box 25 | The Katyn massacre

In April and May 1940 about 15,000 prisoners, mostly regular and reservist officers from the Polish Army and police, were executed by the Soviet NKVD (secret police). The shootings were committed at three sites, but it was the mass grave of a third of these victims, in the Katyn forest near Smolensk in western Russia, that was found by the Germans. This was in April 1943, three months after the fall of Stalingrad, and the discovery was immediately publicised by Berlin for propaganda purposes. The Soviets countered by charging that the Poles had actually been murdered by the Germans in the autumn of 1941, when they occupied the region. The German forensic evidence contradicted this, but during the war the British and American leaders, for reasons of military expediency, accepted the Soviet version of events.

The Katyn victims had been held at the nearby Soviet Kozel'sk prison camp. The two other NKVD mass execution sites, much deeper in European Russia, were not known about for many years: Starobel'sk (near Khar'kov in the Ukraine) and Ostashkov (near Kalinin/Tver'). The 'Katyn' massacre was one of the worst war crimes of the twentieth century, but it was also a capital political miscalculation on the part of the Russians. The killing of the prisoners had been approved by the Soviet Politburo in March 1940, when neither the revival of an independent Poland, nor a break with Germany, nor future co-operation with Britain and France had been anticipated. This was indeed a time when France was arguing for armed help to Finland against the USSR in the Winter War. The explanation must also lie with the institutional culture of Stalinist Russia; the NKVD had committed even bigger 'mass operations', especially in 1937–8, when 680,000 Soviet citizens were shot, many of them 'class enemies' or minority peoples from the suspect borderlands. It was also the case that throughout the 1920s and 1930s the Poles had been seen as one of the most likely military enemies of Soviet Russia.

When the Katyn crime was revealed, Soviet relations with the Polish government-in-exile in London were already difficult. This was due to historic hostilities and to the events of 1939, when Nazi Germany and the USSR had partitioned Poland. Many Poles could never accept the Curzon Line as their eastern border. Polish questions and complaints about Katyn led in April 1943 to a final break in relations between Moscow and the Polish government-in-exile. The death of the Polish Prime Minister, General Sikorski, in a plane crash in July 1943 removed the individual who had most influence with the 'Big Three'. The great powers decided at the Teheran Conference in November 1943, without Polish involvement, that the territory the Soviets had taken over in 1939 would remain part of the USSR. The Poles would be compensated by lands taken from Germany. The Russians set up their own *de facto* government-in-exile in Moscow, and installed it in power in Poland at the start of 1945; Communist-dominated governments ruled Poland until 1989.

The Katyn massacre was such an embarrassment to the Soviet government (which was 'allied' with Poland from the late 1940s onwards) that it did not admit responsibility until the time of Mikhail Gorbachev in 1990. The great Polish film director Andrzej Wajda made a major film, *Katyn*, in 2007.

Germans had fallen back into Estonia and Latvia only after giving up the close investment of Leningrad. But with the complete destruction of German power in the Ukraine it was obvious that the 'balcony' in the north and centre of the front would not hold out for long. It was only a matter of months before all Soviet territory would be liberated and the invasion of Central Europe could begin.

Russia and its allies

While these dramatic battles were being fought out in late 1942 and 1943, the relations between the western and eastern halves of the so-called 'Grand Alliance' developed apace. The relationship was originally marked by mutual fear and a degree of contempt. On top of Britain's century-old legacy of Russophobia were twenty years of conflict with Communism and the bitter experience of the Nazi–Soviet Pact of 1939–41. Much public opinion in the United States had been vigorously hostile to the atheist and Communist USSR. Moscow, for its part, had seen London as the centre of world imperialism, and until the 1930s the British Empire as its leading potential enemy. Aside from the ideological fears, Britain and America were for some months dubious about the Red Army's ability to hold out. This was based partly on intelligence reports from their diplomatic and military representatives in Russia, and partly on Hitler's previous run of successes. Meanwhile, from Stalin's point of view the Western Allies seemed to offer little of military value, especially after the Japanese attack set off a British-American catastrophe in East Asia and the Pacific. At the start of November 1942 (before TORCH), Stalin publicly noted the discrepancy of effort; while there were 179 German divisions facing Russia, the only German ground forces actually fighting the Western Allies were four divisions in North Africa. Even the supplies that Britain and America promised through Lend-Lease were slow in arriving; the Germans were able to seriously interrupt what was at first the main route to the USSR, the convoys to North Russia (see Chapter 9).

After the Red Army's Stalingrad victory the Soviet leaders took an even harder line. Stalin felt strong enough in April 1943 to break relations with the London-based Polish government-in-exile, mainly over the latter's (accurate) charges about the Soviet 1940 massacre of Polish officers at Katyn (see Box 25). Stalin had in the meantime rejected invitations for an early meeting with the two other top Allied leaders. This may have been partly because he did not wish to negotiate at a time of only limited Russian military success, but in any event it was very hard to find a mutually acceptable site for a conference, and Stalin was genuinely needed in Moscow to oversee the war effort. Roosevelt and Churchill met without him at Casablanca in January 1943. Even without a conference, Stalin attempted to defuse the ideological tension. In May 1943 he disbanded the Comintern, maintaining that this would end charges that the USSR wanted to 'Bolshevize' other countries. Occupation zones for Hitler's Reich were informally agreed in late 1943, with the zone allotted to the Red Army taking in the eastern third of Germany. Finally, at the end of the year, after Stalingrad and Kursk, the 'Big Three' gathered at the Teheran Conference.

At the time of Teheran the USSR was still bearing the brunt of the ground war against Germany, and it was pushing the Wehrmacht rapidly back in the Ukraine. Stalin was in a strong position at the conference and in general got his own way, especially over the post-war Soviet–Polish border. Britain and the United States accepted that the USSR would keep the territories east of the Curzon Line (the annexation of 1939); the Poles would gain land in the west at the expense of a defeated Germany. Teheran also marked the end of the long argument with Moscow about the second front, when the British and Americans committed themselves to a cross-Channel landing in May 1944 (see Chapter 12). The conference, and the greatly improved Allied military situation towards the end of 1943, ended apprehensions about a separate peace between the USSR and Germany. The Grand Alliance would survive for many more months.

The fall of the British naval base at Singapore in February 1942 was a key moment in World War II and in the downfall of the European overseas empires. The Japanese made great play of the triumph of 'Asiatics' over Europeans. This photograph shows the British commander at Singapore, General Arthur Percival (far right), walking out to surrender under a white flag and with the escort of a Japanese colonel. The surrender party were on their way to the headquarters of the victorious General Yamashita Tomoyuki.

Singapore was Churchill's worst military defeat. Yamashita had cut through the British Empire's forces on the Malayan peninsula and taken the supposedly impregnable fortress-island from the land side. Some 130,000 Empire troops – Indian, Australian, and British – were taken prisoner in Malaya and Singapore.

Japan's lunge for empire 1941–1942

Timeline

1940	September	Germany, Italy, and Japan sign the Tripartite (Axis) Pact
1941	December	Japan attacks US and Britain. Pearl Harbor
1942	February	Japan captures Singapore from the British
	March	Japanese finish conquest of Netherlands Indies
	April	Main US forces in Philippines surrender
	June	Japanese naval defeat at the Battle of Midway

Japanese strategic choices

From June 1941 all the European powers were at war in a titanic struggle for their continent. The major non-European states, however, were not yet directly involved. China was preoccupied with its struggle for survival. The United States was providing Britain and Russia with arms and other supplies, but public opinion opposed a declaration of war on Germany and Italy. The Japanese had been fighting China since 1937, but they were observing a position of neutrality with respect to the European conflict; this was true despite the fact that they had signed the Tripartite Pact with Germany and Italy in September 1940. Japan had also signed a Treaty of Neutrality with the USSR in April 1941. It would, however, be decisions made in Tokyo that finally joined together the Sino–Japanese war and the European war into World War II, a global conflict which directly involved all world major powers, including the United States.

A counter-factual Japan can be imagined, one which, like Franco's Spain, remained neutral. That, indeed, is what a number of British and American leaders expected. Japan had been an aggressive regional power, but it did not have to throw itself into the global war. Like Italy, Japan was influenced by Germany's victories, but unlike Italy it would be left to fight – if it made that choice – on its own against two world powers, the British Empire and the United States, and possibly a third, the USSR. All the while the war with China would go on.

There were long-term and short-term factors that led Japan to enter the global war, and in a particular way. The long-term factors have already been discussed (Chapters 1 and 2): Japan lacked raw materials, and in the view of the country's leaders – especially the military – it needed hegemony over East Asia in order to survive in a world of struggle. The major powers had not recognised the gains which the Empire had made since 1931. Expansion into Manchuria had increased available resources, but Japan was still dependent on the outside world for oil, rubber, tin and nickel (crucial alloy metals), and bauxite (aluminium for aircraft). These strategic raw materials were available in Southeast Asia. On top of this there was the stalemated war in China, which could be won – it now seemed – only by encircling Jiang Jieshi's Nationalists and preventing meddlesome outsiders from giving help to them.

As to the short-term factors, Tokyo was confronted by a rollercoaster of events in Europe in 1939, 1940, and 1941, the strategic perspective changing almost from month to month. First came the German–Soviet Pact of 1939, which seemed to make a war between Japan and the USSR less likely; Russia was now apparently working as a close political and economic partner of Japan's friend Germany. Then, with the defeat of France in May–June 1940, Germany suddenly emerged as the dominant state in Western and Central Europe. The Western colonial powers were profoundly shaken. The Netherlands and France were occupied by Germany; Britain was under such pressure that it could not protect its Mediterranean interests, let alone its East Asian possessions. Then, in June 1941, Germany attacked Russia. In the course of late 1940 and early 1941 these developments were drawing Japan to the south and towards confrontation with the forces of the 'old order'; in September 1940 Japan sent troops into northern French Indochina and a week later it signed the Tripartite (Axis) Pact with Germany and Italy.

The unexpected German invasion of the USSR in June 1941 revived another option for Tokyo. The Japanese might have joined in Hitler's attack against their old enemy, but estimates of Russian abilities varied. Some Japanese leaders thought German victory was inevitable with or without the Empire's involvement; the majority thought that the Germans had underestimated the Soviet powers of resistance. The Imperial Navy had never been keen on a 'northern' strategy. In any event Soviet eastern Siberia promised Japan no resources comparable to those of the Southeast Asia, and certainly no oil. This – a Japanese attack on the USSR – is another counter-factual. Would an alternative decision in Tokyo have led to Axis victory? We have already seen Russia's desperate situation in late 1941 (see Chapter 5). Given the immense distances involved, the Japanese Army did not present an immediate threat to Soviet vital areas on the European side of Lake Baikal, but the Soviet Stavka might have delayed transferring high-quality troops west to defend Moscow. It is certainly questionable whether in a Japanese–Soviet war America would have intervened on the side of the USSR.

In the event, by the start of Operation BARBAROSSA on 22 June 1941 a strategic momentum was already pulling Japanese forces to the south; the occupation of northern Indochina in late 1940 was especially important. In addition, the German attack on the USSR actually encouraged the Japanese southern advance, as there was now less reason for Imperial GHQ to fear a war on two fronts, with a Red Army attack in Manchuria. On 2 July 1941 an Imperial Conference made a fateful – and fatal – decision not to attack Russia but to press on to the south, beginning with the southern part of Indochina:

Box 26 | The Greater East Asian Co-Prosperity Sphere

The Greater East Asian Co-Prosperity Sphere (*Dai To-A kyoeiken*) was the practical embodiment of the concept of the 'new order' in Asia which Prime Minister Konoe had put forward at the end of 1938. The Co-Prosperity Sphere became a cornerstone of Japanese national policy in November 1940, and it was a fundamental element in Japan's top-level discussions about whether to go to war with Britain and America.

The original concept took in only Japan, Manchukuo, and China (i.e. the pro-Japanese Nanjing government), but the weakening of the European empires broadened the focus out from Northeast Asia. The Co-Prosperity Sphere eventually embraced Burma, Indochina, Indonesia, the Philippines, and Thailand; anti-British Indian political exiles also played a part in the work of the organisation. In 1942 a Greater East Asia Ministry was established in Tokyo, paralleling the Foreign Ministry. Two Greater East Asian conferences were held, one in November 1943, the other in 1945.

The Co-Prosperity Sphere was several things: an institution by which the Japanese elite justified the war to itself, a noble cause around which to mobilise the Japanese population, and a mechanism for winning over the Asian population (or at least alienating them from the 'white' Allies). The declaration made by the November 1943 conference has been compared to the Atlantic Charter of 1941.

Most of this was window-dressing. The occupiers, in practical terms the Japanese Army, behaved with arrogance towards the peoples who came under their control. The Co-Prosperity Sphere was a shell for economic exploitation. Japan milked the captured regions of labour, raw materials, and foodstuffs in the same way the European imperialists had. There was little local enthusiasm for the Japanese cause. Unlike the British, the Japanese could not raise effective military forces from among the peoples in whose interests they claimed to act.

'Various measures relating to French Indochina and Thailand will be taken, with the purpose of strengthening our advance into the southern regions. In carrying out the plans outlined above, our Empire will not be deterred by the possibility of being involved in a war with Great Britain and the United States.'[1] The overall national objective was the establishment of a 'Greater East Asian Co-Prosperity Sphere' (see Box 26).

The prize: European and American colonies on the Pacific Rim

What were the economic and strategic prizes for which the leaders of Japan were prepared to risk so much? Indochina – now Vietnam, Laos, and Cambodia – would be a cockpit of world history in the late 1960s and early 1970s, during the Vietnam War; it was also in 1940–1 a region that pushed Japan, Britain, and America towards open conflict. Indochina was made a colony by the French in the 1850s and 1860s. The pre-war population was 23 million, including 40,000 Europeans. France was a great power and an ally of Britain, and its territory was inviolable before June 1940. Defeat changed everything. Indochina was now controlled by a small French colonial force loyal to the pro-German government in Vichy. In the long term Indochina had value to the Japanese as a rice-producing area, but in 1941 its occupation had more to do with military strategy. The Japanese Army entered Tonkin, the northern part of Indochina, in September 1940. This region was seen as vital to the war with China; a supply railway from Haiphong (the port of Hanoi) connected Jiang Jieshi's base in southwestern China to the outside world. Indochina, especially the southern part, was also an essential military base for any Japanese expedition against the British Empire. It provided vital air and naval bases to control the South China Sea and the approaches to Singapore.

The Netherlands Indies (*Nederlands-Indië*, now Indonesia) were a more important economic objective for Tokyo. Above all, the islands could make Japan self-sufficient in oil. The wells of the Netherlands Indies, mostly on the island of Sumatra, produced nearly 60 million barrels in 1940. The huge colony also had abundant resources of non-ferrous metals, including bauxite, and foodstuffs. The Dutch had been the dominant European power in the region since the middle of the 1600s. Unlike the colonial authorities in Indochina, those in Batavia (now Djakarta) were not subservient to the Germans; a government-in-exile for the Netherlands had been set up in London. The vast archipelago of 18,000 islands and a land area of 730,000 square miles was, however, impossible to defend with the tiny forces available. The total population was 70 million; there were only 250,000 Europeans, and they were concentrated on Java.

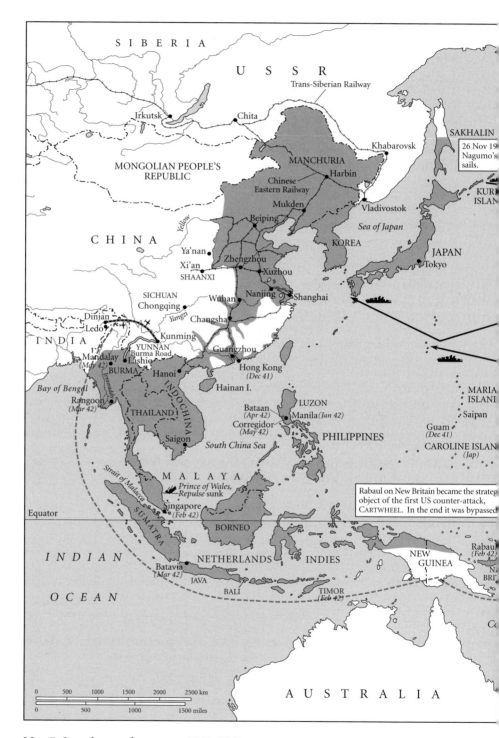

Map 7 Japan's war of conquest, 1941–1942

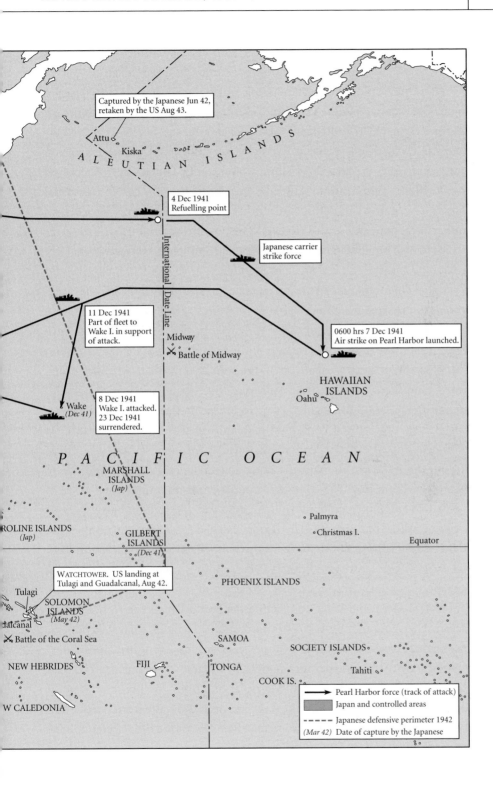

Captured by the Japanese Jun 42, retaken by the US Aug 43.

Attu

Kiska

A L E U T I A N   I S L A N D S

4 Dec 1941
Refuelling point

Japanese carrier
strike force

International Date Line

11 Dec 1941
Part of fleet to
Wake I. in support
of attack.

Midway

Battle of Midway

0600 hrs 7 Dec 1941
Air strike on Pearl Harbor launched.

HAWAIIAN
ISLANDS
Oahu

Wake
(Dec 41)

8 Dec 1941
Wake I. attacked.
23 Dec 1941
surrendered.

P A C I F I C   O C E A N

MARSHALL
ISLANDS
(Jap)

Palmyra

Christmas I.

Equator

CAROLINE ISLANDS
(Jap)

GILBERT
ISLANDS
(Dec 41)

WATCHTOWER. US landing at
Tulagi and Guadalcanal, Aug 42.

PHOENIX ISLANDS

Tulagi

SOLOMON
ISLANDS
(May 42)

Guadalcanal

Battle of the Coral Sea

SAMOA

SOCIETY ISLANDS

NEW HEBRIDES

FIJI

TONGA

COOK IS.

Tahiti

W CALEDONIA

→ Pearl Harbor force (track of attack)

Japan and controlled areas

- - - - Japanese defensive perimeter 1942

(Mar 42) Date of capture by the Japanese

It was not certain, given Britain's straitened wartime position and American isolationism, that London or Washington would go to war to defend a Dutch colony. The Netherlands Indies, however, were important to them. The islands contained valuable resources, and they were close to British colonies. Together with British Malaya, Singapore, and Borneo, the Netherlands Indies formed a strategic 'Malay barrier', blocking Japanese expansion south and west. Western New Guinea, also under Dutch control, covered the northern approaches to Australia. Not unreasonably, Tokyo calculated that a move against the Netherlands Indies would probably provoke a British military reaction, and so this needed to be pre-empted.

The British imperial possessions in East and Southeast Asia were even more numerous and varied than those of the French or the Dutch. Britain would certainly fight for them, and the Japanese had to assume that the United States would join in such a conflict. Britain's interests in northeastern China were relatively limited, and had already been swamped by the Japanese advance in the 1930s; the same could be said of the region around Shanghai. Britain did, however, possess a long lease on the southern port city of Hong Kong, near Guangzhou. Further south still were Malaya and the British colonies on the north coast of Borneo, effectively the modern state of Malaysia. The British possessions contained a wealth of critical raw materials. At about this time (1938) they contained, together with the Netherlands Indies, 75 per cent of the world's natural rubber and 43 per cent of the world's tin, a metal vital as an alloy. The combined annual crude oil production (1935) of the British and Dutch colonies in the region was 145 million barrels, about the same as that of Romania. The region also had great strategic importance to Britain. Singapore, at the southern tip of the Malay peninsula, was in 1941 the main British naval base in the Far East. Built up slowly since the 1920s, Singapore was located at a critical 'choke point' of the Malay barrier, the Strait of Malacca: the strait connecting the South China Sea to the Indian Ocean. This 'Gibraltar of Asia' possessed unique facilities – naval dry docks, fuel storage, barracks, airfields – for the 'forward' basing of British forces.

Another British colony, more remote from Japan, was Burma. This had less economic importance than Malaysia, but from the point of view of Japanese grand strategy it contained the last overland route from Europe and America to China, the Burma Road (see Box 27). At the other geographical extreme, 4,000 miles to the east, were the Pacific island possessions of the

Box 27 | The Burma Road

The Burma Road held great symbolic and strategic importance, as the last link between China and the outside world. The road was created by the Chinese government in 1938 as a 'back-door' route to the Indian Ocean after the Japanese closed the big eastern seaports. It ran from Kunming (Yunnan Province) to Lashio in Burma. From Lashio a railway ran to Mandalay on the Irrawaddy River, and from there rail and river routes led south to Rangoon and the Indian Ocean. The Japanese used diplomatic pressure to close the road in 1940, and at the start of the 1942 they cut its access to the sea. Much of Allied strategy was devoted to reopening the road.

The only alternative access to China was the so-called 'Hump', a 550-mile air route from India to Yunnan. Transport aircraft had to climb over 15,000-foot (5,000-metre) mountain ranges, which took them to near their maximum altitude. One large merchant ship could have been loaded with more tonnage than the Hump carried for most of 1942, although throughput increased in 1943.

The USA built an alternative road from Ledo in India across northern Burma to meet the old Burma Road above Lashio. This was less adequate even than the original Rangoon–Mandalay–Lashio route, as it had to rely on a primitive railway from ports in Bengal to Ledo. The 'Ledo Road' entered service only in January 1945. Within six months the Japanese had pulled out of Burma, and the old route from Rangoon was open.

British Empire, including eastern New Guinea (Papua and the territory of 'New Guinea' proper), the Solomon Islands, and the Gilbert Islands. These varied territories had little immediate economic value to the Japanese (or to the British and Australians). For the Japanese Navy, however, they were the southeastern corner post of the Pacific zone.

Further away from Japan were other major elements of the British Empire. India lay beyond the hills and jungle of northwest Burma. Australia and New Zealand, 'white' Dominions, were to the south of the Netherlands Indies. The Japanese Imperial GHQ (Army) did not have a serious interest in operations in these distant territories, or any short-term plan for incorporating them into the Japanese Empire's political and economic sphere. Nevertheless they would need to be neutralised to prevent British and American counter-attacks.

Like the British and the French, the United States had vulnerable colonies. There were small island colonies west of Hawaii, notably Midway, Wake, and Guam, but these were only stepping stones. They led to the most important possession, the Philippine Islands, which had been taken from Spain in 1898. The Philippines had a large population – some 17 million – but the islands were of no immediate economic value to either the Americans or the Japanese; there were only about 9,000 American residents. The strategic importance of of the Philippines, however, was great. The islands flanked the sea lanes from Japan to Southeast Asia. Should Washington abandon neutrality, American ships and aircraft in the Philippines would threaten the lines of communication of the Japanese forces attacking the British and Dutch in Southeast Asia. In the longer term they endangered the route by which raw materials from the captured zone would be shipped back to the home islands. Naval bases in the Philippines would also be nearer Japan than any others held by the Americans or British; they were potentially much more dangerous than Singapore or Pearl Harbor. Developments in aviation increased the value of the Philippines; long-range American bombers based on Luzon (the northern island of the archipelago) might pose a threat to Formosa (Taiwan) and even to Japan proper.

The Philippines, then, could not be left in the hands of a potential enemy. Here was the essence of the Japanese strategic dilemma: Tokyo could not obtain the riches of the southern area without fighting Britain, and it could not fight Britain without fighting America.

America and the world at war

The United States would be a formidable enemy. It possessed the most powerful economy in the world, and it was technologically very advanced. In 1940, while still emerging from a decade of Depression, America produced 60 million tons of steel, 4.8 million motor vehicles, and 180 million tons of oil. As an oceanic power America had access to global resources. Japan, in contrast, had a pygmy industrial economy producing 5 million tons of steel, 43,000 motor vehicles, and 2 million tons of oil.

The Axis powers counted on the fact that time would be needed to convert America's factory output into military power, and that even then it would be difficult for the USA to project its forces out to distant battlefields. In 1939 the United States standing army numbered 190,000 regulars, and there were another 200,000 in the National Guard; the combined force was considerably smaller than the Belgian Army. The Japanese Army, in contrast, would number 2.1 million men in service at the end of 1941. The US Navy, while large, had not been built up fully to the 1922 treaty limits. Both the Germans and the Japanese – with political systems which stressed martial 'spirit' – doubted the readiness of the American people to put up with prolonged sacrifice. Their doubts were secretly shared by some officials and politicians in Washington.

America's main short-term worry in 1939–41 was the conflict in Europe. Washington's original assumption in 1939 had been that the British and French would easily see off Germany. Then Hitler triumphed in the West in the summer of 1940, Italy joined the war on his side, and Britain came under air bombardment and naval blockade. This European war seemed much more threatening to the American government than the distant tumult in the Far East. Europe was closer, Germany was a much greater economic and military threat than Japan, and most Americans had close cultural ties with the European continent, especially with Britain.

The events of May and June 1940, and the drastic shift of the European balance of power in Germany's favour, led to a steep increase in US military spending. In May 1940 President Roosevelt made a speech in which he called for American industry to produce 50,000 aeroplanes a year (actual production in 1941 would be 26,000), and in July Congress passed a long-term plan to construct a 'Two-Ocean Navy', able to dominate the Atlantic and the Pacific simultaneously. In October 1940 the country began peacetime conscription, which allowed the US Army to increase its strength to 1.7 million by the end of 1941. US armaments production had grown in the late 1930s, partly to supply European orders, partly as a form of New Deal public works.

Especially important here was the expansion of the US Navy, which began in the late 1930s, two or three years before the 'Two-Ocean Navy' plan. This relatively early start (compared to the US Army) was important, because warship design and construction involved long lead times. One often neglected factor in assessing Japanese attitudes in 1941, especially that of the leaders of the Imperial Navy, is that this first American construction programme was about to reinforce the US Navy. No fewer than five new

Figure 15 | **President Franklin D. Roosevelt**

Franklin D. Roosevelt became President in early 1933. Throughout the 1930s 'FDR' was preoccupied with domestic politics. In
the war years, too, he had to devote much time to managing
the political system of the world's largest democracy. 'Isolationist'
currents were stronger among the Republicans than among Roosevelt's Democrats, but Roosevelt still wished to avoid moving too
far ahead of public opinion. In the US system the President was also
Commander-in-Chief. Roosevelt had a good knowledge of military
affairs, having served as Assistant Secretary of the Navy in 1913–
20. He was, however, the most 'civilian' of the wartime leaders,
and he had not seen active military service. He delegated military
planning to others – more so than did Churchill or Stalin – and
he kept the same advisors (General Marshall and Admiral King)
throughout the war. Fortunately, America's military situation did

not require desperate Presidential decisions. Roosevelt's one crucial intervention was to order the American commanders to accept the British plan for a landing of North Africa (Operation TORCH). The President's loose control led to unresolved command conflicts, and to some duplication of effort. The 1944 photograph opposite shows the President flanked by General MacArthur and Admiral Nimitz, the leaders of the competing South and Central Pacific theatres.

Roosevelt was influenced by the internationalist views of Woodrow Wilson (President in 1913–21), and he believed in both the maintenance and the reform of the existing global order. He was sharply critical of the Japanese and German challenges to that order, and it was important that such a man sat in the White House in 1939–41. He committed neutral America to support for Britain, and he pushed forward massive peacetime rearmament. By the autumn of 1941 the President had declared economic sanctions against Japan and committed the US Navy to an undeclared Atlantic war. These actions were both necessary and provocative. Their outcome was a German declaration of war following a Japanese attack on American territory; with this a unified American people entered the war.

Roosevelt hoped to renew the international order through the UN, and under the supervision of the great Allied victor powers. His project included co-operation with Stalin and the dismantling of European colonialism. Following George Washington's precedent, Roosevelt should have retired after his second term, in 1940. Instead, he ran for a third term, and – because he wanted to oversee the peace settlement – for a fourth term in 1944. Exhausted, he died of a cerebral haemorrhage in April 1945; he was only 63.

American fast battleships and a new aircraft carrier were due to enter service by the spring of 1942. Japan enjoyed a short-term naval advantage in the western Pacific, but its options would be much more limited in 1942 and 1943.

Diplomatically, the government in Washington proceeded with caution. From the summer of 1940 the Roosevelt administration extended its support to Britain, exchanging fifty old destroyers for the use of British Atlantic bases. President Roosevelt (see Figure 15) had won his third term in November 1940 on a platform of staying out of the war – especially the European war – and he was keenly conscious of public opinion. After the election had been won Roosevelt made a speech about America being the 'Arsenal of Democracy', and in March 1941 Congress passed the Lend-Lease Act, which in effect allowed the transfer of weapons and supplies to Britain and other friendly states without direct payment (see Chapter 11). American troops took over the occupation of Iceland in July 1941, and more and more of the US Navy was moved from the Pacific to the Atlantic to protect convoys against U-boats and German surface raiders; by the autumn America was fighting an undeclared naval war (see Chapter 9). American–British military talks, held first in extreme secrecy, and then directly between the President and the Prime Minister – off Newfoundland in August 1941 – concentrated on the immediate German-Italian danger rather than a hypothetical and distant threat from neutral Japan.

Europe was the priority, but in the course of 1941 the United States had also become the main counter-weight to Japan. France had been defeated. The Russians had signed a neutrality pact with Japan in April 1941, recognising Tokyo's control of Manchuria; from June they were preoccupied with their own battle for survival. Britain, too, had been overwhelmed by the European war, and any forces available were required for home defence or the Mediterranean. Washington used the one weapon it had readily to hand, economic power. In 1940 and 1941 Japan signed the Tripartite Pact and sent troops into Vichy Indochina; America responded by putting limits on shipments of strategic raw materials like scrap iron and oil. The critical moment came in July 1941, after the Japanese occupation of bases in southern Indochina. It could be argued that this was formally no different from the British occupying Iceland in May 1940, or Lebanon and Syria (both, like Indochina, under Vichy French control) in July 1941, or the British and Russians occupying neutral Iran in August 1941. Washington chose to interpret this as an act of aggression, froze Japan's assets in the USA, and ended oil exports. It was a fateful decision.

Japan and the United States, after June 1941 the two great remaining neutrals in the 'European' war, had not been able to find a common ground. Nine months of negotiations in Washington between Japanese Ambassador Nomura Kichisaburo and Secretary of State Cordell Hull could not produce a formula for accommodation – not least because the Japanese made their move into southern Indochina in the middle of the talks. The American retaliatory sanctions had the opposite effect from that intended. In the minds of Japan's leaders they confirmed a national requirement for reliable supplies of strategic raw materials (especially oil), and they stimulated a determination to act while action was still possible.

This was particularly important for the Imperial Navy; the fuel oil for its ships and the aviation petrol for its aircraft would soon run out. In early September 1941 an Imperial Conference set mid October as a deadline for the diplomatic route. Prince Konoe resigned as Prime Minister in October rather than take the ultimate decision for war; he is sometimes depicted as a man of peace, but the truth is that he only declined to follow his own hawkish policies through to their bitter conclusion. The dangers of war led even the new cabinet of the more decisive General Tōjō (see Figure 16) to hesitate. On 5 November, however, Tokyo decided to cross the Rubicon and take active steps for war against Britain and America. In late November Secretary of State Hull recapitulated his government's terms to Tokyo, including Japanese withdrawal from China and abandonment of the Tripartite Pact. These terms were inflexible, but in themselves they made no difference: Japan's Hawaiian attack force was already at sea.

In moral terms the Americans were right. The Japanese government was dominated by irresponsible imperialists and militarists. Moreover, the Americans knew of Tokyo's own inflexibility through covert reading of the Japanese diplomatic code (the so-called MAGIC intercepts). In practical terms, however, Washington might have been wiser to stall or appease the Japanese; time was on the side of America. The effect of the policy of Roosevelt and Hull was not deterrence but provocation; the end result was a full-scale Japanese move into Southeast Asia and a supporting strike against Pearl Harbor.

Figure 16 | **General Tōjō Hideki**

In American wartime propaganda General Tōjō personified Japanese aggression and perfidy. He would be hanged by the Allies in 1948, as a war criminal. Tōjō, however, became Prime Minister only in October 1941, after the decision to attack America and Britain had essentially been made (although previously, as Army Minister, he had pushed for that decision); he resigned in July 1944, a year before Japan's final agony.

As a professional officer (and son of a general) who served as Prime Minister, he embodied the military caste's strong role in the Empire's political system. During most of Tōjō's time in office he did not actually lead the Japanese Army; indeed, his combat experience was limited. He was regarded as an able administrator, and he attempted – with only limited success – to rationalise the Japanese national security system; he was simultaneously Prime Minister and Army Minister, and at one time or another he was also Minister of the Interior and Minister of Munitions. In a most unusual break from the normal Japanese division of authority Tōjō held the post of Army Chief of Staff for five months from February 1944. This followed the military crisis in New Guinea; another defeat – at Saipan – led to his fall from power.

Tōjō attempted suicide when he was first arrested by the Americans in 1945, but he recovered, to be put on trial and hanged.

Disaster in the Pacific

The spectacular attack against Pearl Harbor on 7 December is understandably what preoccupied Americans, but it was not the centre of gravity of the Japanese offensive. Japan's leaders had made two decisions, one more fundamental than the other. The fundamental one was *strategic*, to advance south to the economic resource area defended by the British in the Netherlands Indies and Malaya, meanwhile eliminating the American threat in the Philippines. The second decision was *operational*, to enable the main offensive by striking the American Pacific Fleet based at Oahu Island in the Hawaiian Islands, at Pearl Harbor.

The southern advance required a long preparation time. This was one of the most complex military campaigns of World War II; Imperial Japan was taking over a whole region of the world. Half a dozen major operations were mounted simultaneously against Malaya and the Philippines in the first weeks of the war, and a second wave of attacks on the Netherlands Indies and Burma began from mid January 1942. All the while the Japanese Army had to keep its ground forces in place in China and leave some forces in the north covering against the Red Army. The campaign was an organisational triumph made possible by the skill of the Japanese planners, the (unusually) close co-operation of the Army and the Navy, the morale of Japanese personnel, and their prolonged experience of war in China.

The demands of this vast attack ought to have led the Japanese to concentrate their naval forces in the western Pacific and Southeast Asia. The British had just sent a new deterrent fleet to Singapore. Many of the planned Japanese landings were beyond the effective range of land-based aircraft, and would have greatly benefited from the support of planes from the carrier fleet; this had been the pattern in China. All the more daring, then, was the decision to send the most powerful carriers, six vessels in all, to strike 4,000 miles away on the other side of the Pacific, to the Hawaiian Islands, which the Japanese had no intention of invading. The inspiration came from the C-in-C of the Combined Fleet (the main naval battle force) Admiral Yamamoto Isoroku. Yamamoto believed, in general, in decisive action, and he was an advocate, in particular, of carrier air power.

Everyone knows the basic story. At dawn on Sunday, 7 December, the carrier force (1st Air Fleet) which had been sent to Hawaiian waters under

Admiral Nagumo, caught the US forces on Oahu unprepared. To achieve surprise, Japanese diplomats had continued talking in Washington until the last moment. They delayed delivery of a statement ending negotiations until an hour after the attacks on airfields and ships on Oahu began. This was partly due to a technical miscalculation, but even the note the American government was belatedly given did not amount to a declaration of war. The attack badly damaged six out of the eight battleships in Pearl Harbor, and of these *Arizona* and *Oklahoma* were total losses. As with the Red Army Air Force in June, large numbers of aircraft were destroyed or damaged on the ground. Most were from the US Army (responsible for the air defence of the Hawaiian Islands); the planes had been lined up in compact rows to minimize the danger of sabotage. Japanese losses were small. Some twenty-nine aircraft were lost and no ships – apart from some midget submarines. The Hawaiian operation seemed more brilliant because of US incompetence. Although the Americans, with some reason, did not expect a mass carrier attack on Oahu, they did believe there was a high probability of Japanese attacks against Malaya and the Netherlands Indies, and they knew that this might well bring an attack against the US possessions of the Philippines and Guam. Their Pacific Fleet should have been on a war footing.

The Japanese Hawaiian operation was a stunning piece of military planning. It matched the German Army's 'Sickle Cut' operation in France in May 1940 – as an equally daring 'operational' solution to a huge strategic challenge. Unlike 'Sickle Cut', however, the Hawaiian attack was a failure at all but the tactical level. Yamamoto's main target had been the three American aircraft carriers in the Pacific, and they were all away from Pearl Harbor on 7 December. *Arizona* and *Oklahoma* were over twenty years old. The American battleship fleet in Pearl Harbor would in any event have been too slow to escort the carriers; the five new fast battleships were in the Atlantic Fleet or in the final stages of construction at East Coast shipyards. The greatest Japanese failure, however, was political and psychological. Yamamoto had launched a surprise attack on United States territory, on a Sunday morning, without a declaration of war; thousands of American sailors had been killed. This was indeed a 'day of infamy', as President Roosevelt described it to Congress on 8 December. Nothing could have been more calculated to arouse and unite American public opinion for a war of revenge against Japan.

Germany's declaration of war on the United States three days later was in some respects as remarkable as Japan's surprise attack. Roosevelt, after all, had asked the US Congress to declare war on Japan; he did not request action against Germany and Italy. Nevertheless, on 11 December Hitler delivered a scathing attack on the United States in the Reichstag, and Germany issued a declaration of war, accusing America of blatant violation of its neutral status over the previous two years. Japan had attacked American territory without warning; now Germany had declared war and thrown in its lot with Japan. The voices of the American Isolationists were silenced. So convenient was this sequence of events that conspiracy theorists have linked Pearl Harbor to a plot by the Roosevelt Administration to stampede the country into the war (see Box 28).

Roosevelt certainly tried to mould public opinion, and his neutrality was indeed one-sided. But Japan had its own reasons for attacking America and Britain, and Hitler had his own reasons for declaring war. The German dictator could not have known on 11 December how successful the Japanese attack on Britain and America was going to be (in the short term), but there was logic in his decision. Hitler despised Roosevelt. He thought the United States was already doing a great deal to help Britain materially and could do little more even if it were a belligerent. He probably thought America would shortly go to war against Germany anyway, and he wanted to seize the moral initiative. While the Führer was hardly a man to base his actions on treaties, he had made commitments to Japan in the 1940 Tripartite Pact, which was designed for precisely this eventuality. Finally, after the setback in the Battle of Moscow in December 1941 it suited Hitler for the Axis to regain the strategic initiative.

In the first months of the Pacific war Hitler's decision seemed sound. The American performance in the Philippine Islands was at first even less competent than at Oahu. The US Army had long recognised the Philippines as indefensible, and the Navy had only a few surface ships there. Douglas MacArthur, a retired US Army Chief of Staff seconded to the Philippines, commanded a mixed force of American and Filipino troops; he concentrated on defending the large northern island of Luzon. There was some hope that a force of four-engined B-17 'Flying Fortress' bombers might be a 'quick fix' to America's strategic dilemma. After all, in Norway and the Mediterranean the Luftwaffe had demonstrated the value of land-based air power. The B-17s could supposedly sink an invasion fleet or, even more ambitiously, deter the Japanese in general by threatening long-range attacks on the home islands. In the event, on 7 December Japanese medium bombers from Formosa (Taiwan)

Box 28 | Pearl Harbor: conspiracy theories

Ever since December 1941 there have been conspiracy theories about the background to Pearl Harbor, in particular regarding why the US forces were so effectively ambushed. The main thrust of this interpretation is that President Franklin D. Roosevelt manoeuvred the United States into World War II. Knowing that isolationist American opinion ruled out a declaration of war by Congress on Germany and Italy, 'FDR' followed a policy of provocation. When the Germans failed to rise to the bait he provoked an attack on American interests by Japan, Germany's near ally, through the drastic policy of embargoing exports of oil and other key raw materials.

The most extreme version of the conspiracy theory has it that the President and his closest advisors knew about the planned Japanese attack on Pearl Harbor from radio intercepts but deliberately withheld this information from Admiral Husband Kimmel and General Walter Short, the two commanders on Oahu. Washington, it is alleged, made sure that only older battleships were in port on 7 December, and in particular that the three Pacific Fleet aircraft carriers were safe from attack. A variant suggests that Prime Minister Churchill knew about the attack plan from British intelligence sources, but did not warn Washington.

Some ten official inquiries about Pearl Harbor were held in the United States, including a large Congressional Inquiry in 1945–6, and an investigation instructed by the arch-conservative southern Senator Strom Thurmond as late as 1995. They were held to investigate an unprecedented American military catastrophe, to follow through the accusations against President Roosevelt, and finally – in the case of the 1995 inquiry – to clear the names of Kimmel and Short, who had been blamed for major failures and effectively dismissed from the service.

It is certainly plausible that Roosevelt – who we should not forget was on the side of the angels – wanted to manoeuvre either Germany or Japan into firing the first shots. His policies in both Europe and Asia can indeed be seen as 'provocative'. It would seem, too, that raw signals intelligence was richer than once suggested; this is clear from the material published in Robert B. Stinnett, *Day of Deceit* (1999). Hardcore conspiracy theories, however, assume that President Roosevelt and other senior officials in Washington, including officers of the US Army and Navy, deliberately put their forces at extreme risk. They also assume a remarkably secret scheme, whose members never broke their silence.

There are more convincing and straightforward explanations for the Pearl Harbor fiasco, explanations which rely less on hindsight. American government and military leaders expected that an escalation of the war in the Far East was imminent, but they thought that this would take the form of a Japanese occupation of Thailand, an attack on the Dutch or British colonies in Southeast Asia, or possibly an attack on the US possessions of Guam and the Philippines. They also underestimated the competence of the 'Asiatic' Japanese. The Pearl Harbor attack was an unprecedented and extremely daring operation, mounted at very long range, using a largely new means of attack. Even senior Japanese naval officers opposed it as being too risky. The American intelligence system was not able to piece together the concrete threat against Pearl Harbor, against all the other background information available; the best account of the systemic and institutional problems is the classic work of Roberta Wohlstetter, *Pearl Harbor: Warning and Decision* (1962). Wohlstetter stressed the role of 'static', i.e. false leads, information which after the event proves to be irrelevant but which drowns out the really important intelligence. Finally, Kimmel and Short did indeed fail to deploy their forces effectively to obtain advance warning of attack and to minimise the damage when the raid occurred; a related factor was the notoriously poor co-operation between the two American armed services.

were able to destroy much of MacArthur's air force on the ground, including many of the big bombers. The weather forced the Japanese to mount their air attack on Luzon ten hours after the Hawaiian attack, when all advantage of surprise should have been lost.

General MacArthur did not conduct the ground campaign with the inspiration he would show later in the war, but he had limited forces. The main fighting on Luzon was over by January 1942, when the defenders were compressed into the Bataan peninsula west of Manila and the small fortified island of Corregidor at the mouth of Manila Bay. Nevertheless the Philippines campaign was the one attack which took longer than the Imperial GHQ (Army) had expected. MacArthur left for Australia in March. The Bataan defenders gave up in early April (the biggest mass surrender in American history – 12,000 Americans and 66,000 Filipinos). The smaller garrison on Corregidor capitulated in early May.

The Japanese occupied much more quickly two vital way stations to the Philippines, Wake Island and Guam in the Mariana Islands. Guam was unfortified and indefensible; it was remote from help, and close to the Japanese-held

Box 29 | Tokyo goes to war

Robert Guillain describes a street scene in Tokyo on 8 December 1941. (Japan was west of the International Date Line and a day 'ahead' of Hawaii.) Guillain was the representative of the French Havas news agency in Japan from 1938.

A [suburban electric] train passes over the viaduct, and the first passengers finally appear at the station portico. Alerted by the bell, they head straight for the [news]vendor, pay their two cents and grab their papers. It is a very small sheet, more like a flier. It contains nothing but the astonishing announcement, in a few vertical lines of big Chinese characters: 'At dawn today, the Imperial Army and Navy entered into a state of war with the forces of the United States and England in the waters of the western Pacific.'

I watch the people's reactions. They took a few steps, then suddenly stopped to read more carefully; their heads lowered, then recoiled. When they looked up their faces were again inscrutable, transformed into masks of seeming indifference. Not a word to the vendor, nor to each other. This was Monday, and the war had stricken these people as they were returning peacefully to work after a fine, sunny Sunday . . .

I know them well enough to understand their reaction. The astonishment and consternation they felt was visible under their impassive expressions. They had instigated the war and yet they did not want it. Out of bravado, and to imitate their leaders, they had talked constantly about it, but they had not believed it would happen. What? A new war? Another war? For it was now added, superimposed, on the China war that had dragged on for three and a half years. And this time, what an enemy: America!

(From Robert Guillain, *I Saw Tokyo Burning: An Eyewitness Narrative from Pearl Harbor to Hiroshima* (London: John Murray, 1981), pp. 1–2.)

island of Saipan. Tiny Wake, however, 2,300 miles west of Hawaii, was in the process of being reinforced and, like Midway Island, could have been an important forward air base. The US Navy would have fought for Wake had the Pearl Harbor shock not been so great, but in the end the small Marine garrison was overwhelmed.

Disaster in Southeast Asia

The attacks on America were actually – at least as far as the Japanese Army was concerned – something of a sideshow. The British Empire and its forces were what stood in the way of the southern advance. Singapore was too far from Japanese air bases for an effective attack (and the carrier force was not immediately available – the price of sending Nagumo's force to the distant Hawaiian Islands). Nevertheless the Japanese Army was able to move troops into ports in southern Thailand and northeastern Malaya from bases on Hainan Island (China) and from Indochina. The Thai government offered only token resistance. The British, although they knew an attack was likely, let pass an opportunity to pre-empt it and occupy the strategic Thai ports. As in the Philippines, the British Singapore commander lacked effective air power to block the enemy approach.

Britain's Pearl Harbor was the destruction on 10 December of naval Force 'Z'. This was a deterrent force of two fast capital ships ordered to the Far East in October 1941, when it had become clear the Japanese might be serious about moving south. *Prince of Wales* and *Repulse* reached Singapore a few days before the outbreak of war. Admiral Phillips took his ships out to intercept the invasion convoys; he had been one of the Royal Navy's chief planners, but he lacked operational experience. It was the third day of the war, so there was no strategic surprise. The unexpected element was the long-range killing power of Japanese torpedo bombers flying out of Indochina; they were much more effective than their Italian and German counterparts in the Mediterranean. Phillips was killed, and his two ships lost. *Repulse* was an elderly battle cruiser. *Prince of Wales*, however, was a brand-new fast battleship (she had carried Churchill to his meeting with Roosevelt in August 1941); she was the only modern Allied battleship lost during the whole war. With Force 'Z' perished any chance of early British naval resistance east of Ceylon.

After the initial paralysing attacks at Oahu, at Luzon, and off Malaya, the Japanese began their advance. The scale of fighting was very different from in Europe. The German Army had attacked France, and then Russia, with about 150 divisions; the Japanese Army, under the overall command of General Terauchi Hisaichi (HQ Saigon) conducted its 'southern operations' with a mere 10 divisions. Some 25 divisions were kept in China, and another 13 in a strengthened force facing Russia. General Yamashita Tomoyuki, the 'Tiger of Malaya', had only 2 infantry divisions, with attached regiments of light tanks. This force was considerably smaller than that of the British defenders. Yamashita's supply lines were very extended; the British had a long-term base in Singapore. The rapid progress through the jungles and plantations of the Malayan peninsula in January 1942, against a numerically superior British/Indian force, was the greatest triumph of the Japanese arms during the whole war. The attacking troops were no more experienced in tropical fighting than their opponents, but they had been blooded in combat in China. A concentration of the Japanese Army's aircraft provided support which demoralised the defenders. Repeatedly outflanking their road-bound opponents, and advancing on bicycles, the Japanese infantry emerged after a 400-mile advance, on the southern tip of the Malayan peninsula, opposite the island 'fortress' of Singapore.

Once southern Malaya had been lost, Singapore itself was impossible to defend. It was a big flat island, 27 miles from east to west, 13 miles north to south – about twice the size of Malta. Unlike Malta it nestled into the mainland, separated from it by the narrow Straits of Johore – effectively a river some 15 miles long and only three-quarters of a mile wide. A rail and road causeway bridged the Straits. The often repeated story that the guns of the naval base could fire only out to sea is not true, but the batteries were inadequate to deal with the small boats carrying the Japanese over the narrow Straits. British ground and air reinforcements were too little and too late. The Japanese crossing onto the island was effected, and in mid February the British commander, the inept General Percival, capitulated. One factor was the presence of about 900,000 civilians in Singapore city (most of them Chinese), but in any event there was no stomach for an extended siege, and no chance of evacuation: 80,000 British, Indian, and Australian troops were captured on Singapore, in addition to the 50,000 taken on the mainland. General Yamashita, the conqueror of Malaya, was hanged as a war criminal in 1946. His last command (1944–5) had been the defence of the Philippines, and he was held responsible for acts committed by Japanese units there. Yamashita actually had greater responsibility for atrocities at Singapore in late February 1942, when tens of thousands of ethnic Chinese men regarded as anti-Japanese activists were massacred (what the Chinese called the *Sook Ching*, or 'purge').

Prime Minister Churchill regarded the loss of Singapore as his greatest defeat of the war; he had not expected it. The inept campaign demonstrated the failings of the British Imperial military system; it was one thing to be beaten by the Wehrmacht, another to be beaten by 'second-rate' Asiatics. Above all Singapore was the most dramatic example of Britain's 'Imperial overstretch'. The Empire could not protect its East Asian possessions, and the attempt to do so was based on diplomatic wishful thinking, a desire to demonstrate resolution to the Americans, and a – racially based – underestimation of the Japanese. Hong Kong also fell, its small Imperial garrison (British, Canadian, and Indian troops) sacrificed. Oil-rich British Borneo shared the fate of the Netherlands Indies. Malaya, Singapore, Hong Kong, and Borneo would remain in Japanese hands until the 1945 surrender.

The collapse of British power at Singapore also led to the loss of Burma. The Japanese Imperial GHQ (Army) was initially only interested in southern Burma, to cover the flank of the advance into Thailand and Malaya and to cut the route from Rangoon to the Burma Road. British resistance was so weak that the Japanese pushed with two divisions further up into the north of the country. By May 1942 the Japanese held nearly all of Burma. The small size of the invading force, supply problems, very difficult terrain, and the build-up of defending forces across the border precluded any further advance into British India proper, into Assam and Bengal. But Burma was held as the western march of the Japanese Empire.

The invasion of the Netherlands Indies – the ultimate Japanese economic objective – met little military opposition. Only a couple of Japanese divisions were involved, broken up into regiments and battalions. The campaign saw the creation – in January – of the first, and very unsuccessful, joint command of the new alliance, 'ABDA' ('American-British-Dutch-Australian'), but it was disbanded in March. After a series of successful naval battles the Japanese landed on Timor and Bali in February, and then at the start of March on the main island of Java. The valuable islands with their oil wells and refineries would remain firmly in Japanese hands until after Hiroshima. As a last step the Japanese Navy established in February 1942 a southeastern strategic anchor at the harbour of Rabaul, off New Guinea, overwhelming a small Australian force. Neither the Japanese nor their enemies could know that Rabaul would be the eye of the whole Pacific storm in 1942–3.

The complex joint operation of the Japanese Army and Navy to overwhelm the Western colonies on the Pacific Rim had been a triumph. Imperial Japan now had its resource base. The Allies had first failed to deter Japan, and then they had been unable to hold the Malay barrier. Although only small Japanese ground forces were involved, the defenders were even weaker. Certainly a part was played by better Japanese experience; Japan had been at war for four years and possessed experienced soldiers, sailors, and airmen. Britain had had few troops to commit to Asia, and the United States had been at peace. Now, however, it was America's turn.

The Japanese aircraft carrier *Zuikaku* manoeuvres under heavy American air attack during the Battle of the Philippine Sea, 20 June 1944. The Japanese high command regarded the Mariana Islands as a vital sector of the defensive perimeter established in 1941–2. The American landing at Saipan in the Marianas triggered a long-planned operation, A-GŌ. The Japanese Navy hoped for a decisive battle west of the Marianas, in the Philippine Sea, using its carrier fleet and land-based aircraft. In the event three of its carriers were sunk by US submarines and aircraft, and most of its trained carrier air crews were lost in fruitless strikes against American Task Force 58. The defeat in the battle and the subsequent fall of the Marianas led to the resignation of Japan's main wartime leader, General Tōjō.

Defending the perimeter: Japan, 1942–1944

Timeline

1942	July	Beginning of the Allied New Guinea campaign
	August	US invasion of Guadalcanal. Beginning of the Solomon Islands campaign
1943	November	US invasion of Tarawa. Beginning of the Central Pacific offensive
1944	March	Japanese Army invasion of India from Burma. Battles of Imphal and Kohima
	June	US invasion of the Mariana Islands. Naval Battle of the Philippine Sea. Resignation of Tōjō
	October	US Philippines invasion. Naval Battle of Leyte Gulf

US strategic choices: Germany or Japan?

All the global powers had – by definition – to think about war on more than one front. This was as true for the United States as for the others, and the challenge was especially hard immediately after Pearl Harbor, when American military resources were limited. As we have seen, Washington's pre-war focus had been on Europe rather than the Pacific. The outbreak of war did not immediately change this. Germany and Italy – as well as Japan – had declared war on America. America's British allies also stressed Europe, despite the disaster to their empire in the Far East. In the background was the need to keep Russia in the war.

British-American joint grand strategy was first formally worked out at the Washington Conference of December 1941 and January 1942, code-named ARCADIA. Churchill came across the Atlantic in a battleship, and his experienced British planners dominated the discussion. As we will see (Chapter 9), the American strategists (especially General Marshall) had a particular vision; they hoped for a direct attack across the English Channel into France. The British preferred to wear the enemy down on the periphery, especially in North Africa. But both sides agreed that the main priority had to be Germany, and that the Asia/Pacific war would be defensive: 'It should be a cardinal principle of [American-British] strategy that only the minimum of force necessary for the safeguarding of vital interests in other theatres should be diverted from operations against Germany.'[1] ARCADIA, it is true, took place before the fall of the Malay barrier; at the conference Churchill had still thought he could hold Singapore. But this basic strategic view continued into the spring of 1942.

Reality was not so simple. By the end of 1942, despite the 'Germany First' policy, as many divisions and air groups of the US Army had been sent to the Pacific as to Europe. Most of the US Navy was sent to fight the Japanese. At the Casablanca Conference in January 1943 (see Figure 17) the basic 'Germany First' strategy survived – and the US Army were now actually fighting the Wehrmacht in Tunisia. But it was decided, against the better judgement of senior British officers (see Box 30), that a larger proportion of resources than originally planned was to go to the Pacific, and that major offensive operations could be mounted there against the Japanese. This turnabout had come from a number of reasons, the most important of which were the continuing military pressure of the Japanese and the delays in mounting immediate and decisive actions against Germany. Admiral Ernest King, head of the US Navy throughout the war, was a powerful decision-maker in Washington and an officer committed to all possible action against Japan. The Navy had trained for a sea war against Japan, and it could play a bigger role in the Pacific than in the Atlantic.

There were 'opportunity costs' arising from this compromise strategy. American divisions and air groups sent to the Pacific were not available for the decisive cross-Channel attack which the US Army high command wanted to mount. Shipping and amphibious forces necessary for Pacific offensive operations could not be used for landings in Europe. Escort ships deployed in the Pacific could not screen Atlantic and Arctic convoys, which were extremely hard pressed by German U-boats in 1942–3. On the other hand the United States had already made a huge investment in the construction of heavy ships – aircraft carriers, battleships, and cruisers. These would become available from mid 1943, and they were not needed in European waters after the destruction or neutralisation of the Axis battle fleets.

The revolution in naval warfare

The American–Japanese conflict turned out to be the greatest sea war in history. The admirals of the American and Japanese navies shared a common theoretical outlook. Both navies embraced a concept of sea power modelled on the British Royal Navy, in a form transmitted to them by the writings of the American strategist and historian Alfred Thayer Mahan (1840–1914). Sea power was to be the crucial element in national power, and victory would be won by a decisive naval battle of capital ships. Trafalgar (1805), where Nelson annihilated the Franco-Spanish fleet, was such a battle. For the Japanese the model was the Battle of Tsu-shima (1905), where the Russian Fleet was destroyed and this defeat forced the Tsar to sue for peace. Other forms of naval warfare, especially commerce raiding and commerce defence, were given a lower priority. (The trade war in the Atlantic and the Pacific is discussed more fully in Chapter 9.)

More narrowly, most senior officers attached great importance to the traditional big-gun ship. The US and Japanese navies, like the fleets of all the other major powers, had ambitious battleship construction programmes

Figure 17 | **The Casablanca Conference**

The Casablanca Conference (codename SYMBOL), was held on 14–23 January 1943. Roosevelt and Churchill had already held three summit meetings in North America. Casablanca, however, was the President's first wartime trip abroad, and French Morocco was 'liberated' territory. Stalin was invited, but said his attendance was not possible due to the situation at the front; the Battle of Stalingrad was raging.

On the whole the British got their way at Casablanca, especially with the decision to continue the Mediterranean strategy by invading Sicily once North Africa had been cleared. It was agreed that a cross-Channel invasion would probably not be practical in 1943 unless Germany collapsed. At Casablanca the British also accepted that the US would mount more than just a defensive holding operation in the Pacific. Plans for an operation against Burma were discussed – but later abandoned at the TRIDENT Conference in May 1943.

During a press conference at the end of the Casablanca Conference, President Roosevelt demanded the 'unconditional surrender' of the Axis powers, citing the example of the American Civil War. Although 'unconditional surrender' was put forward partly to balance Allied dealings with the French collaborator Admiral Darlan in North Africa, and partly to reassure the Russians, it was later blamed for stiffening Axis resistance. By this time, however, a negotiated peace – certainly with the main enemy – was very unlikely.

The photograph opposite shows the key Allied leaders at Casablanca. Seated at the front are President Roosevelt and Prime Minister Churchill. Standing behind the politicians are the top British and American military leaders (left to right): General Arnold (US Army Air Forces), Admiral King (US Navy), General Marshall (US Army), Admiral Pound (Royal Navy), Air Marshal Portal (RAF), General Brooke (British Army), Field Marshal Dill (COS representative in Washington), and Admiral Mountbatten (Royal Navy).

Box 30 | Germany first?

The following exchange took place at the Casablanca Conference in January 1943. General Sir Alan Brooke was C-in-C of the British Army (CIGS), and General George C. Marshall was US Army Chief of Staff.

SIR ALAN BROOKE inquired how far forward the U.S. Chiefs of Staff envisaged it would be necessary to go in order to prevent the Japanese from digging themselves in. He feared that if operations were too extended it would inevitably lead to an all-out war against Japan and it was certain that we had not sufficient resources to undertake this at the same time as a major effort against Germany. Would it be possible for the forces at present in the Pacific to hold the Japanese without incurring the additional drain on our resources which would result from pushing forward from our present defensive positions?

GENERAL MARSHALL explained that it was essential to act offensively in order to stop the Japanese advancing. For example, in New Guinea it had been necessary to push the Japanese back to prevent them capturing Port Moresby . . . It was very difficult to pause: the process of whittling away Japan had to be continuous.

(From *Foreign Relations of the United States*, 1943, Supplement 3 (Washington: GPO, 1968), p. 553.)

in the late 1930s, and this was not without reason. Until the leap in aviation technology in the late 1930s, aircraft (especially carrier aircraft) lacked the range and payload to even damage heavily armoured ships; only battleships could sink battleships. The Japanese went to the extreme of secretly building two super-battleships, *Yamato* and *Musashi*. The standard of the 1922 Washington Treaty – to which the first six new American battleships would be built – was 35,000 tons displacement and 16-inch calibre guns; *Yamato* displaced 64,000 tons and carried 18.1-inch guns. Against expectations, however, the aircraft carrier turned out to be the essential 'weapons system' in this Pacific naval war (see Figure 18). Both the American and Japanese navies had, to be sure, seen the importance of carriers, if not as 'capital ships' then at least as a vital scouting element for the fleet. The American and Japanese navies had their own air arms in the 1930s and developed effective carrier aircraft. British carrier aircraft, in contrast, were controlled until 1938 by the RAF, which had other priorities; Royal Navy aviation never caught up. The Japanese Navy also began the war with deadly long-range land-based torpedo bombers. (By inter-service agreement these were forbidden to the US Navy, as before the war land-based aircraft were the monopoly of the US Army.)

Pearl Harbor both demonstrated the potency of carrier air power and forced the Americans to structure their operations around the undamaged carrier force, deploying it in rapidly moving 'task forces'. Although overall American and Japanese carrier losses were similar in 1942, America had vastly superior shipyard capacity to replace losses. Moreover, ships that had been ordered before Pearl Harbor became available in 1943–4. America put eighteen new 'Essex' class fleet carriers into Pacific service by the end of the war. The Japanese surprised the Allies in 1941 with the quality of some of their carrier aircraft, notably the long-range Mitsubishi 'Zero' (A6M) fighter (which the Americans codenamed 'ZEKE'). Nevertheless American aviators held their own in 1942, and by the middle of 1943 they had carrier fighters in service that were better than the A6M. Above all, the Americans had many more planes and pilots. It was especially important that – against expectations – US carrier-based planes could outperform Japanese land-based ones. This eventually allowed the US Navy to overwhelm the long Japanese defensive perimeter at any point.

The naval situation in the Pacific was different from that in the Atlantic. The two sides were more evenly matched at the outset, at least in the western Pacific. In Europe the German surface fleet was tiny, and neither the Germans nor the Italians put aircraft carriers into operation. Land-based aviation played a bigger role in the confined waters off the European coast than it would in the open Pacific. The big naval engagements in the Pacific were dominated by air carrier power. The Battle of the Coral Sea in May 1942, fought at a range of several hundred miles, was the first fleet-versus-fleet action in which the surface ships of the two sides did not even see one another. The two decisive naval battles, Midway (June 1942) and the Philippine Sea (July 1944), were also fought at long range.

Overall, Pacific distances were much greater than Atlantic or Mediterranean ones, and naval war against Japan was also remarkable because the US Navy developed floating support forces, the 'fleet train'. This logistic revolution made the American exercise of sea power much more flexible and far-reaching – especially from 1943 – than the Japanese had ever expected. The US Navy was functionally like the battle fleets of Nelson's era, which could

Figure 18 | 'Essex' class aircraft carriers

The 'Essex' class carriers dominated the Pacific in the second half of the war. Both the Japanese and the Americans began the Pacific war with four or five fleet carriers (designated as CVs). Big ships of 20,000–30,000 tons, they were capable of a speed of over 30 knots and operated 70–90 aircraft. The fleet carriers turned out to be the new capital ships, able to cruise vast distances, to destroy all other enemy vessels, and to neutralise land-based air power – at least in the Pacific.

The first ship in a new class, USS *Essex* (CV-9) was laid down in April 1941 and entered Pacific service in the middle of 1943. What was remarkable about *Essex* and her sisters was not their design but their number. No fewer than eighteen had joined the Pacific Fleet by V-J Day, built in great shipyards in Virginia, Pennsylvania, New York, and Massachusetts. This famous photograph bore the enthusiastic wartime title 'Murders Row' and shows five of these ships – *Wasp* (2), *Yorktown* (2), *Hornet* (2), *Hancock*, and *Ticonderoga* – at Ulithi Atoll in late 1944. (The term 'Murders Row' had earlier been applied to the powerful batting line-up of the New York Yankees baseball team of 1927 – including Babe Ruth and Lou Gehrig.) None of the 'Essex' class were sunk, although one (*Franklin*) was damaged beyond repair. The Japanese put only one comparable carrier (*Taihō*) into service after Pearl Harbor, in 1944.

sail great distances away from their land bases. Sailing ships had not needed to refuel; American task forces could stay away from their main bases for long periods, refueling at sea from fast tankers or refitting at advance floating bases set up in empty Pacific atolls. The 'short-legged' British Royal Navy did not develop such a capability and would find itself in great difficulties when it operated in the North Pacific in 1945.

Both the American and Japanese fleets stressed 'balance', the need to have enough cruisers and destroyers to protect and supplement the capital ships. Japanese light forces – cruisers and destroyers – were highly efficient. Japan had invested heavily in this category of ships in the 1920s and 1930s to make up for a perceived battleship inferiority. Japanese light forces were well trained, and equipped with outstanding 'conventional' equipment, excellent optics and a superb long-range torpedo. Surprisingly, in view of Japan's huge success in consumer electronics from the 1960s, its navy was poorly equipped with radar and radios. The great test of light forces would be the seven-month campaign of attrition in the Solomon Islands in later 1942 and early 1943 – beginning at Guadalcanal. Losses of cruisers and destroyers here were about equal, but the industrially weaker Japan could not afford this ratio.

Flow and ebb of Imperial Japan, 1941–1942

The Japanese Empire's continuing success in the spring and summer of 1942 resulted from the experience and efficiency of its forces, the paralysing effect of the first strikes, and above all from the early weakness of the Allied opposition. A Japanese carrier task force sent into the Indian Ocean in April 1942 paralysed for many months any British offensive attempts from that quarter. But there was now a significant Japanese dispersal of effort, and the initial impetus was spent. The Imperial Navy tried to secure its perimeter to the west (the Indian Ocean), the south (New Guinea), and the east (Midway). Even the extraordinary mobility of the carrier task force would not permit all of this, and with hindsight the Japanese would have been wiser to consolidate their position in New Guinea and the Solomon Islands.

The Japanese suffered their first setback in early May 1942, when a proposed Army landing near Port Moresby (in southeastern New Guinea) was blocked, as already described, by an American carrier task force in the Battle of the Coral Sea. The Japanese Operation MO had been strategically sound,

Map 8 Japan's defensive war, 1942–1945

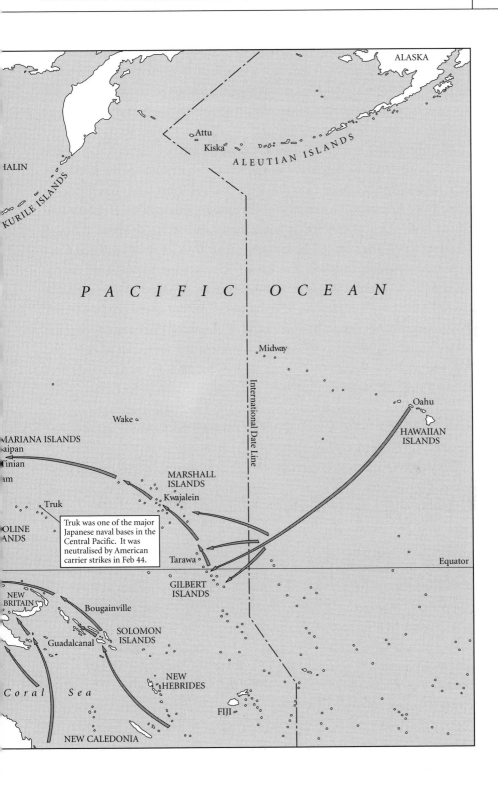

Truk was one of the major Japanese naval bases in the Central Pacific. It was neutralised by American carrier strikes in Feb 44.

as it would have completed the conquest of New Guinea. The Japanese suffered lighter naval losses – they lost a small carrier, the Americans lost a big one (*Lexington*) – but the crucial landing had to be called off. Two big Japanese carriers were badly damaged and unable to take part in the Midway operation in the following month.

The Americans meanwhile had taken advantage of the vast size of the Pacific theatre and the detours of the Japanese carrier force to the south and west. In mid April General Doolittle led a raid on Tokyo and other Japanese cities, flying Army medium bombers off a carrier. Although the Doolittle raid caused little physical damage, it had momentous strategic effect. Admiral Yamamoto prevailed on the Naval General Staff to let his Combined Fleet mount an operation beyond the Empire's new eastern perimeter in the Central Pacific. The focus was to be the American air base on Midway Island, 850 miles west of Pearl Harbor. Midway was a tiny dot in the ocean, without civilian inhabitants, but in Japanese hands the air base there would cover the distant eastern approaches to Japan and imperil the Hawaiian Islands. The threat to Midway, Yamamoto hoped, might lure part of the American fleet out for a decisive Mahanian battle.

The Battle of Midway, fought in early June 1942, was indeed 'decisive', if any battle can be called that, but not in the way the Japanese admiral had expected. US Navy dive bombers had the good fortune to sink all four carriers (two fleet carriers, two light carriers) in Yamamoto's main force; the Japanese carrier fleet would never again have a clear-cut superiority. The outcome, combining logic and luck, was less 'miraculous' than it is sometimes made out to be. The Americans had a roughly similar carrier force (three fleet carriers) to the Japanese, their fleet had air-search radar (unlike the Japanese fleet), and they had some land-based aeroplanes on Midway. They had access to vital intelligence as a 'force multiplier'. Intercepted signals told them the enemy were coming; the Japanese meanwhile thought some of the American carriers were still in the South Pacific. Even if the losses of the two sides had been more equal, even if the Japanese had occupied Midway, this would not have changed the course of the war. Whatever happened, within twelve months a much larger American carrier force would have begun to enter service. It is true, though, that with a less dramatically successful outcome at Midway the Americans might not have been able to begin their South Pacific rollback in 1942. The Japanese would have had more time to fortify their island bases and build airfields, and the Pacific War could have lasted a year longer.

Midway secured the eastern Pacific for the United States. It did not, however, lead to the immediate implementation of the pre-war US concept of a drive west through the Marshall Islands – War Plan ORANGE. Guam and the Philippines had fallen to the Japanese and there were no forward US bases. American naval forces, after losses at Pearl Harbor, the Coral Sea, and Midway, were not strong enough for such ambitious operations. Moreover, the United States was also committed to the 'Germany First' strategy in which major new offensive undertakings against Japan were not to be contemplated. There was less strategic inhibition, however, about *defensive* operations, protecting the sea routes from the USA to Australia. The Japanese never seriously considered an invasion of Australia, primarily because their Army was not prepared to release the required divisions. Australia had a European population of 7 million (with another 1.5 million in New Zealand) and a huge area. Unlike the Netherlands Indies and Malaya, Australia did not contain resources vital to Japan. The Imperial Navy, however, was more ambitious. Before Midway the admirals reached the planning stage for operations deeper into the South Pacific, against Fiji and New Caledonia; the first stage of these operations was to be the establishment of a forward airfield at Guadalcanal in the eastern Solomon Islands. This was not just mindless aggression or 'victory disease'; interrupting the sea and air ferry route from the American West Coast would have greatly slowed the build-up of US forces in Australia.

A month after Midway a US Joint (i.e. Army-Navy) directive was issued for an offensive against the new Japanese base at Rabaul, north of New Guinea; this general operation was codenamed CARTWHEEL. A month after that, in early August, a large American ground force (a Marine division) was suddenly committed to operations in the eastern Solomon Islands, seizing the former British administrative centre on the small island of Tulagi and the airfield that the Japanese had begun to construct on nearby Guadalcanal. This initial attack in the Solomons was not like the later American assault landings against fortified Japanese islands. The Japanese Navy had been in the eastern Solomons for just two months; only a company of Japanese naval infantry was on hand. Imperial GHQ (Army), for its part, had not even known that the Japanese Navy was building an air base. Guadalcanal was a big island (roughly the same size as Crete) but very sparsely inhabited; ground fighting was confined to its northwest corner. The Marine landing achieved tactical surprise, but the Japanese responded quickly with naval and air strikes and with the piecemeal reinforcement of Guadalcanal, now with Army units. The Americans called the enemy supply convoys and bombardment forces the 'Tokyo Express'. Neither side had effective control of the sea. For the Japanese, Guadalcanal proved to be 'an island too far'. It was at the extreme range of Japanese Navy aircraft operating from the nearest friendly base, Rabaul. (The distance from Rabaul to Guadalcanal was some 550 miles, roughly that from Britain to Berlin.) The American Marine and Army aircraft could fly from the now completed air base on Guadalcanal (renamed Henderson Field).

American numbers began to tell in the struggle of attrition on land, at sea, and in the air. It lasted from August 1942 until February 1943. Imperial GHQ (Army) finally decided it could not afford the shipping to support the reinforcements it had sent – too late – to Guadalcanal. At this stage in the war the Japanese command still operated rationally; it knew when to cut its losses. To the surprise of Imperial GHQ (Army), many of their surviving soldiers on Guadalcanal were successfully extracted. Nevertheless the Japanese had made their first withdrawal; the tide of the war had turned. (They would also withdraw an exposed force in the Aleutian Islands, southwest of Alaska, in the following summer.)

Without pushing the historical analogy too far, the Japanese had made the same 'mistake' as the Germans and in just the same period of the war. Both Axis powers were desperately over-extended; both split their forces. The Germans split their (much larger) forces between Stalingrad and the Caucasus; the Japanese split theirs between New Guinea and the Solomons. The unexpected Battle of Guadalcanal in the eastern Solomons had required whatever forces the Japanese Navy and Army had available. The price paid was the abandonment of the campaign 900 miles to the west against Port Moresby on New Guinea. In each case the eventual strategic cost was very high; like the Germans after Stalingrad, the Japanese lost the overall initiative. The Americans and Australians were now able to advance gradually towards Rabaul on two lines, up the chain of the Solomons and around the coast of New Guinea. They were supported not by Navy carrier aircraft but mainly by land-based fighters and bombers operating from rapidly built jungle airstrips. In April 1943, during the fighting in the western Solomons, the Americans assassinated Admiral Yamamoto, the Combined Fleet C-in-C and architect of the Pearl Harbor raid. Their knowledge of the Japanese codes allowed Army fighters to intercept an aircraft transporting the admiral on an inspection trip to a forward base.

Admiral Yamamoto is reported to have told Prince Konoe in September 1940 of his fears for the outcome of the war: 'If I am told to fight regardless of the consequences, I shall run wild for the first six months or a year, but I have utterly no confidence for the second or third year.'[2] And so it turned out. The Japanese Navy did not win the decisive battle that would shatter the resolve of the Americans. United States forces built up in the southwestern Pacific much more rapidly than the Japanese (or British) expected. There was no sign of a diplomatic route to recognition of Japan's 'new order'. Far from that, at the Casablanca Conference of January 1943, a few days before the evacuation of Guadalcanal, the Allies demanded the 'unconditional surrender' of their enemies.

False hopes for China

Today there is still controversy in Japan about what to call the war. The Japanese government, which had claimed to be involved only in an 'incident' in China, declared in December 1941 that it was now fighting the 'Greater East Asian War' (*Dai To-a sensō*). Whatever the political merits of the term it is geographically more accurate (and less American-centred) than simply calling the conflict the 'Pacific War' (in Japanese *Taiheiyō sensō*). In the end the attack against Japan would indeed come from the east, across the Pacific Ocean. But that might not have been predicted in 1942. Both the Japanese and the Americans (if not the jaded British) attached great importance to China. In general, the Japanese diplomatic conflict with the United States and Britain had come from the war with Jiang Jieshi. The actual fighting with the Western powers in 1941 was partly an attempt (a very misjudged one) to end the stalemate in China. For some months the gamble seemed to have worked. The Japanese occupation of Rangoon in early 1942 cut the last major land route (the Burma Road) from the outside world to Jiang Jieshi's rump territory in southwestern China.

Tokyo also persevered with a political strategy in China. A Japanese-sponsored government had been set up in Nanjing in 1940 under Wang

Jingwei. This government had nominal control over eastern China. The great Chinese cities – Beiping, Tianjin, Shanghai, Nanjing, Wuhan – were located within its territory, while Jiang Jieshi was based in provincial and poor Chongqing. As many as a million Chinese served in auxiliary forces maintaining order in the Japanese-occupied zone. The Japanese gave Wang a prominent place in the Greater East Asian Co-Prosperity Sphere, especially from 1943.

The Imperial GHQ (Army) also had hopes at the end of 1942 for a military solution to the China problem, an offensive to take Chongqing. This might have been mounted in the spring of 1943, but the plan was abandoned in December 1942 – the result of the worsening situation in the Solomons and New Guinea – and probably of the stronger position of the USSR after the Stalingrad counter-offensive (November 1942) and the consequent need to face down the Red Army in Manchuria. Neither political nor military pressure, then, had forced Jiang to the peace table. Jiang's diplomatic position and personal resolve were enhanced once it became clear – by the end of 1942 – that Japan and its allies were on the defensive in most of the other theatres of war.

For the Allies too, however, the situation in China was mixed. Churchill and the British had little time for Jiang Jieshi. The Nationalist government, for its part, was almost as much opposed to the British imperialists as it was to the Japanese variety. The Americans were more open-minded – or naive – about Jiang and Nationalist China. China featured prominently in American propaganda as one of the 'United Nations'. Washington needed a regional partner for the time after the expected defeat of Japan. In November 1943 Jiang was seemingly accepted as one of the main Allied leaders, when he met Roosevelt and Churchill in Cairo, just before the Teheran Conference. In a declaration the three leaders publicly specified that at the end of the war Japan would have to give up not only Manchuria, but also Korea and Formosa. Later, when the United Nations Organisation was created in 1944–5, Jiang's China was elevated to the diplomatic heights as one of the four (later five) permanent members of the Security Council.

On the military level, too, Washington initially had high hopes. China had three apparent assets: huge manpower, popular hatred of the Japanese, and geographical closeness to Japan. To some American leaders China was seen as a parallel with Russia. A senior American general, Joseph Stilwell, a close friend of General Marshall's and an old 'China hand', was sent to advise Jiang in early 1942. Stilwell attempted to train and equip a core of Chinese troops to an American level, and to use some of them for a counter-attack in Burma. 'Vinegar Joe' famously fell out with Jiang (whom he privately called 'the Peanut'), and he accomplished little before his relief in late 1944. But although certainly the wrong man for the job, Stilwell was not the basic cause of failure.

General Claire Chennault, another American advisor to the Nationalists (and a rival of Stilwell's) believed that American fliers and aircraft could turn the tide of the ground fighting, stiffening Jiang's troops and attacking Japanese supply routes as far east as the South China Sea. More grandly, as late as 1943 some planners in Washington saw China as the key to victory over Japan. A breakthrough in Burma and the capture of one of the Chinese southeastern ports, aided by Jiang's apparently massive ground forces, would make it possible to base a large US strategic bomber force within range of Japan. A model was the use of North African and Italian bases in the air campaign against Germany. In the end big airfields would indeed be built in southwestern China (around Chengdu), using Chinese peasant labour. Groups of the new long-range B-29 'Superfortress' bomber were deployed to China in the early summer of 1944 in Operation MATTERHORN.

These visions of Stilwell and Chennault proved impractical. China was on the other side of the planet from the British and American industrial centres – the nearest big port was Calcutta in eastern India. Worst of all, any supplies had then to be flown from India into China using the difficult 'Hump' air route over a spur of the Himalayas. Compared to China, even Russia was easy to supply. Meanwhile the fighting effectiveness of Chinese ground troops did not improve, and many were under the control of regional warlords rather than Jiang Jieshi. Fighting continued in China, but the Japanese position was not seriously challenged in 1942 or 1943, even when Jiang's army was given air support by Chennault. The nadir of Jiang's local fortunes came in April 1944, a few months after his meeting with Roosevelt and Churchill at Cairo, when Imperial GHQ (Army) launched a large-scale and highly successful ground offensive codenamed Operation *ICHI-GŌ* ('Operation No. 1'). This was at the same moment that Japanese Army divisions and air regiments were being cut to ribbons by the Americans in western New Guinea. The Japanese objectives in China were strategic, to deny potential air bases to American long-range bombers and to improve overland communication routes with the southern resource area. Both aims were achieved, as Jiang's armies were pushed aside. A number of the forward American air bases had to be abandoned, and the Japanese opened the rail line in the north from Beiping to Wuhan, and then from Wuhan to Guangzhou and Hanoi.

Meanwhile, Generalissimo Jiang Jieshi had been unable to budge the Japanese from the positions they had held since 1939. He did little to help, from the Chinese side, in opening the supply line across Burma. He made what Washington saw as unreasonable demands for equipment, financial subsidies, and strategic support. The military failure is often blamed by outsiders on the corruption and inefficiency of Jiang Jieshi's government and on his desire to preserve his best divisions for the eventual resumption of civil war against the Communists. That said, the Chinese government was also exhausted by a devastating struggle for national survival, begun two years before the British entered the war, and four years before the Russians and the Americans; Jiang's best troops had been wiped out by 1941. Jiang was also in a uniquely difficult geographical and logistical position. His economy was in a bad state, with high inflation. The Japanese kept control of the most developed parts of China. Driven back to a group of provinces centred on Sichuan province, Jiang had virtually no war industry and no means of receiving foreign arms and supplies in any quantity.

Northwestern China's outlying Shaanxi province continued to provide a secure central base for the Communists, with Mao's headquarters at Yan'an (Yenan), but the Russians provided little military aid to their comrades. The lorry route to Soviet Central Asia and Mongolia was long and primitive. Stalin was dubious about Mao ideologically, and he saw Jiang Jieshi as a more likely partner against Japan, both during and immediately after the war. Above all the Soviet leader did not want to provoke the Japanese until he was ready; in April 1941 Moscow had signed a neutrality pact with Tokyo. Although some American advisors felt that the Communists might provide a better partner than a corrupt Nationalist regime, in the end the Chinese Communist Red Army had no more impact on the Japanese occupiers than the Nationalist Army.

In the early twenty-first century, when China is an emerging economic superpower, a different perspective on its role in the war might be considered. The Sino–Japanese front is certainly ignored in many Western histories.

However, we should not go to the other extreme and assume that Chinese resistance was somehow a hidden factor that determined the outcome of the 'Greater East Asian War'. Japan's forces in China did number a million troops, but the Empire did not suffer from a shortage of infantry soldiers. Japan's weakness on the Pacific islands had to do with shipping and supply rather than manpower. There is little point in speculating about a counter-factual situation in which Japanese troops were not committed to China and free for use elsewhere; it was the continental involvement that had led Japan to war with Britain and America in the first place.

Stalemate in Burma

British India's place in World War II, like that of China, is often neglected. London's huge imperial possession had a population of 320 million in 1941. ('India' in 1939–45, of course, included modern Pakistan and Bangladesh; the 'Indian Army' included many Moslem troops.) The political situation was complex; there were powerful forces at work which would lead to the independence and partition of the subcontinent in 1947. British India had been moving towards self-government since 1935, under pressure from local elites; the process was complicated by tensions between Hindus and Moslems, and by differing views in the British Parliament. In the 1930s Winston Churchill – then a parliamentary backbencher – was an outspoken opponent both of the Appeasement of Hitler and of Indian 'home rule'.

During World War II, both before and after the fighting spread to Asia in December 1941, tensions were heightened between the British rulers and the most significant nationalist group, 'Mahatma' Gandhi's Congress Party. The British were able to deal with this challenge by arrests of the Congress leaders and the use of direct rule. Despite the Congress's 1942 'Quit India' campaign, Japan's 'new order' had little practical appeal for most Indian nationalists and less still for the Indian masses. The Japanese found a figurehead in the radical and energetic Congress politician Subas Chandra Bose, who reached Tokyo (via Germany) in the summer of 1943. Bose was allowed to found a government-in-exile in Singapore (later Rangoon) and he took part in the meetings of the Greater East Asian Co-Prosperity Sphere. More practically he led an Indian National Army (the INA), formed from prisoners of war. Nationalist rhetoric, however, could not be converted into mass action. British rule in India was mortally wounded by the war, but in the short term it was still possible to greatly enlarge the British 'Indian Army' on a volunteer basis and to develop a large military base area in India. There was a terrible famine in Bengal in 1942 – caused by wartime dislocation – but no serious internal disturbances.

The Japanese Army had, to the surprise of its own commanders, ended up on the border with northeastern India when it occupied Burma in the spring of 1942. Burma is often regarded as a 'forgotten front', and in strategic terms there are perhaps good reasons for this. Burma, and Southeast Asia more generally, were perhaps the least successful 'Allied' theatre of operations except China. At the junction of routes to China, India, and Southeast Asia, Burma looked on the map to be of great strategic importance. The region was, however, at the end of very long supply lines, both for the Japanese and for the Allies. The Japanese had to develop a tenuous land route from Thailand up through southeastern Burma; this included as a new link the infamous Siam–Burma railway (including the 'bridge on the River Kwai'), built partly by POW labour and at great human cost. For the British and Americans the supply lines to the Burma front extended halfway around the world in either direction. The terrain within Burma was mixed and often very difficult, with mountain ranges covering the approaches to and from China and India. The Japanese controlled the main transport arteries of the Irrawaddy River and the (north–south) railway lines, and the main entry port at Rangoon. Heat and monsoon rains made operations difficult for much of the year. About three-quarters of the 'British' ground troops were from the Indian Army – with British and Indian officers and Indian NCOs and soldiers (see Box 31).

For most of the war the Japanese Army had no serious capability for a further advance into India. Allied planners, for their part, drew up a number of schemes to 'liberate' Burma or other parts of Southeast Asia facing the Indian Ocean. By the end of 1942 the Japanese Army had lost air superiority, and the British had stronger local naval forces. What the Allies lacked was sufficient ground forces to beat back the effective Japanese defenders and – even more – to overcome the severe terrain and climate. There were never sufficient amphibious forces to turn the Japanese flank, given the competing demands of the Mediterranean, the cross-Channel invasion plan, and the Pacific. The British, more than the Americans, were committed through

Box 31 | The Indian Army

The Indian Army played a vital but largely forgotten role in the war in Asia. It was a key resource that allowed Britain to punch above its weight in World War II; British India possessed a population base twice that of the USSR. Of all the great powers, only the British were able effectively to muster large forces from its colonial possessions. The Indian Army was a complex force, reflecting the ethnic diversity of the subcontinent and the fragmented nature of the British *Raj*. Units had British senior officers (in a career structure outside the main British Army), and indigenous NCOs and soldiers. None of the soldiers (*sepoys*) were conscripts, and the force – which at peak strength numbered 3 million – has been called the largest all-volunteer force in history.

First-line Indian Army units fought in the Middle East in 1940–1, mostly as infantry. The great tragedy of the Indian Army was in Malaya and at Singapore in 1941–2, where raw replacement units were outfought by hardened Japanese forces. Eight Indian brigades were destroyed, and a large number of captured troops went over to the enemy. The defence of Burma was also a failure. After reorganisation, training, and re-equipment, a large and effective force was created under the command of General 'Bill' Slim (himself an Indian Army officer). This 14th Army held off the Japanese *U-GŌ* offensive in 1944 and then pursued the enemy back to Rangoon. Indian Army units made up about three-quarters of Slim's ground forces.

necessity to a 'Germany First' grand strategy. To the extent that they considered operations in Burma, they favoured the sensible course of taking the country from the south, by an amphibious landing. The Americans, in contrast, were concerned with the air and ground line of communications across northern Burma from India to China. Washington might urge action, but the USA was unwilling to commit ground troops in more than token numbers. The Japanese easily rebuffed the first attempted British offensive in the Akyab coastal region of northwestern Burma in early 1943, and this and global shipping shortages led to the cancellation of a planned amphibious attack on Rangoon (Operation ANAKIM) at the end of the year. A land operation to the Chindwin River in northern Burma was cancelled, and a planned amphibious landing in the Andaman Islands off Burma eventually came to nothing. Prime Minister Churchill enthused about a landing even further south on the tip of Sumatra – something similar to his isolated advocacy of an attack in northern Norway – but his generals were no keener on Sumatra than they were on Norway. Various techniques were contemplated or attempted, including conventional ground force attacks, amphibious landings, air assaults, and 'special penetration' forces (the British 'Chindits' and the American 'Merrill's Marauders'). None of this seriously threatened the Japanese hold on Burma.

There was a confusing mesh of 'Allied' – British, Indian, Chinese, American – interests and command responsibilities. Jiang Jieshi was jealous of his own forces and reluctant to send them into action into eastern Burma from Yunnan; the American General Stilwell notionally controlled some Chinese troops re-equipping in India. The British also had their own interests and command structure in India. The Americans were the source of the supplies that would make operations possible, but Stilwell was squabbling with Chennault. The region was generally known to the Americans as the 'China-Burma-India Theatre' (CBI) and there was in 1942–4 an American command of this name, but it had virtually no ground or naval forces attached to it. In October 1943 a South-East Asia Command (SEAC) was set up in Delhi under the young Admiral Louis Mountbatten, the former head of British Combined Operations and a favourite of Churchill's, but it would be two years before SEAC made significant gains.

Burma was a place where Tokyo's grand strategy worked; the Japanese Army established a defensive perimeter, and the Allies lacked the co-ordinated will and the means to breach it. Behind this frontier, in Southeast Asia, the Japanese attempted with some success to woo local nationalist politicians. In Burma the nationalist Ba Maw, a pre-war prime minister, served as head of the civil administration under the Japanese occupiers and attended the conferences of the Co-Prosperity Sphere. In August 1943 Burma – with the Philippines – was allowed by Tokyo to declare its independence.

In the end the Japanese were the authors of their own defeat. They unexpectedly, and rashly, lunged out of Burma with a major offensive into Maripur State on the eastern edges of British India in March 1944 (Operation U-GŌ). This coincided with the start of Operation *ICHI-GŌ* in China. Imperial GHQ (Army) had various aims in Burma: to pre-empt an Allied offensive, to cut British railways in Assam (in India) thus severing the link to China, and to seize Indian territory as a symbolic base for anti-British Indian nationalists. The commander of the Japanese 15th Army (a force that was actually no bigger than a corps) vainly hoped that supply problems could be overcome by the Japanese 'spirit'; unfortunately for his soldiers this was not the case. The British command made effective use of its superior (American-supplied) air power. The invaders were able to surround the British/Indian forward strong points at Imphal and Kohima, but in contrast to what had happened in 1942 the defenders stood firm and received supplies and reinforcements by air. The siege lasted until July 1944, when the Japanese, battered and starving, finally fell back. They were pursued now by British/Indian troops of the British 14th Army, under the effective command of General 'Bill' Slim. The fighting was fierce, and the siege and pursuit heroic, but the scale was small and should not be exaggerated. Total British Empire ground force losses in Burma between October 1943 and December 1944 were only about 8,000 killed and missing, of which three-quarters were suffered by the Indian Army. Still, Japanese losses were thirty times those suffered in their successful 1942 advance into Burma.

This was probably the Japanese Army's worst defeat in a land battle during World War II, although the defeats at the hands of the US Army in New Guinea (1943–4) and on Leyte in the Philippines (1944–5) were on a comparable scale and had worse immediate consequences. (The rout of the Kwantung Army at the hands of the Russians in Manchuria in August 1945 was even more devastating, but Tokyo was by then in the process of surrendering.) In the event it would be nine months after the turnaround at Imphal and Kohima before the British Empire's troops got to the town of Mandalay in central Burma (March 1945). Rangoon, the capital, was taken in May 1945 – three days after Berlin; the Japanese had abandoned the city and fallen back towards Thailand. The war as a whole was virtually over, and the fate of Japan had been determined elsewhere.

The South Pacific offensive, 1942–44

In Asia and the Pacific, just as in Europe, there were disagreements about basic theatre strategy for the counter-offensive against the Axis. But while the European arguments were between Britain, the USA, and Russia, those in the Pacific were mainly within the American military. The British and Chinese might have had more influence about decision-making had the Burma–China route to Japan been developed, but for reasons already mentioned, that approach was impractical. Surprisingly an attack on the East Indies, to directly deprive Japan of its resource base, was not considered. The direct North Pacific route to Japan – through Alaska, the Aleutian Islands, and the Kurile Islands – was ruled out by geography, the severe climate, and the unwillingness of the Russians to co-operate. (In the later part of the war the Russians were less worried about a Japanese attack. On the other hand about half of their Lend-Lease supplies from the USA, by tonnage, came through Soviet Pacific ports, and they did not want that flow interrupted.)

There were effectively only two alternatives. One was a continuation of the 'defensive-offensive' begun in the Southwest Pacific (south of the equator), up the ladder of the Solomons and along the northern coast of New Guinea towards the Philippines. The other was a direct offensive by the US Navy across the Central Pacific (north of the equator), along the lines of the pre-Pearl Harbor ORANGE and RAINBOW 5 war plans. This drive would take the US Navy through the Gilbert, Marshall, and Caroline Islands to the former US possessions in the western Pacific. These two broad alternatives pitted the US Army against the US Navy, and also involved powerful and committed personalities: General MacArthur (C-in-C of the 'Southwest Pacific Area' and based in Australia), Admiral King (C-in-C of the US Navy, serving on the Joint Chiefs of Staff in Washington), and Admiral Nimitz (C-in-C of the Pacific Fleet, and based in Hawaii). The Southwest Pacific Area was where the existing forces of the USA, Australia, and New Zealand were actually operating, after the successful battles on Guadalcanal and New Guinea. The Central Pacific, however, provided the shortest route to Japan, and was the best place for using the new heavy ships of the US Navy.

In Europe, as we will see, the American military, especially General Marshall (the US Army C-in-C), argued from 1942 for concentration of effort, a single drive against Germany. In the Pacific this principle was ignored, and the Americans mounted twin offensives across the great ocean. The two prongs of the Pacific advance had many features in common, despite the fact that one was run by the US Army and the other by the US Navy. They had the same general geographical objective, the Philippines. They both benefited from an over-stretched and weakened enemy, who did not know where the next blow would fall and who was repeatedly caught unprepared. More than anywhere else in the war, success on both Pacific axes depended on mobile air power. The southern pincer relied on Army bombers and fighters based on quickly developed island airfields, and the northern one on the Navy's new aircraft carriers; in each case the attackers were able to neutralise and bypass heavily defended positions. Both had the advantage of superior American signals intelligence.

There was in fact a close analogy with Allied strategy in western Europe. In Europe there were two choices, a direct cross-Channel landing or a more roundabout and cautious approach involving North Africa and the Mediterranean. In the Pacific the alternatives were a direct drive across the Central Pacific, versus a roundabout approach through the Southwest Pacific. In both cases the 'ideal' direct advance was impractical in 1942 due to the balance of military strength (with the Axis) and the place where Allied forces had initially been deployed. As a result what might be called a campaign of expediency was begun in the 'peripheral' theatre (Operation CARTWHEEL against Rabaul and Operation TORCH in North Africa). Once the peripheral campaigns had begun, the momentum of strategy and logistics kept them going, at the expense of the direct attacks.

MacArthur's advance in his Southwest Pacific Area is less well remembered today than the Central Pacific advance. It began a year earlier, however, and was a most successful example of three-dimensional mobile operations. New Guinea is the second-largest island in the world – three times the size of the island of Great Britain – but with a primitive population of only a few million inhabitants. During 1943, in a series of attacks, MacArthur leapfrogged his forces around eastern New Guinea. In September, military and political leaders in Tokyo, meeting in the presence of the Emperor, agreed to delineate an 'absolute national defence zone' which included western New Guinea, as well as Burma in the west and the Carolines (with the base at Truk) in the Pacific. Rabaul (off eastern New Guinea) and the Solomons were no longer to be part of this national defence zone. As it happened, however, the month before this the US Joint Chiefs had decided that Rabaul would not have to be taken. In the spring of 1944 MacArthur managed a series of further amphibious jumps into central and western New Guinea. Although reinforcements had been rushed in, the Japanese Army was unready. Key air bases and whole Japanese divisions were cut off. Rabaul, even further to the east, was left in isolation with its garrison of 90,000 Japanese troops.

The Central Pacific offensive, 1943–1944

Meanwhile in the autumn of 1943 the battle fleet of Admirals King and Nimitz had been built up by new construction. The most important addition were the 'Essex' class fleet carriers and new light carriers. Nimitz could now project his fleet's power into the Central Pacific, beyond the range of US ground-based tactical aircraft. The route to the west lay through the island groups that the Japanese had acquired as League of Nations mandates (from Germany) after 1918. The main target was the heart of the Empire's Central Pacific complex, the huge Truk Atoll in the Carolines (now the Chuuk island group in the Federated States of Micronesia). Although not comparable to the facilities on Oahu (with Pearl Harbor), Truk had airfields and submarine bases, and a safe lagoon big enough to shelter the entire Japanese Combined Fleet. The Japanese had also had lesser (pre-war) facilities flanking Truk, in the Marshalls and Gilberts to the east, and at Palau and Yap to the west. To the north, arching towards Japan, were the larger and now better-known Mariana Islands. Through all these islands – unsinkable aircraft carriers – the Imperial Navy could stage land-based fighters and bombers.

In line with pre-war US plans (and the logic of geography) the first American jump was west into the Gilbert Islands and the Marshall Islands. The islands on Nimitz's route were much smaller and further apart than those in the South Pacific. Many of the points on the Japanese outer perimeter were simply coral atolls, with islets only a few feet above sea level and just large enough to build an air strip, or with a lagoon in which to base flying boats and naval ships. Some were initially uninhabited, or had just a few dozen villagers. Unlike the islands of the South Pacific, these places had been controlled by the Japanese before December 1941. Fortunately for the Americans, the Empire had done little to prepare the defences of the 'South Seas' (Nan'yō) until just before the war; even then it devoted few resources to the task. In the 1930s the attention of Japanese leaders, and certainly of the Army, had been focused on the Asian mainland. Even most of 1942 passed with little defensive preparation, as a result of the complacency which followed the Pearl Harbor triumph and then of the demands of the South Pacific. So it was that the Japanese Army and Navy spent only a year – 1943 – fortifying this outer crust of their defensive system, before it came under

attack. The island garrisons consisted of small elements – battalions, regiments, or brigades – and they were only a fragment of the ground forces of
Imperial Japan.

All the same, the islands of the Central Pacific were a formidable challenge
to the Americans. The essence of classic amphibious warfare is to strike
the enemy at his weak points (Guadalcanal was an example of this). Such
a choice was impossible here. The lines of potential attack on individual
islands were predictable, and if it was impossible for the Japanese garrisons
to retreat, there was also no way they could be tactically outflanked. The
defenders – soldiers and naval infantry – fought for these small islands with
a tenacity seen nowhere else in the war, even on the Russian front. They
fought to the death – and were in any event shown little mercy by attacking
American Marines and soldiers.

Against this defensive system the Americans deployed a new kind of warfare, the amphibious *assault*. Although the US Marine Corps (USMC) had
spent the 1920s and 1930s mostly as a police force in the Caribbean, it was
an integral part of the US Navy, and its Pacific role was an essential part of
the Navy's pre-war ORANGE plan. Senior Marine officers had developed
techniques for amphibious warfare. After Pearl Harbor the Corps was developed far beyond its Japanese or British equivalents; it was bigger (eventually
with six divisions) and more lavishly equipped (the USMC had its own air
force). At the same time the Navy developed techniques of massive fire support using naval guns and carrier aeroplanes. British 'combined operations'
developments in 1940–1 provided the designs of many of the special landing
vessels required – the LST, LCI, LSM, LCT, and LCVP (see Chapter 10).

The first amphibious assault was mounted against Tarawa Atoll in the
Gilbert Islands (see Box 32). The attack (Operation GALVANIC) took
place in November 1943, fifteen months after the Guadalcanal landing. The
Marine assault on the main island, Betio, was steadfastly opposed. Both sides
were better prepared than the year before in the Solomons. The Marines
now had more specialised equipment, but the Japanese Navy garrison had
artillery and were protected by log bunkers. In American terms it was a very
bloody operation, with nearly 1,000 Marines killed in three days of fighting;
only 17 Japanese from a garrison of 5,000 survived. The American learned
important lessons from Tarawa, and the main landing in the Marshalls, at
Kwajalein in January 1944, was less costly for them.

Box 32 | **Tarawa**

American war correspondent Robert Sherrod describes the first day of the invasion of Tarawa, 20 November 1943:

Another young Marine walked briskly along the beach. He grinned at a pal who was sitting next to me. Again there was a shot. The Marine spun all the way round and fell to the ground, dead. From where he lay, a few feet away, he looked up at us. Because he had been shot squarely through the temple his eyes bulged out wide, as in horrible surprise at what had happened to him, though it was impossible that he could ever have known what hit him.

'Somebody go get the son-of-a-bitch,' yelled Major Crowe. 'He's right back of us here, just waiting for somebody to pass by.' That Jap sniper, we knew from the crack of his rifle, was very close.

A Marine jumped over the seawall and began throwing blocks of fused TNT into a coconut-log pillbox about fifteen feet back of the seawall against which we sat. Two more Marines scaled the seawall, one of them carrying a twin-cylindered tank strapped to his shoulders, the other holding the nozzle of the flamethrower. As another charge of TNT boomed inside the pillbox, causing smoke and dust to billow out, a khaki-clad figure ran out the side entrance. The flamethrower, waiting for him, caught him in the withering stream of intense fire. As soon as it touched him, the Jap flared up like a piece of celluloid. He was dead instantly but the bullets in his cartridge belt exploded for a full sixty seconds after he had been charred almost to nothingness.

(From Robert Sherrod, *Tarawa: The Story of a Battle* (Fredericksburg, TX: Admiral Nimitz Foundation, 1973), pp. 73f.)

The island air-base system, the 'unsinkable aircraft carriers' on which the Japanese tried to base their defence of the Central Pacific, proved weak. The Imperial Navy had not fully developed its airfields sufficiently before they came under attack from Nimitz's carriers. As soon as one Japanese-held island or atoll in an island group had been taken, and a US air base quickly constructed, the others in the group were relatively easy to suppress and isolate. The surviving Japanese garrisons, immobile and cut off, were reduced to trying to feed themselves, Robinson Crusoes in an American ocean. The Imperial Navy was even forced to stop using its pre-war main forward base at Truk in the Carolines. The local air defences could not stand up to a big American carrier raid mounted in February 1944. The now obvious vulnerability of Truk shocked Imperial GHQ (Army), which realised that any claims by the Navy to be in control of the situation had to be discounted. The Americans had originally planned to invade Truk. They now decided that, as with Rabaul, they could just neutralise the air bases and leave the place to 'wither on the vine'.

In contrast to the experience in the Solomons – and as a result of losses suffered there – the surface ships of the Japanese Navy were inactive in the first stages of Nimitz's drive across the Central Pacific. The Imperial Navy was short of fuel (mainly due to a growing lack of tankers), and it was trying to rebuild and retrain its carrier force. The Combined Fleet did not use its main forces to contest the landings in the Gilberts and Marshalls in the winter of 1943–4. The second decisive naval battle of the Pacific war, perhaps even more important than the Battle of Midway in 1942, was what the Americans call the Battle of the Philippine Sea and the Japanese the Battle of the Marianas. The Mariana Islands were an important part of Japan's 'absolute national defence zone'. The islands (except Guam) had been controlled by Japan before the war, and they had a population of Japanese civilians. In enemy hands they could be used as an advance base for surface ships and submarines cruising in Philippine and Japanese waters. They were big enough and close enough to the home islands to serve as airfields for US strategic bombers.

The Imperial Navy, with its main force now organised on American carrier task force lines as the 1st Mobile Fleet, was to be committed to a decisive battle to defend the Marianas. Flying his flag in the new armoured fleet carrier *Taihō* was Admiral Ozawa Jisaburō. Ozawa hoisted the same Nelsonian signal Admiral Togo had used at the great Battle of Tsu-Shima in 1905: 'The fate of the Empire rests on this one battle. Every man is expected to do his utmost.' As at Midway, the plan was that the defending side would supplement its carrier strength with land-based aircraft based on island airfields. This time, however, the defenders were Japanese rather than American, and the attackers had even larger forces at their disposal. The Japanese were overwhelmed by the quantity and quality of American ships and aircraft. The Americans benefited from huge pilot-training programmes and from technological advantages: radar-based fighter direction, proximity fuses on anti-aircraft guns, a powerful new American carrier fighter plane (the Grumman F6F Hellcat).

Although the Japanese defensive operations in the Marianas were supposed to involve unprecedented co-operation between the Army and Navy air forces, at the last moment the Navy diverted several hundred aircraft to a separate operation at Biak Island off western New Guinea. Japanese local commanders and air crews increasingly lost touch with reality, dramatically exaggerating their successes and failing to report failures. In a six-hour battle, which the Americans mockingly called the 'Great Marianas Turkey Shoot', the Japanese lost 243 attacking planes to the fighters and anti-aircraft guns of the US Navy's Task Force 58, and they were unable to inflict any damage on the fleet; 31 defending American planes were lost. The American carrier counter-strike, plus the activities of the now effective US submarines, achieved major successes. *Taihō* and 2 other carriers were sunk (Admiral Ozawa survived). On the opposite side Admiral Raymond Spruance had 6 brand-new 'Essex' class carriers (plus the pre-war *Enterprise*), along with 8 new light carriers; none was even damaged. Although there would be another wide-ranging naval action in the Philippines in October 1944, around Leyte Gulf, the Battle of the Philippine Sea was the last meeting of roughly comparable and symmetrical 'battle fleets'. At the end of this engagement Japan had ceased to be a modern naval power.

The main land campaign on Saipan Island, which covered some 70 square miles (about three times the size of Manhattan Island), was prolonged (three weeks) and bloody. After the Japanese naval defeat, however, the outcome was inevitable. An especially grisly feature was the mass suicide of Japanese soldiers and civilians in the last days. As a result of these defeats in the Marianas General Tōjō was forced to resign as Prime Minister in July 1944, after nearly three years in office. Within four months of the landings the Americans had completed the first stage of a huge airfield complex on Tinian, Guam, and Saipan islands. Groups of B-29 bombers were flown in, and committed to the bombardment of Japan. The Marianas were as close to the Japanese homeland as central China; compared to the bases in China they were secure and easily supplied. (For the B-29 campaign see Chapter 13.)

Return to the Philippines

The next major American jump was into the central Philippines, where MacArthur and Nimitz's paths from the South and Central Pacific converged. The original American intention had been to hold off the recapture of the Philippines until 1945 (after the planned defeat of Germany). By now, however, the Japanese were perceived to be so weak that the invasion date was moved forwards. The two biggest islands in the Philippines were Luzon and Mindanao, but the initial American objective was the smaller central island of Leyte, where US Army forces landed towards the end of October 1944. General MacArthur waded ashore, accompanied by photographers, fulfilling his famous promise of 1942: 'I shall return.'

The Battle of Leyte Gulf was the biggest naval engagement ever fought. The main American fleet, now under the operational command of Admiral 'Bull' Halsey, had been free to roam at will over the western Pacific. In mid October 1944 Halsey's Task Force 38 raided Formosa, partly to prevent the enemy from staging aircraft through Formosa to reinforce the Philippines. The Japanese believed – incorrectly – that counter-strikes by their Army and Navy aircraft from Formosa had crippled the American fleet, sinking a number of carriers. Celebrations were held in Japan to mark this great 'victory', and the claims were taken seriously by the Japanese high command. The grossly exaggerated combat reports distorted the Japanese response when, a few days later, the Americans descended on Leyte. The Philippines were for the Imperial Navy a final trial. It no longer had an effective carrier force, but there was a fleet of battleships and cruisers and a large number of land-based aircraft. The battleships, including the huge *Yamato* and *Musashi*, had been at the centre of inter-war planning but they had not been used in earlier battles. They were too highly valued and too slow, and they used too much fuel. As at Midway in 1942, the Japanese Navy devised a complex plan involving feints and multiple forces. The remnants of Ozawa's carrier fleet, coming down from Japan but with very few planes on board, were intended to lure off Halsey's task force. By this time the Empire's fuel system was so dislocated that the fleet had to be divided to ensure supply, with many ships based in the south to be near the fuel oil of the East Indies. The Japanese battleship fleet, in two forces, steamed up from its base off Singapore and through the Philippines to attack the American landing area off Leyte, in Leyte Gulf.

Some elements of the plan succeeded. Halsey took the bait and sent his big carriers and fast battleships north against Ozawa's carriers. The two other Japanese forces had been attacked by US submarines and pummelled from the air by repeated carrier strikes as they came through the central

Philippines. The super-battleship *Musashi* in Admiral Kurita Takeo's central force was sunk by swarms of dive bombers and torpedo planes, and the Americans thought the Japanese had turned around. The smaller southern force, with two old dreadnoughts, got as far as the narrow southern entrance into Leyte Gulf. before they were intercepted at night by a fleet of similar vintage American battleships, some of them salvaged from the bottom of Pearl Harbor. History's last battleship-versus-battleship action was fought out, and the Japanese were annihilated. Meanwhile, however, Kurita's central force, less *Musashi*, had reversed course again and approached Leyte Gulf from the north with only a thin screen of US escort carriers and destroyers in its way. Then, in a decision that made pointless the whole operation, Kurita reversed course and headed home. Operating blindly and low on fuel, he had called an end to the naval battle.

During the Battle of Leyte Gulf the local naval air commander organised the first suicide 'kamikaze' (*tokko*) attacks on the American fleet. Fortunately for the invaders this first experiment was carried out piecemeal. Although several ships were sunk, the kamikazes did not affect the course of the naval battle. There then followed a month of ground fighting for Leyte Island, into which the Japanese Army threw most of its reserves in the Philippines. In the end this effort too was unsuccessful, and the Americans were left in control of the central Philippines. (The mass use of kamikazes and the 1945 campaign for Luzon, in the northern Philippines, will be discussed in Chapter 13.)

• • •

Between 1942 and 1944 the Japanese dream of an East Asian / Pacific empire, surrounded by an impregnable defensive perimeter, was broken. The front against the British on the Burma–India border was firm until 1944. In China the Japanese Army held its own until 1945, in part because it succeeded in cutting off – as intended – all surface routes to Nationalist territory. Against America, however, it was clear by the late summer of 1942 that the war was going badly wrong. The Army and the Navy never worked out a coherent joint strategy. At Midway and in the Solomons the Imperial Navy had pushed the assault too far; they gambled and lost. The Americans were able to mount counter-offensives much earlier, and with greater force, than even the pessimists in Tokyo had expected. The US Army and Navy had actually done this using only their pre-war forces. By 1943 the products of American war industry, first a large number of new aircraft and then a new fast-carrier fleet, began to reach the Pacific.

Did the Americans achieve their success (and invalidate Japanese assumptions) by flouting the 'Germany First' strategy? The Pacific did take a bigger share than had been intended back in 1941, but the European theatre still got most of the personnel and equipment. Although historians will go on debating this, the American planners were right, and the British – who wanted to keep the Pacific offensive within tight bounds – were wrong. Even the dual assault (by MacArthur and Nimitz) made sense, given America's immense material resources. The unbroken American offensives in the Pacific after the middle of 1942 made the eventual task of defeating the enemy easier; the Japanese were constantly wrong-footed. The Japanese Army and Navy never had time – as they hoped – to harden the outer defensive ring. This led to defeat in the Pacific Ocean, and defeat in the Pacific meant defeat for Japan.

A convoy of American troopships heads east into the Atlantic in February 1942, photographed from an escorting aircraft. USS *Neville* steams in the foreground. Built in 1918, the vessel was a typical cargo-passenger ship of the inter-war years; in the 1930s she was operated by the Baltimore Mail Steamship Co. as SS *City of Norfolk*. She was converted into a US Navy troopship and later into an attack transport (APA-9); as such she could land about 1,300 troops. *Neville* operated all over the world. Six months after sailing in several convoy runs across the North Atlantic she took part in the landing at Guadalcanal in the South Pacific. She carried American forces to the invasion of Sicily in 1943, to Tarawa in the Central Pacific in 1943, and to Kwajalein, Eniwetok, and Saipan in 1944.

The 'world ocean' and Allied victory, 1939–1945

Timeline

1939	September	Allied blockade of Germany begins
	November	German Navy allows unrestricted submarine warfare
1940	September	USA–Britain 'destroyers for bases' deal
1941	May	ULTRA becomes a major factor
	September	US warships engage U-boats
1942	Spring	U-boat 'Happy time' off the American east coast
	July	Destruction of Russian-bound convoy PQ17
1943	March	Height of Atlantic convoy war
	Spring	Beginning of effective American submarine operations against Japanese shipping
	May	'Black May'. U-boats withdrawn from North Atlantic
1944	November	Americans land in the Philippines, cutting Japanese convoy routes

Mackinder and Mahan

The 'battle fleet' mentality of the followers of Alfred Thayer Mahan in Japan and the United States has already been mentioned (Chapter 8). Captain Mahan was also an advocate of sea power, more generally, as the instrument by which states become great powers. *The Influence of Sea Power Upon History, 1660–1783*, written in 1890, used as its model the Royal Navy and the British state.

In 1904 the British geographer Halford Mackinder provided an alternative view. In a much-read article, 'The Geographical Pivot of History', Mackinder emphasised new developments of land communications – especially the railways. He argued that these had transformed the importance of the Eurasian land mass and of the 'continental' powers. The 'Columbian age', according to Mackinder, had lasted from the end of the fifteenth century until the end of the nineteenth. During those centuries seaborne trade had been the only way to move goods. Now the key to world dominance was control of concentric ring of territory centred on northern Eurasia and the so-called 'pivot area'. Mackinder's ideas influenced the German geographer Karl Haushofer, and indirectly Adolf Hitler himself and his idea of *Lebensraum*.

World War II can be seen as an immense test of the rival conceptions of Mahan and Mackinder. In Mackinder's geo-strategic terms the Germans controlled the Western European land mass – and aspired to control the pivotal area of the 'heartland' by the conquest of Russia. The Germans, with a central position, could move ground and air forces rapidly from direction to direction using land transport to project their power. The German railways were the logistical pivot of Hitler's war system. In contrast, two of Hitler's main enemies were great naval powers; Britain and America controlled what geographers call the 'world ocean'. The Allies moved forces around a long perimeter, ranging from northern Russia to the Persian Gulf, using sea transport as the vital instrument.

Geography certainly played a critical role in determining who would win the war, but this black and white conflict between sea power and land power is oversimplified. Control of Mackinder's European 'heartland' was in 1941–5 actually contested between Germany and the USSR, so World War II was not a fair 'test' of his concept. (The border of the 'pivot area' – on the famous world map with which Mackinder accompanied his 1904 article – ran through the city that became Stalingrad.) Nevertheless, the fact that the Wehrmacht had to fight for the 'heartland' while at the same time being blockaded by the maritime powers shows just what a challenge Hitler's Third Reich faced.

Neither Mahan nor Mackinder provided much guidance about Asia. Nevertheless the Japanese Army gained and kept control of the eastern end of what Mackinder called the 'inner or marginal crescent' – Manchuria, Korea, eastern China, Indochina, Malaya, and Burma. In August 1945 those possessions were subject to a Russian attack from the 'pivot area'. But in a sense they had already proved to be irrelevant. By the end of 1944 the Japanese island state was under close blockade, and its economy – even before the bombing – was collapsing. Among other causes, the land-transport revolution which Mackinder described had only just begun in mainland Asia; coastal shipping was still essential. In any event, in Asia as in Europe sea power proved to be a powerful and decisive factor.

Britannia rules the waves

Britain began World War II with a powerful Royal Navy. Thirteen 'capital ships' survived from World War I, ten battleships and three battle cruisers; some of them had been modernised in the 1930s. Two further battleships were completed in the late 1920s. Five new battleships of the 'King George V' class would enter service from early 1941 onwards. Five aircraft carriers dating from the 1920s served with the fleet, one new fleet carrier (*Ark Royal*) was available from 1938, and four more were under construction when the war began. The largest cruiser force in the world – some fifty vessels – protected Britain's Empire and shipping routes. The German surface forces were completely outnumbered. In 1939 Admiral Raeder had available two recently completed battle cruisers, *Scharnhorst* and *Gneisenau* (fast ships but under-gunned), and three 'pocket battleships' (large cruisers) designed in the Weimar period. None could stand and fight with any of the British capital ships.

Despite strategic ups and downs the Royal Navy kept control of the Atlantic. The Norwegian campaign crippled the small German surface fleet. The defeat of France was a great setback for Britain, but the French Navy could not be used by Germany. Some French ships were destroyed or neutralised by British action in 1940, and those that remained in Vichy hands were scuttled by their own crews two years later. The Italian entry into the war divided British strength, but the Royal Navy was still able to control both the eastern Atlantic and the Mediterranean; the Strait of Gibraltar bottled up the Italian surface fleet. The Japanese attack on Britain stretched the Navy in a new direction and soon cost two capital ships and a carrier – as well as British colonies in Southeast Asia. But it also brought America into the war. Within six months the position in the Pacific had stabilised with the Battle of Midway. The US Navy tied down the Japanese fleet, and only second-class Royal Navy forces were required to defend the Indian Ocean. Meanwhile new American heavy ships reinforced the North Atlantic in 1942–3.

The overwhelming naval superiority of the Royal Navy, and then of the Allied navies, made possible a blockade. The term 'economic warfare' was invented by the British in the 1930s, but this was a very traditional part of their strategy. The main target was German overseas trade. The land route across neutral Russia offered the Reich a partial substitute in 1939–41, but that 'leak' was sealed in June 1941. The Allies developed complex financial machinery to block exports to Germany 'at source' in countries not involved in the war: in particular, they tried to limit deliveries from adjacent neutral states – Portugal, Spain, Sweden, Switzerland, and Turkey. The British resisted humanitarian demands to provide food and other essential raw materials to the states that had been overrun by Germany. As Churchill ruthlessly put it in August 1940: 'Let Hitler bear his responsibilities to the full, and let the people of Europe who groan beneath his yoke aid in every way the coming of the day when that yoke will be broken.'[1]

Whether the blockade was a war-winner – on its own – is open to debate. Hitler's European conquests did give him a *Grossraum* that was largely self-sufficient. The ingenuity of German scientists and engineers provided synthetic replacements (notably oil and rubber). The Third Reich did not collapse through an economic crisis, it was defeated by the invasion of superior Allied ground and air forces. Arguably, however, the blockade impacted heavily on the conquered regions of Western Europe, which had been more dependent than Germany on overseas resources. This in turn prevented Berlin from exploiting them fully. Post-war historians of the blockade argued that in the *long term* the German war economy would have collapsed. And fear of Allied sea power was one factor that led Hitler to seek a 'blockade-proof' resource base in Russia, and to fight a disastrous campaign there.

There is less contention about another result of the British and American domination of the 'world ocean': the Allies could use it for their own purposes. Transport shipping was crucial to the war effort of the British, and eventually to that of the Allies as a whole. One feature of Britain's superpower status in 1939, aside from its financial role and a global empire (and – less obviously – advanced technology), was the commercial shipping fleet or 'merchant navy'. When war broke out in Europe in 1939 the world pool of shipping was 61.4 million tons. Britain possessed much the largest share of this, 16.9 million tons (27 per cent), and the British Dominions another 1.7 million tons. With an average of about 5,000 tons a ship this amounted to nearly 4,000 vessels. The United States did not depend to the same extent on overseas trade, and its merchant fleet was only half the size of Britain's, at 8.7 million tons. The French merchant fleet was only 2.7 million tons. The British benefited from the German conquests in Europe in 1940–1 to take over a major part of the big merchant fleets of Norway, Denmark, the Netherlands, and (later) Greece. British-controlled shipping had risen to 23 million tons in September 1940.

The German counter-blockade

Whatever the underlying importance of the Allied blockade, much more has been written about what was, in effect, a counter-blockade, mounted – mainly – by the Third Reich. Going back to Mahan, naval theorists contrast the war of the Nelsonian 'battle fleet' to the 'commerce war', the *guerre de course*. The commerce war had been favoured by the French in the seventeenth and eighteenth centuries, and Nazi Germany used its small fleet largely for this same purpose. This was not from any 'continental' lack of comprehension of sea power, as is sometime argued. Hitler and the German Navy C-in-C, Admiral Raeder, were battleship enthusiasts. The problem was that big ships could not be built quickly, and Germany's western enemies had a great head start. Hitler and his *Kriegsmarine*, realistically, had to settle for what is now called 'sea denial' rather than 'sea control'.

In the early part of World War II individual German surface ships were used for oceanic raiding in this commerce war. A small number of auxiliary

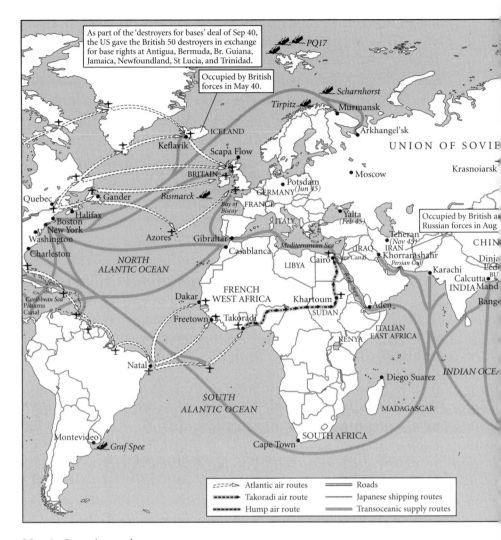

As part of the 'destroyers for bases' deal of Sep 40, the US gave the British 50 destroyers in exchange for base rights at Antigua, Bermuda, Br. Guiana, Jamaica, Newfoundland, St Lucia, and Trinidad.

Occupied by British forces in May 40.

Occupied by British and Russian forces in Aug

Map 9 Oceanic supply routes

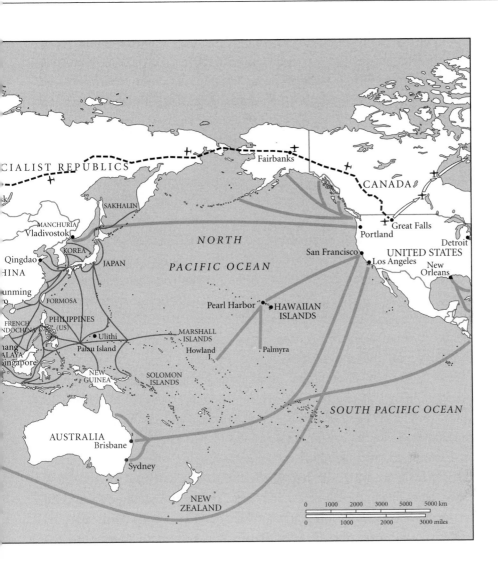

cruisers – merchant ships armed with hidden guns – attacked commerce in distant seas, until they were rounded up with the help of ULTRA intercepts. Unlike in World War I, German heavy warships also took part in oceanic raiding. Some were successful (the pocket battleships *Lützow* and *Admiral Scheer*), some were not (*Graf Spee* and *Bismarck*). The big ships originally had to operate from a confined base in the North Sea. Attempts to base battleships and cruisers in captured western French ports in 1940–1 proved very risky. The first full-sized German battleship, *Bismarck*, became operational in early 1941, but she was stopped and sunk by British carrier aircraft and battleships in May *en route* to France. She had broken out into the Atlantic via the Greenland–Iceland gap. *Scharnhorst* and *Gneisenau* had to effect a dangerous escape home from France in February 1942. Although this dash up the English Channel was a tactical humiliation for the British, *Gneisenau* was so badly damaged that she was never used again. From 1942 Hitler concentrated the surviving German heavy ships – notably *Bismarck*'s 1941 sister ship, *Tirpitz* – in the north of Norway to protect that country against invasion and to threaten supply routes to Russia.

Hitler's pre-war shipbuilding programme had included a large aircraft carrier, the *Graf Zeppelin*, but although launched (in December 1938), she was never completed. The German Navy was not air-minded, and the Luftwaffe command was loathe to commit resources to 'secondary' tasks. The use of land-based aircraft in the long-range anti-shipping role was half-hearted. The German Air Force was highly effective as a 'sea denial' force at short range, especially in the Black Sea, the Baltic, the central Mediterranean, and off northern Norway. By mid war it had even developed 'smart' anti-shipping weapons in the form of radio-controlled bombs and cruise missiles. But the Luftwaffe was stretched in many other directions, over the land fronts from 1941 and over the Reich itself from 1942 to 1945. Rushed preparation for war, and technical failure, meant that Hitler's airmen had few long-range patrol aircraft. German air cover effectively projected only a few hundred miles out into the Atlantic.

The U-boat threat

The most important German instrument for sea denial – as in World War I – was the U-boat (*Unterseeboot*) (see Figure 19). Germany's late start, this

Figure 19 | **Type IX U-boat**

This extraordinary photograph from an attacking US Navy Liberator patrol bomber depicts the Type IXD *U 848* under attack in the South Atlantic in November 1943. Commissioned in Bremen in February 1943, *U 848* was on her first combat mission, to join a 'wolfpack' (submarine group) in the Indian Ocean. The German Navy C-in-C, Admiral Dönitz, had removed his boats from the well-defended Atlantic routes, where they were suffering prohibitive losses. This did not save the *U 848*, which went down with her entire crew of 63 men.

The Type IX U-boats belonged to one of the two largest German submarine classes. They were intended for long-range oceanic operations; the Type IXD version displaced 1,600 tons on the surface and 1,800 tons submerged. The most common German submarines were the smaller Type VIIs, which displaced 770 tons on the surface and 870 tons submerged. Some 568 Type VIIs were commissioned, compared to fewer than 200 Type IXs.

A Type VIIC (*U 96*) is the subject of *Das Boot*, the 1979 novel by Lothar-Günther Buchheim and the 1981 film by Wolfgang Petersen. Another Type VIIC, *U 995*, survives at the *Marine-Ehrenmal* at Laboe, near Kiel. *U 505*, captured by the Americans in 1944 and now on display at the Museum of Science and Industry in Chicago, is a Type IXC. *U 2540*, a Type XXI, was raised from the bottom of the Baltic after the war and is preserved at the *Deutsches Schiffahrtsmuseum* in Bremerhaven.

time in submarine construction (in 1935), and the 'premature' war, meant
that the U-boat fleet was small when the fighting began. Admiral Raeder's
despairing note to himself in September 1939 has already been mentioned:
'The submarine arm is still much too weak, however, to have any decisive
effect on the war' (see Box 9 in Chapter 3). As late as the spring of 1941
the U-boat C-in-C, Admiral Karl Dönitz, had only seventy operational boats
at his disposal, of which a third could be on station in the Atlantic at any
one time (the other two-thirds were *en route* to and from their stations or
refitting in port).

According to the 1936 London Protocol, signed by a number of states,
including Britain, Germany, Japan, and the USA, submarines could not sink
merchant vessels 'without having first placed passengers, crew and ship's
papers in a place of safety'.[2] For diplomatic reasons Hitler originally ordered
the U-boat force to limit its attacks to military targets. When *U 30* torpedoed the British liner *Athenia* without warning off Scotland on the first day
of the war – with the loss of 128 lives, including 28 Americans – Germany
denied responsibility. However, once it became clear that the war would be
prolonged, the standing orders were changed and unrestricted submarine
warfare was allowed; in November 1939, U-boat commanders were ordered
not to take the risk of rescuing survivors.

The British, despite their great loss of shipping in World War I, had at
first assumed that the U-boats would not be a serious threat. The German
submarine force was small and bottled up in the North Sea. The convoy
system had eventually proved effective in reducing shipping losses in World
War I. Further advances had been made since 1918 in detecting submerged
U-boats through echo-ranging and sound detectors – what the British called
ASDIC and the Americans Sonar. The British also had some hopes that the
warring governments would observe the London Protocol. Several factors,
beyond the control of the British Admiralty, changed the situation. At the
strategic level, the success of the German Army and the Luftwaffe gave the
German Navy forward bases in Norway and on the French Atlantic coast.
At the tactical level, Dönitz ordered his boats to attack convoys at night on
the surface, greatly limiting the effect of ASDIC. At the operational level, U-
boat headquarters (in Lorient, France) increasingly co-ordinated the battle
by radio. This was the famous multi-submarine 'wolfpack' (the Germans
themselves used the more descriptive term *Rudeltaktik*, 'rake tactic'). In a

Box 33 | The loss of SS *Avoceta*

The British 3,400-ton cargo liner SS *Avoceta* was sunk north of the Azores by *U 203* late on 25 September 1941. She was carrying 87 passengers, including women and children; most died, along with many crew members. Rear Admiral Kenelm Creighton, who wrote this account, was the commodore of the convoy HG 73 from Gibraltar to Liverpool. Some 10 out of 25 ships in HG 73 were sunk.

A few minutes later... I was about to go to the upper bridge to see the master and officer-of-the-watch. A violent tremor went through *Avoceta*. She staggered like a stumbling horse and shuddered to a lurching stop as a violent explosion came from the direction of the engine-room aft. My years were buzzing from the crash of the exploding torpedo – I had no doubt but that that was what it was. My left arm was numb from being thrown against the side of the bridge ladder. The vicious scream of escaping steam smothered some of the unearthly gargling sounds coming from the drowning and tearing squeals of those trapped in the scalding agony of the engine-room. All these sounds darted into my ears during the two or three seconds before I picked myself up and stumbled across with Signalman Erskine to fire the distress rockets as an indication that we had been hit. As they whizzed up I glanced after and saw the stern was already under water and the dreadful noises were ceasing from that part of the ship. The escape of steam was easing now as *Avoceta* sat back on her haunches and the bows rose to an ever more crazy angle into the air. No boats could be lowered. There was complete pandemonium; the thunderous bangs and crashes of furniture and cargo being hurled about below decks all mingled with the ghastly shrieks of the sleeping people waking to their deaths. As the bows went higher so did the shrieks. I clung to a stanchion feeling sick and helpless as I had to look on while the children were swept out into the darkness below by the torrent of water which roared through the smoking-room.

(From Kenelm Creighton, *Convoy Commodore* (London: William Kimber, 1956), pp. 144f.)

spectacular operation by five boats against Atlantic convoys SC 10 and HX 79 in October 1940 the Germans sank 32 ships. This period, when British escorts were few and inexperienced, was recalled in the U-boat service as the 'happy time' (*die glückliche Zeit*).

By the autumn of 1940, engaged in a prolonged war fought alone and at arm's length with the Germans and Italians, the British realised that the submarine menace was the most immediate threat to their survival. Although the Germans still had only a small number of boats, it was known that they had a large building programme. The U-boats were sinking several hundred thousand tons of shipping (30–50 ships) each month. 'It is, therefore,' Winston Churchill wrote, 'in shipping and in the power to transport across the ocean, particularly the Atlantic Ocean, that in 1941 the crunch of the whole war will be found.'[3]

The Atlantic war had an important impact on the neutral United States. An earlier U-boat campaign had precipitated American entry into the 'European war' in 1917. President Roosevelt had set up a 'neutrality patrol' in September 1939, and with South and Central American neighbours declared a security zone extending 300 miles off the coast of the Americas. When Churchill increased requests for American support at the end of 1940 he stressed the threat to British shipping. Roosevelt had already, in September 1940, agreed to provide 50 'mothballed' World War I destroyers in exchange for long leases to bases in British colonies in the Western hemisphere. US active naval forces in the Atlantic were built up, and Roosevelt extended the security zone to the line 26° W (east of Greenland) which took in the greater part of the North Atlantic. In July 1941 this zone was extended to the waters around Iceland, which was occupied by US troops (replacing a British garrison).

In the summer of 1941 American warships began to escort British convoys in the western Atlantic, and they were soon confronting U-boats. Many historians have seen this as Roosevelt's attempt to provoke Hitler into war. On 4 September 1941 USS *Greer* engaged *U 652* west of Iceland, and two torpedoes were fired at her. In a subsequent radio address the President described the event as an act of 'piracy legally and morally' and condemned the 'rattlesnakes of the Atlantic'. 'It is the Nazi design', he declared, 'to abolish the freedom of the seas, and to acquire absolute control and domination of these seas for themselves.' American vessels were given authority to 'shoot on sight' at German ships and submarines in the security zone.[4] For better or worse *Greer* had apparently been stalking the U-boat in co-operation with a British aircraft, and after the initial torpedo attack she had dropped depth charges. In October another US destroyer was damaged by a German torpedo, and at the end of the month – and five weeks before Pearl Harbor – the destroyer USS *Reuben James* was sunk by *U 562* with the loss of 100 men while escorting a convoy. This undeclared naval war was a factor that Germany cited in the declaration of war on 11 December: 'Vessels of the American Navy, since early September 1941, have systematically attacked German naval forces.'[5]

Box 34 | The Battle of the Atlantic

These two tables give the essential statistics about German and Allied forces between 1939 and 1945.

A German U-boats: status and losses

	1939	1940/1	1940/2	1941/1	1941/2	1942/1
Trials/training	8	24	23	67	93	158
Operational	49	32	28	22	65	91
Total U-boats	57	56	51	89	158	249
Losses	9	14	8	12	23	21

	1942/2	1943/1	1943/2	1944/1	1944/2	1945
Trials/training	191	181	208	268	246	281
Operational	140	212	207	168	188	144
Total U-boats	331	393	415	436	434	425
Losses	66	113	124	128	111	151

Note: 1940/1 is the first half of 1940, 1940/2 is the second half. etc. Figures are for the start of the half-year period; note that newly commissioned boats had to go through a trials and training period before they were ready for operations. The 1945 losses figure includes many U-boats destroyed in port by bombing.

B British, Allied, and neutral merchant shipping: losses and construction (1,000s of gross tons)

Losses and construction (below) have to be seen in comparison with the original size of the British merchant fleet. In September 1939 there were 18.71 million tons of shipping sailing under the British flag (counting just dry cargo ships over 1,600 gross tons). Britain also gained much tonnage from German-conquered states, e.g. Norway, the Netherlands, and Greece. In September 1940 the British flag total had reached 23.5 million gross tons. The US merchant fleet was considerably smaller at the start of the war, with about 10 million tons.

Monthly North Atlantic losses

	Jan	Feb	Mar	Apr	May	Jun	Jul	Aug	Sep	Oct	Nov	Dec
1939	–	–	–	–	–	–	–	–	195	196	174	191
1940	215	227	107	158	286	505	365	353	404	418	294	323
1941	310	369	517	381	437	415	113	103	254	196	85	114
1942	296	441	562	494	645	652	533	543	533	560	573	315
1943	205	315	539	253	206	30	188	26	55	61	41	54
1944	43	17	42	48	17	83	49	61	38	2	17	91
1945	76	88	111	82	10	–	–	–	–	–	–	–

	Total losses N. Atlantic	Global	Construction Total	UK + CW	USA
1939	756	756	1,042	666	376
1940	3,655	4,180	1,391	862	529
1941	3,294	4,332	2,309	1,277	1,032
1942	6,147	7,789	7,471	1,991	5,480
1943	1,973	3,390	13,588	2,140	11,448
1944	508	1,046	10,900	1,612	9,288
1945	367	437	6,376	536	5,840

Note: This includes losses from all causes; U-boats accounted for about 70 per cent. A typical merchant ship was 4,000–6,000 tons; for example, the peak figure of 652,000 tons lost in June 1942 took in 131 vessels. Under 'Construction' the column 'UK + CW' stands for United Kingdom and Commonwealth. (From S. W. Roskill, *The War at Sea, 1939–1945*, 4 vols. (London: HMSO, 1954–61).)

The eighteen months after Pearl Harbor saw continuing German success. What the U-boat crews called the second 'happy time' came in the spring of 1942 when Admiral Dönitz mounted an offensive off the American coast. German success owed much to American mistakes, inexperience, and complacency. The U-boat fleet continued to grow – from 22 operational boats in January 1941 to 91 in January 1942, and 212 in January 1943. Allied shipping losses in the Atlantic from March 1942 onwards were running at 500,000 tons a month – over 100 individual merchant ships. Especially at risk was the North Atlantic. This was a region through which Allied convoys had to pass *en route* to Britain but which was still beyond the range of Allied patrol aircraft – the so-called 'air gap'. At the Casablanca Conference in January 1943 the Allied leaders resolved that the defeat of the U-boat threat was to be the most important single strategic objective of the Allies.

Defeating the U-boats

Submarines – of all navies – in the World War II era had a number of inherent weaknesses which made them vulnerable to anti-submarine warfare (ASW). They were 'submersibles' rather than true 'submarines'. When running submerged on battery-powered electric motors they were slower than many merchant ships. Until the very end of the war they had to spend part of their time on the surface, either to recharge their batteries (while running on their big diesel engines) or to manoeuvre into an attack position. In order to co-ordinate their attacks the submarines needed to use their radios to send and receive orders, and this was especially true of the German 'wolfpacks'.

The U-boat danger was finally contained by the Allies in the spring of 1943, and this development, crucial for the outcome of the war as a whole, had a number of causes. The British decryption of German naval signals (so-called ULTRA intelligence) was certainly a factor, both in breaking the back of the U-boat campaign in 1943, and in limiting its damage in earlier years (see Box 35). As important, however, were other Allied advances in electronic warfare, notably radar and radio direction-finding (DF) (see Box 36). The Allies also supplemented World War I depth charges with more effective weapons, such as the British-designed HEDGEHOG (which

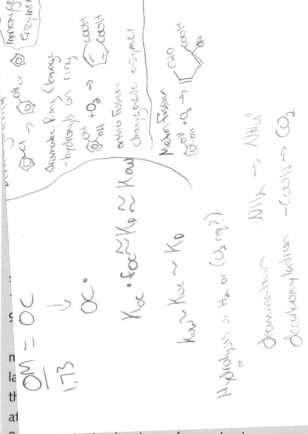

..rs, the war at sea is the most ..ably had its greatest impor-.. the codename used by the ..nciphered enemy radio mes-.. of secrecy) was used by the ..terial which the Wehrmacht ..he war both the Americans ..material from any high-level .. analysis was located from ..was a large enterprise; some ..ar.

..emy had to transmit many ..ss to messages carried over ..nan Navy signals than with ..e to decrypt messages only ..speed up the process. The British also took advantage of procedural errors made by German signals personnel and material captured on German vessels; the taking intact of *U 110* in May 1941 was an important development.

The sudden drop in British merchant ship losses in July 1941 (down from 415,000 tons to 113,000 tons) – despite a growing number of available U-boats – was partly due to the success of ULTRA. Changes in German communications procedures could, however, suddenly cut off ULTRA intelligence, as happened from February to December 1942, and briefly in March 1943. The renewed decryption of U-boat signals at the end of March 1943 was of great importance, although only in connection with other factors such as improved radar and a larger number of escorting ships and aircraft. Signals intelligence (SIGINT) played a vital part in Allied offensive operation in the Pacific, latterly also under the codename ULTRA. The Americans, in particular, were able to decrypt many Japanese merchant ship convoy messages.

ULTRA (or at least the British side of it) was one of the last secrets of World War II and was not revealed for nearly thirty years. The French intelligence officer Gustave Bertrand published a book about it in 1973, and this was followed by an account written by one of the British participants, [RAF] Group Captain F. W. Winterbotham, *The Ultra Secret* (1974). There followed a great outpouring of information, notably the multi-volume *British Intelligence in the Second World War* (1979–90), edited by the Cambridge University historian F. H. Hinsley (himself a Bletchley veteran).

Box 36 | Technology and the Allied victory at sea

In the war at sea the balance of advantage changed over time. The most striking developments were in the field of sensors and communications. (ULTRA decryption is discussed in Box 35.)

Radar had been developed in the 1930s. Although anti-submarine radar was carried by ships and aircraft from 1940, a crucial refinement in the war at sea was the development of centimetric radar, which could more accurately detect submarines on the surface, or even just a periscope. The original CHAIN-HOME radar stations, which were so important in detecting large German bomber formations during the Battle of Britain, operated at a wavelength of 12 metres; the first 'microwave' radar operated at 10 centimetres. The key component in centimetric radar was an electronic valve called the cavity magnetron, which was developed in Britain in the summer of 1940. The 10-cm Type 271 radar was mounted on escort ships in 1941–2. Centimetric radar was installed in patrol aircraft, together with powerful searchlights, and this proved a lethal weapon system against U-boats from early 1943 onwards. As centimetric radar was also vital to strategic night bombing, there was competition with Bomber Command to obtain this scarce equipment; the best-known RAF bombing system, available from 1943, was H2S.

A second major Allied electronic weapon in the Battle of the Atlantic was radio direction-finding (DF). This allowed the location of enemy submarines from their high-frequency (HF) radio transmissions. The technique was known as HF/DF or 'Huff-duff'. Co-ordinated attacks by U-boats required radio communications (for example, reporting sighting of a convoy). Co-ordinated Allied interception stations ashore could, by triangulation, tell the approximate position of the transmitting submarine. Even if these messages could not be decrypted, direction-finding indicated where the enemy submarines were operating. It enabled the naval command to detour convoys around the threat and guide escort groups to an attack. In 1942 HF/DF began to be mounted on ships; operating closer to the target, it allowed more accurate triangulation.

allowed a pattern of explosive charges to be laid down ahead of the attacking escort ship and which allowed more effective use of ASDIC).

Victory would also not have been won without the deployment of large numbers of ships and aircraft. The force of escort ships was limited at the start of the war – the scale of the German submarine danger being, as we have seen, unexpected. British, Canadian and finally American shipyards built a very large number of dedicated escort ships which grew in size and potency as the war progressed. In the initial emergency the British improvised with a pre-war whalecatcher design which they called a 'corvette'. In 1940–2, some 137 served under the British, and 79 with the Royal Canadian Navy. The corvettes were succeeded by larger, faster, and more effective 'frigates' and 'sloops'. A great number of 'destroyer escorts' or DEs (about 450) were built in US shipyards and put in service from the spring of 1943; over 100 were supplied to the Royal Navy under Lend-Lease.

As the war progressed, the British, and then the Canadians and Americans, were able to move more and more aircraft over the Atlantic: long-range flying boats and bombers, and then shorter-range planes carried on improvised 'escort' aircraft carriers (CVEs). By mid 1943 long-range bombers had closed the North Atlantic gap, although there had been a considerable administrative battle with those who wanted to reserve these aircraft for strategic bombing. The CVEs, the so-called 'Woolworth carriers', were built on large merchant-ship hulls and carried 15–20 aircraft. The Royal Navy operated its first escort carrier (*Audacity*) in late 1940; by the end of 1943 Britain had no fewer than 40 in service, mostly supplied under US Lend-Lease. The US Navy received about 65 CVEs in 1942–4, many deployed in US Navy 'hunter-killer' groups in the Atlantic.

This huge force of convoys, escorts, and aircraft was effectively integrated. Like the U-boats they adopted new tactics and weapons. ASW forces on both side of the Atlantic were put through effective training. The Royal Navy and the RAF coastal command in the Atlantic were co-ordinated by Western Approaches command, set up in April 1941 and eventually based in Liverpool under Admiral Max Horton.

To the considerable surprise of the Allied leaders, the Germans had largely lost the Battle of the Atlantic by the summer of 1943. British, Canadian, and American ASW had become so lethal in the mid Atlantic that Admiral Dönitz was forced to withdraw his U-boats to less well-protected ocean areas like the

South Atlantic and the Indian Ocean. The Germans now spoke not of 'happy days' but of 'Black May', when 41 U-boats were lost. Losses of merchant ships in the Atlantic fell from 539,000 tons in March 1943 to 253,000 tons in April, and from the later summer of 1943 monthly losses were seldom more than 50,000 tons – 10–12 ships – a month. The Allied liberation of most of France the following year was a further blow. Although the Wehrmacht held on to some French ports as pockets of resistance until near the end of the war, they were of little use as submarine bases.

In the first four years U-boats sank 2 British battleships (one inside the Scapa Flow base), 3 fleet carriers, and 5 cruisers. Nevertheless, compared to their early devastation of merchant shipping the German submarines were relatively ineffective against fast and well-escorted warships. More remarkably, the U-boats could do little to stop British and American amphibious operations, from Operation TORCH (the invasion of North Africa) onwards. The Allied invasion fleets were normally able to achieve operational surprise, and they were well escorted. The U-boat force in the Mediterranean was small, and it could not interfere effectively with landings in Algeria, Sicily, Italy, and the south of France. By the time of the big European invasion operations of 1943–4 the balance of technology and equipment mass had clearly turned in favour of the Allies. Even though on paper the Germans still possessed nearly 200 operational U-boats in mid 1944, there was very little the submarines could do to interfere with the Normandy landings; Allied ASW forces were able to seal off either end of the English Channel.

Hitler had hopes for a second round of the submarine war. The U-boats were fitted with the *Schnorkel*, in effect a complex ventilation tube which allowed them to recharge their batteries while running just under the surface; the exposed head of the *Schnorkel* was nearly invisible to radar. Dönitz, meanwhile, had been able to convince the Führer of the need for investment in a new generation of U-boats, the Type XXI and the coastal Type XXIII U-boats. These boats had a streamlined hull and extra batteries, giving them a longer underwater range and a higher underwater speed that allowed them to outpace the Allied escorts. The plan was to prefabricate these boats in very large numbers. As with aircraft production, plans were not matched by operational capability. In the end the submarine programme was even more pointless than the V2 missile or the Me 262 jet fighter, both of which at least saw some operational service. Some 118 Type XXI boats were commissioned, but only one actually put to sea from Norway in April 1945, and it did not sink anything.

The U-boats were a major part of the war effort of the Third Reich, certainly its main weapon on the world's oceans. Altogether, the *Kriegsmarine* commissioned 1,170 submarines, of which 630 were lost in action and 81 were sunk in harbour. Some 30,000 German crew members were lost at sea. Hitler's U-boat force was overwhelmed by superior technology and by vastly superior industrial capacity, as well as by remarkable achievements in communications intelligence.

The failure of Japan's commerce war

Oceanic communications were also of great importance in the war in Asia and the Pacific. There was one striking contrast between the Japanese war effort, and that of the Germans: the Imperial Navy made only a feeble attempt to block Allied shipping routes. On the map the Allied position in 1942 looked precarious enough. From San Francisco supply ships had to travel 2,100 miles to Hawaii, and 7,200 miles to Brisbane in eastern Australia. British ships had to cross the Indian Ocean, some 5,400 miles from Cape Town to Fremantle on the Australian west coast. But the Japanese did not mount a maritime blockade of Australia and New Zealand, or seriously threaten America's Pacific shipping.

The major Japanese attack on Allied supply lines was made in the Indian Ocean. Some submarines of the Imperial Navy operated as far as the East African coast, from a base 3,900 miles away at Penang in Malaya. Between January 1942 and November 1944 Japanese boats sank a total 500,000 tons of Allied shipping in the Indian Ocean (roughly what the Germans sank in the Atlantic in each month of 1942). In 1943 and 1944 the average sinkings were only 10,000 tons (one or two ships) a month – some attacks accompanied by the massacre of survivors in lifeboats. The small German U-boat force that began to operate in the Indian Ocean from Penang in 1943 sank many more ships. In the Pacific Ocean (excluding the Netherlands Indies campaign) the Japanese submarines sank only 280,000 tons of shipping up to February 1945, an average of only one merchant ship a month. In the eastern Pacific from January 1942 until February 1945 they sank a grand total of seven merchant ships, only two of which were off the American west coast. From 1943 the US Navy ceased convoying merchant shipping in Pacific rear areas.

Counter-factually, an energetic and well-supported submarine campaign by the world's third-ranking naval power might have slowed the American counter-attack and forced the creation of an extensive ASW system in the eastern Pacific. The Germans did urge their allies to attack merchant shipping. Various factors explain the extraordinary neglect by Tokyo of the 'commerce war'. One was naval doctrine. Attacks on enemy shipping (and defence of Japanese shipping) were regarded by the Imperial Navy as secondary tasks. The Japanese admirals were imbued with the sea-power concepts of Mahan, who stressed the battle fleet and the decisive battle. This coincided with Japanese military tradition. The Japanese submarine force had been designed from the 1920s to fight alongside the battleships of the Combined Fleet, supporting them as they engaged the American fleet advancing across the Pacific.

Even in this fleet-support role, the Japanese submarine force had only limited success. No fewer than 25 submarines were concentrated around the Hawaiian islands at the time of the December 1941 air attack, ready to ambush the US Pacific Fleet when it left port. They had virtually no effect. The Japanese boats had only one success at the turning-point defeat at Midway (*I-168* finished off the crippled carrier *Yorktown*); US code-breaking had allowed the American fleet to move into position before the Japanese submarine ambush line was ready. Fast warships were inherently difficult to attack, and ASW markedly improved. American ships and aircraft used the counter-measures developed in the Battle of the Atlantic. The US Navy also made effective use of ULTRA intercepts. The Japanese lost 18 submarines in 1941–2, 25 in 1943, and 50 in 1944. Japanese submarines could not influence the great naval battles of 1943–4, or block the island invasions. Some 16 submarines (half the surviving operational boats) were deployed in the 1944 defence of the Philippines; against the largest fleet of warships and transports ever assembled they sank only one American destroyer escort.

Technical factors on the Japanese side also limited the effectiveness of their submarines, both against warships and against merchant ships. Designed for the decisive-battle support role, most Japanese submarines were very large and clumsy. The last pre-war class were 2,600 tons (surface displacement) in size, compared to 740 tons for a Type VII U-boat or 1,500 tons for an American wartime 'fleet' boat. This meant fewer Japanese boats, and more vulnerable ones. The tiny scout planes some of them carried were useless, although one did drop incendiary bombs on Oregon forests in late 1942.

The submarines had good torpedoes – and towards the end of the war they embarked manned (suicide) torpedoes, the *kaiten*. But they lacked surface-search and air-search radars.

Another important factor limiting effectiveness was the paradox of Japanese strategy. From late 1942 onwards many submarines were tied down bringing supplies to isolated Navy and Army island garrisons. Thanks to the over-ambitious Japanese onslaught in 1941–2 and the quick recovery of American air and sea power, these garrisons could no longer be supplied by surface ships. Latterly the Japanese Navy – and even the Japanese Army – developed purpose-built transport submarines.

The ultimate reason for the failure to attack US shipping was – it should not be forgotten – industrial weakness (see Chapter 7). The Japanese began the war against America and Britain with only 48 large 'cruiser' (*I*) type submarines, and 15 medium-sized (*Ro*) boats, at a time when Germany had about 90 operational U-boats (and many more under construction). With only a modest wartime building programme the Imperial Navy never went much beyond the pre-war total. The balance of new construction and losses kept Japanese strength at only 60–70 boats in 1942 and 1943; in 1944 the net loss was over 20.

America's U-boat war in the Pacific

Unlike the situation in Europe, it was Axis rather than Allied shipping routes that came under attack in the Far East. Japan after the winter of 1941–2 occupied much of East Asia and had control over more economic resources than it could use. Even less than Germany could it really be described as 'blockaded'. It is worth recalling, however, that the Americans had tried hard to use the economic weapon against the Japanese in the months *before* Pearl Harbor, notably with the embargo on oil and other commodities. Japan's war effort, like that of Germany, was in part concerned with making Japan 'blockade-proof'.

The economy of the home islands and the pre-war empire (Korea, Manchuria, northern China, Formosa) was heavily dependent on sea-going and coastal shipping. Exploitation of the resources captured by Japan in 1941–2 required the establishment and defence of new maritime trade routes. By the winter of 1944–5, six months before heavy bombing of Japanese industry began, the economy was in grave trouble, and this was largely due to the interruption of Japanese shipping. Lack of available merchant ships and loss of imports had so dislocated the economy that output of raw materials peaked in 1943 and output of finished products peaked in 1944. Military operations were affected by the lack of aviation petrol and of fuel oil for warships. The economy was further hit by declining movements of coal, iron ore, and other raw materials. Even food imports were becoming a serious problem.

There was a paradox here: Japan's problems began with her successful conquests. In September 1939 the Japanese had had a modern merchant fleet of 5.4 million tons, the third biggest in the world, and nearly 9 per cent of the world total. Japan's pan-Asian conquest of December 1941 required the mobilisation of a large part of the civilian shipping pool. The Army and Navy together took about half of the available tonnage. Heavy shipping losses were suffered in the South Pacific from the autumn of 1942, and more cargo vessels were pressed into service as the Japanese Army rushed to reinforce its island garrisons. (The British had had similar problems with the dispersal of merchant shipping to support the war in the Middle East in 1940–2, and later – alongside the Americans – to support amphibious operations in several theatres. The Allies, however, began with a much larger pool of ships, and the United States had much greater shipbuilding capacity.) The strategic defeats in the great battles of the Pacific war in 1944 completed Japan's shipping disaster. The resource base in the south – Malaya and the Netherlands Indies – was never invaded, but the capture of Luzon in the Philippines in late 1944 completely blocked the south–north shipping artery.

The Japanese shipping problem, then, came originally – in 1941–2 – from wastage and mismanagement. Ultimately, in 1944–5, US invasions strangled the main north–south shipping routes. In between, however, it was the American submarine force that played the vital role. Up until the middle of 1944 these boats were the only means of directly interdicting the flow of resources from the southern resource area back to Japan, and in the end they accounted for about 60 per cent of Japanese shipping losses, nearly 4.8 million tons. They eventually played a role very like that of the U-boats in the Atlantic, but they had greater success. The US Navy started the war in December 1941 with 111 submarines, about half in the Pacific; a further 73 were under construction. They still had fewer than 100 boats until the beginning of 1943. As in other areas of the war the great increase in

American strength came in 1943–4; by the end of the war the Pacific force had reached 169 boats. The main wartime submarine design, the 1,500-ton 'Gato' class, was roughly comparable in size to the German Type IX U-boat. The American boats were well designed, and from 1942 equipped with effective surface-search and air-search radar.

Many months would pass, however, before the boats of the US Navy began to have serious effect. Overall the Japanese achieved more with their submarine force in 1942 than the Americans did, sinking two fleet carriers and a cruiser. The large American force assembled in the Philippines in 1941 – no fewer than 28 boats – achieved very little. The submarine base at Pearl Harbor was 3,000 to 3,500 miles from Japan and its nearby trade routes, and Fremantle and Brisbane in Australia were also distant from the main shipping lanes. Success was also blunted by one of the worst American technical failures of the war. The Mk 14 torpedo had multiple faults, which were not discovered for a long time; they were not fully corrected until the autumn of 1943. Until then submarine torpedoes frequently hit Japanese ships and failed to explode.

In late 1943 and 1944, however, the impact of the submarine campaign on Japanese shipping became much greater. (Here there is a chronological parallel with the American air campaign against Germany.) Monthly Japanese shipping losses (mostly from submarines) doubled, from about 100,000 tons a month in June 1943 to twice that in most months of 1944 (see Box 37). The Americans made increasing use of ULTRA intelligence to pinpoint Japanese convoys and even individual ships, and they began to use 'wolfpack' tactics. From the beginning of the war the United States Navy practised unrestricted submarine warfare – in violation of the London Protocol. (This point would be successfully used by Admiral Dönitz in his defence at the Nuremberg trial.)

The growing number of American boats made it possible for the force to have a dual role, attacking the Japanese battle fleet as well as merchant ships. During the war as a whole American submarines sank a Japanese battleship, 8 carriers, and 11 cruisers. Their role in the decisive 1944 Battle of the Philippine Sea was especially important. In turn, the American advance provided forward operating bases (latterly in Guam and the Philippines) for boats attacking Japanese trade in home waters, even in the Sea of Japan. The Americans achieved this at relatively low cost; they lost only 33 boats to Japanese action, compared to 630 German U-boats sunk by the Allies.

Box 37 | Japanese merchant shipping

The table below gives monthly figures for Japanese merchant shipping lost in combat from all causes, i.e. surface ships and aircraft as well as submarines. The table also shows annual construction. A typical Japanese merchant ship, at 3,000–5,000 tons, was somewhat smaller than a typical Allied ship in the Atlantic.

Losses and construction need to be seen in comparison with the original size of the Japanese merchant fleet. In December 1941 Japan had a merchant fleet of 6.4 million tons. Total shipping losses were 4.8 million tons. For the war as a whole Allied submarines accounted for 60 per cent of this, although in 1943 the proportion was 80 per cent and in 1945 only 24 per cent. The peak losses of 503,000 tons in February 1944, and 504,000 tons in October 1944, coincided with air attacks on the Japanese base at Truk (February) and the great battle in the Philippines (October).

To be fair, the Japanese did put a major effort into merchant ship construction. Production in the record year of 1944 was comparable to that of the British Empire, but only about 15 per cent of the Allied total. In sharp contrast to the Allies in the Atlantic the Japanese shipyards were not able to meet wartime merchant ship replacement demands, after commitment to combat theatres and losses.

Combat losses (all causes) (1,000 gross tons)

	Jan	Feb	Mar	Apr	May	Jun	Jul	Aug	Sep	Oct	Nov	Dec	Losses Total	Built Total	
1941	–	–	–	–	–	–	–	–	–	–	–	49	49	238	1941
1942	57	40	83	23	97	29	53	84	53	151	145	69	885	361	1942
1943	131	84	123	128	130	100	78	95	171	137	286	204	1,666	1,111	1943
1944	314	503	238	122	244	276	238	273	398	504	405	178	3,694	1,600	1944
1945	431	91	173	110	250	220	290	156	–	–	–	–	1,722	180	1945

(From Mark P. Parillo, *The Japanese Merchant Marine in World War II* (Annapolis, MD: Naval Institute Press, 1993), pp. 240, 243f.)

The Japanese ASW effort was much inferior to that of the Allies in the Atlantic. The Imperial Navy's failure to successfully defend its own trade routes was related to its failure to attack Allied merchant shipping: trade protection had a low priority. The British, in contrast, had had the experience of 1914–18, and attention to the submarine problem was focused early by the U-boat successes in 1940. In general the Japanese did not expect an effective submarine campaign against their shipping, and the mediocre American performance in 1942 and early 1943 did not give them great cause for alarm. In 1942 there were only two months when Japanese merchant ship losses from American submarines were over 50,000 tons.

Japanese ASW effort did not have the advantage of a major intelligence breakthrough like ULTRA. Although the Imperial Navy eventually developed radar, its performance was greatly inferior to that of Allied equipment and it was not available on anything like the same scale. More remarkably, the Japanese did not undertake an escort construction programme on the lines of the British effort in 1940–2. The first wartime ocean-going escorts (comparable to the 1940 British corvettes) entered service only in March 1943, and the first escort destroyer only in April 1944. Japanese shipyards produced about 200 smaller escorts by the end of 1944, and only a dozen escort destroyers. They had few maritime patrol aircraft, and only five escort carriers, four of which were sunk by US submarines. It was only in November 1943 that a Grand Escort Headquarters (separate from the Combined Fleet) – comparable to the British Western Approaches command – was established under a senior admiral. Control of shipping was disputed between Army, Navy, and civilian authorities until May 1945.

One final feature of the American blockade of the Japanese home islands was the aerial mining campaign that began in earnest in 1945. This was like the Luftwaffe's attacks against Britain in 1939–40, but on a much larger scale. American B-29s from the Marianas, each carrying 8–9 mines, dropped some 12,000 of the deadly weapons in Japanese waters. They accounted for a high proportion of the Japanese shipping losses in the last months of the war.

Allied global logistics: survival

The defeat of the U-boats was more important than the failure of the Japanese submarine force. The U-boats were a much more difficult challenge in terms of numbers and technology, and had they severed the Atlantic route the consequences would have been much graver. But, for the Allies to take advantage of sea control, what was required was not only the defeat of ocean predators but also a huge effort of shipbuilding and port construction. An essential contribution was made by American industry, which was already expanding rapidly in December 1941 due to British orders. The Americans were able to more than match shipping losses with new construction. Especially important were the 'emergency' Liberty ships, designed to a British specification and built by American and Canadian yards in huge numbers using mass production methods (see Figure 20). The first 'Liberty' ship was launched by President Roosevelt himself in September 1941. Later in the war, production was supplemented by the less basic 'Victory' ship. British shipbuilding, although considerable, could not keep pace, and by the middle of the war the British merchant navy depended on transfers from the USA.

While general-purpose 'Liberty' and 'Victory' ships provided the basic mass tonnage required, the shipbuilding effort was much more complex. There were times when faster vessels were required (the Libertys could only steam at 11 knots). Tankers were essential to transfer oil. Large and fast passenger liners, of pre-war construction, were most suitable for moving troops efficiently and safely, although many wartime troopships were constructed. Assault ships (mother vessels for small landing craft) were a special category that had to be entirely created during the war; these went from a few British prototypes in 1940–1 to fleets of converted and purpose-built vessels in 1943–5. Ocean-going landing ships, especially the LST (Landing Ship Tank), were built in large quantities. The famous 'fleet train', which allowed the US Navy to operate freely in the western Pacific, was made up of converted merchant ships. The convoys and invasion fleets required hundreds of escorts. On top of this the shipyards had to produce (and repair) the major warships that were required to ensure naval supremacy over the Axis. All these projects competed for shipyard space, steel, and labour.

Less obvious was the need to build new port facilities and infrastructure. The ports on the west coast of Great Britain had to be expanded to make up for the closure to oceanic shipping of London and other British ports that were threatened by the Luftwaffe. Port facilities and rail and road systems had to be constructed in parts of the world that did not figure in the pre-war trade routes. Two striking global examples are the elaborate transhipment facilities that had to be built in Iran to facilitate Lend-Lease shipment to the USSR, and the artificial harbours (MULBERRY ports) built in Normandy in 1944. Harbour facilities in the Pacific had to be constructed virtually from scratch.

Figure 20 | Liberty ship

The backbone of the British-American global war effort was merchant shipping, and the most important type was the Liberty ship. The official type designation was EC-2, with 'EC' standing for Emergency Cargo. They were simple ships, built to a British design, displacing about 7,200 tons, coal-fired, single shaft, and capable of only 11 knots. In the end (up to September 1945) some 2,751 of these vessels were built. Their total of 19 million gross tons has to be compared with the total pre-war US Merchant Marine of about 10 million tons. Welding, prefabrication, and 'Fordist' production-line methods made it possible to proceed from laying down to launch in as few as 40 days. Some 19 shipyards, all along both the North American coasts, were involved. The vessels were not expected to serve more than five years, and indeed some of them suffered structural failures. Later in the war, Liberty ships were superseded by faster and better-built Victory ships.

The Liberty ship SS *Carlos Carrillo,* launched in Los Angeles in January 1943, was scrapped in 1963; she is depicted above in rather shabby condition at the end of the war. Several other Liberty ships are preserved as museum ships, notably the sea-going SS *Jeremiah O'Brien* in San Francisco.

Control of the world's sea lanes played a crucial part in the Allied victory. First of all, sea power in the Atlantic protected the British Isles from invasion and kept the country from starvation. Isolating Britain was probably the only way the Germans could have won the European war, other than a political or military collapse in the USSR. The United States could not have intervened against Germany without its British 'base'. The tragic alternative would have been 'hemispheric defence', defence of the Americas. Britain required annually about 25 million tons of imports, including grain, iron ore, and timber. Despite German hopes – and some British fears – the U-boats did not come close to starving out Britain. This was thanks to the (initially) small U-boat force, the British ASW effort, the huge shipping pool, assistance from the Empire and (from 1940 onwards) from America, and Britain's remarkable (and unexpected) ability to reduce required imports of food and raw materials. Some 20 per cent of British munitions came by sea from America and Canada in 1942, and 35 per cent by 1944.

The oceanic supply chain was important for even the most 'continental' of struggles, in Soviet Russia. Allied convoys sailed through the Atlantic and the Barents Sea to Murmansk and Arkhangel'sk, around Africa to Khorramshahr in the Persian Gulf, and across the North Pacific to Vladivostok. Capture of Arkhangel'sk and Astrakhan – Hitler's original BARBAROSSA concept – would have largely cut the USSR off from the outside world and probably fatally weakened it. The ability of the Red Army to mount a rapid counter-attack in 1943–4 was the result of the arrival of military and economic aid (see Chapter 6).

The Germans had some of their most spectacular anti-shipping successes against the Arctic supply routes to Murmansk and Arkhangel'sk in North Russia. The summer hours of daylight in the high north were long, and the convoy route was closer to German bases than Allied ones. Combined attacks by Luftwaffe bombers, U-boats, and the surviving German surface ships could be devastating to the monthly convoys. The greatest success was against convoy PQ 17 in July 1942, when 24 of 35 merchant ships were sunk. The British, who bore the main weight of organising and escort-ing the northern convoys, responded by cancelling sailings except in the months of winter darkness. The Allies also gave first priority to escorting the TORCH invasion of North Africa (in November 1942). Many of the

American and British aid promises could not be kept, and Stalin complained bitterly.

Fortunately the threat was gradually reduced and the number of available merchant ships and escorts rose. Following a long pause which began in March 1943, the northern convoys resumed again in November. They ran for the rest of the war except for a break in high summer of 1944 at the time of the Normandy landings. The British immobilised the battleship *Tirpitz* in September 1943 and sank *Scharnhorst* in December. Meanwhile the promised amount of Lend-Lease aid to Russia was delivered by other routes. Longer but much more secure links were established through the Persian Gulf and, more surprisingly, through Vladivostok in Siberia. On the Vladivostok route the ships sometimes passed through Japanese waters. The United States transferred some 90 cargo ships and tankers to the 'neutral' Soviet flag, although this route could not be used for 'finished' weapons like tanks and guns. In January 1945 a route though the Turkish Straits to Odessa was opened.

Global logistics: counter-attack

Finally, global logistics were necessary to move troops and supplies to defend Allied overseas possessions and – much more of a challenge – to mount the eventual counter-attacks. As far as the British and American forces were concerned, every soldier, every tank, every artillery piece, had to be moved across the sea and into battle, along with most of their supplies.

Control of the seas allowed Britain to maintain its presence in the Middle East in 1940 and 1941. The cross-Mediterranean route was curtailed in 1941 – latterly due to German air power – but a viable supply route extended 13,000 miles around the Cape of Good Hope and through the Red Sea. These were the monthly WS convoys, named after the Prime Minister himself (Winston Spencer Churchill). Other shipping routes enabled the Empire to channel manpower to the main combat theatre through the Indian Ocean and the Red Sea (especially from Australia, India, South Africa, and New Zealand). A major role in troop movements, especially in the first half of the war, was played by a dozen big pre-war ocean liners, which the planners called the 'monsters'. The outstanding examples were the 81,000-ton *Queen Mary* and the 84,000-ton *Queen Elizabeth* (which entered service in 1936 and 1940, respectively). These two ships could carry as many as 10,000 troops in one voyage. The big liners steamed too fast to be intercepted by submarines. The only serious loss was the 42,000-ton *Empress of Britain*, torpedoed west of Ireland in October 1940 after she had been immobilised by a Luftwaffe bomber; fortunately she was returning from the Middle East with few passengers on board. The 22,000-ton liner *President Coolidge* was sunk by an American mine in October 1942 while entering the harbour at Espiritu Santo in the South Pacific. She was carrying 5,000 American reinforcements, but all were safely evacuated. A major challenge in troop movement was the very large number of motor vehicles, tanks, and supply trucks, which modern Allied mechanised forces needed to function, but these were effectively moved in transport ships.

The global Allied pool of shipping was by 1942 being scattered in different directions. Even in the year after May 1940 Britain was torn between maintaining the basic Atlantic supply route to Britain and developing the supply lines to the Middle East (Suez) from Britain, at a time when losses from the U-boats were increasing. The Japanese attack set off a crisis in the winter of 1941–2, as troops had to be rushed to the Far East, and direct American help to Britain was temporarily reduced. Once the situation in the Pacific stabilised, American ground and air forces had to be built up in the United Kingdom (Operation BOLERO), partly with an early cross-Channel invasion in mind. Meanwhile there was now strong pressure to supply the Red Army and keep the USSR in the war.

The decision to mount the first Allied overseas offensive in North Africa late in 1942 (Operation TORCH), created big challenges for the global shipping system. A large number of merchants ships and escorts were required, and the TORCH operations dragged out much longer than anticipated. Meanwhile the US Navy insisted on mounting offensive operations in the South Pacific. As it happened, losses to U-boats in 1943 were lower than expected, as were British import demands. But shipping to North Russia was reduced, and the build-up of US ground forces in Britain halted for much of 1943.

The Allies took a risk by allowing Admiral King to unleash the South Pacific counter-offensive in the second half of 1942. This was especially demanding in terms of merchant shipping, warships and aircraft, and meanwhile the victory over the U-boats was uncertain and the Russian–German front seemed unstable. Fortunately, the pool of available shipping and escorts increased with time. Technological advances, intelligence, and the escort build-up broke the back of the U-boat offensive, and the Japanese made no serious attempt to interdict Pacific shipping. The reopening of the Mediterranean in mid 1943 meant ships were no longer tied down in the long voyage around Africa. By the summer of 1944 the shipping network was keeping the global Allied economy functioning, sending the required amount of supplies to Russia, and supplying simultaneously four active campaigns in the Mediterranean, northwestern Europe, the Central Pacific, and the South Pacific.

Some Allied requirements could not be filled. The terrible Bengal famine in northeast India in the summer of 1943 was set off by the dislocation of Imperial shipping. Operation ANVIL/DRAGOON, the invasion of the south of France, was confused and delayed by a lack of shipping. British operations in the eastern Mediterranean and in Southeast Asia were cancelled. There was a final shipping 'crisis' at the end of 1944, brought on partly by the delay in clearing continental ports and partly by the movement to Europe of the mass of the United States Army (arriving at the rate of two or three divisions a month). But in the end this was successfully overcome.

The Axis and the oceans

Axis global activities were minimal. In contrast to the Allied effort, in which the USSR and even (to some extent) China were integrated, the Axis powers after Pearl Harbor fought two completely self-contained wars, economically and strategically. Transport links were effectively severed when Germany invaded the Soviet Union in June 1941. German and Italian leaders could never meet with those of Japan to discuss strategy. Communications, especially between Berlin and Tokyo, would be conducted only by radio, and they could be and were intercepted by the Allies. The messages of the Japanese ambassador in Germany, General Ōshima Hiroshi, proved an important source of strategic intelligence. (The Allies had the advantage of being able to use the secure global submarine-cable network.)

There were fears in the summer of 1942 that the Axis powers might effect a link in the Indian Ocean. A Japanese carrier raid against Ceylon (now Sri Lanka) in late March and early April 1942 demonstrated the weakness of the British Empire's forces in the Indian Ocean. In May 1942 the British rushed forces to the Vichy French naval base at Diego Suarez on Madagascar, off the east coast of Africa. The Japanese Navy did mount a midget submarine attack on Diego Suarez (launched from two 'mother' submarines) a month later. But with hindsight it is evident that an Indian Ocean link was not a real threat. Madagascar was, after all, 3,900 miles across the Indian Ocean from Singapore, and even without the unexpected turnabout at Midway in June 1942 a Japanese surface fleet could not have been committed for any time into the Indian Ocean.

A handful of blockade runners passed furtively through the thinly patrolled waters around the Cape of Good Hope, both before and after Pearl Harbor. This traffic dried up in 1942 as Allied patrols improved – and more intelligence was received from ULTRA. Even the submarine route was dangerous. Only one Japanese boat succeeded in making the round trip of 30,000 miles between the Far East and Europe. *I-8* left Penang in July 1943 and reached Brest in September; she returned to Singapore in December. *I-30* had reached France a year earlier, in August 1942, but she was sunk on the return trip. A handful of technicians were exchanged, but the only 'political' transfer was Subhas Chandra Bose, a well-known Indian nationalist. Bose had escaped from house arrest in India and travelled to Germany in early 1941 via Afghanistan and the USSR, in an extraordinary series of adventures. The journey back to Asia was as hazardous; Bose transferred from a German to a Japanese submarine south of Madagascar in April 1943. In May 1943 *U 511* sailed from Lorient in France as a gift to the Japanese. She arrived safely in July with Admiral Nomura Noakuni, a senior military representative to Germany, on board; the submarine was transferred to the Imperial Navy. A small U-boat flotilla did operate in the Indian Ocean from Penang from the autumn of 1943. In the whole war this was the only example of 'combined' operations between the European and Asian Axis powers.

Global air routes

Global air transport was just beginning in the late 1930s. Despite the Depression, intercontinental air networks had been laid out, especially by (British) Imperial Airways and Pan American Airways, mainly using big flying boats. Pan American began scheduled flights across the North Atlantic only in June 1939 (the service was interrupted by the outbreak of war), and across the Pacific in 1941.

The Allies could use intercontinental air transport to move key personnel. Churchill, the oldest of the Big Three leaders, was the most enthusiastic air traveller. As well as making a number of trips to North America and the Middle East, he flew twice to Moscow. In 1942 Molotov, the Soviet Foreign Commissar, flew to Britain and then to America in a Soviet heavy bomber. By the middle of the war Allied long-range transport aircraft, four-engined land aircraft like the C-54 (DC-4) and C-87 (Liberator), were becoming available in considerable numbers.

A larger logistic role within individual theatres was taken by medium-range aircraft. The main cargo aircraft involved was the pre-war Douglas DC-3 airliner, known to the US Army Air Forces (USAAF) as the C-47, and to the RAF as the 'Dakota'. The American DC-3 was also manufactured by the Japanese and the Russians (under pre-war licences). Air transport was used when there was no alternative (for example, supplying China) or when the priority was high. The DC-3/C-47 could carry only 5 tons of cargo – the contents of two standard army trucks – compared to 12,000 tons for one Liberty ship.

More important was the Allied ability to ferry new aircraft over long distances, saving shipping space and time. Bombers and even long-range fighters could be flown from factories and training bases to forward theatres. The Takoradi air route across Central Africa was used for the critical build-up of Allied air forces in the Middle East in 1941–2. The even more extraordinary ALSIB (Alaska–Siberia) route from October 1942 brought 8,000 new American fighters and bombers over the Bering Strait from Alaska and across Siberia to European Russia. The American bomber forces in Britain and the Mediterranean were all flown across the Atlantic, mostly using a route through Newfoundland and Labrador in Canada and then Greenland and

Iceland (or in winter using a longer but safer route across the South Atlantic). By 1944 the B-29 force was flown around the world from the United States to bases in China and the Central Pacific.

The Luftwaffe had a large fleet of Junkers Ju 52 transport aircraft, which it used very effectively within Europe. The Germans pioneered air supply of rapidly advancing ground troops, although it is perhaps two failures of long-range air supply in the winter of 1942–3 that are best remembered: Stalingrad and Tunisia. The Wehrmacht high command used interior lines to rapidly pivot combat air groups from front to front within Europe. The Japanese Army and Navy, too, hoped to use flexible air formations to reinforce and help defend their new island possessions.

Both Germany and Italy had had pre-war interest in air routes outside Europe (Lufthansa and LATI airlines respectively). Indeed, the Germans pioneered intercontinental flight from the late 1920s using airships. But the Axis did not have workable global air links after the outbreak of war in 1939–40, and especially after the invasion of the USSR. An Italian Air Force Savoia-Marchetti S.75 transport with a crew of five made a flight from Rome to Tokyo in early July 1942. The longest leg, between the eastern Ukraine and Inner Mongolia, was 3,600 miles; the Italians returned to Europe two weeks later. The Japanese were embarrassed, however, because the plane had had to violate neutral Soviet air space, and the Tokyo government was very wary of damaging its relations with the Russians. The flight was never repeated. It was no more than a daring adventure, and it showed up a basic weakness of the Axis powers.

·   ·   ·

Mahan was right that oceanic warfare could be conducted in a positive way only by states that had large navies. 'Sea denial' on its own had only restricted value. The western Allies *were* the maritime powers, with a rich legacy of naval history between them. When the war broke out they were the ones with the largest existing fleets of warships and merchant vessels. The main Axis states, in contrast, were positioned at the opposite ends of Eurasia and could not sever the oceanic links which tied the Allies together.

Global air supply routes were, even for the Americans, only a supplement to the all-important shipping arteries. Control of this worldwide transport system – and denial of it to their enemies – gave the Allies a fundamental economic and strategic advantage. The western Allies could pool their forces, and operate where they wanted. The ability to choose when and where to fight, coupled with the ability to use the seas as barriers against invasion, enabled the British and Americans to conduct the war at much lower human cost than the continental powers. The debates between Allied leaders could be heated, and their shipping resources were not unlimited, even in 1943–4. Nevertheless, sitting in Washington or London, or at one or other of their great conferences, they could instruct movements of ships and troops all over the globe.

Italian soldiers trudge across Libya in the spring of 1941. This could be a photograph from Europe in World War I were it not for the helmet of the leading man, the little SPA CL39 lorry – and the desert setting. Despite the fame of the German General Rommel and the *Afrika Korps*, the majority of Axis forces in North Africa in 1941–3 were Italian, for the most part fighting as the infantry. This chapter is also about other 'peripheral forces' – Vichy French, Romanian, Bulgarian, Finnish – which were caught up in Germany's war. Part of the drama of 'peripheral' warfare was that in 1943–4 those governments which had thrown in their lot with the Third Reich tried – with varying degrees of success – to change sides. The Italians had perhaps the worst failure. They ended up with a two-year battle between the Germans and the Allies on their home territory.

The European periphery 1940–1944

Timeline

1940	September	British–Italian fighting begins in North Africa
1941	February	German troops arrive in North Africa
	April	Germany attacks Yugoslavia and Greece
1942	October	British victory at El Alamein in Egypt
	November	Allied invasion of Morocco and Algeria (TORCH)
1943	May	Surrender of all Axis forces in North Africa
	July	Invasion of Sicily (HUSKY); Mussolini overthrown
	September	Invasion of Italy at Salerno (AVALANCHE)
1944	June	Allies capture Rome
	August	USSR invades Romania, begins Balkan campaign

Italy and North Africa, 1940–1941

The periphery of Europe – North Africa, the Balkans, Scandinavia, and the Baltic, arguably even Italy and southern France – was important throughout the war. For some planners it provided an alternative to a direct assault on Germany, and in 1942–3 it led to some of the most heated strategic debates of the war. It was also the object of a muffled struggle for post-war influence, especially between the British and the Russians.

The idea of fighting the European war on the periphery of the continent had been attractive to many Allied leaders since the very beginning of the war. The British and the French hoped to be able to attack Germany in Scandinavia and the Balkans (see Chapter 4) rather than endure a bloody repetition of the 1914–18 Western Front. As it happened, France was defeated, and Britain would have no choice but to fight on the periphery and – initially – in much less favourable strategic circumstances than had originally been expected.

Mussolini's declaration of war against France and Britain in June 1940 seemed to serve Italian interests; France was about to be defeated, and the British were isolated. It soon became clear, however, that the Italian forces were over-extended and unready. In late October 1940, without discussing the matter with Hitler, Mussolini launched an attack from Albania (occupied by Italy in early 1939) into northwestern Greece. Operating in difficult mountain terrain, the Greek Army stopped the Italian advance and then drove the invaders back. With German help Greece was finally knocked out, but in the end thirty Italian divisions were tied up in occupation duties there and in Yugoslavia.

The fighting in North Africa was even more difficult for Italy. The Italian forces had a considerable base in their colony of Libya, which they had seized from Turkey in 1911. But Italian (and later German-Italian) forces in North Africa had to transport all their reinforcements, munitions, supplies, and fuel across the sea. The British were, crucially, able to keep 'marginal' naval control of the Mediterranean. The colony at Malta provided a vital base from which aircraft, submarines, and even surface ships could interdict the north–south Axis convoy routes. Mussolini had a large navy, with four small but modernised World War I battleships and two new battleships just being completed; there were numerous cruisers and destroyers, and a large submarine force. Fuel oil for ships, however, was available in only limited quantities, and was increasingly rationed as the war progressed. The Italian Navy had no aircraft carriers. The independent Air Force had some anti-shipping aircraft and coastal bases in the central and eastern Mediterranean, but co-ordination with the Navy was poor.

The British had a much larger fleet, but they could devote only part of it to the Mediterranean. The Royal Navy had the advantage of two gifted and aggressive commanders, Admirals Andrew Cunningham and James Somerville. A night torpedo air strike against the southern Italian base of Taranto in November 1940 had remarkable success. The slow British biplanes put three Italian battleships out of action (one permanently) and forced the withdrawal of the Italian fleet to better-protected but much less useful bases in the north. A second naval defeat in March 1941, off Cape Matapan (see Box 38), confirmed British supremacy and made Mussolini use his surviving fleet very cautiously.

Meanwhile there had been a remarkable turn of events in the ground war in North Africa. The Italians had considerable forces – about 15 divisions – in Libya, of which 5 were sent into Egypt. Mussolini urged on the attack, but the Italian commander, Marshal Graziani, advanced only cautiously in September 1940, complaining to Rome of his supply problems. General Sir Archibald Wavell (Middle East theatre commander) originally had only two divisions, but he could bring in troops from the wider Empire east of Suez, from Australia, India, and New Zealand. In December 1940, a British surprise attack hit the exposed Italian positions just inside the Egyptian frontier in the 'Western Desert'. The British surrounded large numbers of enemy troops and rapidly drove forward 400 miles across Cyrenaica (the eastern province of Libya). By the beginning of February 1941 they had taken about half the coastline of Libya and established themselves beyond the port of Benghazi. Some 130,000 Italian troops and much equipment were captured; British Empire losses were insignificant.

The British Empire had meanwhile won another victory 1,500 miles to the southeast in Italian East Africa. This was the extreme periphery, the only large overseas territory held by a European Axis power. With a large garrison, 90,000 Italians and 250,000 local troops under the Duke of Aosta (a cousin of the Italian King), Italian East Africa was a threat to Britain's colonies and to shipping through the vital Red Sea artery. Fortunately the Italian colony was itself cut off by Suez. An offensive by Imperial troops from Sudan, Kenya,

Map 10 The Mediterranean and North Africa, 1941–1944

ROMANIA

Belgrade
(Aug 44)
SERBIA
Danube

Bucharest
(Aug 44)

Anti-German palace
coup in Aug 44.

Black Sea

YUGOSLAVIA

riatic Sea

BULGARIA

Sofia
(Oct 44)

Russians declare war
on Bulgaria in Sep 44.

Monte
Cassino
Naples
(Oct 44)
no
43)
Taranto

ALBANIA

Salonika

Aegean Sea

TURKEY

LANCHE,
43.

GREECE

IONIAN ISLANDS

Italian invasion,
Oct 40.

Athens
(Oct 44)

DODECANESE ISLANDS

ILY

SKY, Jun 43.

MALTA

British arrive, install
government Oct 44.

Battle of ✕
Cape Matapan

RHODES

CYPRUS

SYRIA

LEBANON
Beirut

CRETE

Haifa

ta was crucial to British strategy in 1940–2. From
e British aircraft, surface ships, and submarines
cked Axis supply convoys to North Africa.

Mediterranean Sea

Limit of the Axis advance
into Egypt in spring 42.

PALESTINE

Benghazi
(Nov 42)

Tobruk

Sidi
Barrani

Alexandria

*Suez
Canal*

CYRENAICA

Battle of ✕
Alamein

Cairo

*Qattara
Depression*

EGYPT

LIBYA

Limit of the British counter-
attack into Libya in Feb 41.

Limit of the Italian advance
into Egypt in Dec 40.

Nile

Box 38 | The Battle of Cape Matapan

In March 1941 a large Italian fleet attempted to attack British convoys from Egypt to Greece. Instead, the British Mediterranean Fleet under Admiral Andrew Cunningham surprised it off Cape Matapan (the southern tip of mainland Greece). On 28 March the new battleship *Vittorio Veneto* was torpedoed and damaged by an air strike from the aircraft carrier *Formidable*. During the night Cunningham's ships encountered and sank three Italian heavy cruisers and two destroyers; the British suffered virtually no losses.

The Royal Navy had the benefit of a great naval tradition: Cunningham's three battleships – *Barham*, *Valiant*, and *Warspite* – had all fought at Jutland. Cunningham had other advantages; he had learned through ULTRA that a large Axis operation was under way, and the Italian admiral did not learn until too late that Cunningham's big ships had left Alexandria in Egypt. Radar gave the British a great tactical edge in the night action. The historian Correlli Barnett called Matapan 'the Royal Navy's greatest victory in a fleet encounter since Trafalgar'.[a] The Italian Navy never again tried to mount such an ambitious challenge to British supremacy.

The following is from the report of the action.

At 2111 a Radar report was received from the VALF [commander of the scouting force] of an unknown ship stopped about 5 miles to port of him; the C-in-C [Cunningham] at once altered course to pass nearer to the position ...

At 2210 what was apparently the same ship was detected by *Valiant*'s Radar 6 miles on the port bow. The C-in-C decided to investigate and at 2213 the battle fleet altered course together to 240°, the destroyer screen being ordered over to the starboard side.

At 2225 two large cruisers [*Zara* and *Fiume*] were unexpectedly sighted on the starboard bow, with a smaller vessel, thought at first to be a 6-in cruiser ahead of them. The battle fleet were turned back to 280° into line ahead, and at 2228 when the enemy were on the port bow at a range of about 4,000 yards [destroyer] *Greyhound* illuminated one of the enemy cruisers with her searchlight, and *Warspite* opened fire. [Aircraft carrier] *Formidable* hauled out of line to starboard and the battle fleet engaged. The enemy were seen to be two cruisers of the 'Zara' class on an opposite course; they were apparently completely taken by surprise and their turrets were [trained] fore and aft. *Warspite*'s first 15-in broadside hit the rear cruiser with devastating effect, five out of six shells hitting. Both cruisers were thereafter repeatedly hit, set severely on fire and put out of action ....

The battle fleet ceased fire at 2235 and was re-formed into line ahead on a course 010°; *Formidable* was ordered to rejoin the line at 2310. The four screening destroyers (*Stuart, Havock, Greyhound* and *Griffin*) were released at 2238 and ordered to finish off the two cruisers seen to be on fire.

> (From Michael Simpson, ed., *The Cunningham Papers* (Aldershot: Ashgate, 1999), vol. I, pp. 321f.)

[a] Correlli Barnett, *Engage the Enemy More Closely: The Royal Navy in the Second World War* (New York: Norton, 1991), pp. 344f.

and Aden began in January 1941. Adis Ababa was taken in April, and Italian resistance quickly ended.

Churchill followed his winter victory in Egypt and Cyrenaica with his worst strategic mistake of the war. Wavell was ordered to send several of his best divisions to Greece to buttress the Athens government. The British could possibly have completed the capture of Libya in the spring and summer of 1941. They could at least have consolidated their position in Cyrenaica, from where the RAF could have supported Malta. Instead there would be eighteen months of see-saw fighting.

Hitler had (in December 1940) planned intervention in Greece (Operation MARITA) as his first major ground campaign after France. Part of the object was to protect the southern flank of the Reich, and especially the oilfields and refineries in Romania. Although German planning was confused by a pro-British coup in Yugoslavia in March 1941, the attack went ahead in early April. The Wehrmacht crashed quickly through southern Yugoslavia and Bulgaria (Germany's new ally) and then into Greece. Yugoslavia, divided by ethnic conflict and poorly prepared, requested a ceasefire after six days. In Greece, despite the mountainous terrain and the arrival of several British Empire divisions, the German forces made rapid advances. By the third week the German Army was in Athens, and the British Army had had to perform another hasty evacuation. Britain was now thrown off the continent altogether for two years.

The last episode of this campaign was the seizure of the island of Crete in May 1941, Operation MERKUR (see Box 39). The Germans flew a division of airborne forces 150 miles from mainland Greece. Parachutists and glider troops seized the key airfields, and transport planes landed reinforcements.

Box 39 | Crete

Friedrich August *Freiherr* von der Heydte (1907–94) commanded a battalion of the 3rd Parachute Regiment in the Battle of Crete in May 1941. Von der Heydte's unit was dropped near the crucial British airfield at Maleme on the morning of 20 May. The eventual capture of the airfield allowed German reinforcements to be flown in from mainland Greece, and this determined the outcome of the battle.

Von der Heydte later commanded a parachute regiment in the defence of Normandy and was captured in the Battle of the Bulge in December 1944. After the war he was a reserve general in the West German Army.

Next came the order, 'Ready to jump!'

In two strides I was at the door, my men pressing close behind me, and grasped the supports on either side of it. The slipstream clutched at my cheeks, and I felt as though they were fluttering like small flags in the wind.

Suddenly, a lot of little white clouds appeared from nowhere and stood poised in the air about us. They looked harmless enough, like puffs of cotton-wool, for the roar of the planes's engines had drowned the sound of the ack-ack shells' detonation.

Below me was the village of Alikianou. I could see people in the streets staring up at us, others running away and disappearing into doorways. The shadows of our planes swept like ghostly hands over the sun-drenched white houses, while behind the village there gleamed a large mirror – the reservoir – with single coloured parachutes, like autumn leaves, drifting down towards it.

Our plane slowed down. The moment had come.

'Go!'

I pushed with hands and feet, throwing my arms forward as if trying to clutch the black cross on the wing. And then the slipstream caught me, and I was swirling through space with the air roaring in my ears. A sudden jerk upon the webbing, a pressure on the chest which knocked the breath out of my lungs, and then – I looked upwards and saw, spread above me, the wide-open, motley hood of my parachute. In relation to this giant umbrella I felt small and insignificant.

(From Friedrich von der Heydte, *Daedalus Returned* (London: Hutchinson, 1958), pp. 59f.)

The British and Greek defenders had not had time to fortify the airfields. They were poorly co-ordinated and lacked heavy weapons and, especially, tactical air power. The overall commander, the New Zealand General Bernard Freyberg, had a clear picture of German intentions from ULTRA intelligence, but he failed to use it effectively. Within ten days the British survivors were scuttling to evacuate the island. All the same, the battle for the airfields had been closely contested, and the German airborne troops suffered prohibitive losses, some 4,000 men killed or missing. The Wehrmacht never mounted airborne attacks on this scale again. There turned out to be little point to the sacrifice, as four weeks later the main emphasis of Hitler's war turned to Russia. The Royal Navy prevented a seaborne landing on Crete, but it was swamped by the superior Luftwaffe and lost many ships.

The Germans in North Africa

Churchill's Greek blunder was made worse by Hitler's earlier decision to send military aid to the retreating Italians in North Africa. A Luftwaffe force deployed to Sicily, and it provided the air support for the Mediterranean sea war which the Italian Air Force could not. More famous was the participation of German ground troops, initially a couple of German mobile divisions – the famous *Afrika Korps*. General Erwin Rommel arrived at Tripoli with an advance party in February 1941. By the middle of April he had, supported by fresh Italian ground forces, counter-attacked and driven the weakened and over-stretched British back to the Egyptian border. Rommel was a gifted general, but his advance went against the intentions of the German high command, which had ordered only the defence of Tripolitania (western Libya).

If British strategists had argued the advantage of a peripheral strategy, the German experience in Greece and North Africa showed the advantage of operations on 'interior lines'. Pivoting on the central position of the Reich, the Germans were able to move their forces in all directions with apparent ease. A Luftwaffe air corps (*Fliegerkorps*, about 300 aircraft) that fought off Sicily in one month could be based deep in Russia in the next. The continental transport network, mainly the railway system, could be used effectively to transport ground troops. The British, for their part, had to operate – more slowly – along the extended edge of the European periphery. Their task was made much harder by the limited availability of the lateral Mediterranean route, now confined largely to desperate convoys from Gibraltar and Alexandria to Malta, itself under close siege. Supplies and reinforcements for Egypt and the 'Desert War' had to go around the southern tip of Africa and through the Red Sea.

Did Hitler, in the winter of 1940–1 and the following spring, have the option of following his own peripheral strategy in the Mediterranean? After all, Hitler's main enemy at this time was the British Empire, and he would in June 1941 attack Russia partly to eliminate a possible ally for the British. Would it not have been wiser to attack Britain's imperial possessions? A counter-factual strategy looks plausible enough: the capture of Gibraltar, Malta, and the Suez Canal, securing the Mediterranean as an enclosed Axis lake and opening the route to the oil resources of the Persian Gulf. Admiral Raeder, the C-in-C of the German Navy, put the case to Hitler for just such an advance. This is evidently what Stalin, in the early summer of 1941, expected Hitler to do – as well as to mount an invasion of Britain. Hitler did indeed issue Directive No. 18 in November 1940 for an operation against Gibraltar, Operation FELIX.

The failure even of FELIX showed the extent to which Hitler's position in the Mediterranean was a fragile house of cards. Germany had no surface ships in the Mediterranean, and it would send U-boats only in the autumn of 1941. German ground forces, however strong and battle-tested, could not cross the Mediterranean in any numbers. Franco, the Spanish dictator, was not prepared to help, despite a meeting with Hitler in the Pyrenees in October 1940. Franco demanded a price, territory in French North Africa, which would have cost Germany the support of the Vichy government. French support, in turn, was necessary to control Northwest and West Africa and key places in the Levant. Attempts to cultivate the French also conflicted with the Vichy's fear of Italian ambitions in Tunisia and elsewhere. Any German Mediterranean operations would require the help of the Italians, but soon after Directive No. 18 the Italian Army suffered heavy defeats in Egypt, Cyrenaica, Greece, and East Africa, and the Navy took crippling losses at Taranto and Matapan. The Balkan states were not unfriendly to Germany, but they disliked the Italians. It would cost a serious military operation and the risk of alienating the neutral USSR if Germany were to attempt to take control of that region.

There were more fundamental considerations. Mussolini had his own imperial vision in the Mediterranean, and wanted a 'parallel war' there. Hitler's short-term and more basic strategic interests lay elsewhere. In the long term the geopolitics of the Third Reich – and probably strategic common sense – drove it towards the mineral and food resources of Russia rather than the Mediterranean. The oil of the Middle East was not the huge asset it became later in the century; it was not even essential for British supply. Another lure of Russia was the Jewish-Bolshevik racial enemy, absent from the Mediterranean. German also faced a military threat from the east, not from the south. If Germany was to fight the USSR it needed to do it as soon as possible, or a 'neutral' USSR – even one that had pledged non-aggression – would always inhibit Axis initiatives in the eastern Mediterranean. In Russia alone, in the absence of an ocean-going German Navy, could the full weight of the German Army and the Luftwaffe be applied. From Hitler's point of view the British were a major enemy, but they could temporarily lose the eastern Mediterranean, even the Suez Canal, and the loss would not be fatal; after all, the British Mediterranean sea route had already been effectively blocked.

By the spring of 1941 – probably even before Rommel arrived in Tripoli – the Wehrmacht was irrevocably committed to BARBAROSSA, and at that point there is no further counter-factual argument. Hitler's mind was made up. However, three events in the eastern Mediterranean on the very eve of the Russian invasion further demonstrate the limits of German power. Rommel's small force was stopped on the Egyptian border, without even being able to take the advanced port of Tobruk in Cyrenaica. A second event was the capture of Crete, which cost the German airborne forces such high casualties that they were never used again on a large scale. Finally, Berlin could do little to help the anti-British rebellion which broke out in Iraq in April–May 1941. The Luftwaffe sent a handful of aircraft, staged through the Italian island of Rhodes and Vichy French Syria; British Empire forces put down the rising, and then took by force Syria and the Lebanon, defeating the Vichy garrisons.

On 11 June 1941, less than two weeks before the invasion of Russia, Hitler issued his remarkable Directive No. 32, 'Preparations for the period after BARBAROSSA'. An ambitious set of southern operations was projected for the autumn of 1941 and the following winter, after 'the victorious conclusion of the campaign in the East'. Operation FELIX was to be carried out against Gibraltar. Rommel's forces were to be strengthened, mainly with air units, for an advance on Suez. German ground forces were to concentrate in Bulgaria to intimidate or invade Turkey with the goal of passing through that country to threaten the Suez canal from the East. A 'motorised expeditionary corps' was to be sent through the Caucasus to Iraq, and rebellion would be set off in the Arab world. But all of this depended on the prior defeat of Russia.

We know that the Russian campaign cost Germany the war. It does not follow that any alternative strategy – even one in the Mediterranean – would have led to greater success. In any event, with the invasion of Russia in June 1941 the nature of the Mediterranean war changed. There would be no 'period after BARBAROSSA'. The German forces, including the Luftwaffe, were now heavily engaged in a struggle that dwarfed events in North Africa. Each of the eight panzer groups sent to Russia was larger than the *Afrika Korps*. Even the Italians sent troops and aircraft to fight the 'Bolsheviks' – another fatal Mussolini decision – which reduced what was available for the Mediterranean. In the end 80,000 Italian soldiers would die fighting in Russia, four times the number killed in North Africa.

The tide turns in favour of the British

In the second half of 1941 Hitler was preoccupied with Russia. British reinforcements (and equipment supplied by the neutral USA) were gradually built up in Egypt. In November 1941 the British launched Operation CRUSADER. The Axis forces were driven out of Cyrenaica and nearly back to where they had been in February 1941, after the first Italian catastrophe. CRUSADER was, indeed, the first victory of the British Army against German ground forces. Unfortunately, outside events again intervened. The Japanese attack in early December 1941 slowed the build-up of Allied forces in the eastern Mediterranean, especially from Australia, New Zealand, and India. US equipment was diverted to American forces in other parts of the world. Hitler also daringly recalled an air corps from Russia to contest control of the Mediterranean narrows. Over twenty U-boats arrived in the Mediterranean in the autumn of 1941, and they inflicted heavy damage on the Royal Navy. Rommel, again out-fighting the British Empire forces, drove them back across most of Cyrenaica in January and February 1942.

In May–June 1942 Rommel achieved his most remarkable victory at Gazala, 100 miles inside Cyrenaica, overcoming superior British numbers in an extraordinary battle of movement. He then took the forward port of Tobruk (which had withstood an eight-month siege in 1941) and chased the

British back 200 miles, deep into Egypt. German-Italian forces were stopped only at the line of El Alamein, 100 miles west of Alexandria and the Nile Delta; this July engagement is known as the First Battle of El Alamein. Hitler had made Rommel a field marshal for his capture of Tobruk, but the forces of the 'Desert Fox' were now over-extended.

It was unlikely that Rommel could have moved any further towards the Nile Delta. The Germans and Italians were poorly supplied because of the vulnerable Mediterranean sea link. The British held a key bottleneck, only 40 miles wide, between the sea and the impassable Qattara Depression. The new British command team of General Alexander (Middle East command) and General Bernard Montgomery (8th Army) finally had enough men and material, and they had won local air superiority. They also began to make much more effective use of ULTRA to gain inside knowledge of Axis strength and supplies and to attack Rommel's shipping.

Rommel's unsuccessful attempt in early August 1942 to batter his way through Montgomery's lines at the Battle of Alam Halfa demonstrated his weakness. Then in late October 1942 Montgomery launched his own offensive at the Second Battle of El Alamein, one of the turning points of the war. Hitler ordered Rommel to stand fast. Ten days into the attack Rommel's position tipped. With no chance for a measured retreat, Rommel now had to fall back towards his bases, closely pursued by the British. The German forces (although not the Italians) escaped capture by the cautious Montgomery, but this time there would be no strategic rebound. By late November Rommel had been pushed out of Cyrenaica; at the end of January 1943 he had to give up his main base at Tripoli and had withdrawn west from Libya into (French) Tunisia. The famous 'Western Desert' campaign was over.

British-American strategic choices: France or the Mediterranean?

The British Western Desert campaign had been fought from a pre-war Imperial ground base in Egypt, although one that had to be further built up and supplied. The next stage of operations, even in Africa, would require a fundamentally new element, 'amphibious' warfare, or what the British called 'combined operations'. Indeed this element would now become a defining feature of the war in Western and Southern Europe.

Large-scale amphibious warfare was a difficult technique in the age of modern land transport. In theory, the defender could rapidly move forward troops to contain and then destroy the beachhead. High defensive firepower also worked against the invader. The largest landing in World War I, at Gallipoli in Turkey, had been a failure. Accepted military opinion between the wars was that later developments (after 1918) made landing operations even more impractical; these included the new element of (defensive) aviation and the need to transport and unload tanks and other motor vehicles.

The British forces continued to think about landing operations in the 1920s and 1930s. Surprisingly, some lessons came from the Far East. The Japanese (mainly the Japanese Army) had developed specialist amphibious forces, and their use in China from the summer of 1937 was watched with interest by the British. All the same, the Allied Norwegian campaign in April–June 1940 (see Chapter 3) had not inspired confidence in expeditionary warfare. The small forces sent had been unable to retake Narvik or Trondheim or hold out against German ground and air forces moving up from the south.

The fall of France in June 1940 created a radically new situation. A full-scale British amphibious counter-offensive across the Channel against an un-weakened Wehrmacht was, to be sure, unthinkable. Churchill, however, was eager to carry the war to the enemy with raids on his coastal periphery. This furthered the development of amphibious doctrine and equipment, and in turn evolved into something much more substantial. For 'raiding' purposes the British had a few small barge-type vessels to carry platoons and individual vehicles ashore, and they now constructed a handful of mother ships to carry these 'landing craft' across the ocean to remote objectives. The first improvised operation with these vessels was mounted against the strategic Vichy French port of Dakar in West Africa in September 1940. That expedition, however, had to be abandoned in the face of strong defences. For the following two years nothing more than raids could be mounted, but a considerable capability was developed. The first successful British amphibious operation – where hostile territory was permanently held – came as late as May 1942, and was mounted against another Vichy French target, the port of Diego Suarez, on Madagascar in the Indian Ocean. (The first Allied amphibious landing on an operational scale was actually mounted by the *Russians* against Kerch' and Feodosiia in the Crimea in December 1941.) On the Western European coastline a large-scale but very costly raid was mounted, largely by Canadian troops, against the town of Dieppe in August 1942.

American involvement, first as a neutral arms-supplier (through Lend-Lease) and then as a fighting partner, meant that British-designed 'raiding' vessels – LSTs, LCTs, LCIs and others – could be made available to the Allies on a substantial scale by the middle of 1943, and on a vast scale by the summer of 1944 (see Figure 21). This was true despite the fact that the bigger vessels had to compete for shipyard space with emergency merchant ships and anti-submarine ships. The tying down of the bulk of the German Army in Russia and the entry of the United States into the war meant that not just raids, but amphibious operations on the largest scale, including the invasion of the European continent, could be contemplated. This was a development as radical as the German Blitzkrieg.

There was, however, a crucial debate between British and American leaders about where and when they would mount their amphibious counter-attacks. General Marshall (see Figure 22) and the US Army (and later Stalin) were for the direct approach, across the English Channel and through northern France, what was known as the 'single line of action'. The American planners opposed 'scatterization' or 'periphery-pecking'. The historian Russell Weigley and others have been argued that Marshall's view was based on an 'American way of War' which stressed a concentration of force in a decisive theatre. The British leaders, in contrast, still favoured the periphery and the Mediterranean. Churchill in the House of Commons publicly praised the 'wide encircling movement in the Mediterranean' which had as 'its object the exposure of the under-belly of the Axis, especially Italy, to heavy attack'.[1] (Churchill is usually misquoted; to his credit, he did not underestimate the task by speaking of a 'soft' under-belly.)

The debate was affected by setbacks on the battlefield (retreats in North Africa and the Far East) and serious shipping losses to U-boats. It was also complicated by the need to plan for both 1942 and 1943 – i.e. for both the short and the medium/long term. There were also 'political' or 'grand strategic' factors, the need to keep the USSR in the war and the need to concentrate American public opinion on the struggle against Germany (rather than the one against Japan), and the need to keep down British casualties. In the end the British won the argument. The final decision, reached in July 1942, was to go ahead with a long-projected 'peripheral' British-American

Figure 21 | **Landing Ship Tank**

The best-known type of vessel in the huge amphibious flotilla built by the Allies was the LST or 'Landing Ship Tank' (as opposed to the LSI, 'Landing Ship Infantry'). The LST was designed to carry about 20 tanks or other vehicles, up to a total of 500 tons, and land them through bow doors on to an open beach. A dozen LSTs are shown in this photograph of the Normandy beaches. The main version was powered by locomotive diesel engines and could manage only 9 knots; with grim humour it was said that LST stood for 'Large Slow Target'.

The LST was a uniquely Allied (British-American) affair. The concept came from the British in late 1940. They had already developed short-range landing 'craft', able to operate in coastal waters or be slung on the lifeboat davits of carrier ships (converted merchantmen). Now they wanted a sea-going 'ship' that could carry tanks and other vehicles and even piggy-back smaller landing craft. The first three LSTs were converted tankers, and three more were built in British yards. In the autumn of 1941 – before Pearl Harbor – the British had ordered under Lend-Lease a simpler version (Mk 2) for mass production in the United States. The first American-built LST completed its trials in November 1942, and this version was first used in combat at Sicily in the following summer.

LST production was almost entirely confined to the United States, where nearly 1,000 were built during the war. British building capacity was concentrated on smaller landing 'craft' (and on ASW vessels). The Royal Navy received 115 LSTs under Lend-Lease. LSTs were not normally first-wave assault ships, but they brought in vehicles, artillery, and stores immediately after a beachhead had been seized. LSTs were basic building blocks of Allied grand strategy. After the 1944 Normandy landings, with damaged ports and a damaged artificial harbour, the LSTs allowed bulk transfers of equipment across the open beaches. Although they were originally designed for a European mission, their range also made them a vital element in the cross-Pacific campaign.

Figure 22 | General George C. Marshall

An uncharacteristically informal photograph of General Marshall (centre) with three of his colleagues at the Casablanca Conference in January 1943. On the left is the famous General George S. Patton, who commanded the Western [Moroccan] Task Force in Operation TORCH. On the right is General H. H. 'Hap' Arnold, the head of the US Army Air Forces. The art deco Hotel Anfa, venue of the conference, stands in the background.

Marshall (1880–1959) played a central part in US and Allied war-planning. From July 1939 until November 1945 he was Chief of Staff of the United States Army. Roosevelt was not interested in detailed military planning, and Marshall was in effect C-in-C of the US Army. As a key strategist he was a strong advocate of the 'Germany First' strategy, and also a believer in a direct approach to the enemy through a cross-Channel landing. He was forced to give way to the pressure of the British (who favoured a peripheral Mediterranean strategy) and of the US Navy (whose leaders wanted more forces sent to the Pacific).

He was a staff officer in World War I, and a protégé of General Pershing. Training posts in the inter-war years gave him a good knowledge of the officers to whom he would assign key field commands during World War II. Becoming Chief of Staff of the US Army just before the invasion of Poland, Marshall supervised the extraordinary expansion of the next two years. At one time it seemed that he might command the invasion of Europe, but he was by then in his mid-60s, and President Roosevelt wished to keep him as an advisor in Washington. General Eisenhower – who had long experience of working with Marshall – was appointed instead.

To a later generation he is better known for the Marshall Plan, the Cold War foreign aid programme which he announced in 1947 when serving as Secretary of State to President Truman. Marshall won the Nobel Peace Prize in 1953.

amphibious operation mounted against Vichy French North Africa – Morocco and Algeria.

Operation TORCH (originally bearing the less inspiring name GYMNAST) was a very large enterprise compared to the Allied amphibious operations that had gone before. The equivalent of six divisions would be landed in the three widely distant landing zones in Morocco and Algeria. (The nearest European parallel was the April 1940 German invasion of Norway, with widely spaced and simultaneous landings mounted at long range; as with Norway the invader relied heavily on the element of surprise.) TORCH made use of Allied oceanic control, and indeed part of the attacking forces came directly from North America. American planners had feared that hostile forces might block the Strait of Gibraltar, but Franco did not intervene, and the Germans did not make a move into Spain. (Thereafter Spain ceased to be a significant strategic factor for either side in the war.)

The operation was (like the German invasion of Norway) aimed at a relatively 'soft' target. The opposing forces were Vichy French. There was no German military presence in Morocco, Algeria, or Tunisia in early November 1942. The Western Allies, for the first time in the war, achieved strategic surprise when they landed on 8 November. The Germans had no time to use U-boats or aircraft in strength against the invasion convoys, nor did they have any bases nearby. The Allied troops came ashore on largely undefended beaches, and they did not require specialised landing craft. The Vichy armed forces put up some resistance, but this ended after a few days.

Operation TORCH met its objectives. It brought American troops into successful action in 'Europe' in 1942 – a key political goal of President Roosevelt. Coupled with the final success of the British in Libya and Tunisia, the Allies eventually cleared the whole of North Africa. Some 240,000 Italian and German troops were captured, numbers comparable to those taken at Stalingrad. TORCH also gave the US Army essential combat experience; raw American troops suffered a sharp defeat at Kasserine in Tunisia in February 1943. The African element of the Vichy *Armée de l'armistice* was eventually transformed into eleven American-equipped divisions.

On the negative side the final campaign in the central part of the North African coast took much longer than expected, until May 1943. The Americans had been reluctant to risk a landing too far to the east, and the Vichy French command dithered, which allowed the Germans to reinforce Tunisia.

Hitler – unexpectedly and against obvious military logic – sent 50,000 German troops to Tunisia. By the time General von Arnim surrendered in May 1943 – Rommel having been called home – the final decision had been made by the Allies to cancel a cross-Channel landing in that year.

TORCH was the first of six major Allied amphibious landings in Southern and Western Europe, but it was also a 'first' in another sense for the Allies. It raised the political issue of how Axis-controlled peripheral territories could change hands. To what extent could the Allies work – before or after the invasion – with elements who had 'collaborated' with the Germans? How could a territory leave the Axis? Who would run the 'liberated' territory? What would be the political balance between right and left, between the military and civilians? How could the Germans – ever quick to react – be prevented from rushing in forces to buttress or replace a defecting ally? This problem that appeared in French North Africa would repeat itself in a more extreme form in Italy in 1943, and in Romania, Bulgaria, Slovakia, Finland, and Hungary in 1944.

The TORCH planners had hoped that the French would take part in their own 'liberation'. To get around the British–French bad feeling left over from 1940, TORCH was portrayed as an 'American' operation. The C-in-C was an American, the unknown General Dwight D. Eisenhower (see Figure 26). Serious efforts were made by the Americans to woo or subvert the Vichy military. But this effort had only limited success in the short term. The Vichy commanders in North Africa could not be told where and when the Allies would come, and in what strength. They hoped that by observing strict 'neutrality' they would prevent the Germans from taking the 'unoccupied zone' in metropolitan France itself. An attempted *coup de main* in Algiers was only partially successful. As it happened, however, Admiral Darlan, overall C-in-C of the Vichy armed forces, was in Algiers when the Allies landed nearby, and after several days he arranged a ceasefire. Darlan's writ did not run in Tunisia, and the Germans were able to establish a large presence there. The Americans, continuing their cultivation of Vichy, were content to make Darlan 'High Commissioner' for North Africa. De Gaulle's 'Free French', who had not been directly involved in TORCH, were outraged. Darlan was a very senior 'collaborator', who had been Pétain's closest assistant and had worked enthusiastically with the Germans. There were echoes of this outrage in the Allied home countries.

Admiral Darlan was 'conveniently' killed by a lone assassin in December 1942, but this did not end the political rivalry between the Gaullists and with those more mainstream officers who had been involved with the Vichy *Armée de l'armistice*. The Americans favoured General Henri Giraud, whom they had smuggled into North Africa before TORCH. De Gaulle eventually formed in Algiers a political organ which notionally spoke for all Frenchmen, the *Comité Français de Libération Nationale* (CFLN), and edged out the politically inept Giraud. President Roosevelt maintained a strong dislike for the leader of 'Fighting France' (*France Combattante*) but, surprisingly, the Soviets gave de Gaulle significant diplomatic support, and he was able to work with the French Communist Party. In May 1944 de Gaulle's CFLN in Algiers declared itself the Provisional Government of all France; and in June it began to exercise local authority in the homeland (see Chapter 11).

Sicily invaded, Mussolini overthrown

The British–American debate about strategy continued after the initial success of TORCH. The Americans, and especially General Marshall, still gave priority to ROUND-UP, the codename for the cross-Channel landing. The British argued that much would be gained by following up successes in the 'under-belly of the Axis', opening up the Mediterranean, wearing down total German forces, and perhaps knocking Italy out of the war. If a cross-Channel landing was to be attempted in 1943 most of the ground forces employed would have to come from the British Empire, and Churchill and his commanders thought such an operation was neither practical nor desirable. By the spring of 1943 concern about a possible Russian defeat had become less of a factor – and there were as yet few political worries about the Red Army arriving first in Eastern Europe. At the Casablanca Conference in January 1943 the British largely got their way; the decision was made to continue the peripheral strategy and to invade Sicily after Tunisia had been cleared (see Box 40). This did not formally rule out a cross-Channel landing in 1943, but that was the logic of the commitment of troops and landing craft to the Mediterranean (and a consequence of the protracted campaign in Tunisia).

The invasion of Sicily, Operation HUSKY, begun on 10 July 1943. The two Allied armies, led by the British General Montgomery and the American

Box 40 | Allied conferences

British and American global strategy was co-ordinated at inter-Allied conferences held between 1941 and 1945. The conferences at Casablanca, Tehran, Yalta, and Potsdam are the most famous, partly because they touched on high politics and the post-war settlement. But there were military conferences as well, where the British and American High Commands met together as the Combined Chiefs of Staff (CCS).

The conferences are often referred to by their codenames:

ARCADIA	Washington	December 1941 – January 1942
SYMBOL	Casablanca (Morocco)	January 1943
TRIDENT	Washington	May 1943
QUADRANT	Quebec I	August 1943
EUREKA	Tehran	November 1943
SEXTANT	Cairo	November–December 1943
OCTAGON	Quebec II	September 1944
ARGONAUT	Malta/Yalta	February 1945
TERMINAL	Potsdam (Berlin)	July 1945

General Patton, overran Sicily by the middle of August. The campaign could have been more decisive, as four German divisions and 60,000 Italian troops were eventually able to escape intact across the Strait of Messina to continue the fight on the mainland. Overall, however, the results of HUSKY were very positive.

Allied amphibious warfare in Europe came of age. As with TORCH, the invasion of Sicily had achieved strategic surprise. Successful Allied 'deception' operations had forced the Axis to spread their defensive forces across a range of targets from Sardinia to the Peloponnese (southern Greece). HUSKY involved seven Allied divisions – British, American, and Canadian – and several thousand ships. Allied amphibious technique was impressively demonstrated, including naval gunfire support and the first wide-scale use of purpose-built landing vessels (LSTs, LCTs, LCIs) and amphibious trucks (DUKWs). Allied airborne forces were used for the first time on a large scale. Unlike TORCH, the HUSKY landing was mounted against an area defended by a significant number of Axis soldiers and aircraft. Initially there were two German divisions on Sicily and four mobile Italian ones. Fortunately the beach defences were negligible. The British command originally assigned the fresh Americans troops only a supporting role, but the latter showed that they could fight as effectively as Montgomery's North African veterans.

The Allied strategic gains from the occupation of Sicily were also extremely important. The Luftwaffe was driven from its key bases, and the Mediterranean was reopened as a practical west-to-east shipping artery. Even the Japanese high command, far away in Tokyo, reassessed the threat to themselves on the basis of this development. HUSKY also opened the Italian mainland to invasion; from new forward air bases in Sicily, Allied fighter planes could cover the next amphibious leap. Most important, HUSKY triggered Italy's departure from the war. The start of the invasion of Sicily on 10 July was followed by the fall of Mussolini on the 25th, and by the ceasefire of Italian forces which came into effect on 8 September.

The overthrow of Mussolini followed from the defeat of Italian forces on all fronts, and now the imminent loss of Sicily. The position of the *Duce* had never been as strong as that of Hitler, and his 'totalitarian' system had had to accept the surviving power of non-Fascist forces like the King, the church, and the armed forces. Mussolini was now challenged by disgruntled Fascist leaders, then arrested by the King. The new Prime Minister chosen by King Vittorio Emanuele III was the elderly Marshal Badoglio. Badoglio announced that he would continue to fight on alongside Germany, but both he and the King were already seeking a way to get out of the war. Senior Italian officers were sent south to open secret negotiations with the Allies. Hitler, for his part, could in the short term only accept the change of government, but he secretly prepared to send his forces through the Brenner Pass to restore the situation.

Mainland Italy

What happened next was a repetition, on a larger and bloodier scale, of French North Africa. It would have been very advantageous to the Allies – and to the Italians – if the new government in Rome had been able to change sides neatly. There were hopes that the Italian Army could hold the Brenner Pass through the Alps, or at least some readily defendable line in the northern Apennines north of Rome. It was not to be. The so-called

'45 Days' (between Mussolini's removal and the Italian armistice) turned out to be a wasted opportunity. The Allies could not, for reasons of military secrecy, give the new Italian government advance details of their plans to invade the mainland, but the underlying problem was that the Italian military were as inept at making peace as they had been at making war.

The first British landing, in the extreme south, opposite Messina in Sicily, came on 3 September. The Allies intended to make their main landing further north, but not high enough up the Italian boot to take Rome; they did not want to operate beyond the cover of their fighter planes based on Sicily. Negotiations to fly an American airborne division into Rome's airports fell through. The King and Marshal Badoglio fled towards the zone taken by the Allies in the extreme south – without giving instructions to their subordinate commanders.

The main Allied effort came six days later at Salerno, just south of Naples, in Operation AVALANCHE (9 September) (see Box 41). The first British and American troops landed on the day after the armistice was announced. The two invading corps, the British in the north and the Americans in the south, secured a beachhead about 45 miles long. The Germans nearly drove them back into the sea a few days later. The Allies eventually stabilised the situation – partly with naval gunfire and partly by dropping parachute troops directly into the beachhead. Once the Germans saw that the landings were consolidated they pulled back to a strong defensive line across the Italian peninsula, and the Allies took control as far north as Naples.

Hitler moved reinforcements into Italy, tripling the six divisions originally on hand. The Wehrmacht had drafted contingency plans – Operation AXIS – for dealing with an Italian collapse, and they now ruthlessly put them into effect. Most of the Italian Navy was able to cross over to the Allies, although the new battleship *Roma* was sunk *en route* by a Luftwaffe guided missile. The Italian Army in the centre and north of the country, some 25 divisions, was disarmed by much smaller German forces. In some of the out-lying islands, German Army garrisons massacred Italian forces which had originally outnumbered them; some 4,800 were killed on Cefalonia (Kefalonia) in the Ionian Islands. Even Mussolini escaped. Interned by the new Italian government, he was plucked from a mountain prison by German airborne special forces. The *Duce* was then used as a figurehead for what had become a German occupation regime in the north, the so-called 'Italian

Box 41 | Salerno

Mortimer Wheeler (1890–1976) was a well-known British archaeologist; he was knighted in 1952. This excerpt from his memoirs describes the landing at Salerno (Operation AVALANCHE) before dawn on 9 September 1943. Wheeler had fought in World War I as an artillery officer, and went back into the regular army in 1941. He served in North Africa and by 1943 commanded the 12th Anti-Aircraft Brigade. Wheeler sailed to Salerno from Tunisia aboard a British LST which carried many of the men, vehicles, and guns of his brigade.

A penetrating jolt, as though the ship had struck a rock, nearly threw me from the bed and a second jolt brought me to my feet. We had been closely straddled by two bombs, and as I climbed to the bridge hell was let loose. Rocket-ships were hurling blazing salvoes at the unseen coast; monitors, cruisers, and destroyers were blasting the blackness and intensifying it by their lightning flashes. The first landing-craft, including one of my light [AA] batteries, was groping shorewards. The flickering night was alive with hidden activity.

Dawn, after a sudden faint start, grew slowly amidst the mist and smoke. Detached fragments of mountain began to appear in the intermittent rifts; I remember the greedy delight with which my eyes, mountain-starved by two years of African desert, feasted momentarily upon a jagged crest of the Apennines. Now we were zigzagging towards the beaches, evading the black, sinister mines which, loosened from the sea-bed around us by our devoted minesweepers, clustered like fishes' eggs amongst the waves. And now we were under shell-fire. In front of us a landing-craft with tanks aboard slowly rolled over and sank. A destroyer coming inshore to the rescue was likewise hit. Then the Navy closed in and gave the offending battery everything. (When I visited the spot later in the day, I found the German guns knocked to all points of the compass and their plucky crews splashed about them.) Meanwhile, another German battery, four 88-millimetres, had got the range of our craft over open sights as we moved slowly in, awaiting our turn at the beach. The captain of the next landing-ship beside us was killed by a direct hit on the bridge. Another ship beyond was struck forward and received a number of casualties. Our turn was next. The rounds came over in sharp salvoes and bracketed us with perfect precision, sending showers of spray over us as we changed course cumbrously to vary range. The troops lay flat on the deck or were mildly screened in the hold. The naval commander [Lt. Commander Sprigge, RNR (Royal Navy Reserve)] and the brigade commander [Wheeler] on the bridge took it in turns, salvo by salvo, to stand and watch the beach ahead, making the usual fatuous and self-conscious jokes which are appropriate to such an occasion, and taking turns ceremoniously also with the single tin-hat which we shared. At length the awaited sign flashed from the beach; the commander signalled 'full speed ahead' and we struck the beach fairly and squarely. Sprigge, RNR, had brought us in to a nicety.

(From Mortimer Wheeler, *Still Digging: Interleaves from an Antiquary's Notebook* (London: Michael Joseph, 1955), pp. 167f.)

Social Republic'. Some 600,000 Italian soldiers were sent as forced labourers or internees to the Reich.

In the south of Italy political developments echoed those of North Africa. Just as the Allies had first placed their hopes on Darlan and other Vichy authorities, so they used the authority of King Vittorio Emanuele III and Marshal Badoglio. The King had invited Mussolini into government in 1922 and had reigned through two decades of Fascism. Marshal Badoglio had commanded Mussolini's Army, until he was retired after the first setback in Greece in 1940. The arrangement fitted uneasily with 'unconditional surrender'. Remarkably, however, even the Italian Communists (in the spring of the beginning of 1944) supported the Salerno-based Badoglio government, just as they supported de Gaulle in Algiers. In the spring of 1944 the Communist leader Togliatti returned from exile in Moscow and entered the government. As in French North Africa the British and Americans disagreed about the course of events, although in this case Churchill backed the more conservative camp. In the summer of 1944, when Rome fell, a more broadly based and less compromised government was formed under the veteran socialist politician Bonomi. At about the same time Vittorio Emanuele III yielded his own power to Crown Prince Umberto, as regent. Both would abdicate, one after another, in 1946, and the unpopular Italian monarchy came to an end. A limited number of Italian troops supported the Allies as 'co-belligerents', but with much less effect than the French divisions formed in North Africa.

But the main events were taking place elsewhere in Italy. After the German occupation of Rome and the stabilisation of the Allied zone, the 'Italian campaign' proper began. In the era of the Blitzkrieg this fighting seems a throwback. It involved twenty months of foot-slogging up the Italian peninsula, from September 1943 to May 1945. Various factors allowed the Germans to hold up the Allied advance. First, the Italian peninsula is only about 100 miles wide, and the difficult spine of the Apennines meant that much of the fighting had to be done on the easily blocked 30-mile-wide coastal plains to the east and west. Secondly, as in North Africa after TORCH, Hitler decided to pump in reinforcements. He did so despite the crisis in Russia (after the Battle of Kursk) and the threatened landing in France. Once again the Germans could operate on their 'internal lines'. By June 1944 there were 27 German divisions in Italy, compared to 60 in France. The Germans were well led. Field Marshal Kesselring was in overall command; he was a Luftwaffe officer, but a man with an Army background. Meanwhile, the Allies' thrust northward was weakened by the redeployment of their best formations to Britain in preparation for the cross-Channel invasion.

The Germans held the Allies through the winter and spring of 1943–4 on the GUSTAV line (across the peninsula, halfway between Naples and Rome). The American-led 5th Army was on the west coast, the British 8th Army on the east. The heaviest battles, between January and May 1944, were for the town of Cassino. Set in rugged terrain, Cassino was fought for by infantry from many Allied countries – including Britain, the United States, New Zealand, France, India, and Poland. In an infamous episode, the famous hill-top Benedictine monastery above Cassino was carpet-bombed to prevent it being used as a German observation post. An Allied attempt to use their naval superiority to outflank the GUSTAV line by a two-division landing at Anzio/Nettuno southwest of Rome in January 1944 was not a success. The invaders were trapped in a small coastal pocket for three months. Not until early June 1944 – two days before D-Day in France – did the Allied main force finally punch through to Rome. Even then Field Marshal Kesselring was able to pull his armies back to another position, the GOTHIC line north of Florence, taking in the northern Apennines.

The British General Alexander, the Allied Mediterranean Theatre commander, latterly argued for Allied forces to be kept in Italy to move north and eventually effect a strategic breakout to the northeast, through the so-called Ljubljana Gap (in modern Slovenia), and drive on towards Vienna. Later, in the Cold War, it was argued that such a strategy would have prevented Soviet control of much of East Central Europe. But it is unlikely that such a campaign could have yielded decisive results in time, especially on the evidence of the slow pace of advance in the previous two years in Italy. In any event more American and French divisions were pulled out of the peninsula for the August 1944 invasion of southern France (Operation DRAGOON). German Army Group 'C' held the GOTHIC line for another winter, until the final collapse came about in March–April 1945. Turin, Milan, and Venice stayed in German hands until the last weeks of the war.

The Balkans

Histories of World War II, even of the periphery, devote little space to the Balkan peninsula. Yet this outlying region of Europe was of strategic importance throughout the conflict. In 1939 France had hoped to create a Balkan front against Germany. After the fall of France, however, several Balkan states slid under German protection, notably Romania and Bulgaria. Italy, which already controlled Albania, invaded Greece in late 1940, and took a large part in the occupation of the Balkans until 1943. The region, meanwhile, had been a source of tension between Hitler and Stalin during the period of the Nazi–Soviet Pact. Hitler allowed the Russians to take back Bessarabia (Moldavia) from Romania, but he secretly sent German forces to the remaining part of that country. Germany, Italy, and Russia had also vied for influence in Yugoslavia before April 1941. In any event the German spring Blitzkrieg of 1941 overwhelmed Yugoslavia and Greece. With the expulsion of the British from Crete in May 1941 and the Soviets from Bessarabia in the following month, Germany and Italy made themselves dominant in the Balkan region.

The Balkans were important for their resources and for historical and geostrategic reasons, at least as far as the European states were concerned. (The region had decidedly less importance for the United States.) The Germans got much of their oil from Romania, and there were important resources like bauxite (for aluminium) in Yugoslavia. A major German supply route to North Africa in 1941–2 went through the region. Historical factors also made the Balkans important. Austria-Hungary, one of the antecedents of the Third Reich, had been a Balkan power. The Russians had historical relations with some of their fellow Slavs of the Balkans, and the British had 'interests' in Greece and the Levant in general. Of particular importance to all concerned was the effect that gains or losses in the Balkans would have on neutral Turkey.

For a time after the summer of 1941 there was little the Allies – Eastern or Western – could do to influence events in the Balkans. This was due to the Allies' weakness, the concentration of their forces on other fronts, and the distance of their bases from the region. In the late summer of 1943, however, the British and Americans took control of southern Italy across the Adriatic. Various Allied deception plans tried to convince the Germans that an Allied landing in the Balkans was imminent. The collapse of Italy (and the Italian occupation army) left a power vacuum. The Germans had to increase their garrison in the Balkans after the Italian surrender; by June 1944 they had twenty-five divisions there. Churchill despatched a brigade in an attempt to seize the Italian-held island colonies of Rhodes and the Dodecanese Islands, on the far side of the Aegean, in September 1943. The Germans moved faster, and in a humiliating defeat for this stage of the war, in November 1943, the British either evacuated the islands or (in the case of Kos and Leros) surrendered to the Germans.

The Americans had refused to get involved in the Aegean venture. The British, preoccupied with the war of attrition in Italy, had no significant forces to send. What the Allies were able to do was to extend their bombing attacks to the Balkans from North Africa and Italy. Long-range terror raids on Sofia and Bucharest brought home the reality of the war to the smaller Axis governments. More important, American bombers eventually destroyed the oil refineries at Ploesti in Romania. But it was not until the second half of 1944 that Allied ground forces reached the Balkan periphery, and they arrived in the form of the Red Army.

Stalin repeatedly criticised Churchill's reluctance to commit to a 'direct' cross-Channel invasion. But for all this, Stalin was not averse to straying from the direct route to Berlin when it suited him. In August 1944, two months after the main summer Soviet offensive in Belorussia, Operation BAGRATION (see Chapter 12), the Red Army caught the Germans by surprise in a second devastating offensive out of the southern Ukraine towards Romania (the Iasi–Kishinev operation). This was a parallel with North Africa and Italy, although this time it was the Russians who were putting on the pressure. The Russian successes provoked a palace coup in Bucharest in which the Romanian 'Mussolini', the dictator Marshal Antonescu, was overthrown. The new royal government immediately sought an armistice.

The comparisons with Italy in 1943 were striking, but events in Romania went much more badly for the Germans. Unlike the British-American invasion of Sicily, the initial Russian offensive had trapped most of the front-line Axis forces, including twenty-five German divisions. Hitler, who had counted on Romanian anti-Bolshevism, was caught unprepared. Very few German ground troops were stationed in the central part of Romania around Bucharest. The Wehrmacht was by this time struggling for survival in France and Poland and was unable to send reinforcements to fill the Romanian vacuum. Unlike the British and Americans in North Africa in 1942 or in southern Italy in 1943, the Russians had large ground forces ready to throw forward. In a matter of weeks Soviet spearheads had dashed into Bucharest, and the remains of the Royal Romanian Army had changed sides.

The surrender of Romania opened a whole new avenue towards the Reich, up the Danube River valley and through Hungary to Vienna (see Chapter 12). It also meant that the Red Army could move into the Balkans. One well-trodden path of Tsarist Russian expansion led south towards the Turkish Straits. In September 1944 the USSR declared war on Bulgaria. Another political coup, this time in Sofia, eased the passage of the Red Army. Although Bulgaria had not been formally at war with the USSR, it had occupied parts of Yugoslavia and Greece, and had allowed German forces to operate from its territory.

From Bulgaria and western Romania another peripheral route led the Red Army into the territory of pre-war Yugoslavia. In October 1944 the Russians' left-flank armies took the city of Belgrade, which lies on the northeastern edge of the country. Yugoslavia, despite the pitiful performance of its national army in April 1941, had became the scene of the most successful anti-German guerrilla campaign in Europe (see Chapter 11).

The Soviet advance across the northern Balkans put the German outpost forces in Greece and the Aegean at great risk. The main railway line from Central Europe to Greece and Turkey (via Belgrade and Salonika) – route of the peacetime 'Orient Express' – was threatened and then cut, leaving only tortuous road routes. The Germans began in the late summer of 1944 to abandon their untenable forward positions.

This part of the European periphery now became a focus of diplomatic activity. The British, and Churchill in particular, believed that the way forward was to agree in advance to spheres of influence with the Russians. London now accepted that there would inevitably be a major Soviet role in Eastern Europe, especially in those states which had been active partners of Germany. The initial proposal, early in 1944, was that Britain would accept predominant Soviet influence in Romania, while Britain would have predominant influence in Greece. In October 1944, after Romania and Bulgaria had been occupied by the Red Army, and the German garrison had pulled out of Greece, Churchill took the 'spheres' approach a step forward. He flew for the third time to Moscow and made the so-called 'percentages agreement' at a one-to-one meeting with Stalin (the TOLSTOI conference). The name of the agreement came from Churchill's description of political influence in percentage terms, and this now took in the whole Balkan/Danubian area. Britain and the USSR would have an equal interest (50 per cent) in

Yugoslavia and Hungary; Russian interests would predominate in Romania (90 per cent) and Bulgaria (75 per cent); the British would predominate in Greece (90 per cent). Roosevelt, engaged in the last stages of a Presidential election, distanced himself from the 'deal'.

The Churchill–Stalin agreement coincided with the final Allied move into the Balkan periphery, the unopposed British landing in Greece. This began in mid October 1944, following on from the final German withdrawal. Greece was in a unique situation. After the defeat by the Germans in April 1941 King George II had formed a government-in-exile with British support. Politics in Athens had been fractious before the war, and many Greeks disliked the monarchy. The resistance movement, too, was split. The largest organisation, the Communist-led EAM (National Liberation Front), which developed in 1942, was hostile to the King and the government-in-exile. It had a considerable guerrilla force, the ELAS (National People's Liberation Army) (see Chapter 11).

The British brought home the émigré government in October 1944, but the EAM leaders walked out of a coalition government in which they had been assigned a subordinate role. Demonstrations and disturbances followed in Athens. Churchill, who had strong positive views about King George II, flew to the Greek capital for an extraordinary visit in December 1944. Street-fighting between ELAS and royalist forces worsened, with the latter being supported by British air strikes and armour. In December 1944 and January 1945 the British Army forced the disarmament of the ELAS.

The Kremlin raised no objections, and this was in line with the 'percentages' agreement. In January 1945, in a telephone conversation with Georgi Dimitrov, the Bulgarian co-ordinator of the various Communist parties, Stalin criticised the withdrawal of EAM-ELAS from the Greek coalition government: 'They were evidently counting on the Red Army coming down to the Aegean. We cannot do that. We cannot send our troops into Greece, either. The Greeks [i.e. EAM-ELAS] have acted foolishly.' The truth was that elsewhere in the Balkan periphery the 'percentages' deal suited Stalin. He controlled Bulgaria. His Communist allies were the effective government of Yugoslavia. The Red Army already held most of Hungary. In February 1945 Stalin tightened his grip on Romania by sending his own tanks into the streets of Bucharest to install a more pliable government. The shape of the Cold War Balkans was already clear.

Scandinavia

We normally think of the 'periphery' as Southern Europe, because the Mediterranean littoral is where the main 'peripheral' fighting took place. In grand-strategic terms, however, Scandinavia – especially Norway, Sweden, and Finland – and perhaps the Baltic states were also on the edge of Europe, and the importance of the region had not been ended by Germany's April 1940 Norwegian campaign.

Sweden – like Spain, Portugal, and Turkey – was able to keep its neutrality, although it did give the German forces limited transit rights to northern Norway. Estonia, Latvia, and Lithuania, small independent states in 1940, were in the unique position of having been annexed by the USSR and effectively 'liberated' by the Wehrmacht. They had no governments-in-exile, and hardly any anti-German resistance movement. Although Estonia was not on the main axis of the Soviet advance, Latvia and Lithuania were, and the Russians wanted part of East Prussia as well. One of the last German bastions was in western Latvia; Army Group Kurland was the remnant of the Army Group North which had besieged Leningrad. Whatever the sense of the 1941 Atlantic Charter – the signatories of which promised that they sought 'no aggrandizement, territorial or other' – Moscow reincorporated all three Baltic states back into the USSR in 1944. There was no protest from the British or the Americans.

Norway had lost its special economic importance (as seen in 1939–40) with the German occupation of even better bases and mineral resources in France (see Chapter 4). However, the country had a new strategic importance after June 1941 as a base for German aircraft and ships operating against the 'peripheral' supply lines to the North Russian ports. Norway had a government-in-exile and a substantial resistance movement, but neither shook the German hold on the country. Churchill was a persistent advocate of a landing in Norway – Operation JUPITER – as part of his peripheral campaign. Hitler was worried about Norway, partly thanks to Allied deception operations. In June 1944 the Germans had twelve divisions in Norway. Norway, however, had difficult terrain and was beyond the range of Allied ground support aircraft. In the end the only Allied troops to operate in Norway were Russian; they liberated the extreme north of the country after the October 1944 Petsamo-Kirkenes operation. In the end, in May 1945, central and southern Norway remained another German bastion.

Finland was in a different position from the other Scandinavian states both politically and strategically. The country was an enthusiastic participant in the June 1941 war against the USSR. The Finns called their fight with the Red Army the 'Continuation War' (continuing – or rather undoing – the Winter War of 1939–40). The Finns advanced considerably beyond their 1939 border, although they never seriously pressed home the attack on Leningrad from the north. Finland suffered very high losses, nearly 90,000 military deaths in a population of only 3.6 million.

Like the Italians and the Romanians, the Finnish leaders in 1943–4 were looking for ways out of the war and out of their alliance with Hitler. The Germans had clearly lost the war, and the Red Army was ready to mount a counter-attack. Fortunately for the Finns the Germans could not physically enforce a compliant government in Helsinki. There were seven German divisions in Finland, but they were all in the far north. Finland was also politically more stable than the other Axis allies. It was evident to the Russians that the British and the Americans (as well as the Swedes) were more sympathetic to the Finns than any of the other Eastern European states. Fortunately for the Finns, too, their country did not lie on the strategic route to anywhere else.

In September 1944, after the Soviet summer offensive, the Finns capitulated. Aside from giving up territory to Russia, they also undertook to evict the Wehrmacht from Finland using their own army. The positive side of this was that the Red Army would not enter Finland. Some fighting took place between the two former allies, but in the end the Germans withdrew their forces across Lapland to northern Norway (the opposite route of Daladier's planned expedition of 1940). There they would await the end of the war. As for Finland, it was the only European state with a long border with the USSR that was able to avoid a Communist government after 1945.

· · ·

On all sides the Allies had completed the process of 'closing the ring' around the Third Reich – to use the expression of Prime Minister Churchill. His final stages, 'liberating the population' and 'final assault of the German citadel', were yet to come (see Chapters 11 and 12). For the British and Americans this peripheral conflict had been an alternative – a probably unavoidable alternative – to a direct assault on the Reich and its inner defensive core. The Russians had been fighting deep within their own country, but they too had fought peripheral battles in the Balkans. Peripheral fighting also involved Hitler's erstwhile Allies changing sides, or at least attempting to do so. This political change developed in a variety of ways and had weighty implications for the post-war world.

American B-24 Liberators bomb an oil refinery at Ploesti. Romanian oil was identified as a potential Achilles' heel of the German war effort even before the war began. More generally, the Allies hoped that destroying German factories and resource centres by bombing or sabotage would 'wear down' the Nazi war effort, causing the enemy's economy to collapse, shattering civilian morale, and allowing the eventual defeat of the powerful Wehrmacht.

Unfortunately for the Allied planners the 'wear down' strategy took a long time to achieve results, and this was as true in Romania as elsewhere. Ploesti was remote from Allied airfields and was eventually heavily defended. A low-level B-24 raid in August 1943, Operation TIDAL WAVE, was extremely costly for the Americans; 54 out of 177 attacking aircraft were lost, and little permanent damage was achieved. Later attacks, in 1944, succeeded in shutting down Ploesti, but this came late in the war.

Wearing down Germany 1942–1944

Timeline

1940	July	Formation of British Special Operations Executive (SOE)
	December	Roosevelt's 'Arsenal of Democracy' speech
1941	March	US Congress passes Lend-Lease Act
	June	Invasion of USSR; development of Communist Resistance
1942	February	Speer given key role in German war economy
	May	'Thousand bomber' RAF raid on Cologne
1943	January	Goebbels' 'Total War' speech
	July	Bombing of Hamburg
1944	February	'Big Week' of USAAF bombing campaign
	July	Peak of German war production
	July	Attempted assassination of Hitler

Bombers and saboteurs

Two opposite ends of the technological spectrum – long-range bombers and lightly armed guerrillas equipped with little more than a burning hatred of the occupier – had a related part to play in World War II. Both strategic bombing and popular resistance were considered by national leaders as alternatives to mass conventional armies. Both seemed to offer the anti-Hitler coalition, and especially Britain, a means of bypassing the powerful conventional forces of the Wehrmacht and victory at a lower cost.

The common element was called 'wear down'. An important statement of this strategy were the decisions made at the first Washington summit meeting in December 1941, the so-called ARCADIA conference. The Americans and British agreed that 'essential features' of the strategy included 'Wearing down and undermining German resistance by air bombardment, blockade, subversive activities, and propaganda'. Although extreme advocates of air warfare thought bombing could shatter German civilian morale, and extreme advocates of subversion hoped for a large-scale popular uprising, 'wear down' normally meant wearing down the economy of the enemy. The production of the Third Reich would be crippled by bombing and sabotage. Blockade, of course, would also play a role in the strategy; this was discussed in Chapter 9.

World War II, especially in Europe, was seen by many political and military leaders as an economic struggle as much as a military one. This fitted within Field Marshal Ludenforff's concept of total war (see Box 4), and the British even coined the term 'economic warfare'. Victory in the war of machines would go to the side that maximised its own production and was best able to reduce the output of the other side. 'Wear down' through bombing and sabotage seemed a particularly effective way of bringing about that reduction.

The economic strategies of the two sides in Europe did not change, despite ups and downs in the fortunes of war in 1940 and in 1942–3. The 'new order' powers had aimed to gain and exploit economically a larger resource base. This was a central part of Hitler's thinking about strategy. In 1943 the Axis offensives seemed to be over, but Germany had its *Grossraum*, economic 'space' – a larger European 'empire' than that of any previous state. Meanwhile as late as 1942–3 the Germans devoted resources to limiting the economic potential of the Allies, cutting shipping lanes with their U-boat fleet and occupying key economic areas of southern Russia with their panzer divisions. Germany's enemies also stressed this economic conflict. Allied strategists differed among themselves on the extent to which a ground force campaign would be necessary. They were in complete agreement, however, that a major part of winning the war involved organising superior global Allied economic resources.

Economic warfare: raw materials

Traditionally, the key raw materials of the Industrial Revolution were coal and iron, and here the Third Reich was well supplied. Germany had coal in abundance (even on its original home territory). In wartime the mines could be worked by unskilled foreign forced labourers. Coal supply was relatively hard to attack at source, although latterly the movement of coal by rail and canal could be interrupted by bombing. The British, Russians, and Americans also had huge coal reserves, although the Wehrmacht was able to occupy the mines of the Donbass (Donets River basin). Hitler's April 1942 directive for his 'second offensive' in the USSR specified that the aim was to deprive the Soviets 'of the most important sources of strength of their war economy'.[1] Soviet production of coal fell to about two-thirds the pre-war total (and to a third that of Germany) by 1943. Germany also had adequate supplies of iron ore, although this had been considered a highly vulnerable point at the start of the war, when the Allies considered blocking German access to the ore fields of northern Sweden (see Chapter 4). In the end, despite the bombing, German steel production rose through 1943, when it was twice that of Britain, and three times that of the USSR.

In the case of oil products, essential for the operational side of the 'war of motors', the situation was far less favourable for the Reich. The Western Allies controlled the Gulf of Mexico and the Caribbean, which were at that time the global centre of oil extraction (see Box 42). Oil production from the USA alone was 1,400 million tons in 1941, rising to 1,680 million tons in 1944. Meanwhile Soviet oil production, although dwarfed by that of the USA, was considerably more than German-controlled production and enough to provide the needs of the Red Army. It totalled some 33 million tons in 1941, and about 20 million tons in each of the war years. Soviet production was maintained, despite oil being another of the economic 'sources of strength' that Hitler had attempted to attack in 1942; one importance of Stalingrad was that it commanded the oil-barge traffic up the Volga.

Box 42 | Production statistics

The three tables below give basic information about the economic potential and war production of seven of the major wartime states. There are no comparable figures for China.

A Economic potential (1938)

	Population (millions)	Steel (millions of tons)	Energy consumption (millions of tons)	GDP ($ billion)
USA	130	29	697	800
Russia	169	18	177	359
Germany	75	23	228	351
Britain	47	10	196	284
France	42	6	84	186
Japan	72	7	96	169
Italy	43	2	28	141

(From Paul Kennedy, *The Rise and Fall of the Great Powers: Economic Change and Military Conflict from 1500 to 2000* (London: Fontana, 1989), pp. 255, 257–8, citing IUCPSR data at the University of Michigan (steel and energy); Mark Harrison, ed., *The Economics of World War II: Six Powers in International Comparison* (Cambridge: Cambridge University Press, 1998), p. 10 (population and GDP). 'Population' is for home territory. 'Energy consumption' is an important indicator of industrial activity; it is measured in millions of metric tons of coal equivalent. GDP is gross domestic product in international dollars and at 1990 prices.)

B Weapons production (thousand units)

	1939	1940	1941	1942	1943	1944	1945
Germany							
Tanks and SPG	0.7	2.2	3.8	6.2	10.7	18.3	4.4
Combat aircraft	2.3	6.6	8.4	11.6	19.3	34.1	7.2
Britain							
Tanks and SPG	0.3	1.4	4.8	8.6	7.5	4.6	2.1
Combat aircraft	1.3	8.6	13.2	17.7	21.2	22.7	9.9
USA							
Tanks and SPG	–	–	0.9	27.0	38.5	20.5	12.6
Combat aircraft	–	–	1.4	24.9	54.1	74.1	37.5
USSR							
Tanks and SPG	–	–	4.8	24.4	24.1	29.0	20.5
Combat aircraft	–	–	8.2	21.7	29.9	33.2	19.1

(From Mark Harrison, ed., *The Economics of World War II: Six Powers in International Comparison* (Cambridge: Cambridge University Press, 1998), pp. 15–16. SPG are self–propelled guns, i.e. tracked artillery.)

C World crude oil production (thousands of barrels per day)								
	USA	Mexico	Venezuela	USSR	Romania	East Indies	Iran	Others	Total
1935	2,730	110	406	500	169	144	157	317	4,534
1945	4,695	119	885	408	95	27	358	522	7,109

(From Daniel Yergin, *The Prize: The Epic Quest for Oil, Money, and Power* (New York: Simon & Schuster, 1991), p. 830. A barrel is given in this source as 42 US gallons (159 litres).)

The Third Reich lacked oil, for Germany itself, and for most of its allies; it lacked oil, too, for the occupied states, whose pre-war economies had been dependent on imports. The British blockade was tellingly important here. Coping with this anticipated weakness had been the object of a large part of the pre-war German strategic investment, especially increasing production of synthetic oil products (mainly from coal). In 1939 Germany produced just 1.5 million tons of natural oil and 2.2 million tons of synthetic oil; it imported 5.2 million tons. Although the USSR provided large amounts of oil in 1940 and 1941, after June 1941 Germany's main foreign source was Romania, which provided 3 million tons in 1941, 2.2 million in 1942, and 2.4 million in 1943. The German production of synthetic oil was increased to 5.7 million tons in 1943. As we will see, the British and then the Americans identified oil as a choke point, but it was not until the spring of 1944 that their bombers were able to inflict crippling damage on the Romanian oil installations and on the synthetic oil plants in central Germany.

The final general raw material was food. In 1917 Tsarist Russia had dropped out of World War I largely because of a food-supply crisis. The ultimate goal of the U-boat campaign in both World Wars was to starve out Britain, and here the British did seem uniquely vulnerable. The British were, however, able to keep supplies flowing and to increase domestic production. The USA had abundant food supplies, much of which it could export. In the USSR the 'collective farm' system introduced in the early 1930s, whatever its shortcomings, provided a working system of state procurement. Above all the Soviet Union was able to survive the loss of the grain-producing Ukraine, although there was much malnutrition. The Third Reich, too, was able to secure adequate supplies of food. Germany avoided a repetition of the *Steckrübenwinter* (turnip winter) of 1916–17, when even the supply of potatoes ran low. The vast German food-producing region of 1940–1 meant that the oceanic blockade could not cause fatal damage. Bombing could not affect German food production, and until the very end of the war it was difficult to block food distribution. The Germans were able to introduce foreign labour to work in agriculture. They also resorted to the drastic and cruel policy of starving peripheral regions in the East to feed Germans in the Reich and the Wehrmacht in the field.

The German war industry

Germany and Italy had to fight World War II from a position of economic inferiority (see the statistics in Box 42). This was true even when Germany confronted Britain and France in 1939–40. It was clearer still that the three major states which made up the 'Grand Alliance' of December 1941 – the British Empire, the USSR, and the United States – had a marked economic advantage over the 'new-order' Axis powers of Germany, Italy, and Japan. The leaders of Germany and Italy were aware of this relative material weakness. The Chief of the German Army General Staff (General Beck) resigned before Munich in 1938 due to what he perceived as Hitler's rash strategy, given the correlation of forces. In May 1939 the head of German Army weapons supply, General Thomas, spoke secretly about the Axis states' lack of German armaments 'in depth', and the inherent advantage of the 'Western powers' (see Box 42). Mussolini balked at joining the war in September 1939, correctly pleading Italy's lack of economic and military preparations.

Nevertheless a desire to redress the economic/resource balance was a major reason why the 'new-order' powers went to war in the first place. Economic weakness also dictated the strategy and the pace of their actions before and during the war. From the German point of view the war could be won only if rivals and enemies could be knocked off in a series of 'quick decisive blows' (in the words of General Thomas), before they could mobilise their economies and join up their resources. The German leaders hoped that distance and lack of political will would prevent US economic potential from having a serious effect until after the position of the Reich in Europe had been militarily consolidated. Meanwhile the Germans had only a hazy perception of Soviet economic potential, seeing the territory of the USSR as a source of raw materials rather than as an – enemy – manufacturing base.

The German war economy could be made stronger in two ways: through territorial expansion and through investment and reorganisation. On paper the German economic position greatly improved from 1938 onwards, first with the annexation of Austria and the Czech lands, then by gaining control of the advanced and largely undamaged economies of Western Europe – Belgium, the Netherlands, and France – and finally by getting access to the natural resources of the Balkans and western Russia. One recent assessment, by the British economic historian Mark Harrison, calculated the extent of Germany's gains between 1938 and 1942. Germany had a 1938 population of 68 million people and a GDP (gross domestic product) of $351 billion (in international dollars and at 1990 prices). By 1942 the Third Reich had taken over, mainly by military conquest, a European territory with an additional population of just over 200 million people and an additional GDP of nearly $600 billion. About a quarter of this total gain came from the occupied USSR and the rest was from Western, Central, and Southern Europe (measuring population and GDP as of 1938). Germany's European allies provided a further (1938) population of about 95 million people and a GDP of nearly $210 billion. About half this 'allied' population and two-thirds of the GDP were from Italy.

In reality, however, the Third Reich did not gain a great deal economically from the occupations. Germany was not able to develop or exploit significant arms industries in the countries it had taken over, with the exception of the Czech lands. This failure, as we will see shortly, was not primarily the result of successful Allied subversion of the subject populations. Rather, German economic policy in the occupied region was both heavy-handed and short-sighted. Also, the developed economies of Western Europe had been too dependent on outside trade to be quickly set up on a new basis. Above all, the Germans had very little time.

As it turned out, the main industrial gain of Hitler's conquests took the form of forced labour (or 'slave labour' as it would be described in the 1946 Nuremberg indictment). Millions of workers, male and female, were brought to Greater Germany under a greater or lesser degree of compulsion. Some laboured in agriculture, construction, or mining to free Germans for work in the war factories or for service in the Wehrmacht. The first to be drafted in were Poles, who originally worked in agriculture; French POWs followed them in 1940. When the course of the war became more difficult for the Reich

Box 43 | Armament in breadth

General Georg Thomas was head of the Office of Army Weapons (*Heereswaffenamt*). The following extract is from a speech given by Thomas at the German Foreign Ministry on 24 May 1939.

From 1939 to November 1942 Thomas was head of the Defence Economy and Armament Office (*Wehrwirtschafts-und Rüstungsamt*) in the Wehrmacht high command (OKW). Although he was an enthusiastic supporter of Hitler's early conquests, documents compromising him were discovered after the July 1944 bomb plot. He was arrested in October 1944 and imprisoned at Flossenbürg and Dachau concentration camps. He died in American custody in December 1946.

Gentlemen! All the time I have been in charge of my department [Office of Army Weapons, *Heereswaffenamt*], I have always pointed out the difference between armament in breadth and armament in depth.

By armament in breadth I mean the number and strength of the armed forces in peacetime and the preparation made to increase them in time of war.

Armament in depth, on the other hand, embraces all those measures, particularly affecting materials and of an economic nature, which serve to provide supplies during war and therefore strengthen our powers of endurance.

We are clear about our present superiority in breadth and in the initial striking power of our armament; now we must analyse whether we can retain the superiority in an armaments race and thereby achieve superiority in depth of armament.

Allow me first to say a few words about the dangers which can develop if too much attention is paid to armament in breadth at the expense of armament in depth.

We all know that in every war, soon after the beginning of operations, a request comes for new formations and that then all available resources are recklessly released to provide these new formations. At the same time, there is a request for increased amounts of munitions and all the other necessities, and woe betide the leadership of economic warfare if it is not in a position to fulfil these demands owing to a lack of reserves of finished goods or raw materials and semi-finished goods . . . You will understand if, particularly at the present time in which the sections of the armed forces are considerably enlarged every year, I emphasize in all seriousness the need of improving our armament in depth . . .

The information which we have so far received does not indicate that the western Great Powers are as yet pursuing rearmament with the same energy as we are. But should the political situation lead to a long-drawn-out armaments race we must of course realize that the Western Powers, considering the capacity of their economies for producing armaments, will be in a position to catch up with the German lead in 1–1½ years. The combined economic strength of Britain, America, and France is in the long run greater than that of the Axis Powers and in an armaments race the Western Powers will not have the same difficulties which Germany and Italy will always have on account of their lack of raw materials and manpower. If it comes to an armaments race and then to a war the result of the war will, in my opinion, depend on whether the Axis States succeed in bringing about a decision by a quick decisive blow. If they do not succeed in this, if it comes to a struggle like that of the World War [i.e. 1914–18], then the depth of military economic power, that is, the powers of endurance, will decide the issue.

(From Jeremey Noakes and Geoffrey Pridham, *Nazism 1919–1945: A Documentary Reader* (Exeter: University of Exeter Press, 2001), vol. III, pp. 731f.)

after the winter of 1941–2, inhibitions against using non-Aryan labour in German industry were reduced; at the same time the pool of potential forced labour was huge, with the Wehrmacht still holding the western parts of the USSR (mainly the Ukraine and Belorussia). The NSDAP leader Fritz Sauckel was in May 1942 made plenipotentiary for the mobilisation of foreign labour from all over Europe; for this role he would be condemned and hanged as a major war criminal at Nuremberg.

Hundreds of thousands of forced labourers were housed in improvised labour camps, often in poor conditions. An extreme case was the concentration camp system of the SS. It has been estimated that well over 2 million foreign men and women died while working in the Reich, about half of them Soviet POWs. In 1944 over 7 million foreign workers and POWs were in the labour force working in Greater Germany, as well as 500,000 concentration camp inmates. This total included nearly 2.4 million forced labourers from the USSR, 1.4 million from Poland, 900,000 from France and 500,000 from Italy. A third of the workforce in the armaments industry was foreign by 1944. Altogether foreign workers made up a quarter of the whole labour force. Without them the economy of the Third Reich could not have functioned, nor could the Wehrmacht have been manned and supplied.

The other way in which the Germans could cope with the demands of total war was to reorganise their homeland economy and to concentrate on military production. Albert Speer, the supremo of Hitler's war economy, put the position as follows in a late 1943 speech to NSDAP *Gauleiter* (regional party chiefs):

[A rapid increase in production] is urgently necessary, because we are no longer in the happy position as we were after the [1940] French campaign when we could determine what the enemy had to do, but today the enemy dictates to us with his production what we have do. And if we cannot follow this dictation by the enemy then, in the long run, the front cannot hold.[2]

The picture is distorted by propaganda and by the self-publicity of Speer himself. The Germans had actually been preparing for a big war, with crippling investments, since the mid 1930s. The advanced German economy was adapted to war production, albeit at high long-term cost and at a level that practically left Germany no alternative but to embark on wars of aggression. After the Moscow defeat and Pearl Harbor, Hitler appointed Speer to be Minister of Armaments and Munitions (following the death of Fritz Todt), but many of Speer's achievements were the pay-off for the earlier investments. At the start of 1943, Hitler and Goebbels announced a policy of 'total war', but this was aimed more at public opinion than at actual reorganisation. A further propaganda campaign came in the summer of 1944 after critical defeats at the front and the emergence of an anti-Hitler conspiracy at home. Much of this amounted to window-dressing.

The Germans were able to increase their own GDP from $351 billion in 1938 to a peak of $437 billion in 1944, but this was not enough. The growth of GDP – up about 25 per cent – was matched from 1938 to 1944 by that of Britain and the USSR. In contrast the US GDP soared from $800 billion in 1938 to $1,094 billion in 1941 and $1,499 billion in 1944, a total growth of nearly 90 per cent. Even British production of aircraft and tanks had caught up and overtaken Germany – at least in numbers – in 1941 and 1942 (see Box 42). In 1942 and 1943 the Americans and Russians were *each* producing about 2,000 tanks a month, compared to 500–900 for the Germans. In 1943 Germany was producing only 1,600 aircraft a month, compared to 1,800 British, 2,500 Soviet, and no fewer than 4,500 American (many American aircraft were supplied to the RAF, the Red Army Air Force, and other allies). The Americans, Russians, and British all created motorised armies – thanks especially to American truck and Jeep production – while much of the vaunted German Army was horse-drawn or dependent on railway movement.

In 1944, however, and despite the intensification of the Allied bombing campaign, the Germans did achieve massive production figures. German factories produced 1,500 tanks a month, nearly matching the output of US factories; they produced 2,800 aircraft, which was a figure comparable to Soviet production. Even so, in 1944 the US produced three times as many aircraft as the Germans, and the Soviet Union over 50 per cent more tanks. In addition Speer and others had produced high raw output figures by concentrating on standardised weapons. A classic example was the huge-scale production of the Messerschmitt Bf 109G fighter, a ten-year-old design which had no development potential, and for which there were too few trained pilots and insufficient fuel.

The Third Reich also attempted to square the circle by technical innovation, to recapture the edge they had held at the start of the war. German propaganda made much of 'miracle weapons' (*Wunderwaffen*) that would turn the tide and overcome the Allied numerical advantage: V1 and V2 guided missiles, Me 262 and He 162 jet fighters, anti-shipping missiles, and the Type XXI U-boat. The Third Reich famously anticipated many of the weapons systems of the following decades – except atomic weapons – but the work was carried out too rapidly. The new weapons had many teething problems and for the most part were available in only small numbers; none entered service before D-Day.

The Allied war economy

The other side of the coin was the Allied economic war effort. The British economy on its own was about the same size as that of Germany. Unlike the Third Reich Britain did not gain, by conquest, supplies of labour and factory space, but the Empire gave it access to the world's raw materials (although less so after December 1941); there was also some weapons production in Canada and Australia. It is often argued that Britain had the best-organised home front, although the economy was hitting physical limits by 1944, and the post-war situation would be very difficult; Britain was dependent on US imports and credit after 1940. The Soviet achievement was remarkable, given the late historical start of Russian industrialisation (Tsarist in the 1890s, Soviet in the 1930s), and the loss of western territories. As an advantage the Russians had a huge geographical hinterland. The Russians also had a vital head start: their peacetime Five-Year economic plans (since 1927) gave them experience in near-wartime concentration of resources, and they had begun massive rearmament even before the Germans. The ability to evacuate much industrial plant to the east was important. Like the British, the Russians benefited from American supplies, especially from 1943 onwards.

The American population made greater sacrifices than their enemies thought they might, but they also began from a much higher base of raw materials and they could make use of 'Fordist' production techniques (see Figure 23). Their production could be carried out on a huge scale without any interruption from enemy action. War production did not affect the standard of living, and in fact jerked the American economy out of the Great Depression. The Allies were also able to transfer manufactured equipment and resources effectively within the alliance, mainly from the United States to its partners, thanks to their control of the oceans (see Chapter 9). Lend-Lease (see Box 44) provided the main means. As Stalin put it: 'Modern war is a war of motors. The war will be won by whichever side produces the most motors.'[3] US economic power was a decisive factor in the victory of the Allied coalition.

In the economic war – both industrial production and mobilisation of raw materials – the Allies had great advantages over Germany in almost all aspects except technical ingenuity. They also had the singular ability to blockade Germany, without their enemy being able to retaliate effectively. The economic war was not, however, going to achieve rapid victory. Germany probably organised its war economy as skilfully as its opponents, and a good deal more ruthlessly.

Strategic bombing

Strategic bombing was regarded by many military planners, most importantly in Britain and the United States, as a key means of wearing down the economic strength of an enemy and weakening the morale of its population (see Chapter 1). The Japanese and the Germans, however, were the first to attempt a strategic air campaign. Japanese bombers mounted over 100 long-range raids against Chongqing in 1940 (see Chapter 2). The Germans followed later in the year with a much heavier series of air attacks on British targets (see Chapter 4). Some of these Luftwaffe attacks were, broadly speaking, economic, including strikes against ports and aircraft factories. In the later stages of the Blitz the objective became civilian morale, and large urban areas were targeted. In the winter of 1940–1 and through the late spring of 1941 heavy night raids were carried out against British cities.

The subsequent air offensive unleashed by the RAF was not simply a reprisal. 'Strategic' bombing had become an important part of British military theory in the inter-war years. Britain had the first proper independent air force (i.e. independent of the Army and the Navy) under Hugh Trenchard. Throughout the 1930s, and even before the rise of Hitler, some British leaders had seen the RAF as a way by which future wars could be won. Britain was eager to find an alternative to the 'continental' commitment, the massive deployment of ground troops which had been such a feature of World War I. The strategic air power concept also had 'bureaucratic' origins: the independent RAF needed its own mission to win status and justify funding. There were certainly great moral issues to consider in attacks on civilians, but the original conception of 'strategic bombing' had, for the British, a deterrent as much as a 'war-fighting' value. One way to prevent war, or, if war came, to prevent attacks on British cities, was to be able to threaten a potential enemy with unacceptable damage to his own cities.

In the early phases of the war both German and Allied long-range bombing was limited by a lack of resources, by geography, and by a fear of escalation. The Blitz, Hitler's 1940 air attack on British cities, reduced British strategic and ethical restraints, but it did not change the geographical or technical realities. All the same, in the two years between the fall of France and the arrival of significant American ground forces, the long-range campaign of the RAF's 'Bomber Command' was – alongside the naval blockade – one of the few means by which Britain could directly damage Germany. British aircraft production, as we have seen, had reached impressive levels even in 1940–1. By 1942 the British had a bomber force larger than that of Germany, including a number of huge four-engined machines (Stirlings, Lancasters, and Halifaxes). From February of that year, until the end of the war, the RAF effort was led by the C-in-C of Bomber Command, Air Marshal Arthur Harris.

The original RAF plan had been aimed at German civilian morale, but it also had an element of genuine 'economic warfare'. Key elements of the German economy, most notably its synthetic oil plants, were to be destroyed. But Bomber Command could not penetrate the Luftwaffe's air defences – fighter planes and anti-aircraft guns – during the hours of daylight without suffering unacceptable losses. The new Hurricane and Spitfire fighters, which had won the Battle of Britain, did not have the range to escort the bombers

Figure 23 | **Fordism**

'Fordism' comes from the name of Henry Ford (1863–1947), the pioneer of the mass production of motor vehicles. 'Fordism' has various meanings, but it is taken here to be the use of series production on a conveyer belt or 'assembly line' with the simplification of manufacturing processes and the extensive use of machine tools. Rational management, integrated production, and economies of scale are also key features. The first practical motor car was probably German, the 1890s design of Gottfried Daimler (1834–1900), but the Ford Model 'T' car was produced in much greater numbers between 1908 and 1927, using assembly-line methods.

The success or failure of wartime economies of the major powers in the 1930s and 1940s was based on the extent to which they could apply Fordist methods to the production of aircraft, motors, vehicles, weapons, ammunition, and even ships and submarines. The photograph shows one of the production lines for the Boeing B-29 Superfortress. The B-29 was originally built in a huge new plant at Renton, Washington. Another Boeing assembly line was established in Wichita, Kansas, and Martin and Bell built the aircraft under license in Omaha, Nebraska, and Marietta, Georgia. The huge Cyclone GR-3350 (2,200 hp) motors were partly manufactured in a huge new Wright plant in New Jersey and partly built under licence by the Chrysler Corporation in Chicago.

Fordist production methods could be applied by large private firms (as in the USA) or by the state (as in the USSR). The more traditional economies of Germany, Britain, Italy, and Japan struggled to match these achievements. The perverse variant of Fordism in the Third Reich included forced-labour production of V2 rockets in the underground *Mittelwerk* factory at Nordhausen. Both in Germany and the USSR, forced labour – in the second case the GULAG – was important, especially for the construction of industrial plant.

Box 44 | Lend-Lease

Lend-Lease was initially a means by which the affluent United States could support states defending themselves against Germany, without direct American involvement in combat. By the end of 1940 Britain no longer had the funds available to purchase goods from America. The new policy was first publicly mooted by President Roosevelt in a December 1940 press conference, using a folksy analogy: 'Suppose my neighbor's home catches fire, and I have a length of garden hose 400 or 500 feet away. If he can take my garden hose and connect it up with his hydrant, I may help him to put out his fire. Now, what do I do? I don't say to him before that operation, "Neighbor, my garden hose cost me $15; you have to pay me $15 for it." What is the transaction that goes on? I don't want $15 – I want my garden hose back after the fire is over.'[a] A week later, in a radio 'fireside chat', Roosevelt expanded upon this and declared that the (neutral) America should become the 'the great arsenal of democracy'.

This arrangement was an alternative to the US loans that had caused so many practical and political problems after World War I. It also reversed the various isolationist laws that had limited the supply of arms to countries engaged in war (see Chapter 3). The Lend-Lease bill passed Congress in March 1941, and it gave the President extremely broad powers to 'lend' military equipment to states which he decided were vital to the long-term defence of the United States. Britain was the most obvious case. More surprisingly, aid was extended to the Communist USSR when, in October 1941, the President declared the Soviet Union eligible. (Britain provided some aid to Russia from the middle of 1941, continuing a long tradition of subsidising continental allies.) Overall Lend-Lease was an extraordinary indication of how far the neutral USA was leaning in favour of the anti-German coalition.

After the USA entered the war in December 1941, Lend-Lease remained a central element of President Roosevelt's grand strategy, the globalised channel for supplying arms, equipment, and economic aid to allies. It was the main contribution America could make to the war in Europe in 1942, and negotiations about the various annual 'protocols' were central to American diplomatic relations with the USSR. The American leadership had to juggle the interests and assess the relative importance of various allies, as well as the requirements of its own armed forces.

Massive transfers were effected, some $42 billion-worth of war goods and other supplies. Britain received about half the value of the Lend-Lease provision, the USSR about $10 billion, and the French $3.5 billion; only small amounts of Lend-Lease aid could be sent to China. About 55 per cent (by value) of the goods supplied took the form of weapons (including supply vehicles) and munitions, and about 40 per cent was industrial and agricultural products.

After the war the 'garden hose' was rarely returned; Lend-Lease equipment was often just dumped in the sea. Lend-Lease aid was related to broader financial negotiations, and involved significant costs to some recipients. In particular the British had to allow free trade, the consequence of which was the opening of the Empire to imports from America. This in turn set the scene for many of the most important post-war arrangements of the world economy. President Truman's abrupt ending of Lend-Lease in August 1945 had significant effects in both Britain and the USSR.

There was nothing comparable to Lend-Lease on the Axis side, although Germany and Japan supplied small amounts of military equipment to their allies. Probably most important was the aid in weapons and raw materials provided by Germany to Italy, but after 1943 the flow went the other way, as the Reich utilised hundreds of thousands of Italians as forced labourers.

[a] Franklin D. Roosevelt, Press conference, 17 December 1940, Franklin D. Roosevelt Presidential Library and Museum, at www.fdrlibrary.marist.edu.

into Germany. Bomber Command, as a result, had to operate under cover of darkness, and while night attacks reduced RAF losses, they were highly inaccurate. In the summer of 1941 the independent Butt Report concluded that only one aircraft in three was dropping its bombs within 5 miles of the target. The RAF by the beginning of 1942 opted for 'area' targets rather than 'point' ones, in effect cities rather than individual factories. Nazi propaganda called this 'terror bombing' (*Terrorangriffe*), and the term was not inaccurate. The major objective for the British, as for the Germans in the Battle of Britain (and for Douhet back in the 1920s), became political, cracking the morale of enemy civilians.

By the late spring of 1942 Harris was able to send a thousand bombers against the Ruhr city of Cologne (Köln). There was some protest on moral grounds against the indiscriminate bombing of German civilians. The most notable protestor was George Bell, the Bishop of Chichester, who spoke in the

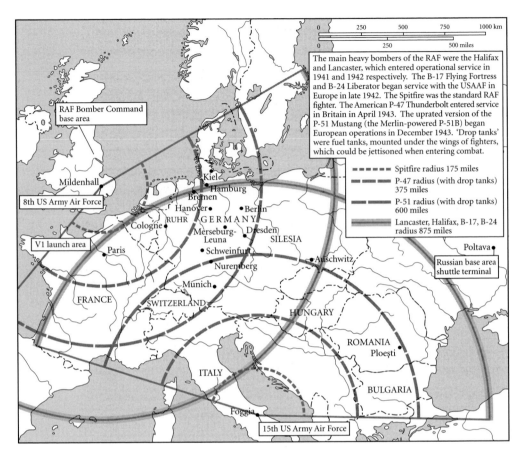

The main heavy bombers of the RAF were the Halifax and Lancaster, which entered operational service in 1941 and 1942 respectively. The B-17 Flying Fortress and B-24 Liberator began service with the USAAF in Europe in late 1942. The Spitfire was the standard RAF fighter. The American P-47 Thunderbolt entered service in Britain in April 1943. The uprated version of the P-51 Mustang (the Merlin-powered P-51B) began European operations in December 1943. 'Drop tanks' were fuel tanks, mounted under the wings of fighters, which could be jettisoned when entering combat.

- - - - - Spitfire radius 175 miles
– – – – P-47 radius (with drop tanks) 375 miles
—— —— P-51 radius (with drop tanks) 600 miles
━━━━ Lancaster, Halifax, B-17, B-24 radius 875 miles

RAF Bomber Command base area

8th US Army Air Force

V1 launch area

Russian base area shuttle terminal

15th US Army Air Force

Map 11 The strategic air campaign in Europe

House of Lords and had letters published in the press. Bell's view was a minority one, especially in the middle years of the conflict. The struggle with Germany was in other respects going badly, and Bomber Command seemed the only weapon that could be used to hit back at the Germans; on balance the RAF attacks were a boost to British morale.

The United States Army, too, built a small pre-war heavy bomber force. The prototype of the famous wartime B-17 'Flying Fortress' flew as early as 1935. As with the British, there were geographical, technical, and bureaucratic reasons for the development of American strategic bombing aviation. America also had the world's most advanced aircraft industry. The USAAF entered the war in 1941 with the same general strategic objective as the RAF, but with tactics different from those that the British had evolved over the first two years of the war. The Americans persevered in a belief in precision daylight attacks, by masses of bombers (up to 300). They trusted that heavily armed bombers (eventually with eleven heavy machine guns), flying in tight formations, would be able to defend themselves without escorting fighters.

Many B-17s were sent to the Pacific before and after Pearl Harbor, but by the late autumn of 1942 the handful of machines that had reached Britain were committed to operations over occupied France or on the edges of Germany (the first US raid on Germany proper came only in January 1943) (see Box 45). They were organised within an American command which became the US 8th Air Force. The USAAF deployment was far enough advanced by the time of the Casablanca Conference (January 1943) for a Combined Bomber Offensive (later called POINTBLANK) to be laid out and given high priority. American aircraft were to strike during the day, and the British ones at night. The stated aim was the 'progressive destruction and dislocation of the German military, industrial, and economic system and [to] undermine the morale of the German people to a point where their capability for armed resistance is fatally weakened'.[4]

Air battle over the Reich

As the war went on, RAF Bomber Command continued to build up its technical expertise for night attacks, in the form of electronic navigation aids, electronic counter-measures, and the 'mix' of incendiary and high-explosive bombs required to inflict maximum damage on German cities. In

Box 45 | The strategic air battle over Europe

Table A shows the growing weight of the Allied strategic air attack. The column 1942/1 denotes the first six months of 1942, 1942/2 the second six months, etc. By comparison with these figures, the Luftwaffe is estimated to have dropped 55,000 tons on Britain in the year beginning July 1940. British four-engined bombers typically carried about 9 tons of bombs, American bombers about half that. This table shows only bombers operating from Britain. A smaller American bomber formation, the 15th Air Force, operated over Southern Europe from bases in North Africa and Italy.

Table B shows the distribution of the German Air Force on the eve of D-Day. It is broken down by operational *Gruppen*; a *Gruppe* (Group) typically numbered about 30–35 aircraft. This table excludes reconnaissance and transport *Gruppen*. This gives some sense of the extent to which the strategic air campaign distracted the Luftwaffe from other fronts.

A Tonnage of Allied air attack, 1940–1945 (thousand tons)

	1939	1940	1941	1942/1	1942/2	1943/1	1943/2	1944/1	1944/2	1945
RAF Bomber Command	0	13	32	20	25	66	92	186	339	182
US 8th Air Force	–	–	–	–	2	8	36	156	233	189

(From Charles Webster and Noble Frankland, *The Strategic Air Offensive against Germany, 1939–1945* (London: HMSO, 1961), vol. IV, pp. 456f.)

B Distribution of the Luftwaffe, May 1944 (*Gruppen*)

	France	Germany	Russia	Norway	Balkans	Italy
Day fighters	8	30	20	2	3	6
Night fighters	6	23	2	0	1	0
Ground attack aircraft	2	1	24	1	0	2
Bombers	22	20	11	0	0	1

(From Alfred Price, *Luftwaffe Data Book* (London: Greenhill Books, 1997), pp. 92–128.)

the summer of 1943 (about the time of the Battle of Kursk and the invasion of Sicily), Bomber Command – with some USAAF assistance – was able to mount an extremely heavy attack on Germany's second city, Hamburg. The attacks lasted for several days, caused a severe 'firestorm' and killed 50,000 people (see Box 46). Before this, a long RAF 'campaign' against the Ruhr industrial region had caused significant disruption to the German war economy. The strategic problem was that attacks could not be sustained long enough to overcome the effectively organised German recovery methods. The attacks were having only a limited impact on the war economy of the Reich, the output of which – as we have seen – continued to grow.

Meanwhile the USAAF was able by mid 1943 to deploy larger heavy bomber forces, with the B-17 and the newer B-24 'Liberator' (see chapter frontispiece). These aircraft were mainly based in Britain. From early 1943, however, North Africa and Italy provided new airfields from which American bombers could attack Axis targets in Southern Europe. It is possible that the American threat in mid 1943 to launch a terror bombing campaign against Italian cities (Rome had hardly been attacked yet) helped push the Italian government to sue for peace (see Chapter 10).

The main campaign, however, was not fulfilling the expectations of the planners. The USAAF bomber self-defence doctrine did not work. The Germans deployed masses of fighters over the Reich and inflicted very heavy casualties on unescorted American bomber formations. In an attempt to hit a supposed bottleneck of German industry, ball-bearing production, the USAAF flew deep into Bavaria to hit the industrial town of Schweinfurt. The first raid, in August 1943, cost 60 out of 376 B-17s despatched, and the second, in October (later known as 'Black Thursday'), cost 60 out of 291. Deep penetration raids into Germany were temporarily abandoned due to these unsustainable losses. It was only by good fortune that a solution was found. Against the technical expectations of the USAAF (and the RAF), effective escort fighters became available for really deep American daytime raids. The most notable of these, the P-51 (see Figure 24), began deep sweeps over the Reich at the end of 1943 and was available in strength by the spring of 1944. The American precision-bombing strategy at last began to pay off. The 'Big Week' in February 1944 was aimed especially at German aircraft production and had considerable effect; heavy losses were inflicted on the defending Luftwaffe fighters. Especially notable were

Box 46 | The bombing of Hamburg

The following is from the Report of the Police President of Hamburg in 1943, describing the air raids of July and August 1943. The attacks had been mounted by the RAF and the USAAF and codenamed Operation GOMORRAH. Total German losses are estimated to have been about 50,000 people.

The scenes of terror which took place in the firestorm area are indescribable. Children were torn away from their parents' hands by the force of the hurricane and whirled into the fire. People who thought they had escaped fell down, overcome by the devouring force of the heat, and died in an instant. Refugees had to make their way over the dead and dying. The sick and the infirm had to be left behind by rescuers as they themselves were in danger of burning.

This sad fate, which befell Hamburg, exceeded in effect and extent any catastrophic fire – with the exception of Tokyo [1923] – of the past. It is distinguished in the first place by the fact that never before in a city of a million inhabitants, every one prepared and equipped for fire-fighting, supported by great experience and great success in fire-fighting in many earlier raids, was waiting at the signal for the sirens for duty and the necessity of fighting the fire. In earlier cases it developed as a rule gradually during many hours or days from a small incipient fire. Here a population ready and prepared for the alarm were literally overwhelmed by the fire which reached its height in under an hour.

Even taking the conditions of those days into consideration, the fire in Hamburg in 1842 bears only a faint likeness to the fire in Hamburg in 1943. The catastrophes of Chicago [1871] and San Francisco [1906], the fire in the Paris Opera House [1887], all these events, of which the scenes of fantastic and gruesome terror have been described by contemporaries, pale beside the extent and uniqueness of the Hamburg fire of [July–August] 1943. Its horror is revealed in the howling and raging of the firestorms, the hellish noise of exploding bombs and the death cries of martyred human beings as well as in the big silence after the raids. Speech is impotent to portray the measure of horror, which shook the people for ten days and nights and traces of which were written indelibly on the face of the city and of its inhabitants.

And each of these nights convulsed by flames was followed by a day which displayed the horror of the dim and unreal light of day hidden in smoke. Summer heat intensified by the glow of the firestorms to an unbearable degree; dust from the torn earth and the ruins and debris of damaged areas which penetrated everywhere; showers of soot and ashes; more heat and dust; and above all a pestilential stench of decaying corpses and smouldering fires weighed continually on the exhausted men.

(From Charles Webster and Noble Frankland, *The Strategic Air Offensive against Germany, 1939–1945* (London: HMSO, 1961), vol. IV, pp. 314f.)

the precision attacks on the synthetic oil plants in central Germany in May 1944.

The strategic air campaign is certainly controversial, although more so now than during the war itself. Morally, the aerial attacks on civilians – men, women, and children – were reprehensible; the Allies, the British especially, were using the bomber force as a 'weapon of mass destruction'. Some 660,000 Germans were killed in the bombing. RAF bombing was heavier for much of the war than that of the USAAF, and more indiscriminate. The fact that residential areas of cities were the only target the RAF could reliably hit did not alter the moral case. The final attacks, like the one on Dresden in February 1945 in which 40,000 civilians were killed, had little economic or military justification.

Another criticism made at the time (especially by commanders of ground and naval forces), and later, was that the strategic air campaign took up too large a share of Allied industrial resources. While America had productive capacity to spare, for Britain there were significant opportunity costs in building up Bomber Command. British factories built long-range four-engined bombers at the expense of tactical aircraft. More fighters, strike aircraft, and medium bombers would have improved the fighting potential of the British Army and of the Royal Navy in the battles fought in the Mediterranean and Far East in 1941 and 1942. They could have supported a second front in northwestern Europe in 1943.

In the end the greatest debate about the Allied bombing campaign is whether it played a decisive role in the outcome of the war. Rather than strategic bombardment being an alternative to invasion, the full effectiveness of the air campaign was achieved only in 1944–5, after the Allies had won in Normandy and Belorussia. German industrial production increased through 1943 and 1944, and still civilian morale did not reach tipping point. On the other hand the air campaign prevented the German war industry from expanding even more than it actually did. Furthermore, the Allied air campaign forced the Luftwaffe to concentrate over Germany, rather than in Russia or the Mediterranean (see Box 44). A large part of the expanded German war production had to go into air defensive weapons like fighters, anti-aircraft guns, and radars.

The Luftwaffe did not have a strategic bomber able to retaliate in kind. Its force was made up mainly of medium (twin-engined) bombers, and from

Figure 24 | North American P-51 Mustang

The American P-51 Mustang was the most important fighter aircraft of the war. It directly affected overall Allied air strategy. The reason for this was that it had high performance and a tactical range which allowed it to escort American bombers very deep into German territory. P-51s based on Iwo Jima even escorted American B-29s over Japan.

In early 1940 the RAF ordered this type from North American Aviation Co. of Los Angeles and named it the 'Mustang'; the engine was an American Allison V-1710. The Mustang was not originally ordered by the USAAF, which had its own fighter procurement programme. Only the fortuitous RAF test conversion of a Mustang to take the Spitfire's Rolls-Royce Merlin engine allowed the highly advanced airframe to reach its full potential. The P-51 (the eventual USAAF designation – 'P', stood for 'Pursuit') could now operate at high altitudes and could outfight and outpace the best German piston-engined fighters. It was significantly superior to the machines of the original USAAF programme, the P-38 Lightning and P-47 Thunderbolt.

The Merlin-powered Mustang entered operational service only in the last months of 1943, but the American aircraft industry quickly shifted to mass production; the Packard Motor Car Company had been manufacturing the Merlin under licence in Detroit since the autumn of 1941. Production of the main wartime Mustang variants in Los Angeles and Dallas amounted to 11,700 aircraft.

This P-51B flew with the 357th Fighter Group, nicknamed 'The Yoxford Boys', after a village near the Group's base in Suffolk. 'Shoo Shoo Baby' was a sentimental popular song by the Andrews Sisters, dating from late 1943, and the name was painted on the fuselages of a number of American aircraft.

mid 1941 these were deployed in a tactical role against the Red Army or in the Mediterranean. The Allied attacks did provoke the Germans into developing, from 1942, expensive 'reprisal' weapons (*Vergeltungswaffen*), the V1 cruise missile and the V2 short-range ballistic missile. The V1 and V2 were technologically very advanced and they were produced in large numbers – latterly in underground factories built and manned by forced labour. The V2 (officially called the A4) was the Third Reich's most expensive single armaments programme, with an estimated expenditure of 2 billion Reichsmarks. The V1 and V2 had warheads of 750 kg and 850 kg respectively, compared to 6,350 kg (14,000 lb) for the bomb load of an RAF Lancaster bomber. The tiny and fast jet-powered V1 was hard to intercept, and there was no defence at all against the V2 rocket. On the other hand the Nazi missiles had a relatively short range (the main targets were London and the strategic cities of Antwerp and Liège in Belgium), they were even less accurate than the RAF's early night bombers, and they could inflict relatively little damage. Both became available only after D-Day. About 6,000 people were killed in Britain by V-weapons (10 per cent of those killed in the 1943 attack on Hamburg alone).

The atomic bomb is a final and neglected feature of the planned strategic air war against Germany. At the end of the 1930s scientists in various countries had become aware of the long-term implications of nuclear energy. Both the American and the British governments were in 1939–40 given warnings, by refugee scientists from Europe and others, that nuclear fission might create a huge destructive force and that Nazi Germany might be beginning practical work in this area. In May of 1941 a team of British experts, known as the MAUD Committee, reported that the development of a uranium weapon was feasible. The report was immediately made known to neutral Washington. The Germans, fortunately, did not move very far towards an atomic weapon. They considered that the engineering problems were insuperable in the short term, and that the project could not be completed in the time-span of the current war. In the latter point they were right. Even on the Allied side the resources lavished on the American-British MANHATTAN project did not produce practical weapons until the summer of 1945, three months after the German surrender. The atomic bomb would, however, turn out to have a vital place in the war against Japan and in the post-war confrontation with the Soviet Union.

Occupation and collaboration

Another possible means – aside from strategic bombing – to wear down or even to defeat Germany was to support resistance in occupied countries. This was not illogical, given the vast span of territory overrun by the Wehrmacht, and its potential contribution to the economy of the Reich. The British initially thought they could exploit the internal political vulnerabilities within German-occupied territory, and even within the Reich itself. Meanwhile tens of millions of Europeans, and many of their leaders, had to decide how they would behave under Hitler's new order.

There was no single pattern of Axis occupation. In early 1939 Czechoslovakia was partly annexed into Germany and Hungary, and partly left as the pro-German puppet state of Slovakia. The western part had valuable industries, and was incorporated into the Reich as the Protectorate of Bohemia-Moravia. A second Slav state, Poland, resisted violently and was treated much more harshly than Czechoslovakia or some of Hitler's later conquests (see Chapter 3). After Poland was partitioned by the Nazi–Soviet Pact the German-controlled area was partly annexed into eastern Germany, and partly left in limbo as an occupied zone run by the SS. There was no civilian collaboration regime, and the Germans behaved with extreme brutality from 1939 onwards. Poland served as an object lesson to leaders of other occupied territories; collaboration seemed to offer a safer course.

In contrast, Denmark was treated the most leniently of Germany's victims. The Danish Army had hardly fought against the initial invasion in 1940, and the King had stayed in the country. Uniquely, there was no government-in-exile. The Danish authorities co-operated with the Reich in the hope of preserving this favourable situation, although direct control was imposed in August 1943 (after the overthrow of Mussolini). Norway fought against the initial German invasion and a government-in-exile was formed (see Chapter 4). The pro-Nazi Norwegian politician Vidkun Quisling exemplified the threat of German subversion, i.e. the 'fifth column', although his role was exaggerated in Allied propaganda. Civilian control was exercised until 1945 by a German *Reichskommissar*. The Third Reich provided a lot of employment, and some Norwegians were prepared for active or passive co-operation with the occupiers. A considerable number of Danes and Norwegians were induced to serve in the German armed forces.

The other German victories in the West in 1940 had great implications. Hitler's initial political treatment of France was in some respects as remarkable as his military campaign. By offering relatively generous terms in June 1940 he secured a quick French capitulation and co-operation from French elites. France was divided into a zone of German military occupation in the north and west (and including Paris), and a small Italian-occupied zone in the southeast. But an unoccupied and neutral rump French state continued in the south, based in the town of Vichy. It controlled the large Navy and a colonial empire with a population of 70 million. The government was not led by a Quisling puppet installed by the Germans. Uniquely in occupied Europe, a figure of national stature, Marshal Philippe Pétain, agreed to act as head of state, and Pierre Laval, who had been a prominent pre-war politician, acted as his Prime Minister. Nearly the whole officer corps of the French armed forces was loyal to *le Maréchal* and to Vichy. A large part of the French elite believed – for many months – that Britain was doomed and that German hegemony was a long-term thing. For them France's priority was to put its house in order through an authoritarian *Révolution nationale*, while at the same time maintaining neutrality in the British–German war. Very few of the French people rallied to the apparently hopeless cause of Charles de Gaulle, and his self-proclaimed government-in-exile in London (see Box 47). If the Norwegian case gave us the word 'Quisling', Pétain and Laval popularised the concept of *la collaboration*. In November 1942, with the Allied invasion of French North Africa (TORCH), the Germans occupied all of France, but left Pétain and Laval as figureheads, alongside a German governor.

Belgium and the Netherlands were also under military occupation. The population at home – at least the non-Jewish part of it – was treated relatively leniently. The Netherlands, like Norway, had a German civilian governor (*Reichskommissar*), while Belgium was under military administration (with northern France). There were local politicians with whom the Germans could work to a limited extent; King Léopold III had remained in Belgium after his government went abroad to London. As in France and Scandinavia, the recruitment of 'Aryan' recruits for the German military (notably the *Waffen-SS*) had some success.

The German–Italian campaign in the Balkans in the spring of 1941 opened a very different area of occupation. (Bulgaria and Romania were already Axis allies.) The pre-war Kingdom of Yugoslavia (inhabited by Serb, Croat, and

Box 47 | **The Resistance**

The following extract is from the memoirs of 'Colonel Rémy', the pseudonym of the Resistance leader Gilbert Renault (1904–84). Renault refused to accept the June 1940 surrender. He left France for Britain shortly after the Armistice, and then returned home to organise a major underground resistance network in the western part of France, the *Confrérie de Notre Dame*. The CND was engaged in intelligence-gathering and other activities.

The conversation was with Paul Mauger (b. 1923), a young man who wanted to join the Resistance. Rémy met him at home in France, along with his mother: 'It was just as if his mother were introducing her boy to the manager of a business and was waiting to know whether her son would be taken on.' Mauger was only eighteen, but had already made one unsuccessful attempt to travel through Spain to join de Gaulle. He served as a resistance fighter but was arrested in May 1942. He was sent to the Mauthausen concentration camp, but survived the war.

I am in no position to get you to England, Paul,' I told him. 'But would you like to work for me?'

'Yes, please,' he replied eagerly.

'You realise that I shall have to give you dangerous things to do.'

'That doesn't matter.'

'You realise, too, that you will be travelling all the time, often very uncomfortably?'

'That doesn't matter.'

'If they ever discover the papers you are carrying, you will be shot.'

'That doesn't matter.'

'Of course they will torture you to make you talk. In no case must you ever say anything.'

The tears came to his eyes. I had already seen much the same look of reproach in Lhermite's eyes.

'I know all that,' was his answer.

'I shall be very exacting, very severe.'

'Yes,' he said.

'Right you are, then, Paul. I'll take you on.'

I can still see the smile on Paul's lips as I agreed to let him work for me. He took to heart what I told him that day.

'From today on I shall give you another name. Among us you will be known as Pierre.'

He was as pleased as if I had given him a medal.

I rose. His mother shook hands with me warmly.

'I am very grateful to you,' she said. 'When can he begin?'

'This evening,' I replied. 'We shall leave together for Brest.'

(From Rémy [sic], *The Silent Company* (London: Arthur Barker, 1948), pp. 128f.)

Slovene ethnic groups) was broken up. Border areas were annexed by Italy, Germany, Hungary, and Bulgaria. Serbia was largely under German military control, and the western territories were under the Italians. Hitler sanctioned the creation of a large pro-German Croat state in the northwest under the Fascist and terrorist Ustaša party of Ante Pavelić. While the Croat regime was undoubtedly devoted to the Axis, it set about an extreme version of what – fifty years later but in the same region – would be called 'ethnic cleansing'. In 1941 the potential victims were the third of the population of the Croat state who were Orthodox Serbs. A German puppet military government was set up in the smaller rump territory of Serbia. Greece was more ethnically homogeneous than Yugoslavia, but like Serbia it had a collaborationist government. Until 1943 the country was largely under Italian military control, but there was a German presence at key points. After September 1943 the German garrisons spread out, albeit thinly, across the whole country.

The western part of the USSR was subjected to direct German conquest, in the second half of 1941 (see also Chapters 5 and 6). Here occupied regions were treated like Poland, run by the German Army and the SS, with native officials only at the lowest level. Two regional administrations were set up, *Reichskommissariats* for *Ostland* (the Baltic and northern Belorussia) and for the Ukraine. The zone immediately behind the front line was under German military rule. Hitler refused to work with local anti-Communist politicians, either ethnic Russians or members of the non-Russian minorities (for example the three Baltic states, Belorussia, and the Ukraine). The Germans did eventually set up a figurehead in the form of a senior Soviet officer captured in 1942, General Vlasov, but he was given little power or political space until after the *Ostheer* had been driven out of the USSR in 1944. All the same, the Germans had a remarkable degree of success in mobilising the human resources of the occupied zone of the USSR for labour service in the Reich and even for the German armed forces.

Finally, there were erstwhile Axis allies who were subject to German occupation from 1943 to 1944, when they tried to withdraw from the war. The most important region was in Italy after the Allied invasion. An ephemeral political centre was set up under Mussolini at the town of Salò on Lake Garda in late 1943, but essentially northern Italy was under German military rule.

Despite great differences, common occupation trends can be detected right across Europe. The subject populations were largely unarmed, the occupiers had a monopoly of force, and the German authorities – the Army, the security organs, and the SS – were prepared to act with extreme ruthlessness (and the regime in Italian-occupied areas could also be harsh). Large numbers of hostages were killed in reprisal for acts of resistance against the occupying forces. The most extreme common factor was the persecution of the Jews and, from the winter of 1941–2, their deportation, ultimately to extermination centres. Another feature was economic exploitation. In extreme cases – notably in occupied Russia – the Germans were prepared to use a policy of starvation. Most important, especially from mid 1942, was the German policy of forced labour conscription (see above). Young people in the regions on all sides of Greater Germany were faced with the prospect of being shipped off to factories, mines, and farms there; in the long term that prospect played no small part in the development of active resistance to the occupation regime.

Resistance in occupied Europe: the first phase

Just as the Axis occupation regime varied in different parts of Europe, so did opposition to it. Some resistance activity, moreover, was spontaneous and internal, some was induced from outside.

In the year between the fall of France and the entry of Soviet Russia and America into the war, subversion was a crucial part of the British grand strategy. The forces of the Third Reich seemed invincible, and it was hard to envisage a time when the British Army could – on its own – liberate the continent. It was not unreasonable to think that Europeans under the 'Nazi jackboot' might readily be aroused for a struggle with the occupiers to free themselves. Churchill was an enthusiastic supporter of irregular warfare, and he set up the Special Operations Executive (SOE). His instructions to Hugh Dalton, the first head of SOE, included the memorable phrase: 'And now . . . set Europe ablaze.' In another crossover from the Asian war Dalton set out as one model 'the Chinese guerrillas now operating against Japan.'[5] Under the 'detonator' strategy of 1940–1, small British landings would eventually set off uprisings by European 'patriots'. SOE would by then have grouped the 'patriots' into 'secret armies' and equipped them with clandestine arms; meanwhile Germany would have been crippled by bombing. As things turned out, SOE had even less success than the early RAF Bomber Command. Although gallant individuals began to organise against the occupation, the 'patriot forces' were still insignificant, and Britain had little help to give.

Early SOE interest in Czechoslovakia and Poland soon waned. The terrain of the Czech lands was unfavourable for guerrilla warfare, and it was difficult for the RAF to fly in even minimal supplies. There was no way in which the Central European underground could interact with British 'detonator' ground operations in the foreseeable future. As it happened, in the early summer of 1942 Czechoslovakia was the scene of two of the most spectacular events in the European battle between occupiers and resistors. Czechoslovak Resistance fighters parachuted in from Britain mortally wounded SS leader Reinhard Heydrich as he drove to work in Prague. Heydrich was Himmler's deputy, architect of the Holocaust, and *de facto* governor of Bohemia-Moravia. The act had been organised by the Czechoslovak government in exile and by SOE. One German response was the atrocity at the village of Lidiče: 200 men were shot, the women were imprisoned, and the village was razed to the ground. Lidiče became an Allied symbol of Nazi terror, but the vicious German action also achieved its goal: terrorising the population and inhibiting further resistance. In the end the Czechs took action only after Hitler's death, when an uprising broke out in Prague on 5 May 1945. The eastern part of pre-war Czechoslovakia did see a significant uprising in the late summer of 1944 when the puppet Slovak Army revolted – as the Red Army approached – but the Slovak National Uprising was put down by the Germans.

Resistance was much stronger in Poland, the worst-treated occupied area outside the USSR. Many Poles were fiercely nationalist, and there was a strong tradition of insurgency. Unlike in most other parts of occupied Europe, there was no 'Quisling' government and only low-level individual collaboration. An energetic and much publicised government-in-exile worked in London, with military forces initially made up of Poles who had escaped to Britain via Romania (1939) and France (1940). Within Poland a 'secret army' was created in early 1940 under the command of the London government-in-exile, and in 1942 this was renamed the Home Army (*Armia Krajewo*, AK). The Home Army undertook sabotage and other forms of active resistance, but the main emphasis was preparation for a future general uprising. The British sent few supplies to Poland, for the same practical reasons that applied in the Czechoslovak case.

Another kind of resistance appeared in June 1941, when a large 'Partisan' (*Partizan*) movement began to take shape in Soviet territory occupied by the Germans. As with the British, there was improvisation and a measure of desperation here, as the Soviets had not expected to fight a war deep in their own territory. The organised Partisan movement expanded to as many as 250,000 combatants by early 1944. There had been some early popular ambivalence about German rule, especially in the western regions inhabited by ethnic minorities like the Belorussians and Ukrainians. Crude German policies, counter-productive reprisals, and deportation of men and women to work in the Reich increased popular resistance. As the war progressed, links between the Partisans and the Soviet 'mainland' were improved. But although the Partisan movement provided long-range intelligence and conducted attacks on the transport system of the *Ostheer,* it did not tie up significant numbers of German front-line troops, seriously interrupt German communications, or prevent the extraction of food and raw materials. There was also no large-scale uprising. The conventional Red Army, not the Partisans, was the force that eventually threw out the invaders.

Resistance in occupied Europe: the second phase

The survival of the USSR over the winter of 1941–2, and the entry of the USA into the war, changed the nature of the European Resistance. Britain's unrealistic plan for European self-liberation would now be replaced by conventional reconquest by mass Russian, American, and British armies. The Resistance would act as a helpful auxiliary, not the key factor. Support for the Resistance was subordinated to conventional strategy, first in the Mediterranean and the Balkans (see also Chapter 10). Paradoxically, as the Resistance became more active in 1942, so did it become less of a force that could win the war on its own.

The Soviet entry into the war furthered the cause of the Resistance outside the USSR. The Comintern (Communist International) and the local Communist parties that it controlled came into play. The European Communists were committed 'anti-Fascists' (despite the zigzags of the 1939–41 Nazi–Soviet Pact). They were relatively well organised, or at least well disciplined, and they were used to working under conspiratorial/illegal conditions. In many European states the 'bourgeois' parties had discredited themselves, especially during the hard years of the Depression, at the time of German conquest, or during the occupation.

The Russians could not send arms or instructions to western or southern Europe, and they had great trouble even communicating with local activists. All the same, their heroic defensive struggle inspired activists in occupied territories, for some of whom the Russians were 'brother Slavs' (the Poles, as we will see, did not share this sentiment). In Western Europe the Comintern was inclined to push for more violent action than SOE or its American equivalent, the OSS (Office of Strategic Services). Moscow's strategic priority was to create immediate problems in the German rear and force the Wehrmacht to pull troops out of Russia; from this remote point of view German reprisals would only make the struggle more intense. The Western Allies were more concerned about keeping Resistance forces intact for the eventual British-American invasion. Meanwhile the governments-in-exile in London did not want to see their own nationals consumed as SOE 'set Europe ablaze'. In Western Europe the Communist Resistance followed Moscow's united front guidance, and generally accepted the lead of the Western Allies, while being given a place in the interim governments. In Eastern Europe the Communists were more independent, and in 1944 they had the political and military support of the Red Army.

The entry of the USSR into the war eventually furthered another development: the formation on Allied territory of regular military units made up of nationals from German-occupied territory. Poles who had been interned in Russia in 1939 were released to serve with the British forces in the Mediterranean. Polish conventional forces played an important part in the fighting in Italy in 1943–5, and in northwestern Europe from 1944. The Russians also created their own conventional Polish units operating alongside the Red Army, and not under the control of the London government-in-exile. The Polish

Figure 25 | **Soviet Partisans**

Men and women Partisans from the Molotov Brigade, a Partisan
unit operating in Belorussia in the western part of the USSR. Viacheslav Molotov (1890–1986) was the Prime Minister of the USSR
in the 1930s, and one of the best-known Soviet leaders. Many of
the original members of the Molotov Brigade were Red Army soldiers who took to the forests to avoid capture after the great Soviet
defeats of mid 1941.

The Soviet government had not expected to fight a guerrilla war on its own territory, so it had made few preparations. After the Germans drove deep into the USSR, the regime at first tried to create a centrally controlled Partisan force, using Communist Party cadres; later, from mid 1942, the slogan became one of an 'all-people's' movement. German policies furthered the growth of the Partisans. The drafting of forced labour for work in the Reich made young men and women of the occupied regions take to the woods, and fierce German counter-insurgency campaigns polarised the population.

By the middle of the war the Soviet Partisans were, by European standards, well equipped. Good radio communications with the 'mainland' were established, and an elaborate system of clandestine air links brought in weapons, military cadres, and medical support. The Partisans sabotaged the Wehrmacht rail system and provided long-range intelligence. Politically they prepared the population for the return of Soviet rule. Many of them were drafted into the regular forces as soon as the Red Army arrived. After the 'liberation', other (nationalist) guerrillas took to the forests of the Ukraine and the Baltic republics to oppose Soviet rule.

The Molotov Brigade was typical of an extreme form of Resistance, armed bands fighting in the forests and hills. Anti-German guerrillas in other parts of Europe – Yugoslav Partisans and *Chetniks*, the French *Maquis*, the Polish Home Army, partisans in Greece and northern Italy – would have looked the same. Elsewhere in Europe guerrilla fighters relied on small arms captured from the occupiers or supplied by SOE and flown in by British and American aircraft. Guerrillas were not confined to Europe. Communist resistance to the Japanese invasion of China took the form of guerrilla warfare, and that struggle was one of the models for the European Resistance.

forces eventually amounted to two field armies operating in Poland and eastern Germany in 1945. The Soviets also began to raise military formations from the large numbers of POWs who fell into their hands, first Czechs and Slovaks, and later Romanians and Hungarians. These 'international' units played a marginal role in the overall fighting power of the Red Army. Nevertheless they were important politically in the establishment of governments 'friendly' to the USSR in 1944–5.

The Communists emerged as a remarkable force in Yugoslavia and Greece, neither of which had had strong pre-war Communist parties (or even a large urban working class). In Yugoslavia the Resistance struggle was stronger than anywhere else in Western or Central Europe. The terrain was rugged, and there was a long tradition of rebellion (originally against the Turks). The extreme racist policies of the Croat Ustaša government drove many Serbs and others into armed opposition. Uniquely it was an inter-ethnic civil war as much as a struggle against Axis occupiers. A 'Partisan' movement (named after the Soviet *partizany*) developed in central Serbia led by the Croat Comintern operative Josip Broz-Tito. It went into action in June 1941 and eventually operated over much of the country.

The military potential of the Partisans in Yugoslavia increased dramatically in 1943 when they obtained weapons from the surrendering Italian garrisons and began to receive deliveries of equipment across the Adriatic from the British; the USSR could not provide any concrete help until late 1944. The Balkans became the highest priority for the Western Allies, as far as the Resistance was concerned. They saw guerrilla war as a means of causing trouble for the Axis, and they did not worry over-much about the human or longer-term political consequences; this was the equivalent of the Comintern attitude in the West. In 1942 Greece was important for Rommel's supply lines, and in 1943 the Allies wanted to stir up unrest in Greece and Yugoslavia to divert German attention from Sicily and southern Italy. In the first half of 1944 the Balkans were important to draw German troops away from northern France. The British eventually favoured Tito's Communist Partisans over a rival Serbian nationalist resistance, the *Chetniks* of Colonel Drava Mihailović. The Partisans were perceived – partly on the basis of ULTRA intelligence – to be killing more Germans than the anti-Communist *Chetniks*. In Yugoslavia in November 1942 the Partisans created their own political authority in the form of the AVNOJ (Anti-Fascist Council of National

Liberation of Yugoslavia), a *de facto* rival to the Yugoslav government-in-exile. But while the Partisans could create bases in inaccessible parts of Yugoslavia, they could not drive the Germans out. When the war ended, the Fascist Ustaša government was still in control of Croatia. Wartime conditions, civil war, and German and Italian counter-insurgency resulted in the death of over a million Yugoslavs – three times the total British wartime losses – out of a population of 16 million.

Greece also had a significant resistance movement from the summer of 1942, brought on by the hard conditions of the occupation. The government-in-exile had limited support, and rival partisan groups appeared. Most powerful, as we have seen (Chapter 10), was the Communist-led EAM (National Liberation Front) with its combat organisation, the ELAS. The EAM/ELAS took power in much of the country when the Germans pulled out, but in the end (in late 1944) Churchill was able to return the government-in-exile to Athens.

Organised resistance in Northern and Western Europe developed more gradually than in Russia, Poland, or the Balkans. The situation began to change in the winter of 1942–3. As we have seen (Chapter 10), the British and Americans were able to make contact with some of the leaders of the Vichy administration in Morocco and Algeria and to ease the TORCH landings. The liberation of French North Africa and the winning over of the French colonies (other than Indochina) meant that by 1943–4 the 'Fighting French' disposed of significant armed forces (including many native North Africans). New French divisions entered combat, first of all in Italy and then in the liberation of France itself – under former Vichy generals. In the course of 1943 and 1944 de Gaulle, based in Britain and North Africa, was able to build up his political and military base, and established working links with underground Resistance organisations in metropolitan France. In mid 1943 this came together in a national organisation, the *Conseil National de la Résistance* (CNR), with a joint political programme, and in the spring of 1944 most Resistance groups came under the control of the Gaullist *Forces françaises de l'Intérieur* (FFI). After June 1941 the Communists (PCF) played an important part in France, but they came to accept de Gaulle's authority.

Armed resistance elsewhere, in the Low Countries and Scandinavia, was limited. The Allies established links and flew in some arms and supplies. As in France the Resistance gathered intelligence and mounted a few acts of sabotage; it also played a role in rescuing downed Allied fliers. The Germans developed brutal or clever police counter-measures. Of the latter the most notable was the so-called *Englandspiel* ('England game'), in which the Germans took complete control of the SOE network in the Netherlands and sent false radio signals back to Britain; for much of the war all agents and supplies dropped to the Dutch ended up in German hands.

Resistance and liberation

As with strategic bombing, the most significant developments of the Resistance occurred *after* all the mass armies had directly entered the war as the main force. Operation BAGRATION in Belorussia in 1944 was the high point of Soviet Partisan activity. And to the surprise of the conventional British and American generals the European Resistance achieved remarkable successes after the Normandy landings. German rail transport was cut, and areas of France away from the main campaign route were taken over by the FFI. The Belgian Resistance took intact the vital port of Antwerp. The Germans conducted reprisals with a cruelty hitherto only seen in the East; Oradour-sur-Glane, a village in central France, was completely destroyed by a *Waffen-SS* division. The *Maquis* – the French Resistance in the countryside of the southeast – could still not hold territory on its own; a *Maquisard* uprising at Vercors, near Grenoble, was fiercely crushed by the Germans. The Resistance uprising in Paris in late August 1944 came about when the back of the German armies had been broken in Normandy; it was a result of the success of the American and British armies, rather than a cause of it. On the other side of the Reich, the Home Army's uprising in Warsaw was a unique example of a prolonged urban rebellion against German occupation (see Box 48). It too came about only after the Red Army burst into Poland.

The final Resistance movement was in northern Italy. It began to develop only after the summer of 1943, with the fall of Mussolini and the occupation by the Germans. Although Italian partisans held some inaccessible areas, they did not seriously complicate the prolonged and stubborn German defence of the peninsula. The big northern cities of the north fell only in the last days of

Box 48 | The Warsaw Uprising

The Warsaw Uprising, which began in late July 1944, was the largest urban revolt against German rule. The Polish 'Home Army' (AK) was the most developed underground force in occupied Europe. The British, however, found it hard to supply the Home Army with arms, and SOE gave preference after 1941 to the Mediterranean and to France; these areas were easier to reach and promised more immediate military gains.

The 1944 rising was a local affair, set off by the Polish underground rather than by the British or even by the government-in-exile based in London. It was aimed directly against the Germans, but indirectly also against the Russians, who were long-term oppressors of the Poles and who had seized eastern Poland in 1939. Moscow had broken off relations with the Polish government-in-exile in London in 1943, and the Soviets set up their own resistance government (the Polish Committee of National Liberation, or PKWN) behind the Red Army front line in Lublin. The poorly armed Home Army had originally planned for a rural rather than an urban revolt, but as the Red Army raced towards Warsaw in July 1944 the Poles hoped to seize the old capital and present the Russians with a *fait accompli*; the bomb plot against Hitler (20 July) suggested that Germany (as in October 1918) was on the verge of political collapse. The Poles built on a national tradition of revolt against occupiers, in 1830 and 1863, and there had been a revolt of Jews in the Warsaw ghetto in 1943.

In the event, the Red Army halted outside Warsaw, and German counter-insurgency forces were able by October to put down the rising. The cost was enormous; perhaps 200,000 Poles were killed, more than three times the losses in the 1939 campaign. It was not in Stalin's interests to support his bitter political opponents in the Home Army, but logistical and strategic factors also played a part in keeping the Red Army from Warsaw, and from western Poland more generally, in the second half of 1944. Whatever the cause, much bitterness resulted from the Russian refusal to allow the Western Allies to stage air supply missions through Soviet bases. Warsaw – an empty shell – was liberated only in January 1945.

the war, after the Germans had left. The Italian Communists, who played an important part in the late-war partisan movement, agreed like their French comrades to take part in the Allied-sponsored provisional government.

Opposition to Hitler

Finally – in terms of opposition to Hitler – there was Germany itself. We know now that Hitler and the Nazi regime held out until 'five minutes past twelve', after the Red Army had taken Berlin. Nevertheless there were hopes, from 1940 onwards, that the Nazi menace would crumble internally, from mass unrest or a military coup, just as the Kaiser's Germany had crumbled in October-November 1918. After the Wehrmacht defeat at the Battle of Moscow in 1941 Stalin made a memorable appeal to the German people (and the German elite): 'The Hitlers come and go, but the German people, and the German state – they remain.'[6] The overthrow of Mussolini in 1943 by other Fascist leaders served as a practical example of 'regime change'. The Western Allies had a plan, RANKIN, for the rapid landing on the continent in the event of a sudden German collapse. However, they made no use of the German opposition to Hitler; they had very limited knowledge of it, and no trust in it. The Soviets had sheltered some of the survivors of the pre-1933 German Communist Party (KPD) in Moscow. The Soviets had rather better spies in Germany than did the British, especially what the Gestapo called the 'Red Orchestra' (*Rote Kapelle*). Moscow also made some attempt after 1943 to cultivate captured German officers and men, and they had a figurehead in the form of General Walter von Seydlitz (captured at Stalingrad).

Hitler himself feared a repetition of 1918. The NSDAP regime, however, kept the lid on internal mass opposition by exploiting nationalism. They played on spectacular military victories in the first part of the war, and on fear of the Asiatic Russian hordes in the later part. They attended to the material needs of the ethnic German population (at the expense of other parts of Europe), and they promised a 'people's community' (*Volksgemeinschaft*). The Nazis also created a large, efficient, and ruthless apparatus of surveillance and repression.

Popular unrest, meanwhile, was unusual. The left-wing parties, the Social Democrats (SPD) and Communists (KPD), had been shattered. Elements in the Army had considered taking action against Hitler during the 1938 Munich crisis, fearing that the adventurous policies of their untested leader would lead to catastrophe. The plotting evaporated with Hitler's diplomatic and military triumph. Opposition in the later part of the war, within the civilian and military elite, was confined to small discussion circles (what the security police called the 'Black Orchestra' or *Schwarze Kapelle*). Even then the 'programme' of the elite dissidents involved unrealistic territorial claims. The most important figure was General Ludwig Beck, who had been Chief of the Army General Staff in the 1930s. Well-connected younger Army officers, led by Colonel Henning von Tresckow, plotted Hitler's assassination, which culminated in the 20 July 1944 'bomb plot'(see Box 49). However heroic the individual actions, and however tragic the fate of the elite dissidents, the term *Widerstand* (the German word for 'resistance') seems inappropriate, if used in comparison with other parts of Europe. The conspirators were leading figures in Hitler's war machine, and outright action against an appalling regime was taken only once.

Roosevelt and Churchill are sometimes criticised for the 'unconditional surrender' policy of January 1943 which made it impossible to find a middle ground or for nationalist officers to build up a credible alternative, but that was a minor element. Other factors kept the Germans fighting, and on Hitler's side. In the end they would all go down together. The victorious Western Allies had difficulty finding uncompromised German leaders. In the end they had to skip a generation and turn to the pre-Nazi era. Konrad Adenauer, the Christian Democrat Chancellor of 1949, was a septuagenarian who had been out of politics for over twenty years.

· · ·

The Allies easily won the battle of production, but neither the morale nor the production of the Third Reich could be fundamentally crippled by the Allied 'wear down' strategy. Allied blockade (from 1939) and Allied bombing (effectively from 1942) were not able to shut down German production, although they certainly slowed it. German terror, and the caution of the occupied

Box 49 | The 20 July 1944 bomb plot

Beginning in the months after Stalingrad, various plots to kill Hitler were developed by a handful of junior and middle-level German Army officers, loosely grouped around Colonel Henning von Tresckow. By the autumn of 1943 these had developed into a plan both to kill Hitler and to effect a military takeover using elements of the so-called Replacement Army (*Ersatzheer*), which was based within the German homeland. Operation VALKYRIE (*WALKÜR*), an official contingency plan to deal with civil unrest, became the outline of a military coup.

In November 1943 Tresckow was promoted to the rank of general and made Chief of Staff of 2nd Army in Russia. However, a major collaborator, General Friedrich Olbricht, worked in Berlin; Olbricht was the head of the Army General Office (*Allgemeine Heeresamt*), located in the Bendlerstrasse. In the months before July 1944 Lieutenant Colonel Count Claus Schenk von Stauffenberg became a leading light in the conspiracy. The devoutly Catholic Stauffenberg was apparently influenced by witnessing atrocities on the Eastern Front. He joined the conspiracy in autumn of 1943, when he left hospital after treatment for war injuries (suffered in Tunisia). At the start of July 1944 the disabled Stauffenberg became Chief of Staff of the Replacement Army and gained physical access to Hitler. In this new situation Stauffenberg decided to carry out the assassination attempt himself. He left a time-bomb in a briefcase in one of Hitler's conferences at his headquarters in Rastenburg in East Prussia. The explosion mortally wounded a number of senior officers, including the Luftwaffe Chief of Staff and Hitler's Wehrmacht adjutant. Hitler himself suffered only superficial injuries.

Hitler's survival doomed the plot. Stauffenberg flew back from East Prussia to Berlin, believing that the Führer was dead. The attempt to seize power, organised from the Bendlerstrasse, was ineffectual. Goebbels rallied loyal forces in Berlin, having restored telephone communications with Hitler. The commander of the Replacement Army came down on the side of the authorities and had Stauffenberg, Olbricht, and other key conspirators summarily executed. General Ludwig Beck, who was to have been head of state in the new regime, shot himself. In occupied Paris the local military commander, General Karl Heinrich von Stülpnagel, had taken more decisive action, ordering the arrest of leading SS and Gestapo officials; they were released when the coup collapsed. In the weeks that followed 20 July, many of those associated with the conspiracy were arrested, publicly tried, and executed.

Hitler had good fortune on 20 July. We cannot know what would have happened had he died at Rastenburg, and whether enough of the Army would have challenged the NSDAP power structure. The affair continues to excite controversy. The feature film *Valkyrie* (2008) told the story of the bomb plot. The cast included Tom Cruise as Stauffenberg, Kenneth Branagh as Tresckow, and Bill Nighy as Olbricht.

population, kept resistance within manageable bounds. The 'wear down' strategy had an effect, but it would not win the war. The Germans, for their part, could do very little to reduce Allied production, except for holding on to parts of occupied Russia and interdicting the British-American shipping routes. The resilience of the Nazi regime meant that the final destruction of the Third Reich would have to be brought about on the ground by conventional armies. The final stage of the war in Europe was about to begin.

Allied military might finally crushes Nazi Germany. Two IS-2 'Stalin' heavy tanks sit parked in front of the Reichstag building on 2 May 1945. The Soviet red flag flies over the ruined façade of the German parliament. Two days earlier, and a thousand yards to the south, Hitler had committed suicide in the Reich Chancellery bomb shelter.

The Reichstag was a surprising symbol of Nazi power. The structure had been burned out in 1933, and it was not used by the regime for the occasional ceremonial meetings of the Reichstag (which usually assembled in the Kroll Opera House). Perhaps it was the best-known and most prominent building in the city, set in a fairly open site near the Tiergarten and the Brandenburg Gate in the centre of Berlin. Hitler's Reich Chancellery, the real centre of power, was set in the relatively narrow Wilhelmstrasse.

In 1999 the Reichstag was reopened as the parliament building of a reunited Germany.

Victory in Europe 1944–1945

Timeline

1944	June	D-Day in Normandy (OVERLORD)
	June	Soviet offensive in Belorussia (BAGRATION)
	August	Paris liberated
	December	Red Army siege of Budapest begins (to February)
	December	German Ardennes offensive (Battle of the Bulge)
1945	January	Soviet Vistula–Oder offensive begins
	March	British and American armies cross the Rhine
	April	Red Army captures Vienna
	May	Red Army captures Berlin
	May	Germany surrenders

Four invasions:
(1a) France and the Low Countries: D-Day

OVERLORD, the cross-Channel invasion, was unlike any military operation in history. Amphibious landings in previous wars had been raids or diversions, aimed to hit the enemy where he was weak or unprepared. This could also be said of the peripheral invasions of North Africa in 1942 and even of Sicily and southern Italy in 1943. OVERLORD, in contrast, was the military 'centre of gravity'. Northern France was well defended and near the German heartland. The Allied landing there was the most anticipated event of the whole war.

The Germans, for their part, had begun to worry about their western marches in the spring of 1942. The setback of the *Ostheer* at Moscow in December 1941 and the entry of the United States into the war ended any serious thoughts of a German invasion of Britain. The Canadian raid on Dieppe in northern France in August 1942, unsuccessful as it was, made the Allied threat more tangible. German Army engineers and the *Organisation Todt* began building up the fixed defences of what German propaganda called the *Atlantikwall*. In 1943 the danger became even greater. In the late autumn of that year Hitler ordered that preparations against a cross-Channel invasion be made the first priority of the Wehrmacht, more important even than the fighting in Russia.

There were differing opinions on the German side about how to deal with the cross-Channel threat. Rundstedt, the veteran Field Marshal who had served since 1942 as C-in-C, West, argued for the concentration of reserves in central locations, back from the sea. From there they could be thrown forward to deal with whichever beaches the Allies landed on. Field Marshal Rommel, the erstwhile 'Desert Fox', and since January 1944 Rundstedt's subordinate for northern France as commander of Army Group 'B', favoured a forward deployment. Rommel aimed to defeat the enemy on the beaches. Although his concept scattered the German forces, he was pessimistic about his ability to move reserves forward over damaged roads and railways and in the face of constant daytime air attacks. Hitler was inclined to support Rommel, but in any event he demanded that Rundstedt's armoured reserves be kept under his own (Hitler's) immediate control.

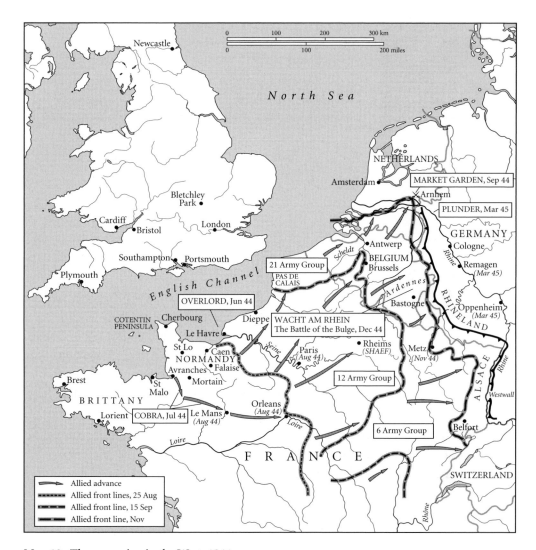

Map 12 The campaign in the West, 1944

Figure 26 | General Dwight D. Eisenhower

For Eisenhower, unlike some other senior American generals, military service was not a family tradition. 'Ike' Eisenhower (1890–1969) came from relatively humble origins; his German ancestors had come to America in the 1740s, and he grew up in Kansas. The US Military Academy at West Point offered him the chance of a higher education; he graduated in 1915, in the middle of his class.

Although he did not see combat in 1917–18, and in the inter-war years never commanded anything larger than a battalion, Eisenhower proved himself to be an efficient staff officer. He came to the attention of General Marshall, who in March 1941 appointed him to the Army's War Plans (later Operations) Division; Eisenhower quickly rose to the rank of general. In June 1942 Marshall assigned him to command the small US Army forces that were building up in Britain.

When Operation TORCH was mounted against French North Africa, Eisenhower was assigned to be its overall commander; given the legacy of bad feeling between Britain and Vichy France, the invasion was made to look as much as possible like an American one. General Brooke, the British Army C-in-C, formed a bad early impression: 'I am afraid that Eisenhower as a general is hopeless!' Brooke recorded in his diary during the campaign. 'He submerges himself in politics because he knows little if anything about military matters'.[a] TORCH did indeed take longer than expected to complete, but it gave Eisenhower crucial experience. Subsequently he was in overall command of Allied operations in Sicily and southern Italy. He did not display brilliant generalship, but he had developed an effective rapport with British and American officers.

In January 1944, after the Tehran Conference, the Allies finally agreed to appoint a commander for the cross-Channel landing. Roosevelt and Churchill settled on Eisenhower. Supreme Headquarters Allied Expeditionary Force (SHAEF) remained Eisenhower's command post until the end of the war. In September 1944 he took direct command of the ground campaign, with three army groups operating under him.

Eisenhower served as President of the United States in 1953–61 (as a Republican) and led the country at a time of unparalleled affluence and international power. He produced war memoirs, *Crusade in Europe* (1948).

[a] Viscount Alanbrooke, *War Diaries 1939–1945*, ed. Alex Danchev and Daniel Todman (London: Weidenfeld & Nicolson, 2001), p. 351.

The Allied planners had begun to look seriously at a cross-Channel operation in early 1942. They were then overwhelmed by the preparations for Operation TORCH in North Africa (see Chapter 10). In February–March 1943, after TORCH and the Casablanca Conference, Roosevelt and Churchill agreed to postpone the cross-Channel operation until 1 May 1944. Forward planning continued, and at the Quebec Conference (QUADRANT) in August 1943 the British and American high command approved an outline invasion scheme. This specified the final landing areas on the Normandy coast, stretching some 50 miles from the city of Caen west to the base of the Contentin peninsula. In January 1944, partly in light of ULTRA information about the strength of the German defences, the planners increased the strength of the initial sea landing from three divisions to five. The build-up and supply of the expeditionary force were going to be crucial, and the Allies hoped to meet this challenge by assembling two huge prefabricated ports (known as MULBERRY harbours) on the Normandy coast (see Figure 27).

Deception planning played a large part in the Allied preparations. The various measures taken were given the codename FORTITUDE. The Allies attempted to convince the enemy that the landing would come somewhere other than Normandy. In particular, they tried to draw the Germans' attention further east along the Channel coast, beyond the Seine estuary, to the so-called Pas de Calais. The Wehrmacht was to be made to think (before 6 June) that the initial landing would come in the Pas de Calais, or (after 6 June) that there would be important follow-up landings there. The Pas de Calais beaches required a shorter crossing from southern England, and they were nearer the eventual Allied objectives.

The Allies set up large dummy formations, complete with radio networks, to make the Wehrmacht command think they had extra forces available for landings in the Pas de Calais. The most important was '1st US Army Group' (FUSAG), under the hero of Sicily, General Patton. Poor strategic intelligence, which led the Germans to overestimate the number of Allied divisions in Britain, made FUSAG more plausible. Thanks to ULTRA, Allied commanders could get a sense of how far the enemy were being taken in by the deception. FORTITUDE worked; the Germans devoted too much energy to fortifying the Pas de Calais, and they held back reserves there until well into the Normandy campaign.

Figure 27 | **MULBERRY harbour**

A port for deep-water ships was needed to bring in heavy equipment and supplies after the initial cross-Channel landings. The Dieppe operation had shown the difficulty of taking one of the existing French ports, and the German engineers could in any event use demolitions to make captured harbours unusable. The solution – deemed essential by the OVERLORD planners – was the secret construction of prefabricated port facilities, codenamed MULBERRY harbours. The design and construction work was carried out in Britain.

The picture above shows the long causeways from one of the deep-water moorings where full-size cargo ships could unload. Further out to sea were caissons and blockships to protect the harbour area. Two MULBERRY harbours were designed and put in place, the American MULBERRY 'A' off Omaha beach and the British MULBERRY 'B' (above) at Arromanches.

The American MULBERRY was very badly damaged by a great gale at the end of June and was thereafter of little use. MULBERRY 'B', further east, continued to serve. As it turned out, it was possible to meet the basic needs of the invading armies by unloading landing ships like LSTs directly on the beaches. Eventually the Allies acquired conventional ports, the most important of which was Cherbourg on the Cotentin peninsula, but it took some time to make them fully serviceable.

The cross-Channel invasion came on 6 June 1944. German naval and air power were now so weak that they could offer no real threat to the invasion fleet. The five landing beaches were attacked just after dawn and secured during the first day. Airborne landings mounted on the night of 5–6 June on either side of the planned beachhead zone were confused, but they achieved their objective of securing the flanks for critical hours. The fighting on one of the American beaches – OMAHA – was the bloodiest, partly because it was well defended. But by the end of the first day some 150,000 Allied troops had come ashore. The Normandy landings were the peak of British effort in World War II. A generation brought up on the 'American' Normandy epic needs to be reminded that three of the five beaches – GOLD, JUNO, and SWORD – were assaulted by British Empire forces, and only two – UTAH and OMAHA – by American forces. Nearly half the aircraft supporting OVERLORD were under RAF control. The overall commanders of the ground forces and air forces were British (Montgomery and Tedder).

The British and Americans secured a beachhead zone about 60 miles wide, and 10–20 miles deep. This had room for forward airfields, and for beach facilities and supply dumps beyond the range of German artillery fire. The ingenious MULBERRY harbours facilitated the early build-up. The Germans had no means to mount serious attacks on them by sea or by air, but unfortunately the weather proved to be a more dangerous enemy. Severe channel storms in late June damaged the British MULBERRY and largely destroyed the American one. Fortunately the availability of large numbers of vehicles and roll-on, roll-off landing ships, especially American LSTs, meant that much of the Normandy build-up could be mounted over the open beaches. A most important strategic development was the early (27 June) American capture of a major port, Cherbourg, west of Normandy, although more than a month was needed to repair German demolitions. The task of capturing the ports further west, like Brest and St Malo, was not as easy or as quick as hoped for. Indeed, St Nazaire and Lorient remained in Germans hands until the end of the war. All the same, the logistic base was sufficient for a series of dramatic Allied victories.

Allied tactical air power came into its own during the Normandy campaign. One factor which had delayed the landings was the requirement for complete air superiority over the landing area – and this was also why the beaches chosen had to be within range of tactical aircraft operating from

Britain. American and British aircraft were able to soften up the German defences, drive the Luftwaffe out of forward airfields, and, as Rommel feared, prevent the rapid movement of German reserves to the landing area. The Allies had 11,500 aircraft available to support OVERLORD at the start of the operation (including 6,000 fighters and the heavy bomber force). The German 3rd Air Fleet in France had only 800 aircraft, with just 300 fighters. The Luftwaffe was able to mount only 100 sorties during daylight on 6 June itself. Although, as planned, the Luftwaffe sent some reinforcements to France, the Allies kept control of the sky throughout the Battle of Normandy. Rommel himself was very badly injured in a strafing attack by an RAF Spitfire in July.

Four invasions: (1b) France and the Low Countries: breakout and pursuit

Despite the generally successful outcome of the initial landings, the subsequent steps could not be taken as quickly as the planners expected. The German command, on Hitler's orders, threw considerable forces into counter-attacks, with little attempt to form a rear line of defence. Allied losses were lighter than had been expected by the planners, but progress was slow. The French town of Caen, at the eastern end of the beachhead, should have been taken by the British on the first day. It was fought over for more than a month. The terrain inland from the beaches, with its now famous *Bocage*, proved to be hard to break through. (The *Bocage* was a Normandy landscape of small fields bordered by dense hedgerows and sunken roads; it was very hard to penetrate.)

The ring of German forces was gradually worn down, however, and Allied forces in the Normandy beachhead area built up. At the start of July Rundstedt was replaced as C-in-C, West, by the more energetic Field Marshal Kluge, commander of Army Group Centre in Russia from late 1941 to late 1943; the change of commander could not save the situation. On 15 July, six weeks after the initial landing and two weeks before the American breakout, Field Marshal Rommel reported to Hitler that the military situation in Normandy was hopeless: 'The troops are everywhere fighting heroically, but the unequal struggle is approaching its end. It is urgently necessary to draw the proper conclusion from this situation. As C-in-C of the army group I feel myself in duty bound to speak plainly on this point.'[1] This operational crisis coincided with the 20 July 1944 assassination attempt on Hitler (see Chapter 11), although that event was more a symptom than a cause of impending military disaster in Normandy.

The Americans under General Omar Bradley had been building up the pressure at the western end of the Normandy beachhead. On 25 July, after a carpet bombing attack by heavy bombers, Operation COBRA began the breakout. Within a week US forces had taken the strategic town of Avranches at the base on the Cotentin Peninsula. At this point (6–7 August) Hitler ordered the last armoured counter-attack in Normandy, Operation LÜTTICH. He finally threw in the forces that had been held back to defend the Pas de Calais. Three panzer divisions and attached battle groups struck west from near the town of Mortain, aiming to drive to the sea and cut the Allied spearheads off from their main forces in Normandy. Forewarned by ULTRA the Allies repelled the Mortain attack. Within days they had out-flanked the panzers from the south and were threatening to encircle them. The Germans were able to pull some of their forces back through a gap in the Allied ring at Falaise, but they suffered heavy losses and were soon in headlong retreat.

When German resistance in Normandy broke in August the Wehrmacht paid the price of its forward deployment. The new American 3rd Army under General Patton exploited the COBRA breakthrough and dashed east to Le Mans, Orléans and the upper Seine. The Germans had to give up the line of the Seine without a serious struggle. Field Marshal Kluge was dismissed in mid August; Hitler feared he might try to make a separate peace in the west. The Field Marshal committed suicide, fearing arrest for his complicity in the 20 July 1944 plot. Rommel, too, recuperating from his injuries in Germany, was obliged to take poison in October, when evidence of his knowledge of the July plot became clear; he was officially reported to have died of his wounds and was given a state funeral. The able Field Marshal Walther Model replaced both Rundstedt and Rommel, but he could do little. The German garrison of Paris could not deal with a spontaneous uprising on 19 August, let alone fulfil Hitler's order to raze the great city. Contrary to his original intentions to bypass Paris, Eisenhower sent relief troops there. The Allied forces, famously led by General Leclerc's 1st French Armoured Division, reached the city on the 25th (see Box 50). All central France was soon under Allied control.

Box 50 | General de Gaulle's walk down the Champs Elysées

The following is an account by French historian Adrien Dansette of the dramatic events in Paris on 26 August 1944, the day of the liberation of Paris.

From the workshops of Montparnasse and the markets of Bercy, from the hovels of the rue Mouffetard and the shops of the Faubourg Saint-Antoine, from the great houses in the Avenue Foch and the hutted camps in the outer suburbs, men, women, children, the people of Paris came up, more and more numerous as they neared the centre, coagulating in a dense swarm. By three in the afternoon they had formed a gigantic crowd, crammed in irregular layers on iron chairs, stools, ladders; waiting, along a way bright with tricolours, for a glorious procession to pass . . .

No doubt, as official processions always do, this one will drive down the Champs Elysées. But no. Loudspeaker cars address the crowd down the route: 'General de Gaulle confides his safety to the people of Paris. He asks them to keep order for themselves, to help in this task the police and the FFI who are weary after five days' fighting.' Four tanks lumber forward, *Lauragais, Limagne, Limousin, Verdelon*. Behind them, blocking the avenue [the Champs Elysées], come forward arm-in-arm policemen, FFI, first-aid men, soldiers, in a human chain; a fireman, a postman, even a negro grinning from ear to ear among them. Behind, in disorder, come motorcycles, sidecars, overloaded jeeps; then after an empty space an usher in a black coat, with a white shirt front and a silver chain, very solemn; behind him, at last, a throng of people with a few officers half-hidden among them. In the front rank there is one man in uniform; he is a head taller than the rest. '*Vive de Gaulle! Vive de Gaulle!*' the crowd yells.

(From M. R. D. Foot, *SOE in France: An Account of the Work of the British Special Operations Executive in France: 1940–1944* (London: Whitehall History Publishing / Frank Cass, 2004), pp. 365f.)

One of the biggest inter-Allied military controversies of the war now broke out, over what step to take next. The British General Montgomery had been the overall Allied ground forces commander in Normandy. In a reorganisation at the start of September Montgomery's 21st Army Group was now joined by a largely American 12th Army Group under General Bradley, and then by a 6th Army Group under the American General Devers, formed from the American and French troops which had advanced from landings in the south of France (see below). General Eisenhower became overall ground forces commander, as well as continuing as 'Supreme Commander' of air, ground, and naval forces in France.

The Allied armies were now on the Seine and facing east towards Germany. Montgomery, with mainly British and Canadian divisions, was on the left flank; Bradley, with the Americans, was further inland. Germany was 250–300 miles to the east, its western border stretching from the North Sea to Switzerland. The original OVERLORD plan had called for the armies of the Allied 'expeditionary force' (AEF) to pause to regroup and consolidate their supply base once they had reached the lines of the Seine and the Loire. Presented with the shattering of German mobile forces in Normandy, Eisenhower now decided against the pause and ordered an uninterrupted pursuit to the Seine and beyond. The Allied advance would of necessity have to be channelled either side of the rough terrain of the Eifel region and the German defences in front of the Ruhr valley (the *Westwall* or 'Siegfried Line'). Montgomery in mid August proposed a concentrated thrust with his forces around the northern end of the *Westwall*, through the Netherlands towards the lower Rhine. His aim was a quick entry into the Reich and an early end to the war. Eisenhower agreed about the importance of this northern wing, but he also favoured what was called the 'broad front'. *Both* the main forces of the AEF – Montgomery, with mainly British forces, and Bradley's Americans – would advance. Montgomery was to take the vital ports, especially Antwerp. Bradley, with Patton's spearhead, was to advance into the Saar region. This would position Allied armies for an entry into Germany on either side of the vital Ruhr industrial region.

Montgomery's approach was more in line with the German thrusts of the Blitzkrieg era or the Soviet 'deep battle' concept. At one point he described this as a 'reverse Schlieffen plan', after the German offensive into France in 1914. His plan emphasised both concentration of effort and pace – maintaining the drive against the Germans before they could assemble defensive forces. The need for a decision to concentrate on one sector or the other was especially important, Montgomery argued, because supplies (especially fuel) coming from the western French ports were still very limited. The Normandy beaches and the main port of Cherbourg were now 200–300 miles to the rear, and the Allies now had 50 divisions ashore in France. Montgomery believed there were larger political factors at work: Bradley and his two American army-level commanders (Hodges and Patton) did not want the US Army to be sidelined. Eisenhower (Montgomery argued) was reluctant to halt rapidly advancing American forces, and he did not want to commit his main effort to a commander who was not an American. A US Presidential election was pending in November. It is doubtful in any event if Montgomery would have been able to win a quick victory with his northern wing, given his supply problems and the recuperative power of the Germans.

Montgomery had a reputation for tactical inflexibility (and personal irascibility). Nevertheless he proposed, and Eisenhower supported, one daring offensive. The hastily organised attack codenamed Operation GARDEN was a narrow thrust by British XXX Corps 60 miles north into the Netherlands to take a bridgehead across the Rhine. The British-American airborne corps was assigned to Montgomery's drive. In Operation MARKET two American airborne divisions were to take vital river crossings along the attack corridor, and a British airborne division was to land in parachutes and gliders for a preliminary seizure of the final bridgehead, on the lower Rhine at Arnhem. The operation began on 17 September. The two American drops were successful, but a combination of tactical problems and unexpected German resistance doomed the landings at Arhem. Some British airborne troops reached the bridge there, but they were unable to hold it against German counter-attacks. Meanwhile XXX Corps was unable to break through to relieve them. After a week of heavy fighting the Arnhem force was mostly captured or killed.

The spectacular Allied setback at Arnhem masked an even more important operational miscalculation: the failure to secure the sea approaches to the big Belgian port of Antwerp. The contradictory weaknesses and strengths of the German Army were shown by this episode. On the one hand the Germans allowed the port and its facilities to fall intact into British hands (two weeks before Arnhem), thanks to the efforts of the Belgian Resistance. On the other hand the German forces tenaciously defended the mouth of the Scheldt River, below Antwerp. They delayed the opening of this vital forward port for nearly three months until late November 1944. In the end, indeed, it was logistics that forced a halt by the American and British on the edges of Germany.

The Normandy campaign was the final one in the European war where the British Empire took even a near equal share. At the end of the Battle of Normandy, in August 1944, there were 6 British or Canadian armoured divisions in action, and 9 infantry divisions; the American contribution was 7 armoured divisions and 14 infantry divisions. Month by month over the following autumn and winter, fresh troops arrived in Western Europe from the United States. By the end of the war, in May 1945, the Americans were very much the senior partner, with 15 armoured divisions and 42 infantry divisions. The order of battle of British-led forces was virtually unchanged – 6 British, Canadian, or Polish armoured divisions and 12 infantry divisions (3 of them Canadian); the British actually had to disband 2 divisions due to manpower shortages. The French had meanwhile put into service 3 French armoured divisions and 9 infantry divisions (with mainly American equipment).

Even so, the American fighting force committed to Europe had limited strength. In late 1943 the planners in Washington, who required manpower for support troops and the preparations for the B-29 campaign against Japan, had decided not to raise the further 15 divisions of combat ground troops that were scheduled. They gambled that a global total of 90 (rather than 105) US Army divisions would be all that was needed to defeat the Axis; of these about 60 would be sent to Europe. (The 'Victory Program' of late 1941, drafted before Japan entered the war, had assumed that over 200 US Army divisions would be required by 1944.) General Marshall decided in 1943 that the higher quality of American divisions and powerful air support would be enough to ensure victory. It was a gamble; had German resistance been stronger than expected, America would have had no reserves. The '90 division gamble' also meant that US Army planners were eager to transfer American divisions as soon as possible from Europe to the Pacific for the invasion of Japan. By way of contrast, the Red Army had at the start of 1945 some 32 tank and mechanised corps (comparable to armoured divisions), and 473 infantry divisions.

Four invasions: (2) The south of France

The Allies mounted a second invasion of France, on the Mediterranean coast. This came ten weeks after D-Day, on 16 August 1944. The planners originally conceived it in the summer of 1943 as a diversionary landing to be mounted before OVERLORD; they gave it the revealing codename ANVIL (OVERLORD being the 'hammer'). The Big Three approved ANVIL at the Teheran Conference, after a considerable debate. Roosevelt and Marshall wanted the southern landings, in order to support the main effort of OVERLORD. Churchill was opposed. He and the British commanders in the Mediterranean theatre wanted to concentrate Allied divisions in Italy,

Figure 28 | **The Sherman tank**

The American 'Medium Tank M4', usually known as the Sherman, was the most important tank used by the Western Allies in the liberation of Europe. Some 50,000 were built, a larger number than any other American or British tank. 'Virgin', pictured above being transferred ashore on the morning of D-Day, was a Sherman that served with the British Army. It has been driven off an American-manned LST (amphibious ship) and transferred to a motorised pontoon called a RHINO for the final trip to shore.

The 30-ton Sherman was not the best tank of the war, nor even the best tank available in large numbers. It entered combat in the summer of 1942, rushed over to help the British in North Africa (and was named by them, after the American Civil War general). At that time the Sherman was a match for the Panzer IIIs and IVs of the *Afrika Korps*. By 1944 the Sherman was obsolescent, and unlike the Russian T-34 or the German Panzer IV it was not significantly modernised. This was partly because the makers of US Army doctrine wrongly thought that a bigger role would be played by fast but weakly protected 'tank-destroyers' like the M10 Wolverine, and partly because of an American underestimation of German tanks. The US Army received a first-class tank – in small numbers – only at the very end of the war (February 1945), when the 'Heavy Tank M26' Pershing was rushed to Germany; the M26 was a 42-ton vehicle with a 90-mm gun.

The Sherman, then, was inferior to the 1943 Panzer V Panther, not to mention the Panzer VI Tiger and King Tiger heavy tanks. The Sherman's protection was inadequate, it was high-sided and vulnerable, and the relatively low-velocity 75 mm gun most Shermans carried was of limited use against the latest German tanks. Thanks to tank plants like the Detroit Arsenal, however, the Sherman was available in huge quantities. Three or four average tanks were able to cope with one above-average tank, especially when they were supported by powerful air forces and artillery. The M4 also had long range, it was mechanically reliable, it fitted into standard ships and landing craft, and it could run over standard bridges. (Some were specially modified to operated as amphibians.)

The Sherman was also the main tank of the British Army from 1943 onwards and was superior as a 'universal tank' to anything the British had available. It was supplied in quantity to the Red Army in the later part of the war.

anticipating an advance into the north Italian plain and even the Balkans. The Americans would have had their way in any event, but it helped that Stalin threw his weight in on their side at the Teheran Conference.

In the event the arguments about ANVIL continued after Teheran and into 1944. Even after the Normandy landings, the Allies were still debating the relative merits of southern France and northern Italy. The Allies had finally begun to move forward again in Italy; they took Rome on 5 June. But the Americans stressed the southern flank of the armies in Normandy and the importance of logistics. The big port at Marseilles, distant as it was from the main front, promised an additional supply route. Logistics became a bigger factor after the Channel storm of 19 June wrecked the American MULBERRY harbour. The final decision to proceed with ANVIL, now renamed DRAGOON, was made as late as 2 July.

The invasion came ashore in agreeable surroundings, between Cannes and St Tropez. Unlike in OVERLORD, the first wave of seaborne troops – three divisions – were all American. The main troops in the second wave were French; new formations raised in North Africa in 1943 and equipped with American weapons. The French involvement is sometimes forgotten by historians, but it was significant. These troops, under General de Lattre de Tassigny, were liberating their own country. As the campaign progressed, the French conventional forces incorporated many Resistance (FFI) fighters.

There was only slight enemy resistance to the southern D-Day. The German 19th Army defending the south of France was now a second-line formation with seven weak infantry divisions stretched along the whole Mediterranean coast, and only one panzer division. The Allies had air supe-riority. They quickly learned from ULTRA decrypts that Hitler did not plan a serious defence of the region. The campaign in the south of France involved relatively light losses – fewer than 1,000 US ground troops were killed.

While the French troops liberated the Riviera towns (Marseilles and Toulon were taken with little damage on 28 August), the more mobile Americans pursued the Germans up the Rhône river valley. They took a considerable number of prisoners, but could not prevent the escape of the bulk of 19th Army. The remnants of the collaborator government in Vichy – including Marshal Pétain – were bundled up and taken back to the Reich. The Germans did not stop retreating until they reached Belfort in the first week of September. There they dug in, covering the approaches to Alsace.

Their resistance was helped by the rough country of the Vosges mountains and by the fact that the Allies were operating at the end of long supply lines. Meanwhile the advancing Americans made contact with their comrades – with the flank of Patton's 3rd Army – in mid September.

The wisdom of ANVIL/DRAGOON is still debated by military historians, especially its effect on the Italian campaign. The Germans would have had to evacuate the south of France anyway, once Patton mounted his spectacular charge across central France from Avranches to the Seine in the first two weeks of August. But this success could not have been predicted at the time ANVIL was approved. There is also no reason to think that leaving the ANVIL divisions in northern Italy would have given better results. The newly equipped French troops certainly fought better in France than they would have elsewhere.

Four invasions: (3) Belorussia and Poland

Leaving aside the afterthought of ANVIL/DRAGOON, the 'invasion of Europe' is often taken to mean the Normandy (OVERLORD) landings and the advance through northern France, Belgium, and the Netherlands towards the Rhine. There was another, and bigger, 'invasion' of Hitler's Europe that summer, a few weeks after D-Day. It was mounted by the Red Army. Most of Hitler's ground forces were still concentrated in the East; on 1 June 1944 there were 156 German divisions in the East and only 60 in France (and 27 in Italy).

The British and Americans had to cross the English Channel. The Russians had to make their 'bridge' into Europe by mounting a huge operation to reconquer Belorussia and to break Army Group Centre, the largest of Hitler's four eastern army groups. Repeated Soviet offensives in this wooded central part of the front had made only limited advances in 1942–3 – and even in the spring of 1944. The stalemate in Belorussia contrasted unfavourably with sweeping Soviet successes on the Ukrainian steppe and even around Leningrad. Stalin tended to reinforce success rather than failure, so – until the spring of 1944 – personnel, equipment, and supplies went to the Ukraine rather than to the front facing Belorussia.

In April 1944 Stalin and the Stavka decided to mount their main summer attack in Belorussia. The Soviet version of OVERLORD was given the

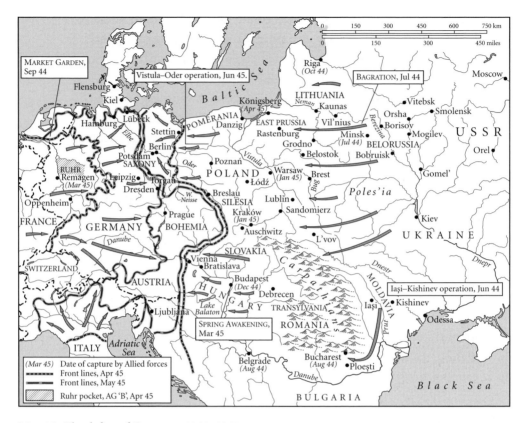

Map 13　The defeat of Germany, 1944–1945

codename BAGRATION (pronounced 'Bagrat-i-on'), after a Russian general of the Napoleonic Wars. The Germans were confused by a Soviet deception plan which was on a similar scale to FORTITUDE. They expected the main Soviet blow to be a continuation of the rolling advance in the Ukraine, on the southern side of the Polesia (Pripiat' Marshes). Five of the six Soviet tank armies were still in the Ukraine. The Russians skilfully masked the build-up of their forces against Army Group Centre: 2.4 million men, 5,200 tanks and self-propelled guns, 5,300 combat aircraft.

Defending Belorussia was one of Hitler's lesser-known senior commanders, Field Marshal Ernst Busch. Busch's Army Group Centre had 51 divisions and over 800,000 men, a force roughly the size of Rommel's Army Group 'B' in northern France. Unlike the defenders of France, Busch had almost no armour, having had to transfer his tanks to the Ukraine. He also had minimal support from the Luftwaffe. Hitler had decided in March 1944 that the key element was to be the 'fortified places' (*feste Plätze*), fortresses that were to be held tenaciously while the enemy's mobile forces swept around them; the fortified place would then be relieved by the German counter-attack. Of particular importance in Belorussia was a line of fortified towns – Vitebsk, Orsha, Mogilev, and Bobruisk.

Operation BAGRATION began on 22 June, two weeks after D-Day (it was the third anniversary of the start of the Nazi–Soviet War). Hitler's 'fortified places' proved to be no more effective than the *Atlantikwall*. The four Soviet army groups under the command of Marshals Zhukov and Vasilevskii (overseeing the southern and northern wings respectively) punched through the German front. Hitler, Busch, and Busch's army commanders were surprised by the strength and pace of the assault. The Soviet tank columns and their heavy American-built supply trucks broke through the gaps between the 'fortified places'. They encircled and destroyed the 'fortified places', trapping many German units in their forward positions. Nowhere was Army Group Centre able to counter-attack.

The Stavka did not intend BAGRATION just to break the crust of the German defences. It was a 'deep' operation, made from a standing start (see Box 51). On 3 July – the tenth day – Soviet troops took Minsk (the capital of Belorussia), and they then continued on to the west. The four Soviet army groups pursued the remnants of Army Group Centre back across 300 miles, rapidly liberating all of Belorussia and moving on to the borders of East

Box 51 | Deep battle

The Red Army did not win its offensive victories in 1943–5 by crude bulldozer tactics. Deep battle was a sophisticated Soviet concept of mechanised offensive warfare developed in the 1930s. It was still the basic concept in 1941, and this partly explains the over-exposed 'offensive' deployment of Soviet forces on 22 June. By mid 1943, when the Red Army had regained the initiative over the Wehrmacht, the Deep Battle concept was the intellectual backbone of the drive across Eastern Europe into the Reich.

Deep Battle (or deep operations) was developed as a means to avoid the static trench warfare of World War I. It is most often linked with Marshal Tukhachevskii, who was its patron, until he was arrested and shot in 1937. The theoretical essence of deep battle was to attack the enemy using very fast-moving mechanised troops, air strikes, and parachute landings. Simultaneous blows were to be struck through the depth of the enemy's defensive system. Deep battle was also partly an attempt to integrate the newest military technology – tanks, self-propelled artillery, motor transport, attack aircraft. Although it had much in common with what we know as the Blitzkrieg, it was a Russian concept, not a copy of a German one.

The Battles of Moscow, Stalingrad, and even Kursk were counter-offensive battles, in which the Wehrmacht held the original operational initiative. Later in the war the initiative passed to the Red Army. The long Ukrainian offensive in 1943–4, Operation BAGRATION in 1944, and the 1945 winter offensive (the Vistula–Oder operation) were all examples of deep battle.

The concept of deep battle has been very influential since 1945, in both Russian and Western military thought. One of the most spectacular examples of this type of warfare was the American Operation IRAQI FREEDOM in 2003.

Prussia (to within 60 miles of Hitler's 'Wolf's Lair' headquarters) and to the Vistula River in central Poland. The spearheads of General Rokossovskii's 1st Belorussian Army Group reached the Vistula on 1 August, the day after Patton began his breakout from Normandy. Warsaw rose in revolt against Germany occupation on that day (see Chapter 11), only three weeks before the Parisians began their uprising.

South of the Polesiia the Ukrainian offensive had reopened in mid July, on a parallel track with BAGRATION. Marshal Konev's 1st Ukrainian Army

Group resumed its march to the west, across the Ukrainian–Polish borderlands. Konev drove back the enemy's Army Group 'North Ukraine'. He overran all the 'fortified places' in front of him, captured L'vov, and then pushed across southern Poland to establish the Sandomierz bridgehead on the far side of the Vistula.

There, on the Vistula, the two wings of the huge Soviet offensive were finally brought to a halt in August 1944. In France the British and Americans were able rapidly to relieve Paris and push beyond the Seine in late August and September. This was because Hitler had burned out the German Army in the Normandy battles and because there was no feasible line of defence west of the German state border. In Poland, in contrast, Rokossosovkii and Konev had to limit themselves to digging in to small bridgeheads on the far side of the Vistula. Indeed, on 29 August all the Soviet army groups in the central part of the Soviet–German front were ordered to halt offensive operations, and they then stood in place for four months (until January 1945).

The reasons for the Soviet halt were complex. At the end of June Hitler had assigned Field Marshal Walther Model to replace Busch in the main eastern command. Model was a tenacious fighter, and he eventually organised an impressive mobile defence east of Warsaw in early August. As we have seen, however, Model was soon sent to the West to replace Field Marshal Kluge. More important as a general factor was that the Germans were now defending a relatively narrow defensive front. The line of the Vistula was easier for the Germans to hold than the line of the Seine. The German defensive front was anchored in the north in East Prussia and in the south by the Carpathian Mountains. The defending troops were much nearer their sources of reinforcement and supply. The Germans rushed reinforcements into the central part of the front (which would fatally weaken their position elsewhere, especially in Romania). Meanwhile the Soviet spearheads (like Eisenhower's) had outrun their supplies, after one of the longest continuous advances since the beginning of the war.

Another explanation for the halt in Poland was that the Stavka had assigned the Red Army to other tasks in the Baltic states and Romania. There was a big battle around Riga in the first weeks of August which might have (but in the end did not) cut off German Army Group North in the Baltic states. In the end the German forces were able to withdraw into a pocket in the Kurland Peninsula west of Riga. In the south the Soviet Iasi–Kishinev operation at the end of August achieved unexpected success. A huge opportunity was presented to the Russians when a royalist coup in Bucharest led Romania to change sides and suddenly opened the Soviet road to the Balkans (see Chapter 10).

These were enormous and very costly battles, on a scale significantly larger than Normandy. In late June, July, and August 1944 Operation BAGRATION cost nearly 180,000 Soviet troops (killed and missing), with another 65,000 lost in Konev's L'vov–Sandomierz operation. By comparison losses in the same summer period for British-led forces in Normandy and northern France were about 25,000, and US losses about 30,000. More to the point, *German* losses were also considerably worse in Belorussia. In Normandy the Germans lost about 23,000 killed in action and nearly 200,000 missing (many of whom were POWs). In Belorussia alone the German statistics give a figure of 26,000 men killed in action and 263,000 missing. Many of the 'missing' died on the battlefield, but for the *Ostheer* there were also an unprecedented number of POWs. In mid July the Russians organised a huge 'parade' of captured German soldiers around the Moscow ring road. These German losses involved the destruction of whole formations. The BAGRATION campaign is sometimes – accurately – called 'the destruction of Army Group Centre'. The Russians claimed that 17 German divisions were completely destroyed in Belorussia and a further 50 lost more than half their combat strength. The Germans would also suffer great losses in the south, as the Red Army marched towards Romania. The fullest survey of military losses, by the historian Rüdiger Overmans, suggests that German fatalities (not counting POWs) in the East were about 590,000 in June, July, and August in 1944, and about 160,000 on all other fronts.

Four invasions: (4) Hungary

The fourth invasion of the German outer defences in 1944 is the least well known. This was the advance of two more Soviet army groups into the southeastern approaches to the Reich, south of the Carpathian Mountains and up the Danube valley through Romania and Hungary. Events in Romania, Bulgaria, and Yugoslavia were discussed in Chapter 10. When the Romanian government changed sides much of German Army Group South Ukraine was destroyed; it was a disaster second only to the destruction of German Army Group Centre two months before. The Soviets were now able to advance south and west into the Balkans.

Hungary was directly exposed to attack. Hitler had taken the precaution of carrying out a military occupation of the territory of his Hungarian ally back in March 1944, when Red troops rolled up to the opposite side of the Carpathian Mountains after the offensive across the Ukraine. Hungary had been since 1920 an authoritarian state, under Admiral Horthy (an admiral of the former Austro-Hungarian Navy). Hungary's government under Horthy had been fiercely anti-Communist (after a Soviet republic in 1919), with powerful antisemitic and anti-Slav sentiments. Hitler had rewarded Hungary for its support for the Third Reich by giving it large territories taken from Czechoslovakia (1939) and Romania (1940) – territories which had been part of Hungary before 1919. In return Horthy had sent a considerable Hungarian expeditionary force to Russia, where it had been destroyed in the winter of 1942–3. When Hitler's troops took up positions in Hungary Horthy was forced to install a government that would do anything the Reich requested. This set off the last terrible wave of the European Holocaust. The German SS, now given a free hand, deported hundreds of thousands of Hungarian Jews to the death camps or to lethal forced labour. After the fiasco in Romania in August 1944, Hitler watched Hungary very carefully. Horthy's belated attempt to negotiate a separate peace with the Allies was blocked. The Admiral was deposed in October by German special forces, and the Fascist Arrow Cross movement was given full power. Most of the surviving Hungarian Army remained loyal to the Axis.

In early October 1944 the forces of the Red Army under two newly promoted marshals, Tolbukhin and Malinovskii, began a major advance northwest into Hungary, given some support on the flanks by Romanian, Bulgarian, and Yugoslav divisions. There was some hope that the enemy's opposition could be easily swept aside – especially if Horthy were able to change sides – and that there might be a triumphal early march into Budapest. The Axis front firmed up, however, and a major Soviet attempt to storm Budapest in the last two months of the year was repelled. At the end of December Marshal Malinovskii – operating at the end of very long supply lines – was able to complete the full encirclement of the Hungarian capital. This was the first time the Red Army had had to besiege a large enemy city (with a population of several million). Budapest held out, blocking the main communications route west, until the middle of February 1945. This was another expensive operation. Some 100,000 Soviet troops were killed in Hungary, the greater part in the winter battles around Budapest. By comparison American losses (excluding POWs) in the better-known Battle of the Bulge in the Ardennes in December were about 15,000.

The four Allied invasions of what might be called the 'inner occupied zone' – France (Normandy and the Riviera), the Low Countries, Belorussia, Poland, and Hungary – had much in common. In each case the invaders, after breaking through the crust of Hitler's forward defences, were able to make a rapid exploitation. The Allied advances were eventually – and inevitably – slowed by the logistic demands of their massive armies, by the narrowing of the German defensive lines, and by the recuperative power of the Wehrmacht. The German defensive task was complicated by insurgencies mounted by some inhabitants of the occupied countries, but the Resistance in its various forms proved to be only a secondary consideration.

Interlude: Hitler's Ardennes offensive

The Third Reich shuddered under multiple shocks in the summer and autumn of 1944. Invading armies broke through its outer defences to the east and the west; nearly all the conquests of 1939–41 were lost. The air campaign became much more intense; the USAAF and RAF would drop twice as many bombs on Germany in the eight months from September 1944 to the end of the war as they had in the preceding five years. Another kind of bomb, exploded in a briefcase in Hitler's conference room on 20 July, revealed a high-level military conspiracy against the NSDAP regime (see Chapter 10).

Germany's position was not totally hopeless. The front line that had to be defended was shorter than ever before. The German forces contained a notional 10 million personnel. War production seemed for the moment healthy; the autumn of 1944 was actually the peak of wartime aircraft output for the Luftwaffe and of tank production for the German Army. The 'wonder weapons' – jet fighters, rockets, advanced submarines – the product of the

Germans' remarkable technical ingenuity, were at last becoming available in some quantities. Nevertheless the military professionals and industrialists could see that the long-term situation was bleak, and Rommel's July plea for Hitler to seek 'the proper conclusion' was the rational view.

Various factors made a 'rational' surrender impossible. Allied hatred of the Third Reich and of Nazi crimes ruled out anything except radical 'regime change', and those in the military and political elite of the Third Reich knew that they had no future after defeat. What also sustained the German war effort, however, was the dread felt by so many members of these elites about a repetition of November 1918. Hitler made his own position clear as early as the day he invaded Poland in September 1939. 'There is one word which I have never known,' he told the Reichstag, 'and this word is: capitulation! . . . I would like to assure the world around us of one thing: there shall never ever be another November 1918 in German history!'[2] For Hitler, and for many others, the sudden surrender of Imperial Germany had been a traumatic event of the utmost importance and tragedy. In the autumn of 1918 the German armies had still been fighting on French and Belgian soil (and Russia had been knocked out of the war). From the 1920s a core NSDAP view had been that German soldiers had been betrayed into a humiliating peace by liberal politicians and socialist revolutionaries. There was thus on the German side an element of what the historian Michael Geyer has called 'catastrophic nationalism': better that Germany be destroyed than that it make a another humiliating surrender.[3]

The events of 20 July 1944, especially, led the Nazis to attempt a re-ideologisation of the Reich, a return to first principles. The NSDAP and its local *Gauleiter* played a greater role than ever before. Goebbels, the Propaganda Minister, assumed extraordinary powers as 'Reich Plenipotentiary for the Total War Effort'. Above all he was to 'comb out' the home front for labour and troops. Himmler, the head of the SS, was to knock the Wehrmacht into shape, taking control of the so-called 'Replacement Army' at home. In September 1944 the *Volkssturm* was announced, a popular militia, run by the NSDAP, and planned to number 6 million men between the ages of 16 and 60 (see Box 52).

The German Army remained, as before, the main force at the disposal of the Third Reich. The Army command was in some turmoil after 20 July.

Box 52 | The *Volkssturm*

The *Volkssturm* was a people's militia, the last desperate military expedient of the Third Reich. Its creation was announced in late September 1944, when the military situation became desperate. Conventional German formations had been smashed in France, Belorussia, and Romania. The Red Army was approaching East Prussia; the British and Americans were in the Rhineland. The 20 July 1944 conspiracy convinced Hitler that many leaders of the regular Army could not be trusted or were defeatists.

The creation of the *Volkssturm* also reflected a heightened Nazi stress on ideology in the last nine months of the Third Reich. The name *Volkssturm* was derived partly from the *Landsturm,* which fought successfully against Napoleon in the campaign of 1813, but the *Volk* (people) was a central concept of NSDAP ideology. In happier times there had been the *Volksgemeinschaft* (People's Community) or even the *Volkswagen* (People's Car). The *Volkssturm* was set up under the auspices of the NSDAP; regional *Gauleiter* were the principle organisers. In theory *Volkssturm* units would defend their local region (*Gau*), in battalion-sized units organised on remarkably democratic lines.

All men between the age of 16 and 60 were eligible for the *Volkssturm*, and it was hoped to involve as many as 6 million. (For contrast, the total strength of the German field army in December 1944 was only about 3.6 million.) Nearly 175,000 men were killed fighting in the *Volkssturm*. Incapable of maneouvre, and poorly equipped and trained, the *Volkssturm* fought rather better in the East against the Russians, notably around Königsberg and Breslau, where the danger was most tangible. In the West, *Volkssturm* units proved to be of little value. The American capture of the vital Remagen Bridge in March 1945 was mainly due to the failure of the local *Volkssturm*.

Effective military units could not be created from nothing. The mass of the population was unenthusiastic, demoralised, and unready for suicidal battles. The *Volkssturm* ended up as a symbol of the bankruptcy of Hitler, the NSDAP, and the German war effort.

Hitler had appointed a new Chief of the Army General Staff, naming General Guderian to replace General Zeitzler. Guderian was no lackey; he had been a brilliant operational leader in France in 1940 and in Russia in 1941. But he had only limited control over strategy in 1944–5 – and indeed there was no strategy that could have saved Germany. Hitler, aided by

Generals Keitel and Jodl, was still in full command of the Wehrmacht and the Army. And the Führer was not without ideas about how to use his surviving forces.

The last gasp of the German Army in the West came in the famous 'Battle of the Bulge', the Ardennes offensive (Operation WACHT AM RHEIN). Hitler had been thinking about this since September 1944. He had assembled in the greatest secrecy what panzer reserves and fuel he had for a counter-stroke in the West, aimed at the newly opened port of Antwerp. The Ardennes offensive looked very like the YELLOW (*Sichelschnitt*) offensive of May 1940. It was to strike unexpectedly from the Ardennes toward the sea, cutting off the most advanced Allied forces. In overall command was Field Marshal von Rundstedt, who had commanded the key Army Group in 1940 (and who had returned as C-in-C, West, in early September 1944). Under Rundstedt was General Model, the experienced commander of Army Group 'B'. Hitler personally supervised WACHT AM RHEIN from an advanced headquarters. The Germans picked the weakest sector of the Allied front, part of Bradley's American army group, and they waited for a spell of bad weather which would neutralise the superior Allied air forces. Hitler was again staking everything on one card, and, as before, there was a logic to this. The odds were very much against the success of the attack, but not to attack meant certain defeat.

The Ardennes offensive finally came on 16 December. It did not play out as a repeat of 1940. Unlike the French in 1940, the Americans were able to redeploy their forces quickly to deal with the attack. They tenaciously held the small town of Bastogne in the middle of the German advance, blocking enemy lines of communication. German tanks exhausted their limited fuel stocks and could not be resupplied. The weather cleared to permit attacks by Allied tactical aircraft. The real crisis was over within ten days, but it took several more weeks fully to deflate the German salient. WACHT AM RHEIN did further delay the British and American invasion of Germany, but at the cost of many of the Wehrmacht's remaining reserves. Allied losses, almost all American, came to nearly 30,000 killed and missing. German losses were about 80,000.

The Ardennes offensive was the last military initiative of the Third Reich that approached rationality. After its failure there was little Hitler's government could do to prepare for the final onslaught, either from the East or from the West. All that was left now was 'catastrophic nationalism'. Hitler's

Box 53 | Yalta

Churchill, Roosevelt, and Stalin met at the resort of Yalta, in the Soviet Crimea, in early February 1945. This meeting has aroused great historical controversy. Some historians see the conference as a Western betrayal of allies in Eastern Europe. Others see it as a remarkable episode of East–West accommodation which might – with some more good will – have been continued into the post-war era.

All the Allies wanted to preserve a united front, in a war that might well run into the summer of 1945. (As we have seen, Hitler's one hope of survival was a split in the Grand Alliance.) They also assumed that they, the great powers, would dominate the international scene after the war. The Western leaders had reasons not to be intransigent about Soviet territorial gains in Eastern Europe. Roosevelt was eager to gain Stalin's support for the creation of a workable United Nations Organisation; this would be achieved at Yalta. He wanted to confirm Russian agreement to enter the war against Japan. Churchill wanted Soviet support to maintain the 'percentages' in southeastern Europe, and he hoped to bring Britain's old Western European ally, France, back to 'great power' status (with a seat on the UN Security Council and an occupation zone in Germany). The Russians for their part realised that the three great powers would need to co-operate over Germany, since it was unlikely that any one of them could dominate the country without bringing about another war. Germany seemed – at the time – to be the greatest danger to a future peace. An agreement was made on reparations from Germany that was generally acceptable to Moscow.

The Western Allies accepted that in the short term the Red Army needed reliable lines of communications, especially through Poland, for the final assault on Germany. By this time, too, the Russians had already set up their own provisional government on occupied Polish territory, at Lublin in July 1944. In January 1945 the Red Army expelled German forces from the entire territory of pre-war Poland and extended the provisional government to the whole country. The Polish nationalist underground had been shattered by the fiasco of the Warsaw Uprising and by Soviet police measures. The question of Poland's borders had already been decided, from above, at Teheran. That decision had never been accepted by the Polish government-in-exile in London, but the remnants of that body now had poor relations with all the Allies. At Yalta the Western Allies limited themselves to adding a few representatives of the 'London' Poles to the pro-Soviet government in Poland. Tito's Communist-led government was in power in much of Yugoslavia. At Yalta the Allied leaders agreed in principle to representative 'democratic' governments, following the principle of the Atlantic Charter in the 'Declaration on Liberated Europe'. Little was done, however, by the Western leaders to challenge growing Soviet influence.

One of the great imponderables regarding Yalta is the effect of the death of Franklin D. Roosevelt two months after the conference. The American President had been confident that he could use his personal relationship with Stalin to ensure a continuing good relationship with the USSR; he hoped that the Soviet leader trusted him.

19 March 1945 'scorched earth' decree, calling for destruction of the German infrastructure, was to be the ultimate absurdity of Nazi strategy.

The Grand Alliance: the last months

By 1945 Hitler's only chance for survival, even for a stalemate peace, was to play his enemies off against one another. He knew this, and so did his closest advisors, although they suggested different ways of effecting the split. As for the 'Great Powers' – Britain, the USSR, and the USA – their advance into the German borderlands, and then into the Reich itself, made it essential to agree preliminary peace terms. This was true despite different territorial interests and expectations, different clients in third-party states, and drastically different ideologies.

As we have seen (Chapter 6), serious discussion of the post-war world began in 1943, as the Allies gained the initiative in Russia and North Africa – although they were still far away from Central Europe. America, Britain, and Russia had not reached a joint decision about the post-war fate of Germany – especially whether it would be permanently broken up into smaller states or not – but they had agreed in 1943 about temporary military occupation zones. There had finally been a face-to-face conference of all the Big Three at Teheran at the end of 1943, and the British, Soviet, and American foreign ministers met several times. The Allies had at Teheran decided the territorial issue of Poland to their own satisfaction, if not at all to that of the Polish government-in-exile based in London. Stalin had

disbanded the Comintern (May 1943), and his accommodating ideological stance had continued – at least in Western Europe. In late 1943, as
we have seen (Chapter 11), he ordered the Italian and French Communist Parties to co-operate with the Resistance committees that had been set
up by the Western governments on partially recaptured territory (Algeria
and southern Italy). The British, and Churchill in particular, believed that
the way forward was to agree in advance to spheres of influence. This was
evident in the October 1944 'percentages agreement' over the Balkans (see
Chapter 10).

The famous meeting of the Big Three at Yalta (see Box 53) confirmed many
of these arrangements and marked a high point of wartime understanding by
the Allies over a range of European and global issues. Differences, however,
soon emerged. Two weeks after Yalta the Soviets installed a more compliant
government in Romania, after applying military pressure. In late March
1945 they arrested the leaders of the Home Army (AK), the underground
movement loyal to the Polish government-in-exile in London. At the start of
April an unpleasant exchange took place between the Americans and Stalin
over a possible separate surrender of the German forces in northern Italy.
Some historians have suggested that in the last weeks of his life (he died on 12
April) Roosevelt was changing his approach to Stalin and adopting a harder
line. In these weeks, however, the President took few political initiatives, and
after he was gone Vice-President Truman (Figure 30) was content to follow
the narrow advice of the officials around him.

Five battles for the Reich: (1) East Prussia, Brandenburg, and Silesia

Westerners often ignore the 'other' fronts (other than Normandy) in the
invasion campaigns of the summer and autumn of 1944. On the other hand,
they exaggerate the importance of the Red Army and the Battle of Berlin
in the climactic last four months of the war, and underestimate fighting
elsewhere and the role of the British and American armies. Hitler's Reich
proper was now enclosed in a tight ring of fronts, and the Allies mounted
attacks from five directions.

The offensive that the Russians now call the 'Vistula–Oder operation' began on 12 January 1945. The Red Army was able to drive west from the Vistula River in central Poland to the Oder, a river well within eastern Germany. It was the start of the Allied invasion of Germany proper. Although the Americans and Russians had first scratched the very edges of 'old' German territory (in East Prussia and the Rhineland) in the autumn of 1944, the pre-war borders of the Reich – with natural and man-made defences – had been left basically intact. Now those defences were being battered in.

The Soviet winter offensive followed the long pause on the central front that had begun in August 1944, when Stalin had called a halt to the thrust across the Vistula, and turned the main effort to the Baltic states and Romania. In November 1944 the Stavka and the Red Army General Staff began consideration of the final Russian campaign of the war. It was timed for January 1945, and was supposed to be the definitive 'deep operation', shattering German resistance in six weeks of devastating offensive. The operation was planned at a time – before Hitler's December 1944 Ardennes offensive – when German powers of resistance seemed broken and the British and Americans were making rapid progress towards Germany. There is some historical controversy about whether the Russians brought forward their winter offensive to help the Americans beat off the mid-December 1944 Ardennes offensive. This was almost certainly not the case, and in any event, the 'Bulge' had been contained and punctured three weeks before the Soviet offensive began.

Command arrangements in the Red Army were radically altered. Rather than co-ordinating several army groups – as he had since 1942 – the formidable Marshal Zhukov was given direct command of the central part of the front, replacing his old comrade Marshal Rokossovskii as commander of 1st Belorussian Army Group. This might appear to be a demotion for Zhukov, but 1st Belorussian Army Group was a huge force with, at peak strength, two tank armies, nine infantry armies, and two air armies. It had as its object the German capital. Zhukov was flanked by two other army groups led by Marshals Konev (1st Ukrainian) and Rokossovskii (2nd Belorussian). (The three Russian commanders were the opposite numbers to Montgomery, Bradley, and Devers.)

Co-ordinating the activities of all three Soviet army groups was Marshal Stalin; he wanted to take personal credit for the final victories of the war. The Soviet dictator was now advised by the acting Red Army chief of staff, General Antonov. Stalin was in effect the equivalent of Eisenhower, but he also kept his other responsibilities as head of the Stavka and the State Defence Committee. Sitting in Moscow, he was far removed from the action; the distance to central Poland was 800 miles. Some of the problems which beset the Soviet winter offensive would come from the want of a professional theatre commander who was close to the scene of the action.

The offensive of 12 January 1945 actually had two elements. The main blow, by Zhukov and Konev, attacked due west across Poland from the Vistula River bridgeheads. The Soviet forces drove through western Poland, eastern Brandenburg and Silesia, towards the line of the Oder and Neisse Rivers and, beyond them, towards Berlin.

The second and simultaneous Soviet blow was towards the north, into East Prussia. Stalin and the Stavka were still concerned about the situation in the East Prussian 'balcony'. Here was a large German-populated territory – part of the old Prussian state – with both natural defences (lakes and forests) and man-made fortifications. In 1914 the Russians had suffered a terrible defeat at Tannenberg in East Prussia, when the Germans saw off an earlier Russian invasion. Unlike France or Poland in 1944, this was core historical and ethnic German territory; the expectation was that it would be defended to last ditch. The Germans had created a strong position around Königsberg. The region might be used as the base for a counter-attack on the northern flank of the Red Army. This was also territory that the Russians claimed as a diplomatic gain of the war (and indeed is still today part of the Russian Federation). The main attack against East Prussia was supposed to come from the east, mounted by 3rd Belorussian Army Group under General Cherniakhovskii. However, Marshal Rokossovskii's 2nd Belorussian Army Group was to help by driving north to the Baltic and cutting East Prussia off from the west; this was in addition to Rokossovskii's main task of pushing west towards Berlin.

The offensive in Poland started well. Soviet-trained Polish forces, fighting alongside the Red Army, captured the ruins of Warsaw. They did so, without much of a fight, on the fifth day of the offensive. Hitler flew into a rage and arrested senior German staff officers. Zhukov advanced rapidly to the west, as German formations disintegrated in front of him. He raced across western Poland to the old defensive line covering the 1939 German–Polish border; it proved to be largely unmanned. Zhukov's tanks bypassed major urban centres of resistance, notably Posen (Poznan), in the hope that those centres would be reduced by follow-up forces. The isolated German garrisons held out, however, covering communications hubs – especially railway junctions.

Further south, Marshal Konev's 1st Ukrainian Army Group made very rapid progress along the upper Vistula. Kraków fell without a battle, and just to the west of the city the Red Army overran what was left of Auschwitz. Beyond was Silesia, a pre-war province of Germany. Konev sent his forces across Silesia to the Neisse River (south of the Oder), but like Zhukov he bypassed major centres of resistance. The most important of these was the regional centre at Breslau (now Wrocław). Compared to Operation BAGRATION in Belorussia, and the great battles to come in East Prussia and Brandenburg, the Red Army suffered relatively light losses here. The total in the Vistula–Oder operation was about 45,000, roughly what the British and Americans lost in Normandy and northern France. The cost to the Germans, in comparison, was very high.

Developments in East Prussia derailed the great Soviet offensive. General Cherniakhovskii seemed to be running into difficulties in his drive on Königsberg from the east. Stalin ordered Rokossovskii to shift more of his forces north to the Baltic coast, away from the western advance. This did enable 2nd Belorussian Army Group to complete the isolation of East Prussia on 26 January. Rokossovskii's success, however, still did not make it possible for the Soviets quickly to reduce the fanatically held East Prussian enclave. More important for the big picture, however, Rokossovskii's forces were no longer fully covering the right (northern) flank of Zhukov's advance towards Berlin.

Worried about his right flank and ordered by Stalin to deploy forces there, Zhukov ran out of steam in early February. Soviet supply lines stretched back to central Poland. A difficult campaign was continuing in East Prussia. The Americans and British were still west of the Rhine and could offer only limited support. Red Army intelligence was not sure of the location of remaining German reserves. Stalin now decided to take a longer view. He ordered Zhukov to divert more forces north into Pomerania to help Rokossovskii clear that large coastal region between central Germany and East Prussia, including Danzig. Hitler, in response, made SS leader Heinrich Himmler commander of a new Army Group Vistula – with a paper strength of thirty divisions – to cover western Pomerania. (Himmler was completely unqualified and in late March Hitler removed him.)

Once it was clear that the Berlin offensive had been postponed, Stalin ordered Konev to consolidate control of Silesia, which was, like East Prussia, an area populated mostly by Germans. Silesia was an important coal-mining region, but it was also the part of the Reich most remote from British and American bomber bases, and many factories had been relocated there for safety. Konev spent much of February and March tightening the noose around Breslau, protecting his southern flank against the still numerically strong German forces in the Czech lands, and bringing up supplies for the next phase of the attack. 'Fortress' Breslau held out until 6 May. Just before he died Hitler named its ruthless *Gauleiter* (Karl Hanke) head of the SS, replacing the disgraced Himmler.

The Battle for East Prussia, meanwhile, turned out to be a long and very bloody affair. General Cherniakhovskii – commander of 3rd Belorussian Army Group – was himself killed in the battles near besieged Königsberg. The fortress surrendered, after a systematic siege led by Marshal Vasilevskii, only in mid April. Even then, German forces, with thousands of civilian refugees, held out on the beaches west of Königsberg until the final national surrender. The battles in East Prussia between January and April 1945 cost 126,000 Soviet soldiers, three times more than were lost in the Vistula–Oder Operation, and 40 per cent more than were lost in the final Soviet April battles for eastern Germany (misleadingly called the 'Berlin Operation').

Another harrowing feature of the battles for East Prussia was the evacuation by sea of much of the civilian population. The remains of the German merchant fleet, some forty large ships and many smaller vessels, were pressed into service. Hundreds of thousands of Germans soldiers and civilians were evacuated, in what remains the largest operation of its kind ever mounted. Terrible incidents occurred; Soviet submarines sank the overloaded civilian ships *Wilhelm Gustloff, General Steuben,* and *Goya,* each with the loss of several thousand refugees on board (perhaps 6,000 souls with the *Goya* in mid-April).

Five battles for the Reich: (2) The Rhineland

The British and American forces, like the Russians, had been held up on the edges of the Reich by logistical problems and by determined German resistance. The top-heavy armies and air forces needed abundant supplies. A major forward supply port, at Antwerp in Belgium, became usable only at the end of November 1944.

With the end of the German Ardennes offensive, the Western Allies began to regroup for their advance to the Rhine and beyond. British, Canadian, American, and French forces had to battle for the belt of territory from the 1939 Reich border east to the Rhine River – the Rhineland region the Germans had 're-militarised' and then fortified in one of the first pre-war crises, in 1936. The Germans had some defences here in the form of the so-called *Westwall* or Siegfried Line, which had been laid out opposite the Maginot Line in the late 1930s. The main fighting here lasted a month and a half, from the beginning of February 1945 until the end of March, when the Allies finally cleared the whole area of German troops. On 7 March an American armoured division from Bradley's 12th Army Group had, unexpectedly, secured an intact (railway) bridge some 300 yards long spanning the Rhine near the town of Remagen. Pouring advance parties over the structure, Bradley's forces secured a hold on the far shore and then laid down pontoon bridges alongside. A furious Hitler sacked Field Marshal Rundstedt – for the last time. Meanwhile further south, towards the Swiss border, Devers's 6th Army Group had finally overrun the southern part of the Rhineland, where Hitler had ordered rigid resistance. Under Devers, Patton's armoured divisions executed a dramatic breakthrough, crushing the enemy's resistance, and making another unexpected crossing over the Rhine, this time at Oppenheim (on 22 March).

According to Eisenhower's master concept, the main Rhine crossing should have been made by planned assault (rather than by good fortune) at the other end of the Allied line, in the north. The attack, Operation

PLUNDER, was mounted by Montgomery's 21st Army Group. Montgomery was well prepared with landing craft and supplies for a river crossing – to be followed by a prolonged drive into Germany, turning around the north side of the Ruhr. The assault crossing was carried out on 23 March. As part of Montgomery's operation another massive Allied airborne assault was mounted (Operation VARSITY), this one much more successful than Arnhem.

The Rhineland campaign (officially running from September 1944 to March 1945) was the US Army's single most costly campaign of the whole war, with nearly 40,000 ground troops killed in action (compared to just over 10,000 in the six weeks after D-Day, and about 15,000 during the Battle of the Bulge). The heavy fighting meant, however, that Hitler expended much of his remaining effective forces west of the Rhine. The British and American advance into Germany east of the river would meet only limited resistance. Alarm bells went off, not only in Berlin, but also in Moscow.

Five battles for the Reich: (3) Western Germany and Bavaria

On 1 April 1945 American formations which had gone around the Ruhr from the north met other American troops that had come up from the south, out of the Remagen bridgehead. The key industrial region of the Third Reich, object of Allied military planners since 1939–40, and target of the RAF Bomber Command's huge air campaign, was now encircled. The Ruhr was the largest German encirclement of the war, reminiscent of what the Wehrmacht had done to the Red Army in 1941. Trapped in the pocket was Field Marshal Model's Army Group 'B', which had defended northern France and had mounted the Ardennes offensive. The surrounding ring grew tighter and tighter. When the Ruhr pocket surrendered, on 18 April, some 320,000 POWs were taken. Model shot himself.

In the north Montgomery's 21st Army Group pushed into northwest Germany, taking Bremen and moving rapidly towards Hamburg. The southern part of the Netherlands remained in German hands, behind a flooded area, and this region suffered a terrible food shortage that winter. On 2 May – after Hitler's death – the British spearheads would reach Lübeck on the Baltic

Sea. The British, and especially the Americans, were now making very rapid progress against little resistance. The troops would sometimes advance 35–50 miles in a day. Only 10,000 US combat troops were killed in Germany and Central Europe in the six weeks between the final Rhine crossing (in the third week of March) and the end of the war.

Eisenhower now turned his attention to the southern part of the Reich. He was worried that the Nazi regime might attempt to stage a fanatical campaign in the readily defended mountain country there, the so-called 'Alpine Redoubt'. Such a German strategy made no military sense, as the defending forces there would have had no war-industry base. There was little supporting evidence from ULTRA. Eisenhower could see, however, that the strategy of the Third Reich was not driven by rational considerations. Marshall and Eisenhower, taking a military perspective, also prioritised the most rapid defeat of the German armed forces rather than the seizure of political objectives. An important consideration for the American military command was freeing Allied ground and air forces in Europe for the completion of what was expected to be a hard final campaign against Japan. President Roosevelt's death on 12 April, five weeks after the Rhine was crossed, and his replacement by the inexperienced Truman, meant that military – as opposed to political – considerations were uppermost. At the start of April Eisenhower contacted Stalin to clarify what was to happen next. Stalin lied and signalled to Eisenhower that in his view Berlin had lost its importance and was now only a secondary target. Eisenhower turned his armies to the southeast. By the middle of April, as the rapidly advancing American spearheads reached the Elbe River in central Germany, some of the local commanders urged a dash to Berlin. Eisenhower again resisted the temptation.

Some historians allege that a naïve and narrowly focused Eisenhower 'gave away' Berlin, and with it the political influence its capture would have brought the Western Allies. We should remember, however, that the zonal division of Germany had already been agreed upon. Greater Berlin was to be a large enclave within the Soviet occupation zone, although an enclave itself divided between the occupying powers. Would capturing the city – only to hand it over to the Russians – have been worth another 10,000 American lives? In addition, the Red Army was so close to Berlin from February 1945 that it was always more likely to get to Hitler's capital first; there was no point in attempting to race it to the Reichstag.

Five battles for the Reich: (4) Austria

The southeastern approaches to the Reich, up the Danube, were a little different from the other directions. The Germans were defending, until very late in the war (March 1945), a non-German area – Hungary. This was partly because Hitler wanted to hold his last source of fuel, the small oil fields of southwestern Hungary. And Hitler as a southerner was especially sensitive to the front on the Danube in Hungary and Austria.

Indeed, the last major German offensive of the war was launched in Hungary on 6 March 1945. Operation SPRING AWAKENING, mounted near Lake Balaton, was intended to retake Budapest. The German force included 6th SS Panzer Army, veterans of the Battle of the Bulge and Hitler's last mobile reserve. SPRING AWAKENING was not dissimilar to CITADEL at Kursk in 1943: after considerable fighting the German attack stalled on the Soviet defences, and the Red Army was then able to go over to the attack. Pursued, the Germans fell back across western Hungary and into Austria. The Soviet Vienna operation began on 26 March under Marshals Tolbukhin and Malinovskii. After heavy fighting the former Austrian capital was captured on 11 April; it cost nearly 40,000 Soviet soldiers. The battle was also the final defeat of the *Waffen-SS* divisions that had defended the city. Hitler, enraged by the loss of his beloved Vienna, ordered the removal of the *Waffen-SS* battle honours. Soviet troops were beginning to push deeper west into Austria when the war ended.

Soviet troops had been in action on the soil of pre-war Czechoslovakia since the autumn of 1944. There was heavy fighting in the east of this country (now Slovakia) as the Red Army tried to break through the Carpathians. Once the Red Army had advanced into Hungary, Soviet troops had also tried to push north into Czechoslovak territory. The Germans, however, had a large garrison in the Czech lands under one of Hitler's most ruthless commanders, General Ferdinand Schörner. The mountainous border areas – to north and south – were relatively easily defended. Prague was in the western part of the country. In the end the Red Army reached the Czechoslovak capital only after the fall of Berlin. On 9 May, the day following the German surrender, Soviet spearheads broke in from the north (Marshal Konev) and south (Marshal Malinovskii) to take Prague.

Five battles for the Reich: (5) Berlin

After Zhukov halted on the Oder in February 1945 and diverted forces to the Baltic flanks, there followed another Soviet pause, this time of two months. The Stavka was apparently looking forward to an attack on Berlin in May, when road conditions would be better and supplies had been built up. Most of Konev and Zhukov's mobile forces had been sent to clear the flanks, to push the German Army out of the Baltic coast and out of Silesia. Plans were suddenly changed when the news arrived that the Americans and British had secured Rhine crossings and were meeting only limited resistance in western Germany. The Stavka order a rapid Red Army redeployment to ensure that Soviet rather than American or British forces reached Hitler's capital first. Stalin was also worried about a separate German surrender to the Western Allies.

After a top-level Soviet military conference in Moscow, Konev, Zhukov, and Rokossovskii were sent back to Germany to prepare the final attack, which was launched on 16 April. What the Russians called the 'Berlin operation' was actually a wide-front attack along a line stretching 300 miles from the Baltic to the old German border with Czechoslovakia. The main blow was assigned to Zhukov's 1st Belorussian Army Group, which was to punch directly through the Seelow heights to Berlin.

The main casualties were suffered not in the Berlin street-fighting but in the approaches to the city, where the Germans again tried to mount a forward defence. The resistance was broken-backed. There was an additional threat to Berlin from the west, as American forces approached the Elbe. The high command (Keitel and Jodl) had been moved out of the capital. Hitler had completely lost touch with military reality and called up non-existent formations in support. Zhukov's army group took the major share of the fighting, and when his vanguard forces linked up with those of Konev west of the city the encirclement was complete.

Hitler's pathetic last days are very well known and need not be recounted in detail. The German dictator had been away from Berlin for most of the war; he returned to his capital in the middle of January 1945. He now spent most of his time in the so-called *Führerbunker*, a giant air-raid shelter built under the back garden of the Reich Chancellery in the Wilhelmstrasse. The Bunker was very uncomfortable, with small rooms, and poor and noisy ventilation; it was the opposite of his residence on the Obersalzberg in the Bavarian Alps.

During April most senior Reich officials fled Berlin for safety – Göring, Himmler, Speer, Keitel, and Jodl. Hitler remained behind with private secretary Martin Bormann and Josef Goebbels, the Propaganda Minister, but he no longer had any control over events. Göring had long fallen from Hitler's favour, and when he tried to assume command of the surviving parts of the Reich he was condemned by Hitler as a usurper. Himmler, who in a half-rational way had been trying to set up surrender talks with the Western Allies, was rejected by Hitler as a traitor. Hitler committed suicide in the Bunker on the afternoon of 30 April, alongside his mistress, Eva Braun. Attempts were made to burn their bodies in the grounds of the garden. Shortly afterwards the Berlin military commander began negotiations to end the fighting; the city surrendered on 2 May. Parts of Hitler's charred corpse were recovered and identified by a Soviet forensic team.

The overall surrender of the German armed forces was a chaotic affair. Although Berlin and the heart of the Reich had fallen, there were still intact Wehrmacht forces in Norway, the Netherlands, Bavaria, western Austria, the Czech lands, and Latvia (Kurland) – the debris of early German triumphs. The delay in the surrender was caused partly by the shattered German command structure, partly by the physical extent of the Allied and German forces, and partly by the incipient distrust between the Allies. On 6 May General Jodl, the operations head of the Wehrmacht high command, was brought to Eisenhower's headquarters (SHAEF) in eastern France at Rheims. Early the following morning Jodl signed a hastily drafted capitulation, agreeing that German forces would cease fighting on the evening of the 8th. The Russians would not accept that this was a full surrender – they were represented at Rheims only by a senior liaison officer. On the evening of the 8th, a few minutes before the ceasefire time, General Keitel, Hitler's Wehrmacht Chief of Staff since 1938, signed another surrender at Zhukov's headquarters at Karlshorst in eastern Berlin. The war in Europe officially ended at 23.01, Central European Time.

The last battles were especially lethal. Of the Allies the Russians suffered much higher losses in 1945 than the Americans or British. Red Army losses (killed and missing) in 1945 were about 770,000. British and American losses were certainly less than a tenth of that. The *Endkämpfe* were also hugely destructive for the German armed forces. The German historian Overmanns suggests losses of 1.4 million killed in the period January–May 1945; if this is correct nearly 30 per cent of the deaths of German service personnel came in the last five months of the war. Six or seven million more soldiers, sailors, and airmen were now prisoners of war, under the control of one or other of the victor powers. The Wehrmacht had ceased to exist.

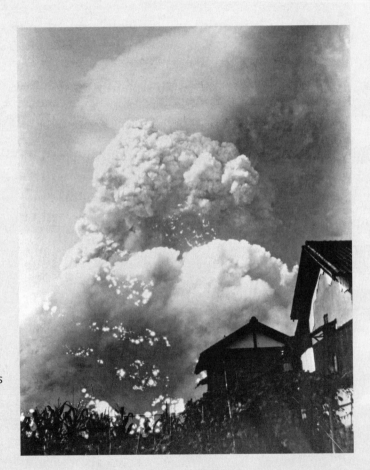

The atomic cloud rises over Hiroshima on the morning of 6 August 1945. This photograph was taken by Matsushige Mitsuo about two minutes after the explosion. Mr Matsushige was standing about $4\frac{1}{2}$ miles from the centre of the blast.

End and beginning in Asia, 1945

Timeline

1945	February	Yalta Conference
	March	Tokyo fire raid
	April	US invasion of Okinawa; death of Roosevelt
	July	Potsdam Conference
	August	Atomic bombs dropped on Hiroshima, Nagasaki
	August	USSR declares war, invades Manchuria, Korea
	August	Japan accepts surrender terms; V-J Day
	September	Japanese surrender on USS *Missouri*

Japan in 1945

At the start of 1945 the rulers of Japan could see only darkness ahead. Their country would soon be fighting on its own against America, the British Empire, and China; it might have to go to war with the USSR as well. Japan's last surviving partner in Europe was in great peril, as Allied troops squeezed the tattered Wehrmacht back into its home territory. Meanwhile Japan's own military position was worsening. With the loss of the Mariana Islands in June and July 1944, and the American landings in the central Philippines in October, the Japanese Pacific empire had effectively ended. The island garrisons further south 'withered on the vine'. The Imperial Navy had been wiped out at the Battles of the Philippine Sea and Leyte Gulf. Carrier task forces of the US Navy roamed the Pacific Rim, raiding as far west as Indochina and Formosa. Submarines and long-range aircraft cut the flow of resources to Japan from the East Indies and Malaya.

Still, the war went on. Another general, Koiso Kuniaki, had replaced Tōjō as Prime Minister in July 1944; the new government declared that Japan would continue the struggle. Koiso was not a powerful figure in the Tōjō mould; he had been Governor-General of Korea in 1942–4 but had played no part in earlier military operations. Koiso did set up a Supreme War Leadership Council in an attempt to rationalise national policy, but this made little difference to the conduct of the war. Tōjō had also been Minister of War and Chief of the Army General Staff; now Field Marshal Sugiyama Hajime and General Umezu Yoshijiro filled these posts and played a dominant role in decision-making.

The American offensive in the Pacific accelerated in 1945. Leyte Island in the central Philippines had been secured by December 1944. After a high-level strategic debate, the planners decided to strike next at Luzon, the main (northern) island in the Philippines, rather than at Formosa (Taiwan). American troops also landed on Mindanao, in the southern Philippines. The north–south Japanese shipping routes could have been cut without these extended operations, which tied down a number of US Army divisions. Washington, however, felt a moral commitment to the Filipinos, as US subjects, living under what was widely publicised in America as a cruel occupation. Many American military leaders, and especially the influential General MacArthur, desired to erase the unique American military

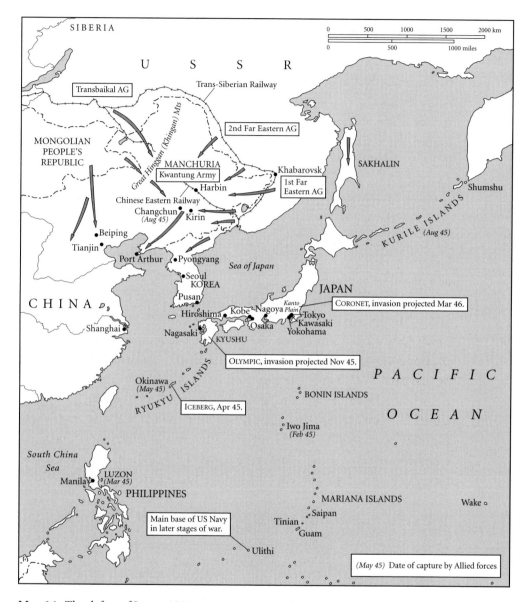

Map 14 The defeat of Japan, 1944–1945

humiliation of 1942. Under General Yamashita – the former 'Tiger of Malaya' – the Japanese 14th Area Army fought with greater tenacity on Luzon than the American and Filipino troops had in early 1942 – although the Japanese had already expended their best ground forces in the earlier battle for Leyte.

The strategic bombing campaign against the Japanese home islands had begun – from China and on a small scale – in June 1944; the background to this has already been discussed (Chapter 7). A second B-29 bomber force, operating from the Marianas, was quickly built up. The B-29 proved, literally, to be a war-winner, but not everything in the programme went according to plan (see Figure 23). The aircraft was rushed from test flight to operational service in eighteen months. The huge piston engines were prone to catch fire, and many missions had to be aborted due to technical problems. The B-29 was supposed to fly at a very high level – 30,000 feet – to extend its range and to let it fly unescorted above the fighters and the flak (the earlier B-17s and B-24s typically flew at 15,000–20,000 feet). But the B-29 was not able to destroy a precision target from 30,000 feet, and until the spring of 1945 the B-29 operations against Japan were little more than nuisance raids.

In March 1945, under the new command of General Curtis LeMay, the B-29s shifted their tactics to lower-level night raids using napalm incendiary cluster bombs. The supposed logic was to hit dispersed Japanese armaments factories by destroying the entire part of the city in which they (and their employees) were situated. The USAAF was adopting the area-bombing terror tactics of RAF Bomber Command – which it had rejected in Europe. LeMay's new approach was devastatingly successful. The Tokyo raid of 9–10 March 1945 destroyed 16 square miles of the Japanese capital and is estimated to have killed 100,000 civilians, more than the Hiroshima or Nagasaki attacks (and more in one night than total Japanese losses in the 1904–5 war). The Tokyo attack was followed by a campaign of similar raids on Japanese cities, limited mainly by supplies of incendiary bombs.

The number of Japanese killed in air raids (including the two atomic attacks) over less than six months was 410,000, more than total US combat deaths in the war as a whole. Beyond the immediate death toll of the 'fire raids' the general dislocation of Japanese society was calamitous; the population of Tokyo, for example, fell from about 6.8 million in 1940 to 2.8 million at the end of the war. There was high absenteeism from the workplace; production plummeted further. The Japanese had only a limited air defence system, with poor radar and few night fighters. In February 1945 the US Navy mounted its first carrier strike against Japan proper (not counting the Doolittle raid of 1942), and these attacks were repeated with growing intensity throughout the spring and summer. By July 1945 US battleships were even coming inshore to pound Japanese coastal targets with their big guns.

The American ground forces moved closer to the Japanese home islands. Iwo Jima in the Bonin (or Volcano) Islands was assaulted in mid February 1945. The month-long island battle is one of the best-remembered of the war, partly because of the intensity of the fighting and partly because of the iconic photograph of four Marines raising the American flag over Mount Suribachi, the high point of the island. Iwo Jima was situated some 650 miles south of Tokyo, and lay on the route from the Marianas to central Japan. The island's value was primarily to support the B-29 campaign, denying the Japanese an early-warning radar site and providing an emergency landing ground for damaged B-29s. Iwo Jima was very small; only 4 miles by 2, with a volcanic peak at one end, and could never be more than an auxiliary airfield. The Americans bought it at a very high cost, nearly 7,000 US Marines – seven times the losses on Tarawa in 1943. Of over 20,000 Japanese Army defenders dug into the island, only 200 were taken prisoner.

Okinawa

The next step in the American offensive was the invasion of Okinawa, in the Ryukyu archipelago, southwest of the home islands. Okinawa was very different from Iwo Jima. A long, narrow island some 450 square miles in area, it was over twice the size of Saipan or Guam. While Iwo Jima had been (before its Japanese garrison arrived) a sparsely inhabited speck of volcanic waste, Okinawa had a large civilian population. Okinawa was big enough to allow the construction of the complex of American air bases needed for the close blockade of the home islands and for the invasion of Kyushu. The initial American landing on Okinawa (Operation ICEBERG) was nearly on the same scale as the Normandy first wave: two Army and two Marine divisions went ashore on 1 April 1945, Easter Sunday.

The Japanese leadership, including the Emperor, attached great importance to Okinawa as a decisive battle. The intention was to shake American will before the main home islands were directly threatened, saving face and allowing Japanese diplomats to negotiate from a position of some strength. But with the need to defend other outlying areas – Formosa, Korea, Manchuria – as well as the home islands, Imperial GHQ (Army) could not send enough troops to build up 32nd Army on Okinawa to the required strength. Okinawa was also a desperate testing ground for new defensive techniques. The Japanese Army's new doctrine – unexpected by the invaders – was not to contest the beaches but to concentrate on inland redoubts. The defenders would counter-attack when the invading fleet had been driven off by Japanese air attacks.

The landings were thus unopposed on land, and the Americans were able in a matter of weeks to take control of most of the island, including the existing airfields. The Japanese forces tenaciously defended the south of the island, an area about 10 miles by 10 and covered by a line of defences which had not been expected by American intelligence. The Japanese were not, however, able to mount the planned counter-attacks. The commander of the Okinawa garrison, General Ushijima, committed suicide on 22 June, after twelve weeks of fighting; his surviving forces had been driven to the southern tip of the island. By American standards Army and Marine casualties were heavy; some 7,600 personnel were killed. Losses included Ushijima's opposite number, General Simon Bolivar Buckner (killed by artillery fire four days earlier). This was for the Americans the worst of any of the Pacific island operations. For the Japanese it was another forlorn hope, another military catastrophe. About 90 per cent of the Japanese garrison of 120,000 died.

More striking even than the Japanese Army's desperate inland defence were the kamikazes (see Figure 29). Compared to Iwo Jima, the American naval force at Okinawa was much closer to air units based in Japan proper. The 'special' (*tokko*) attacks had been introduced by the Japanese Navy in the central Philippines in October 1944, but as an improvisation involving a handful of aircraft. More numerous suicide air attacks were made against the fleet invading Luzon, but the operation that the Japanese mounted against the ships off Okinawa was massive. The Army and Navy had had over six months to organise 'special attack' air units on an operational scale, and these strikes could be flown from numerous airfields on Kyushu. The operation, the biggest suicide campaign that would ever be mounted, was called *TEN-GŌ*. It began six days after the initial ICEBERG landings. The Japanese, ever poetic, called each wave of attacks a *kikusui* ('floating chrysanthemum'). Each of the eight waves – separated by intervals of one or two weeks – contained a mix of several hundred kamikazes and conventional attack planes. No fewer than 1,900 suicide sorties were mounted between April and the end of June. Some 36 ships were sunk, and the American fleet's personnel losses mounted up to half the level of those of the US ground forces. The first *kikusui* was accompanied by the death ride of the Japanese big-ship navy, when the super-battleship *Yamato* sortied to lure off American aircraft from the main kamikaze strikes.

The battle off Okinawa also saw the arrival of the British Pacific Fleet (BPF). Churchill had been keen for the British Empire to play a prominent and direct part in the final stages of the war against Japan, to secure its status as a great power. The Royal Navy, too, wanted to demonstrate its continuing importance within the British armed forces. The Americans were not enthusiastic about British participation, because Royal Navy ships might be a drain on US supplies and because the Americans already had overwhelming numerical superiority. In addition, Admiral King, the US Navy C-in-C, was something of an Anglophobe. After some discussion the British were invited to deploy their fleet, but with the proviso that they would provide their own supply and repair system. The Royal Navy did this (via Australia) but with difficulties that showed how far it had slipped behind the US Navy. Also, many British carrier aircraft were American-built Hellcats, Corsairs, and Avengers. But compared to the earlier hand-to-mouth period in Europe, the BPF was an impressive modern battle fleet, with six new fleet carriers and four fast battleships available for the North Pacific. In the end the fleet (as Task Force 57) played a valuable air defence role off Okinawa; the kamikazes could not penetrate the unique armoured decks of the British carriers. (There were plans to transfer an RAF Bomber Command group to Okinawa – as 'Tiger Force' – but this was not begun before the war's unexpectedly early end.)

Japan: the war goes on

Okinawa was to be the penultimate battle of the war, although no one – on either side – knew it at the time. The beginning of April was not only the time of the initial landing on Okinawa; it also saw changing leaders in

Figure 29 | Kamikaze

A Japanese suicide plane about to crash into USS *Missouri* off Okinawa on 11 April 1945. In the words of the official American historian: 'At 1443 a kamikaze crashed battleship *Missouri* near her starboard quarter about three feet below main deck level. Parts of the plane and the mutilated body of the pilot were strewn over the after part of the ship, but the resulting fire was brought under control within three minutes and damage was confined to scorched paint.'[a] The attacking plane was a Zero [Allied codename ZEKE], the Mitsubishi A6M fighter, which had been the Japanese wonder weapon in the early days of the war. As for *Missouri*, it would be the setting for the Japanese surrender ceremony in September.

The Japanese Navy adopted 'special' (*tokko*) tactics as an emergency measure at the time of the invasion of the Philippines in October 1944. Later, as the situation became even more desperate, this technique was adopted both by the Army and the Navy, not only for mass air attacks but – less successfully – for anti-tank tactics, human torpedoes and suicide boats. In part, suicide missions were a response to overwhelming American technological and quantitative superiority, where even conventional attacks involved a high probability of failure and loss. Aside from the moral bankruptcy of institutionalised mass suicide warfare, the *tokko* tactics were not very effective, especially against armoured ships. No purpose-built American warship larger than a destroyer was sunk by kamikazes, although a number were damaged, and three auxiliary escort carriers (CVEs) were destroyed. However, more American sailors were killed off Okinawa than in the Battle of the Atlantic. Thousands of Japanese pilots and planes were expended.

---

[a] Samuel Eliot Morison, *Victory in the Pacific 1945*, History of United States Naval Operations in World War II, vol. XIV (Boston: Little, Brown, 1960), p. 210.

Japan and America. The Japanese prime minister, General Koiso, had been compromised by a bogus peace feeler from China. A new Japanese cabinet was formed on 5 April, this time under a retired admiral, the seventy-eight-year-old Suzuki Kantaro. The venerable Suzuki had commanded a cruiser at the battle of Tsu-shima forty years earlier. He had served the Court as Grand Chamberlain; the Emperor had often turned to him for advice. Suzuki was not, however, a flexible or dynamic statesman. The hard-liners were still strong. General Anami Korechika, the new Minister of the Army, played a dominant role, supported by General Umezu, who continued as Chief of the Army General Staff. On the other hand the new Foreign Minister was Togo Shigenori, who was looking for a way to end the war. Although he had also been Foreign Minister in December 1941, and would be tried and imprisoned by the Allies as a Class A war criminal, Togo was at least more realistic than the generals. On the American side, President Roosevelt died suddenly on 12 April, two weeks after the Okinawa invasion, and Vice President Truman (see Figure 30) succeeded him. Truman kept most of Roosevelt's advisors; the exception would be in the State Department, where in June Senator 'Jimmy' Byrnes, a powerful and canny Democratic Party politician, took over as Secretary of State.

Japan's continued unwillingness to consider surrender in the spring and early summer of 1945 seems suicidal and irrational. The term 'catastrophic nationalism' has been applied to Germany (see Chapter 12); it fits Japan as well. Japan's leaders seemed to prefer the utter destruction of their state and its population to defeat and surrender. There were also profound cultural differences, a 'clash of civilisations', between Japan and its enemies (which was not true for Germany). And yet there was some logic in the position of the Japanese government. The only Allied terms on offer were those of 'unconditional surrender'. To accept these terms the Japanese political and military elite – and the Emperor – would have to allow the most profound changes. The territorial losses would be comprehensive. Japan would lose what it had gained by conquest in Southeast Asia in 1941–2 – and which had allegedly been required for its national economic independence. It would have to give up what its forces still held in China, including Manchukuo/Manchuria; all the sacrifices of the 1937–45 war would be for nothing. And at the Cairo Conference (1943), Roosevelt, Churchill, and Jiang Jieshi had publicly announced that Japan would have to put the clock back, not to 1931, but to the early

Figure 30 | **President Harry S. Truman**

President Truman (1884–1972) poses for photographs with Churchill and Stalin at the Potsdam Conference in July 1945. Truman had been twice elected to the US Senate from Missouri, in 1934 and 1940. He made a national reputation leading a Senate committee investigating waste in war expenditure. This, plus the fact that he was on neither the right nor the left of the Democratic Party, won him the nomination as Roosevelt's running mate in the 1944 election.

The emergence of Truman as a world statesman came as a surprise to the man himself. Even after becoming Vice President (in January 1945), he had had little contact with Roosevelt. Before the President's death in April he had not been told about the atomic bomb programme. Truman had no experience in foreign or strategic affairs (although he had served briefly as an artillery officer in France in 1918). He relied much more than Roosevelt on his advisors to make important decisions about – among other things – the strategy for bringing the Pacific War to a close.

Box 54 | **The *kokutai***

The Japanese concept of the *kokutai* was an important factor in the final stages of the war in Asia, and in the question of whether or not the Japanese elite would accept surrender. The word *kokutai* has been translated as Japanese 'national polity', and in pre-war Japan national identity was bound up with the person of the divine Emperor.

Hawks and doves in the Japanese leadership interpreted the *kokutai* in different ways. Ultra-nationalists saw the *kokutai* as a mythical notion transcending even the political system. Could Japan exist if it had an Emperor but he was not regarded as divine, or if he did not have constitutionally absolute powers? Was the *kokutai* compatible with the elimination of the Japanese armed forces or with enemy occupation? Less radical leaders defined the *kokutai* more narrowly as the survival of a pared-down Emperor system. In the end the Shōwa Emperor himself came to the view that the peace terms proposed by the Americans would be compatible with the *kokutai*.

1890s. Japan would lose Korea and Formosa, forfeiting the gains of the Russo–Japanese War (1904–5) and the first Sino–Japanese War (1894–5). More profoundly still, surrender meant the removal and likely trial of the politicians, generals, and admirals who were actually running the country, and these were the very people who would have to make the decision to stop fighting. What was involved was the fate of the Emperor and the whole Japanese political system, which was known as the *kokutai* (see Box 52). Hitler and the Nazis had, after all, been in power for only twelve years; elements of the *kokutai* went back for millennia.

It was not only that these potential surrender terms were unthinkable to many Japanese leaders. Until the spring of 1945 Imperial Japan was also not doing so badly in the war, especially if we avoid a purely 'Pacific' perspective. In contrast to Germany's three years of heavy bombing raids (1942–5), the Japanese homeland did not come under serious air attack until March 1945. Japan had, to be sure, been driven out of many of its island conquests; the transport arteries to Southeast Asia had been severed; the ships of the Imperial Navy had been sunk. But Japanese Army ground forces had not suffered decisive defeat, despite heavy local setbacks in New Guinea, the Philippines, and Burma. It had not suffered losses comparable to those of the Japanese Navy, and it was less battered than Hitler's Army in 1945. It was unchallenged in occupied China, Manchuria, and Korea. The Nationalist Chinese armies had not been able to make gains, and indeed had lost territory in southern central China in 1944 as the Japanese moved against the B-29 bases in Operation *ICHI-GŌ*. A limited Japanese Army evacuation of some areas south of the Yangzi River began only in May 1945. Shipping still plied the short sea routes from China to the home islands via Shanghai, Tianjin (Tientsin), and Pusan (in Korea). In Southeast Asia the military situation was more mixed for Japan. Nevertheless Field Marshal Terauchi's Southern Army command still controlled the region comprising Malaya, Singapore, Indochina, and the former Netherlands Indies.

Japan was also less vulnerable to invasion than Germany had been. The British and Americans had 'only' to cross the Channel in 1944. The Russians had a land route to the Reich. In Asia, even the staging posts for an attack on Japan were thousands of miles from the invasion beaches, and the Allied metropolitan territories were on the other side of the planet. Japan still had a vast pool of personnel, especially after the government extended the conscription age. In 1944–5 Japan conscripted 3.4 million men, more than had been called up in 1937–43. Despite the loss of most of its ships the Japanese Navy had 1.7 million men on active service in 1944, compared to 430,000 in 1942. In February 1945 Imperial GHQ (Army) had begun raising many fresh divisions to defend the homeland, increasing the number there from 12 in January 1945 to 60. The Japanese military began developing in early 1945 a plan for the sea, air, and land defence of the home islands, under the codename *KETSU-GŌ* (Operation DECISIVE); an outline was issued to the forces in April 1945, a week after the Okinawa landing. *KETSU-GŌ* assumed fierce resistance, destroying the enemy invading transports at sea, rapidly redeploying forces to meet any invasion threat, and making use of civilians in guerrilla warfare. The nation's leaders believed that the Japanese 'spirit' was unvanquished, and that Japan had discovered in its *tokko* (suicide) weapons a means to inflict unacceptable damage on its enemy. *Tokko* attacks on a massive scale – by air, sea, and land – were a crucial feature of *KETSU-GŌ*.

From the Japanese perspective, the Americans and British might have built up huge armed forces, but they had also suffered great losses in the protracted war in Europe and Asia. The British and Russians, in particular, seemed very seriously weakened. The Americans had thus far, in the eyes of the Japanese Army at least, fought only a 'limited' war in the Pacific; public opinion in the USA might not favour a protracted war with heavy casualties. The war and the creation of the United Nations Organisation in June 1945 had not done away with the international power system. Between the states in the enemy coalition – the United States, Britain, Russia, and Nationalist China – and especially between Communist Russia and the rest – there had to be mutual distrust. Like Hitler and other leaders of the Third Reich a few months before, many Japanese officials believed that the Allies might be played off against one another.

American and Soviet plans

The Japanese were correct to believe that their enemies were divided. Indeed the decisions made in Washington and Tokyo cannot be understood without taking into account a growing tension – especially between America and Russia – which had been heightened by disagreements over Eastern Europe and by the inauguration of the new President. The key leaders in Washington wanted to ensure uncontested American control over Japan, not least because the United States had fought the main counter-offensive on its own. Stalin, for his part, wanted to guarantee his eastern frontier against all potential enemies, and not just the Japanese. He also wanted to restore to Russia at least what had been lost in 1905.

American military leaders had long considered how best to force a Japanese surrender. The original ORANGE war-planning concept in the 1920s had assumed that the war would be limited and that a blockade would eventually compel the Japanese government to accept American terms. At the end of the Pacific War the US Navy and the Army Air Force both thought Japan could be worn down without a land campaign. The US Army ground forces, however, considered that an invasion would be necessary, and this was accepted by the Joint Chiefs of Staff; the JCS began to plan an invasion of Japan in 1944. The strategy of General Marshall in Asia was consistent with his strategy in Europe in 1942; victory was to to brought about by the troops of the US Army in a campaign aimed at the enemy's heartland. Marshall's opinion was that American public opinion would not stand for a long siege. The planners initially hoped the USSR would play a major role in this campaign, tying down Japanese forces in Manchuria and providing advanced bases (especially air bases) for American strikes on the home islands.

The invasion of Okinawa had been mounted mainly to provide air bases from which US Army fighters and medium bombers could support a landing on Kyushu. The next objective was to have been Kyushu itself. The attack was set for 1 November 1945, and the codename was Operation OLYMPIC. If the fall of Kyushu did not force the Japanese government to sue for peace it would be followed by Operation CORONET in March 1946. CORO-NET was a landing in the area around Tokyo (the so-called Kanto Plain), supported by new airfields on Kyushu. It is now debatable whether even OLYMPIC would have gone ahead as planned, as the Americans learned through ULTRA intercepts that the ground defences of Kyushu were being greatly strengthened. One of the themes of the post-war American Hiroshima debate is whether an invasion in Japan would have been very bloody and whether the atomic bombs – terrible as they were – were required to save lives. President Truman could be given only rough estimates of possible American casualties, but they were high. Many more Japanese soldiers and civilians would have been killed in a full-scale desperate land battle than were killed in the atomic attacks, but that argument was not made at the time in Washington.

The other American tool, besides blockade and invasion, was the strategic bombing campaign, and especially the atomic bomb. As we have seen (Chapter 11), the Americans did not develop the atomic bomb in order to drop it on Japanese cities. However, the processing of sufficient quantities of plutonium and enriched uranium had taken longer than expected, and the 'Special' bomb was not ready for use against Germany. Only in the late summer of 1944 could General Leslie Groves (head of the atomic project) set the middle of 1945 as the delivery date for the first uranium and plutonium weapons. The first plutonium device was tested in New Mexico in July 1945; it measured up to expectations. The uranium bomb was technically less complex and was deemed to require no test. A uranium bomb would be dropped on Hiroshima, a plutonium bomb on Nagasaki.

Meanwhile the Russians were considering how they could best achieve their own objectives in the Far East. At the Teheran Conference in late 1943 Stalin had committed the USSR to joining the struggle against Japan after the defeat of Germany. At the Yalta Conference in February 1945 he agreed to enter the war three months after the German surrender, whenever that came. Yalta had involved considerable horse-trading. The Americans – despite the advanced stage of development of their atomic bomb – made significant concessions to ensure Soviet entry into the war against Japan. Stalin asked for, and received, a promise of the return of the southern part of Sakhalin island. He was also given the strategic Kurile Islands, a transfer lacking historical or ethnic justification (like his European gain of Königsberg). Without consultation with the Chinese, Roosevelt and Churchill also promised Stalin the restoration of Tsarist Russia's earlier imperialist gains – control of strategic railways in (Chinese) Manchuria, and a lease on the naval base at (Chinese) Port Arthur. What the USSR was not given was an occupation zone in the Japanese home islands, comparable to those it held in Germany and Austria.

The Red Army had reduced its Far Eastern garrison at the beginning of 1941, more drastically in the second half of 1941, and then again in 1942. Once the initiative had been regained in Europe, Russia began to rebuild its forces in Asia. The Japanese Kwantung Army had gone through a similar process. Japanese forces earmarked for Manchuria had been diverted to China from 1938 onwards, although in 1941 there was a renewed but short-term build-up against Russia. In 1943 more and more of the high-quality ground and air units of the Kwantung Army had been withdrawn for other fronts, to be replaced by new and less well-trained divisions.

In the autumn of 1944 the Soviets began concrete preparations for entry into the war against Japan, setting up the command structures and positioning supplies (much of which came through American Lend-Lease deliveries to Vladivostok). In 1944 Stalin chose Marshal Aleksandr Vasilevskii to be the overall commander of the operation against Japan. Vasilevskii would have three army groups under his command. The intention – laid down in secret Kremlin directives finalised on 28 June 1945 – was to begin the massive and rapid attack in the second half of August.

In the late spring of 1945, even without accurate knowledge of these developments in America and the USSR, the Japanese people and their rulers could see that the war situation was changing decidedly for the worse. The protracted battle for Okinawa, in April and May, brought American forces to the Japanese doorstep, and showed that even massed suicide attacks could not stop them. The B-29 campaign of low-altitude terror bombing began to inflict much heavier damage. On 5 April Moscow informed Tokyo that it

Figure 31 | **The Emperor inspects fire damage**

The Emperor of Japan, pictured above inspecting fire damage in Tokyo in 1945, was one of the most controversial figures of World War II; he certainly had the most extraordinary life of any of the national leaders. Born in 1901, the grandson of the Meiji Emperor, he acted as regent for his father from 1921, and reigned in his own right from 1926. As Hirohito came to the throne, his reign was given the name *Shōwa*, the 'era of enlightened peace'. The name was to prove fatally inaccurate, at least for the first twenty years of the *Shōwa* Emperor.

The Emperor was notionally the centre of the Japanese political system, and there was a state cult of Emperor-worship, but he reigned rather than ruled. Although historians continue to debate this, the *Shōwa* Emperor was probably able to have only an indirect influence on the formation of policy. His most important individual initiative was to force government and military acceptance of the capitulation of August 1945.

The Emperor was, along with Prime Minister Tōjō, the butt of much Allied wartime propaganda. Nevertheless he was not tried as a war criminal. The Americans allowed the *Shōwa* Emperor to remain on his throne, although he renounced his divine status. He presided over the reconstruction of Japan and its transformation into an economic superpower. His death came forty-four years after those of Hitler and Mussolini, in 1989.

would not renew the 1941 Soviet–Japanese neutrality treaty when it expired in April 1946. Any hopes of the Germans conducting a protracted defence of their own homeland had to be abandoned; in May the Third Reich capitulated, and this event passed without evident splits between the Allies. By early June Marquis Kido, one of the Emperor's closest advisers, had come to the conclusion that the war needed to be brought to an end. On 22 June, the day of General Ushijima's suicide on Okinawa and six weeks before Hiroshima, the Emperor told the Supreme War Leadership Council of his desire that steps be taken to end the war.

The Suzuki government – at least the civilians in it – staked everything on using the neutral USSR as an intermediary to bring about a negotiated peace with America, Britain, and China. From the perspective of the Soviet–Japanese antagonism of the 1930s and the Cold War of the late 1940s and 1950s, Stalin may seem a strange middleman. (As it happened, America – in the person of President Theodore Roosevelt – had acted as the middleman in ending Japan's war with Russia in 1905.) But since 1942 America rather than Russia had become the main enemy. The Japanese calculation was that Soviet interests were different from those of the Americans and British; in essence they were employing the traditional Chinese technique of 'playing barbarian off against barbarian'. But Tokyo's plan was a foolish miscalculation which came to nothing. The Japanese never made any clear proposals. Through intercepted signals Washington was aware of the peace feelers sent to Moscow (and their lack of success). Critics of the Hiroshima bombing have made much of this intelligence factor, arguing that Washington knew that the Japanese were trying to make peace; what the Americans actually learned, however, was that Tokyo was not prepared to accept an unconditional surrender.

The Potsdam ultimatum, the atomic bombs, and the Soviet invasion

Events were developing fast in July 1945. August would be three months after the capitulation of Germany, and Soviet entry into the war had been secretly promised for then. The plutonium bomb had been tested; atomic weapons were now a real factor that could be used against Japan. In late July Truman, Churchill, and Stalin met at Potsdam outside Berlin for the third (and last)

Box 55 | The Potsdam Declaration

The following excerpt comes from the declaration issued by the United States, China, and Britain on 26 July 1945, during the Allied conference at Potsdam (outside Berlin). The USSR was not at that time at war with Japan.

The might that now converges on Japan is immeasurably greater than that which, when applied to the resisting Nazis, necessarily laid waste to the lands, the industry and the method of life of the whole German people. The full application of our military power, backed by our resolve, will mean the inevitable and complete destruction of the Japanese armed forces and just as inevitably the utter destruction of the Japanese homeland . . .

There must be eliminated for all time the authority and influence of those who have deceived and misled the people of Japan into embarking on world conquest, for we insist that a new order of peace, security and justice will be impossible until irresponsible militarism is driven from the world . . .

We do not intend that the Japanese shall be enslaved as a race or destroyed as a nation, but stern justice shall be meted out to all war criminals, including those who have visited cruelties upon our prisoners. The Japanese Government shall remove all obstacles to the revival and strengthening of democratic tendencies among the Japanese people. Freedom of speech, of religion and of thought, as well as respect for the fundamental human rights, shall be established.

(From Proclamation, July 26, 1945, Potsdam Conference, *The Avalon Project: Documents in Law, History and Diplomacy*, at http://avalon.law.yale.edu.)

great 'Big Three' meeting. The leaders' declared aim was to discuss the fate of post-war Germany, but the Americans and the British used the occasion to issue, with the Chinese, the Potsdam Declaration of 26 July (see Box 55). Stalin was not asked to sign the declaration; the USSR was not yet at war, and in any event Washington wanted to keep control of Far Eastern policy.

The Declaration was in effect an ultimatum; it laid out the terms of Japanese capitulation, and essentially it carried on from the Hull Note of November 1941, Roosevelt and Churchill's 'unconditional surrender' statement at Casablanca, and the December 1943 Cairo Declaration. The Allies demanded that Japan give up all overseas territory, submit to Allied occupation, and allow prosecution of war criminals. The threatened alternative was 'the complete destruction of the Japanese armed forces and just as inevitably the utter destruction of the Japanese homeland'.[1] There is an historical debate about whether the Declaration was intended more as a justification for the use of the atomic bomb than as a genuine diplomatic approach to which Tokyo was expected to respond. The text was edited to leave out any prior commitment to the Emperor system, and the Soviet Union was not a signatory; both factors made Japanese acceptance of the ultimatum less likely. The day before the Potsdam Declaration was announced President Truman had authorised the US Army Air Force commander in the Far East to drop the atomic bombs on four possible Japanese target cities 'after about' 3 August.

Admiral Suzuki, although now sometimes portrayed as a man of peace, was unsure about what his government should do. Tokyo did not respond diplomatically to the Potsdam Declaration (although neither did it explicitly reject it). On 28 July Suzuki gave a press conference at which he said there was nothing new in the Potsdam Declaration. The Emperor, for his part, took no action.

A week later, on the morning of 6 August, a B-29 (named the 'Enola Gay') dropped an atomic bomb on Hiroshima. This port city of 255,000 inhabitants in southern Honshu was effectively destroyed (see Box 56). The number of immediate deaths is estimated to have been 80,000 people, and many more would eventually succumb to radiation poisoning. The same day a pre-recorded radio message by President Truman was broadcast: an atomic bomb had been dropped on 'the important Japanese Army base' of Hiroshima with a power of 20,000 tons of TNT and 'a harnessing of the basic power of the universe'. (Hiroshima had indeed been the location of the headquarters of Field Marshal Hata's '2nd General Force', the theatre command in charge of the defences of southern Japan, but most of the bomb victims were civilians.) In his announcement Truman threatened the Japanese with further atomic attacks if they did not come to terms.

We are now prepared to obliterate more rapidly and completely every productive enterprise the Japanese have above ground in any city. We shall destroy their docks, their factories, and their communications . . . It was to spare the Japanese people from utter destruction that the ultimatum of July 26 was issued at Potsdam. Their leaders promptly rejected that ultimatum. If they do not now accept our terms they may expect a rain of ruin from the air, the like of which has never been seen on this earth. Behind this air attack will follow sea and land forces.[2]

Box 56 | Hiroshima

The following account of the aftermath of the atomic attack on Hiroshima was written by Dr Hida Shuntaro.

Unexpectedly, the blue sky appeared with the brightness of high noon. I saw that the long bank of the river at Choju-En [Park] was filled with a large number of burned human beings. They occupied the bank as far as the eye could see. The greatest number lay in the water rolling slowly at the mercy of the waves. Most of them must have been corpses. Countless survivors crept toward the river one after another, some crawling over others. The suspension bridge was in flames with black smoke billowing from the structure. Despite this, many flesh-like creatures moved slowly across the bridge at a snail's pace. Many fell into the water as their strength ebbed out of them.

   The Engineering Corps [Building] on the opposite bank was exploding and dark smoke filled the sky above the flames. Sparks coloured the dark cloud accompanied by thunderous sounds, as if a fireworks display had been set off. A number of survivors fell into the water, driven forward by the heavy fire in the city. Others, finding their way barred by the river, also fell into the water. Intending to enter the city, I simply could not take one step forward and would have gone on standing there blankly. I confronted a great many survivors without human faces or a capacity for speech. They walked past me, as best they could, as they tried to flee Hiroshima. Some of the corpses in the river came to the surface, while others stayed suspended beneath the surface. As they floated and swirled down the river, they knocked against my body. Whenever I saw a little innocent baby among them, I looked up to the sky and bit my lip hoping to control myself from crying. Above me rose the enormous mushroom-shaped cloud with its five colours. It seemed to rise to an infinite height where it could touch the blue sky above and leave below the whirling black smoke of our world.

   (From Kai Bird and Lawrence Lifschultz, *Hiroshima's Shadow* (Stony Creek, CN: Pamphleteer's Press, 1998), p. 420.)

The statement also publicly outlined at some length the history of the atomic bomb project.

   Again, the Japanese government did not react immediately. The level of damage at Hiroshima had not yet been assessed, and it was not clear, in any event, that the damage was different from that inflicted on other Japanese cities that had been burned out by mass incendiary attacks. The military hawks doubted – correctly – that the Americans actually had a large supply of nuclear weapons. The next development, less than three days after the bombing of Hiroshima, was the Soviet attack on Manchuria. The Red Army moved just after midnight on 9 August – with a declaration of war, but in violation of the April 1941 Treaty of Neutrality. The Kwantung Army was caught by surprise. About eleven hours after this offensive began, a second American atomic bomb was dropped, on Nagasaki.

The Soviet entry into the war on 9 August made the situation much more dangerous for Japan, and this even the Army and the Emperor could see. The impasse in the government was still unresolved, but the balance of opinion now allowed a diplomatic response to the Allies. On the night of 9–10 August an Imperial Conference, following the direction of the Emperor, agreed to accept the Potsdam Declaration 'with the understanding that the said declaration does not comprise any demand which prejudices the prerogatives of His Majesty as a Sovereign Ruler'.[3] The decision was made despite the objections of the military leaders, who wanted other modifications to the Allied demands, including no occupation of Japan. In any event the American government refused Japan's attempt at 'conditional' surrender, namely an advance commitment to keep the prerogatives of the Emperor. James Byrnes, Truman's new hard-line Secretary of State, repeated that 'the ultimate form of government of Japan shall, in accordance with the Potsdam Declaration, be established by the freely expressed will of the Japanese people'; that is, it could not be conceded beforehand.[4]

Two factors pushed the Emperor into an unprecedented direct involvement in the affairs of state: the lack of consensus among his advisors and a fear of what his military might do. Through broadcasts and leaflet-dropping the Americans made every attempt to make the Japanese population aware of the Allied peace offer and the Tokyo government's initial lack of response. Indirectly this led to the acute danger of a military coup. On the night of 14–15 August, again with the intervention of the Emperor, another Imperial Conference resolved to accept the Allied terms without conditions. The Emperor recorded a 'rescript' (in effect an imperial announcement) to be broadcast to the Japanese people. That night came the last attempt to influence events by die-hard nationalists, an echo of the events of the early 1930s. Young officers attempted to take over the Imperial Palace and set off Army intervention. The Minister of War, General Anami, did not directly support the plotters (he would commit suicide early on the following day). The military units guarding the Imperial Palace resisted the plotters, and at midday on

15 August the Emperor's message was broadcast. Although he did not mention defeat or surrender, the essence of his words was that Japan now accepted the Potsdam Declaration. The description of Japan's military catastrophe was understated: 'The war situation has developed not necessarily to Japan's advantage, while the general trends of the world have all turned against her interest.' 'The hardships and sufferings', the *Shōwa* Emperor admitted, 'to which our nation will be subjected hereafter will be certainly great. We are keenly aware of the inmost feelings of all you, our subjects. However, it is according to the dicates of time and fate that we have resolved to pave the way for a grand peace for all the generations to come by enduring the unendurable and suffering what is insufferable.'[5] This day, 15 August, was what the Allies celebrated as V-J Day – victory over Japan.

Why did Japan surrender?

The end of the war against Japan is – even now – more controversial than the end of the war in Europe. This is partly because of the *de facto* 'conditional' nature of the eventual surrender (the Japanese kept the Emperor) and partly because of the use of nuclear weapons. The question of whether the atomic bomb was more or less important to the Japanese leaders than the Soviet declaration of war cannot be answered; what is undeniable is that the USSR played an important part in the end of the war. The Emperor actually made two important pronouncements. In the first rescript (15 August) he stressed the atomic bombs ('the enemy has recently used a most cruel explosive'). He declared that the Japanese were aiming to save the world from future destruction. Two days later a second Imperial message was broadcast, this time to the Japanese armed forces; it was not clear that the overseas commanders would accept the 15 August rescript. In this second pronouncement the Emperor did not mention the 'cruel explosive' – which officers sitting in China or Malaya might not understand – but only the Russian factor: 'Now that the Soviet Union has entered the war against us, to continue the war under the present internal and external conditions would be only to increase needlessly the ravages of war finally to the point of endangering the very foundation of the Empire's existence.'[6]

We can blame the Japanese, including the Emperor, for taking so long to surrender. They could not have expected the atomic bombs, but as early as

February 1945 Army intelligence had given warnings that Soviet intervention was likely. Whatever the essence of the Potsdam Declaration – whether the Americans intended it as an ultimatum or an excuse – the Japanese had no intention of making a response. Tokyo had put all its efforts into Soviet mediation, and it should have been obvious that this approach was leading nowhere. The Army was intransigent, but was not uniquely to blame. The Emperor had been waiting foolishly for a face-saving local victory (what Okinawa should have been); now he went to the other extreme and made use of two devastating catastrophes – the atomic bombs and the Russian attack – which 'excused' surrender.

No American decision has caused more controversy. In effect the planners decided to kill 70,000–100,000 civilians – men, women, and children. Extreme criticisms have equated Hiroshima and Auschwitz. One could argue that – unlike Auschwitz – the atomic attacks were a means to a rational and positive end, forcing Japanese politicians and military leaders to accept unconditional surrender terms that they would not otherwise have stomached. The incendiary raids on Japanese cities from March 1945 had had the same purpose, and they killed Japanese civilians in about the same quantities as the atomic attacks. A secondary factor – at least for some of President Truman's advisers – was probably a 'working demonstration' to the Russians of this incredible new American agent of destruction. In terms of future world history and the 'atomic age', however, the decision to drop the two bombs on Hiroshima and Nagasaki was not central. The atomic bomb had been developed in 1942–5, and it could not be 'un-invented'; there would still have been a nuclear confrontation with the USSR even if the atomic bombs had not been used against Japan. The American decision to target cities, rather than just demonstrate the power of the bomb over some sparsely inhabited place, was influenced by the limited number of atomic bombs and the desire to maximise the psychological impact on Japanese decision-makers – what, in a later war, would be called 'shock and awe'. The bombing of Hiroshima and Nagasaki achieved that desired effect.

Like Germany after World War I, Japan was occupied only after it surrendered. The first American ground troops landed in Japan on 28 August – after delay caused by a typhoon. A huge Allied fleet – mainly American – had entered Tokyo Bay. On 2 September – three weeks after the atomic bombs and the Russian invasion – the Instrument of Surrender was signed on the battleship *Missouri*. General Douglas MacArthur presided in his new post as Supreme Commander of the Allied Powers (SCAP). Among those MacArthur brought as witnesses were two Allied officers who had just been freed from Japanese POW camps: General Pervical, who had surrendered at Singapore, and General Wainwright, who had been the last US commander in the Philippines in 1942. The Japanese signatories were Shigemitsu Mamoru, the new Foreign Minister, and General Umezu, still the Chief of the Army General Staff (both would eventually be tried and given prison sentences as war criminals). The Japanese diplomats wore top hats; the soldiers wore uniforms but were not allowed swords. MacArthur now embarked on the occupation and transformation of Japan, a task he would continue until early 1951.

The war ends in China and Korea

As we have seen, the fall of Berlin had left some isolated Wehrmacht forces outside Germany. Nevertheless most of the territories that the Third Reich had occupied during the war had already been 'liberated' by May 1945, and Germany's allies had been dealt with. Asia was far more complicated. Even after V-J Day (15 August), millions of Japanese troops were still committed to the overseas adventures in Manchuria, central China, and Southeast Asia, not to mention those serving in isolated island garrisons in the Pacific. Moreover, the political framework in Japanese-occupied territory was often far from clear.

The Japanese government made its decision to surrender before the success of the Soviet invasion of Manchuria – the last campaign of the Second World War – was complete. When the Russian attack began on 9 August the Kwantung Army was ordered to resist. It would be six full days from the start of the invasion before the Japanese central government accepted the Allied surrender terms, two more before the local Japanese command requested a ceasefire, and another two before the Russians agreed and set out terms. Russian historians call the campaign the 'Manchurian operation'; the Red Army did not actually use the codename 'AUGUST STORM', despite the appearance of the term in some modern sources.

In military operational terms the Soviet attack on Manchuria had much in common with the first campaign of the European war, the German invasion of Poland. A weak and unready army was paralysed and overrun from several sides by a force that was technologically a generation ahead of it. The Soviet operational plan was a remarkable example of the 'deep battle' concept, with armoured columns racing through the enemy positions. The most extraordinary feature was the planned 300-mile advance of a large motorised force from the Transbaikal Army Group across the undefended Great Hinggan (Khingan) Mountains of western Manchuria. This was an expanse of territory so wild that the Japanese had not bothered to defend it. The Japanese could only throw a few suicide planes against advancing tank columns. But there was more fighting in the east of Manchuria, where the Japanese, with long-prepared positions, held out in the city of Mudanjiang (Mutanchiang) against the Soviet 1st Far Eastern Army Group.

On the morning of 17 August the last Kwantung Army commander, General Yamada, requested a ceasefire, but this did not include an offer to surrender. The Soviets did not reply to a second Japanese message for two days, and then Yamada's Chief of Staff was flown to Marshal Vasilevskii's headquarters to agree to the ceasefire. The same day small Soviet airborne detachments landed at Shenyang (Mukden), Changchun, and Kirin, and on the 22nd at Port Arthur (Lushun) and Dalian on the strategic Liaodong (Kwantung) Peninsula. Mobile detachments pushed through on land to support the airborne troops.

Small Soviet amphibious landings were mounted against southern Sakhalin, the Kurile Islands, and some of the Korean ports. Especially bitter was the battle for the most northerly of the Kuriles, fortified Shumshu Island, on 18–20 August. Shumshu was the last of many island battles of the Pacific War. The Russian possession of the Kurile Islands has remained, into the twenty-first century, a major obstacle to normalisation of relations with Japan. Stalin seriously considered an improvised amphibious landing in Hokkaido (the northern home island) and the occupation of its northern part. Given the collapse of the Japanese Army, a Red Army division could probably have been put ashore, but this proposal met with robust opposition from Washington. The Americans had specified that it was their forces that would take the surrender of all the home islands. Japan was spared the complication of joint occupation.

The Soviet Manchurian operation demonstrated just how much the balance of military power had shifted, in the Far East and elsewhere. The Soviets deployed 1.5 million men in 80 divisions, organised in a tank army and

11 infantry armies; equipment included 5,000 tanks and 4,000 aircraft. The Japanese had 600,000 men (many of them very recent conscripts) and 1,200 armoured vehicles, mainly light tanks and armoured cars, and only about 50 combat aircraft. The Red Army attack was not a walkover. Total Soviet losses were 8,000 men (mostly suffered on the eastern side of Manchuria), about half what the Germans lost in Poland in 1939. A high estimate of Japanese losses would be 80,000 killed, which, if accurate, is more than the Polish battlefield dead in 1939. The Red Army took over 600,000 Japanese prisoners, again about the number of POWs the Germans took in Poland. Many of the 1945 captives were to spend five years toiling in labour camps in the USSR; about 40,000 died there (compared to 14,000 Allied POWs who died building the Siam–Burma railway). The Russians also seized much industrial plant when they withdrew from Manchuria in 1946. Neither measure was justified by Japanese direct aggression against the USSR or by direct destruction of Soviet property, but Japan had been Germany's ally. The defeat of Japan occasioned one of Stalin's most nationalist speeches. The Russian defeat in 1905, he said, 'left a black mark on our country'. 'We of the older generation have waited for this day for forty years. The day has finally come.'[7] Forty years previously, of course, Stalin had been a young Marxist revolutionary working to overthrow the Tsar and subvert the Russian war effort.

The general arrangements for the Japanese surrender – agreed to by the USA, Britain, the USSR, and China – had been laid out in the so-called Order No. 1 of 15 August. President Truman issued this Order to General MacArthur, as commander of the future occupation forces in Japan. It was under these arrangements that Japanese forces in Manchuria surrendered to the Red Army. The situation in Korea, as outlined by Order No. 1, was different. The Russians were to take the surrender of Japanese troops north of the 38th parallel; those south of the parallel would surrender to the Americans. There was a more fundamental dissimilarity with Manchuria, in that the Americans and Russians had agreed in principle to share a more extended occupation of Korea. All sides now agreed that Manchuria was part of one of the Allied states, China; Soviet military occupation was to last only a few months, until the spring of 1946. Korea, however, had been an integral part of Japan since 1910, and the Allies' declared aim was to make Korea an independent state with the help of the United Nations. Given the later prominence of the Korean question, it seems surprising that the practicalities were not considered until the last minute. It was only on 10 August that the Allies agreed that the occupation zones would be bounded by the 38th parallel. At the start of the Manchurian operation a Red Army force had driven southwest from Vladivostok to the port of Chongjin in northern Korea, cutting one railway route north. A small Soviet advance detachment landed by aeroplane in Pyongyang on 24 August. American troops landed in Inchon (the port of Seoul) on 8 September.

In China both the Nationalists and Communists were surprised by Tokyo's sudden capitulation. The Japanese Army still held virtually all the territory seized in 1937–8; Imperial GHQ (Army) had, however, pulled divisions out of southern China (gained in 1944) to accumulate troops to defend the Chinese east coast, Korea, and Manchuria. The Japanese surrender was signed on 9 September at the Central Military Academy in Nanjing by General Okamura, commander of the China Expeditionary Force (he of the infamous 'Three Alls' search and destroy policy; see Chapter 2), and General He Yingqin (Ho Ying-chin), the C-in-C of the Nationalist Army. Under the terms of MacArthur's Order No. 1, the Japanese in China were to surrender to Nationalist (rather than Communist) forces, which led to much tension on the ground. Here, as elsewhere in Asia, Japanese troops were ordered to stay in place and maintain order until sufficient Allied forces could arrive. With the approval of the Chinese government an American force landed at Tianjin, the strategic port near Beijing. By late September two US Marine divisions were attempting to maintain order in the Beijing–Tianjin area; more than 100,000 US personnel were stationed in northern China at the peak of involvement in early 1946. Meanwhile American aircraft and ships moved Nationalist troops from southwestern China to take control of Nanjing, Shanghai, Guangzhou, and other coastal cities.

Nationalist China and the USSR had signed a thirty-year Treaty of Alliance and Friendship on 24 August 1945. In the treaty Jiang Jieshi had to accept the gains achieved by the Soviet Union at Yalta (including the railway zone in Manchuria and the temporary use of Port Arthur). These had been gained at China's expense, granted by America and Britain without consulting the Chinese government. In exchange the USSR recognised that the 'three eastern provinces' (Manchuria) were an integral part of China. At this point Stalin evidently thought Jiang was his most likely partner in China – rather than Mao and the Communists. It was only with some initial reluctance on Stalin's part that some Chinese Communist forces were allowed to regroup in Soviet-occupied Manchuria; in the end it was here that the smouldering Chinese

Civil War would burst into flame in the spring of 1946. Order No. 1 also provoked some tension between the British and the Chinese. The Nationalist government asserted that according to the letter of the directive it was their forces which should take the surrender of Japanese forces in the British colony of Hong Kong. The British went their own way and a large Royal Navy task force arrived at Hong Kong on 30 August; internees from the pre-war colonial administration had already taken charge.

The war ends in Southeast Asia

The situation in Southeast Asia was mixed. The region fell under the umbrella of Admiral Lord Mountbatten's South-East Asia Command (SEAC); some cynical Americans claimed that the initials stood for 'Save England's Asiatic Colonies'. The reconquest of Burma had already been completed by British-led forces in the summer of 1945. The British part of Borneo had been taken by Australian amphibious landings in the spring and summer of 1945. Malaya and Singapore were still in Japanese hands on V-J Day, but after three and a half years the British finally broke through the 'Malay barrier'. A British naval task force proceeded down the Strait of Malacca to Singapore, using charts of the minefields provided by the defeated Japanese. The Japanese Southern Expeditionary Force still comprised three-quarters of a million troops. An elaborate surrender ceremony was staged by SEAC in Singapore on 12 September 1945. Field Marshal Terauchi, the C-in-C of Southern Expeditionary Force, had suffered a stroke and could not leave his headquarters in Saigon, so it was General Itagaki Seishiro (commander of 7th Area Army in Singapore) who surrendered all Japanese forces in Southeast Asia to Mountbatten. General Itagaki, it so happened, had been one of the masterminds of the 1931 Mukden Incident, through which Japan seized Manchuria. He would be tried as a Class A war criminal in the Tokyo trial and hanged. (In November Mountbatten flew to Saigon and took Field Marshal Terauchi's personal surrender.) There was considerable tension in Malaya, partly due to the restoration of colonial rule, and partly due to conflict between local Chinese and other ethnic groups. The British were nevertheless – in the short term – able to restore their undisputed control.

The handover in Thailand (Siam) was also relatively easy. Thailand was not a colony but an independent state, albeit one which had been allied with Japan since 1942. The Thai government had secretly resumed links with the

Allies in late 1944, and there was no serious inter-ethnic tension within the country. Thailand was, moreover, a strategic backwater. British spearhead detachments from SEAC arrived in Bangkok by air on 3 September. They received a friendly welcome and found their main task was to ensure the disarmament and removal of the Japanese 18th Area Army and the repatriation of Allied POWs.

The big former French colony of Indochina – which had played such a central role in the Japanese–American confrontation in 1940–1 – was far more complicated. Through an accident of history internal control in Indochina had been largely left by the Japanese in the hands of the European authorities; Vichy France had been aligned with Germany and Japan. This situation had also encouraged the Americans – and especially President Roosevelt – to argue for the end of French rule after the war. By the start of 1945 the Japanese had changed their view about the Vichy colonial authorities. De Gaulle's – Allied – government was firmly emplaced in Paris, an American landing in Indochina was a possibility, and in Tokyo the government of General Koiso was grasping at the final straw of Asian nationalism. In March the Japanese rapidly disarmed the French garrison and imprisoned those officials who could not escape into the countryside. Bao Dai, the young Emperor of Annam – the dynasty having been kept on as window-dressing by the French – was prevailed upon by the Japanese to declare independence and preside over a pro-Japanese government incorporating all of modern Vietnam. Meanwhile the disintegration of French colonial rule and the crisis conditions (which included a severe famine) aided the rise of a powerful anti-colonial 'front', the Viet Minh, led by the Communist Ho Chi Minh. With the Japanese surrender after Hiroshima and Nagasaki, Ho mounted the 'August Revolution' in Hanoi. The Viet Minh took power in Hanoi on 19 August, and shortly afterwards gained control of Hue and Saigon further south; the local Japanese garrison – 39th Army – put up no resistance. On 2 September the new government declared the independent Republic of Vietnam.

A further confusing development in Indochina – as in Korea – was the involvement of two different occupation authorities. Order No. 1 laid out that the Chinese would take the Japanese surrender north of the 16th parallel and the British (SEAC) would do so south of it. Unusually, the Chinese got their chance to act outside China's borders as one of the Allied Big Four 'policemen' (alongside the USA, the British Empire, and the USSR). Because the Americans had been lukewarm about the restoration of colonial rule in Indochina, few preliminary steps had been taken to ensure an early French presence. In the second week of September 1945, British forces arrived in Saigon by sea and Chinese forces arrived in Hanoi from Yunnan and Guangxi. The Chinese commander at first accepted Ho's independence government – even though it was Communist-led – and there was less bloodshed than in the SEAC zone to the south. There the British, with their own colonial status to maintain, were more supportive of the French. In the end (in March 1946) Jiang Jieshi ordered that forces arriving from metropolitan France – commanded by General LeClerc, the 1944 liberator of Paris – be allowed to land. A provisional agreement was brokered between the Ho Chi Minh government and the French, with Paris promising autonomy and a minimal French military presence. The Chinese and British departed. By the end of 1946 the French–Vietnamese agreement had broken down, and the long and terrible Indochina War began.

Just as the Allies had not expected the upsurge of nationalist sentiment in Indochina, so they were surprised by what happened in the Netherlands Indies. The situation here was probably the most difficult one British-led forces met in Southeast Asia in the immediate aftermath of the war. On Java, Indonesian nationalists under Sukarno (Soekarno) had co-operated with the Japanese Army through much of the war. The Japanese allowed them to declare an Indonesian Republic on 17 August 1945, in the aftermath of the surrender. The first British ships arrived near the capital, Batavia (now Jakarta), on 15 September. Small numbers of British-led troops (the majority from the Indian Army) then attempted to disarm the Japanese, rescue European POWs and internees, and restore order. The weak strength of the British forces and the rigidity of the Dutch meant that the situation spiralled out of control. British Empire troops would be involved in armed conflict with the nationalists until November 1946 (when the Dutch took over the doomed struggle).

All these events in the first weeks and months after the Japanese 'unconditional surrender' – and especially developments in Indochina and Indonesia – were harbingers of things to come. They would make the failure of some of Japan's war aims less clear-cut. This paradox will be explored more fully in the following chapter.

The first session of the United Nations Security Council meets in London on 17 January 1946. Under the UN Charter the member nations conferred on the Security Council 'primary responsibility for the maintenance of peace and security'. For over sixty years the Security Council has been dominated by the same five permanent members, the victors of World War II: Britain, China, France, the USSR, and the United States.

Conclusion

Timeline

1945 Potsdam Conference

1945 United Nations formally constituted

1947 Italy, Romania, Hungary, Bulgaria, and Finland sign peace treaties in Paris

1947 India and Pakistan become independent

1947 General Agreement on Tariffs and Trade (GATT)

1948 Berlin crisis

1949 Victory of Chinese Communists in Civil War

1950 Beginning of Korean War

1951 Treaty of San Francisco: Japan signs peace treaty with USA and Britain

1973 Conference on Security and Co-operation in Europe opens in Helsinki

Making peace

As has been suggested more than once in this book, World War II was very different from World War I. Not the least difference between the two conflicts was that there was no great peace conference after 1945 – like the Paris Peace Conference in 1919, or the Congress of Vienna in 1814–15. The Berlin (Potsdam) Conference in June–July 1945 was the last summit meeting of the great powers before the Geneva Conference in 1955. The final and formal resolution of many of the European issues did not come until the Conference on Security and Co-operation in Europe met in Helsinki from 1973 to 1975.

The Cold War came on rapidly after 1945, but the USA, Britain, and the USSR were able to agree peace terms with Nazi Germany's European allies, the most important of which was Italy. The Paris peace treaties were signed in February 1947. There remained fundamental disagreements over Germany, which were eventually resolved by making the occupation zones into two separate states, the Federal Republic (West Germany) and the German Democratic Republic (East Germany); outstanding issues were dealt with unilaterally. Resolution of problems was no easier in Asia, even though Japan was not divided into occupation zones. (Korea, to the eventual great misfortune of its inhabitants, *was* divided.) Japan finally signed a peace treaty with the United States, Britain, and a number of other states in 1951. The Soviets took part in the 1951 San Francisco Conference but refused to sign the resulting treaty. The government which was in control of all mainland China did not attend the conference. By this time, indeed, the United States, the USSR, and the People's Republic of China were fighting a proxy war in Korea. Russia and Japan ended their state of war with a joint declaration in 1956, but they never signed a formal peace treaty; this partly explains continuing friction over the Russian-held Kurile Islands.

Historians debate the war

There have been large and small controversies about the history of World War II. Given the public interest in the event, these have never been confined to the academic world. Some of the arguments have now gone on for sixty years. Could Britain and France have stood up to Hitler at Munich in 1938? Why did France collapse in 1940? Was Winston Churchill really a great war leader? Was Hitler to blame for the defeats of the German Army after 1940? Did Stalin plan a pre-emptive attack on Germany in 1941? What was the relationship between the war and the mass murder of the Jews? Why was the US Navy caught by surprise at Pearl Harbor? How significant was ULTRA intelligence in the outcome of the war? Was the Resistance an important factor? Did the strategic bomber play a war-winning role? Could the war in the West have been won more rapidly after D-Day and, in particular, should the Americans have attempted to capture Berlin? Was the United States justified in using the atomic bomb against Japan? Above all, why did the Allies win, and was their victory inevitable? Many of the controversies about particular campaigns and operations, or about the roles of specific individuals, have been mentioned in the main text of this book.

The development of the debates has been influenced by changing perspectives and the greater availability of sources. West Germany became an ally of Britain and the United States, and the West German Army a key part of NATO. A new cohort of German historians appeared, who were fully prepared to criticise the Third Reich. The same thing happened in Italy, where Fascism was totally discredited and much was made of the anti-German *Resistenza* of 1943–5. (The Japanese, on the whole, did not go through the same process of national self-criticism.) Events became clearer with the opening of most Western archives in the 1970s, with revelations about code-breaking in the mid 1970s, and with access in the 1980s to some Soviet archives (including captured documents located in Russia). Other debates have been triggered by anniversaries and exhibitions. Controversy surrounded an exhibition at the Smithsonian Institution in Washington DC, planned to mark the fiftieth anniversary of the bombings of Hiroshima and Nagasaki in 1995. This was to have been centred around the 'Enola Gay', the giant B-29 aircraft that dropped the atomic bomb on Hiroshima. Some Americans argued that the exhibition glamorised an atrocious crime. Others felt that the Smithsonian had gone too far in expressing sympathy for Japanese suffering, and had skimmed over Tokyo's responsibility for the war. In the end the event was withdrawn. (The restored 'Enola Gay' is still on display at an air museum outside Washington.) Another 1995 exhibition, 'War of Annihilation: Crimes of the Wehrmacht 1941 to 1944', aroused heated arguments in Germany. It presented evidence that the German armed forces were systemically involved in the crimes of the Nazi era, including support for the Holocaust and lethal mistreatment of POWs. The organisers, the Hamburg Institute for Social Research, were taken to task both for the premise of the exhibition and for some inaccuracies in the material displayed (a corrected exhibition was mounted in 2001–4).

There has been remarkably little controversy about who 'started' World War II. There was nothing quite like the 'War Guilt' debate after World War I, or even the seemingly endless disputes among historians, from the 1960s onwards, about the origins of the Cold War. The version of responsibility laid out at the Nuremberg and Tokyo war crimes trials has been accepted: that aggressive regimes wanted to expand their territory at the expense of their neighbours, and that the leaders of those countries conspired to take them to war. This view has been accepted both in the Allied countries (on both sides of the Cold War) and in the former Axis ones – despite the fact that some of those hanged for war crimes in Asia are commemorated at Tokyo's Yasukuni war-memorial shrine. Even the Japanese government took a rather more objective view of their country's responsibility after the death of the *Shōwa* Emperor in 1989. The British historian A. J. P. Taylor set off heated argument in 1961, when he suggested that Hitler was more an opportunist than a cunning plotter, and that his foreign policy was little different from that of other German statesmen of the Imperial period. This gadfly view is not taken seriously now, although it has something in common with one side of a vigorous West German controversy of the late 1980s, the *Historikerstreit* (see Box 57).

The Axis leaders generally knew what they were doing, even if the end results were unexpected and unpleasant for them. They were indeed the aggressors. Germany invaded Poland without provocation in September 1939 and Russia in June 1941. Italy declared war on Britain and France in May 1940. Japan made war on Britain and America in December 1941. Few people would dispute the correctness of Britain and France going to war in defence of Poland – although some would accuse them of failing to help their Eastern

Box 57 | **The *Historikerstreit***

One of the most important World War II controversies was the so-called *Historiker-streit* (the historians' dispute) of the late 1980s. Prominent German historians took part on both sides. The discussion was in the press, rather than in academic books and articles, and it aroused widespread interest. In terms of the war as a whole the discussion was fairly narrow, with German scholars focusing on the level of German responsibility. Nevertheless the *Historikerstreit* raised a number of fundamental points. Coinciding as it did with the period just before German reunification, it had much to do with a search for a new national identity.

The arguments had several strands, but one disagreement was whether the Nazi period was an aberration in the German tradition, or a culmination of it. There was also a desire by some participants to consider the Germans as victims, for example, with the post-war deportations of millions of Germans from Poland and Czechoslovakia. Some historians took the view that the Nazi regime was no worse than that of Soviet Russia, and indeed that German excesses were a response to Communist ones.

European ally. The German attack on Russia was not, by and large, intended to pre-empt a suspected Red Army attack.

The one event that is perhaps genuinely contentious is the very beginning of the fighting, when full-scale war broke out in China in the summer of 1937. It can reasonably be said that neither side intended events to unfold as they did (see Chapter 2). But whatever the dynamics of escalation around Peiping and Shanghai in 1937, it was the Japanese who were encroaching on Chinese territory, rather than vice versa.

Who won World War II?

A bigger question, although not always explicitly stated, is this: who should get the main credit for the victory over the Axis? Despite the possible diplomatic impact of the 1945 Soviet invasion of Manchuria, and despite long suffering of the Chinese armies and the Chinese people, the war against Japan was undoubtedly won mainly by the United States. As for Mussolini's

Italy, it was knocked out of the war largely by the forces of the British Empire, although it is debatable whether the government in Rome would have changed sides without the potential might of the USA in the background. But to whom should the main credit be given for the defeat of Nazi Germany?

The British Empire is often overlooked. London's policy was tarnished by Appeasement. Britain was bankrupted within two years of starting the struggle. The British forces failed dismally in the Far East in 1941–3. They made up only a minority share of the great armies that completed the defeat of Germany in late 1944 and 1945. The RAF Bomber Command campaign was overrated. And yet Britain (with France) did stand up over Poland, at a time when the United States did nothing, and when the USSR actually joined in the partition of that unfortunate country. It was crucially important that Britain stayed in the war in June 1940, when France collapsed. The overall European situation looked hopeless, and apparently attractive offers were being made by Berlin. For a year, until June 1941, Britain was the only state doing any serious fighting against Germany and Italy. (Greece might be added over the winter of 1940–1, although its government made every effort to fight Italy and not Germany.) The British Empire produced a huge effort, largely winning the Battle of the Atlantic, mounting the largest element of the bomber offensive until 1944, and providing at least a half share in all the major amphibious operations, including D-Day. To this would have to be added British technical genius, which played a critical part in radar, decryption, anti-submarine warfare, aircraft engines, and the theoretical foundations of the atomic project. Churchill, despite some grumbling at the time by his commanders, and criticism by revisionist historians like John Charmley (and recently by the American conservative pundit Pat Buchanan), was an essential war leader.

The role of Russia in the war is obscured by Western ignorance and distaste, by Soviet secrecy and vainglory, and by the long-term effect of the Cold War. To an historian of the Russian front, however, the war seems almost over when the Allies finally land in Normandy, eleven months before the end of the fighting. The level of suffering in Russia was greater than anywhere else in Europe (except perhaps Poland and Yugoslavia) and it was probably worse than what happened in China. The Red Army lost 10 million personnel, compared to about 300,000–350,000 in the case of each of Britain and the

United States. Meanwhile, the Russians killed a lot more German troops than anyone else. As Churchill put it, in a world radio broadcast of March 1944, 'Not only have the Hun invaders been driven from the lands they had ravaged, but the guts of the German Army have been largely torn out by Russian valour and generalship.'[1]

Had the USSR been defeated by Germany in 1941 or 1942, Germany could have concentrated its efforts on the defence of its conquests in Western Europe. It is hard to see how an Allied invasion could have been mounted, even with the industrial might of the United States and the human resources of the British Empire. Britain might have been subjected to a bombardment and blockade that rendered her powerless. Stalin also pulled off an industrial miracle, creating an industrial base from which Russia could prepare in the pre-war year, and re-equip after the disasters of 1941; Allied Lend-Lease became a serious factor only in the second half of the war. And yet it is worth remembering that the USSR did not enter the war against Germany until nearly two years after it began, and only after Germany launched an attack. Much of the suffering of Soviet soldiers and civilians can be attributed to operational mistakes on the Russian side, and to the consequences of Moscow standing aside while Hitler defeated France.

The role of the United States was different. Roosevelt's 'Arsenal of Democracy' strategy was reasonable from an American point of view, and actually had a huge effect on the outcome of the war. Certainly in the second half of the war American supply was essential to prevent the war from becoming a stalemate and to allow all the Allied armies (except the Chinese) to continue vigorous offensives. America made a uniquely global effort. In one month, June 1944, American troops simultaneously provided half the D-Day force in Normandy, liberated Rome, defeated the main body of the Japanese Navy in the Battle of the Philippine Sea, and began the air bombardment of Japan from China. On the other hand America entered the war even later than Russia, and had a serious operational impact – certainly in Europe – only from the end of 1942. Throughout the war there was a tendency for Washington to divert forces to the Pacific, in conflict with agreed Allied 'Germany First' strategy. The US Army deployed relatively few divisions, and they suffered low losses. Unlike their enemies, the Americans had the luxury of being able to fight a 'capital-intensive' war, rather than a 'labour-intensive' one; they expended equipment rather than human lives.

The fairest assessment must be that all three of the main Allies played an indispensable part. They each did this in different ways, and at different times. The British were most important from 1939 to 1941, the Russians were the centre of the war from 1941 to 1943, and the Americans played a global role from 1943 onwards.

Why did these Allies win? What was the relative role of strategy, on the one hand, and economic production and population, on the other? Able and thoughtful historians, and those involved directly in the great conflict, differed widely in their conclusions. The British historian Richard Overy, although well aware of the economic dimension, made much of chance and strategic decisions: 'Although from today's perspective Allied victory seemed somehow inevitable, the conflict was poised on a knife-edge in the middle years of the war.'[2] Hitler's view was similar. While he always stressed to his subordinates the importance of resources and the 'big picture', he was also prone to take risks, staking everything on an operational gamble even when the odds were unfavourable. Gambles worked for the Führer in his pre-war diplomacy, and they worked in Norway and – most importantly – in France in 1940.

An alternative view stressed deeper factors. Mark Harrison, another British historian, made a subtle distinction between the first period of the war, when 'purely military' factors were predominant, and the period after the winter of 1941–2, when 'economic fundamentals reasserted themselves'. Stalin made much the same point in an article written in early 1942, when he contrasted the early, unsuccessful period of the Soviet–German war, when the invaders had the temporary advantage of surprise, and the later period of the war, when 'permanently operating factors' like size of the army and level of production came into play.[3]

My argument would be that the war turned out as it did because the correlation of potential forces between the status quo states and the new-order states always favoured the former, and this was true even in the first year of the war. Germany achieved only one unexpected large-scale success, knocking France out of the war in June 1940. Japan was also, in comparative terms, weak. The leaders of the Empire went to war with America and Britain in December 1941 partly from a sense that they would soon be overtaken by American military and naval strength. That assessment proved to be fatally accurate, and in 1943–4 the Japanese forces were indeed overwhelmed.

But the Allied victory was also explained by politics. It is not enough to say that the forces of good defeated the forces of evil. Only in the very broadest sense was it the case that the forces of democracy beat the forces of dictatorship. The eminent Marxist historian Eric Hobsbawm wrote that the forces rooted in the 'shared values and aspirations of the Enlightenment and the Age of Revolution' (in which camp he placed Stalin's USSR) defeated those that rejected those values and aspirations.[4] This was a strained argument. What was more important was the extraordinary nature of the German Third Reich, the main regime challenging the established order in Europe. It was not so much the inhuman internal policies of the NSDAP that created a powerful coalition of enemies; these policies reached their full and terrible development only once the war was already in progress. What really mattered was the limitless ambition of Germany's new leaders and the threat of their technology and armed forces. This barred any route to 'conditional' (as opposed to unconditional) surrender and bound together the awkward alliance of opposites – Britain, Russia, and the United States – which opposed the new order. 'Regime change' in Germany was essential to all partners in the Grand Alliance. The politics of the Japanese Empire were also a notable factor. The lack of political control over the armed forces, even by the Emperor, meant that Japan's ambitions in China were in practice unlimited. It was also impossible to establish a *modus vivendi* with America and Britain before December 1941 or to conclude a sensible peace before August 1945.

Who lost World War II?

There is a second sense to this question of winning and losing: who *benefited* and who *lost out* from the outcome of World War II? This might seem an obvious question. Germany and Japan were physically devastated by the war; 'catastrophic nationalism' did indeed lead to catastrophe. The Allies forced unconditional surrender on their enemies. Germany ceased to exist as a state;

it was divided for nearly forty years and never recovered its eastern provinces from Poland and Russia. Japan was occupied until 1952 (when the Treaty of San Francisco came into effect). A number of the supreme leaders of Germany and Japan – those who did not commit suicide – were tried and sentenced to death or long terms of imprisonment; Mussolini was murdered. The ultra-nationalist radical right never reappeared as a serious political force.

Nevertheless, Germany and Japan would survive and within fifteen years achieve unprecedented prosperity. Without its *Grossraum* Germany became the strongest economy in Europe and eventually, in 1989, would even achieve reunification. The success of the Japanese economy, by the early 1960s – and still under the wartime Emperor – was stunning. Stripped of its imperial gains of 1895, 1905, 1931, and 1942, with only limited self-defence forces, Japan went from success to success. The country's GDP increased by about 10 per cent a year from the late 1940s until the early 1970s, and by 1966 Japan had become the world's second-largest economy, after the United States. Italy was less affected by the war than Germany or Japan, although more prolonged fighting took place on its territory. An early surrender in 1943 and the death of Mussolini in 1945 meant that Italy avoided division, occupation, or grand post-war trials. It effected a rapid economic recovery in the 1950s and 1960s, if not on the same scale as Germany and Japan, and it did this without any Mediterranean or East African empire.

Not only did the defeated nations recover, but some of the states on the Allied side fared badly. If the aim of the Allies – as expressed by the 1941 Atlantic Charter – was to defend the independence of nation states and to ensure democratic government, it was not successful in Eastern Europe after 1945. Poland and Czechoslovakia, in particular, rather than being liberated, ended up for two generations under cruel dictatorships imposed from outside.

Within a few years of the great victory of 1945, two of the major Allied states, Britain and China, had suffered grave setbacks. The die was cast for the British in 1940–1, when they continued the war in the knowledge that fighting on meant national bankruptcy. Britain was in the end unable to defend its colonial system against all comers, and the struggle with Germany, Italy, and Japan fatally weakened its hold. The British Empire broke up, with the achievement of independence by India and Pakistan in August 1947, and then with the humiliation of the Suez crisis in 1956. In the long run the Empire would have collapsed anyway, but war certainly accelerated the process. France had a steeper downward trajectory in that it was liberated rather than a liberator. The French gained a permanent seat on the UN Security Council and an occupation zone in Germany, but this was only with British backing. Even more than Britain, France's time as a world power was passing. The French overseas Empire was vulnerable, and fruitless wars were fought in Indochina and Algeria in the 1950s to turn back the clock. The Dutch Empire went the same way.

The government of Nationalist China faced an even more drastic fate: defeat in the Civil War at the hands of the Communists and a humiliating flight to Formosa (Taiwan). Jiang Jieshi had received significant military aid at the end of the war. The Nationalist government had US diplomatic support and held one of five permanent seats on the UN Security Council. In the end, however, the Nationalists were unable to cope; the Japanese occupation accelerated the break-up of Chinese rural society and ultimately the situation played into the hands of the Communists.

The war was immensely costly at several levels to the Soviet Union, whose troops had stormed Berlin in 1945. Victory in what the Russians called the 'Great Patriotic War' greatly expanded – for a time – the scope of Stalinist Communism, giving the USSR a huge 'empire' in Eastern Europe. But Soviet Russia won its victory at a huge cost, losing many more people than did Germany – in all some 27 million. Victory gave the USSR burdens it could not sustain. Soviet control over Eastern Europe was bought at the price of permanent conflict with the West. Triumph in World War II blinded Soviet Russian leaders to the need to make reforms, and by the end of the 1970s the regime was sliding into a crisis from which it never recovered.

There seems little doubt that America was the great winner of World War II, when every other major participant suffered economic, political, or demographic ruin. But victory had a price, even for the United States. The British historian Paul Kennedy, in his 1987 book *The Rise and Fall of the Great Powers*, argued that victory over the Axis led to 'imperial overstretch', which would eventually threaten America's economic supremacy. Overseas commitments, and the need to maintain huge military forces, reduced the ability of the American economy to compete and pulled Washington into new struggles in Korea and Vietnam, and in the Middle East. This was the same way in which world empire had reduced the ability of the British economy to compete in the late nineteenth century. Countries like Japan and Germany, now with lighter military commitments, could gradually outpace America economically. (Kennedy, it must be said, made this case before the collapse of the USSR and before the setbacks to the Japanese economy in the 1990s.) President Eisenhower warned of other threats in his famous 1961 farewell address: 'Until the latest of our world conflicts [World War II], the United States had no armaments industry. American makers of plowshares could, with time and as required, make swords as well. But now we can no longer risk emergency improvisation of national defense. We have been compelled to create a permanent armaments industry of vast proportions.' Eisenhower omitted to say that America had built a navy nearly the size of Britain's after 1916, but he was right that this armaments industry presented a danger: 'In the councils of government, we must guard against the acquisition of unwarranted influence, whether sought or unsought, by the military-industrial complex.'[5]

Before becoming too pessimistic we should recall that the global system did survive, although in the short and medium term without the participation of the Soviet bloc or Communist China. The system worked much better than in the 1930s, and Britain, France, Germany, Japan, and Italy accepted American economic and political leadership, partly because of the existence of the Soviet military threat. More robust international financial institutions were created in place of the economic anarchy of the 1930s. Western Europe benefited from the European Recovery Programme (the Marshall Plan) of 1948–52. The economies of the region were much more closely co-ordinated, moving in 1957 to the EEC and later to the European Union. In the long term even Russia and China were incorporated into the system, the latter with extraordinary success.

The positive impact of the war was not just victory, but transformation. Mao Zedong was at least half right in his 1938 prediction about the conflict: 'The Sino–Japanese war will transform both China and Japan; provided China perseveres ... the old Japan will surely be transformed into a new

Japan and the old China into a new China, and people and everything else in both China and Japan will be transformed during and after the war.'[6] Japan actually changed less than Mao imagined (he expected a revolution), but China would certainly be transformed, through several stages. Europe, too, was transformed, and with it much of the world.

Further reading

This short list is generally limited to works in English. The amount of published work on World War II, even in English alone, is so great that any reading list must of necessity be very selective.

General books

There are a number of general histories of World War II. One of the best, especially on the operational side, is Williamson Murray and Allan R. Millett, *A War to be Won: Fighting the Second World War* (Cambridge, MA: Belknap Press, 2000). Gerhard L. Weinberg, *A World at Arms: A Global History of World War II* (Cambridge: Cambridge University Press, 2005) is an impressive scholarly achievement and especially good on diplomacy and intelligence; its size, however, makes it hard to navigate through.

Richard Overy, *Why the Allies Won* (London: Pimlico, 1995), is a stimulatingly different survey of the war, and Ian Kershaw, *Fateful Choices: Ten Decisions That Changed the World, 1940–1941* (London: Allen Lane, 2007), takes an interesting approach to the middle period of the conflict. R. J. B. Bosworth, *Explaining Auschwitz and Hiroshima: History Writing and the Second World War 1945–1990* (London: Routledge, 1994), is perceptive and thought-provoking, and there is still much of interest in Raymond Aron, *A Century of Total War* (London: Derek Verschoyle, 1954). 'The Future of World War II Studies: A Roundtable', *Diplomatic History* 25:3 (2001), pp. 347–500, provides a recent perspective.

Important collections of essays covering, among other things, aspects of World War II are Paul Kennedy, ed., *Grand Strategies in War and Peace* (New Haven: Yale University Press, 1991); Allan Millett and Williamson Murray, *Military Effectiveness*, vol. III (London: Allen & Unwin, 1988); Williamson Murray *et al.*, eds., *The Making of Strategy: Rulers, States, and War* (Cambridge: Cambridge University Press, 1994); and Peter Paret, ed., *Makers of Modern Strategy from Machiavelli to the Nuclear Age* (Oxford: Clarendon Press, 1984); in the Paret volume, Maurice Matloff, 'Allied Strategy in Europe, 1939–1945', is a useful overview.

For the important 'total war' concept there is Roger Chickering and Stig Förster, eds., *The Shadows of Total War: Europe, East Asia, and the United States, 1919–1939* (Cambridge: Cambridge University Press, 2003), and Roger Chickering *et al.*, eds., *A World at Total War: Global Conflict and the Politics of Destruction, 1937–1945* (Cambridge: Cambridge University Press, 2005).

Relations within the alliances throughout the war are central to an understanding of the outcome. For the British–American partnership, with its ups and downs, there are Warren F. Kimball, *Forged in War: Roosevelt, Churchill, and the Second World War* (New York: William Morrow, 1997); Brian J. C. McKercher, *Transition of Power: Britain's Loss of Global Pre-eminence to the United States, 1930–1945* (Cambridge: Cambridge University Press, 1999); and Mark Stoler, *Allies in War: Britain and America Against the Axis Powers, 1940–1945* (London: Hodder Arnold, 2005). The letters in Warren F. Kimball, ed., *Churchill and Roosevelt: The Complete Correspondence*, 3 vols. (Princeton: Princeton University Press, 1984), are an especially important primary source on this subject.

On the other side see Richard L. DiNardo, *Germany and the Axis Powers: From Coalition to Collapse* (Lawrence: University Press of Kansas, 2005), and Macgregor Knox, *Common Destiny: Dictatorship, Foreign Policy, and War in Fascist Italy and Nazi Germany* (Cambridge: Cambridge University Press, 2000).

The essays in Mark Harrison, ed., *The Economics of World War II: Six Powers in International Comparison* (Cambridge: Cambridge University Press, 1998), provide a useful introduction to the war economies, as well as much statistical data. They supplement the survey by Alan S. Milward, *War Economy and Society, 1939–1945* (Berkeley: University of California Press, 1977). Daniel Yergin, *The Prize: The Epic Quest for Oil, Money, and Power* (New York: Simon & Schuster, 1991), and Robert Goralski and Russell W. Freeburg, *Oil and War: How the Deadly Struggle for Fuel in WWII Meant Victory or Defeat* (New York: William Morrow, 1987), are readable treatments of the vital oil resource.

Richard Overy, *The Air War, 1939–45* (London: Europa, 1980) is a useful one-volume history of this aspect. On intelligence there is Stephen Budiansky, *Battle of Wits: The Complete Story of Codebreaking in World War II* (London: Penguin Books, 2001). A useful collection of published first-person accounts, many of them written when memory was fresh in the first decade after the war, is Desmond Flower and James Reeves, eds., *The War, 1939–1945* (London: Cassell, 1960); this was a starting point for many of the extracts quoted in the present book.

On war losses see Rüdiger Overmans, *Deutsche militärische Verluste im Zweiten Weltkrieg* (Munich: R. Oldenbourg, 1999), and G. F. Krivosheev, ed., *Soviet Casualties and Combat Losses in the Twentieth Century* (London: Greenhill, 1997).

Some English-language journals especially relevant for World War II are *Diplomatic History* (USA), *Diplomacy and Statecraft* (UK), *Intelligence and National Security* (UK), *Journal of Military History* (USA), *Journal of Strategic Studies* (UK), *War in History* (UK), and *World War II Quarterly* (USA).

An indispensable reference is I. C. B. Dear and M. R. D. Foot, eds., *The Oxford Companion to the Second World War* (Oxford: Oxford University Press, 1995). Larger still is Spencer C. Tucker, *The Encyclopedia of World War II: A Political, Social, and*

Military History, 5 vols. (Santa Barbara, CA: ABC-Clio, 2004). For deep background see Richard Holmes, ed., *The Oxford Companion to Military History* (Oxford: Oxford University Press, 2001), and for authoritative suggestions about further reading, Charles Messenger, ed., *Reader's Guide to Military History* (London: Fitzroy Dearborn, 2001).

Atlases are essential for understanding the conduct of the war. Two of the most useful are Martin Gilbert, ed., *The Routledge Atlas of the Second World War* (London: Routledge, 2008), and John Keegan, ed., *The Times Atlas of the Second World War* (London, HarperReference, 1989).

The definitive documentary film about the war, still readily available, is *The World at War*. This was produced by Jeremy Isaacs for Thames Television and first shown in 1973–4 in 26 episodes, each 52 minutes long. The series is a unique combination of intelligently chosen archive film and interviews with survivors, both senior politicians (including Admiral Dönitz, Anthony Eden, Lord Mountbatten, and Albert Speer) and commanders and 'ordinary' soldiers, sailors, and airmen from various countries. The DVD set includes additional material.

The internet contains enormous amounts of factual material about aspects of World War II. One of the best websites for the war as a whole is that of the Imperial War Museum in London, www.iwm.org.uk. The IWM site includes links to subsidiary museums including the Churchill Museum and the Cabinet War Rooms.

The internet also makes primary sources more readily available. Many diplomatic sources are available through the Yale University Avalon Project (Documents in Law, History, and Diplomacy), www.yale.edu/lawweb/avalon/avalon.htm.

A considerable amount of material, predominantly American, is available at the non-government Hyperwar Foundation, digitised by Patrick W. Clancy: www.ibiblio.org/hyperwar/about.html.

The main 'academic' website for military history is H-War, Military History Network, based in the United States. H-War is a member of H-Net, Humanities & Social Sciences OnLine. H-WAR is an electronic newsletter, both a discussion board and a source of useful reviews: www.h-net.org/~war.

Britain

'Official' histories were produced in various countries, but generally they appeared soon after the war, took a national point of view, and were narrowly specialised. Their authors were often unable to cite the primary sources on which they were based. As a result they are generally not listed here. The British, it must be said, published the most systematically conceived series of official histories under the overall title *History of the Second World War*. Still interesting today are the five volumes (in six) published long after the war in 1979–90, following revelations about British codebreaking and other activities: *British Intelligence in the Second World War*, edited by F. H. Hinsley and others (London: HMSO, 1979–90). Volume IV covers security and counter-intelligence, and vol. V (edited by Michael Howard) strategic deception. There is also F. H. Hinsley, *British Intelligence in the Second World War, Abridged Version* (London: HMSO, 1993).

For Churchill's role in this period and later, the essential source is David Reynolds, *In Command of History: Churchill Fighting and Writing the Second World War* (London: Penguin Books, 2005). Reynolds's book is about how Churchill came to write his highly influential six-volume history, *The Second World War* (London: Cassell, 1948–54); the Churchill work is itself an important source for the war. The official biography is Martin Gilbert, *Winston S. Churchill*; for the war see vol. VI, *Finest Hour, 1939–1941* (London: Heinemann, 1983), and vol. VII, *Road to Victory, 1941–1945* (London: Heinemann, 1986). The best-known revisionist treatment of the British leader is by John Charmley; see especially his *Churchill: The End of Glory* (New York: Harcourt Brace, 1993).

Brian P. Farrell, *The Basis and Making of British Grand Strategy, 1940–1943: Was There a Plan?*, 2 vols. (Lampeter: Edwin Mellen Press, 1998), provides a good background, incorporating extensive work in the archives. Eliot A. Cohen, 'Churchill and Coalition Strategy in World War II', is a shorter treatment in Kennedy, *Grand Strategies*.

For an overview of British military posture, see David French, *The British Way in Warfare 1688–2000* (London: Unwin Hyman, 1990), and Williamson Murray, 'The Collapse of Empire: British Strategy, 1919–1945', in Williamson Murray, Alvin Bernstein, and MacGregor Knox, eds., *The Making of Strategy* (Cambridge: Cambridge University Press, 1996). See also the general assessment in Correlli Barnett, *The Audit of War: The Illusion and Reality of Britain as a Great Nation* (Basingstoke: Macmillan, 1986), and David Edgerton, *Warfare State: Britain, 1920–1970* (Cambridge: Cambridge University Press, 2006). For the various armed services there are Correlli Barnett, *Engage the Enemy More Closely: The Royal Navy in the Second World War* (New York: Norton, 1991); David Fraser, *And We Shall Shock Them: The British Army in the Second World War* (London: Hodder & Stoughton, 1983); David French, *Raising Churchill's Army: The British Army and the War against Germany, 1919–1945* (Oxford: Oxford University Press, 2000); and John Terraine, *The Right of the Line: The Royal Air Force in the European War, 1939–1945* (Sevenoaks: Sceptre, 1988). See also the RAF Museum website: www.rafmuseum.org.uk.

China

The most readily available biography of Jiang Jieshi is Jay Taylor, *The Generalissimo: Chiang Kai-Shek and the Struggle for Modern China* (Cambridge, MA: Harvard University Press, 2009). Authoritative articles on wartime China can be found in

Republican China 1912–1949, Part 2, vol. XIII of *The Cambridge History of China*, ed. John K. Fairbank and Albert Feuerwerker (Cambridge: Cambridge University Press, 1986). These are Akira Iriye, 'Japanese Aggression and China's International Position, 1931–1949', and Lloyd E. Eastman, 'Nationalist China during the Sino–Japanese War 1937–1945'. Hans J. van de Ven, *War and Nationalism in China, 1925–1945* (London: Routledge, 2003), is a stimulating new interpretation of Nationalist China. See also the articles in James C. Hsiung and Steven I. Levine, eds., *China's Bitter Victory: The War with Japan, 1937–1945* (Armonk, NY, M. E. Sharpe, 1992).

For military operations, placed in context, there are Edward L. Dreyer, *China at War, 1901–1949* (London: Longman, 1995), and Dick Wilson, *When Tigers Fight: The Story of the Sino–Japanese War, 1937–1945* (Harmondsworth: Penguin, 1983).

France

General works on wartime France are problematic, given the turnabout of national fortunes in May 1940. See, however, Nicholas Atkin, *The French at War 1934–1944* (London: Longman, 2001), and Julian Jackson, *France: The Dark Years, 1940–1944* (Oxford: Oxford University Press, 2003).

The website of the French Army Museum is www.invalides.org.

Italy

Macgregor Knox, *Hitler's Italian Allies: Royal Armed Forces, Fascist Regime, and the War of 1940–43* (Cambridge: Cambridge University Press, 2000), gives an overall view. A biography of the central figure is R. J. B. Bosworth, *Mussolini* (London: Edward Arnold, 2002).

Germany

A multi-volume history began to be published in Germany in 1979, *Das Deutsche Reich und der Zweite Weltkrieg* (*DRZW*); the last instalment, the second part of vol. 10, appeared only in 2008. Work on the project began in 1971 under the auspices of the *Militärgeschichtliche Forschungsamt* (Military History Research Office) of the (West) German armed forces. The series takes no consistent 'line', and the authors within individual volumes occasionally disagree with one another.

Oxford University Press began to publish the *DRZW* series in English in 1990 as *Germany and the Second World War*. Volumes available at the time of writing are: vol. I, *The Build-up of German Aggression* (1990); vol. II, *Germany's Initial Conquests in Europe* (1991); vol. III, *The Mediterranean, South-East Europe, and North Africa 1939–1941* (1995); vol. IV, *The Attack on the Soviet Union* [1941] (1998); vol. V/1, *Organization and Mobilization of the German Sphere of Power* [1939–41] (2000);

vol. V/2, *Organization and Mobilization of the German Sphere of Power* [1942–4/5] (2003); vol. VI, *The Global War* [1941–3] (2001); vol. VII, *The Strategic Air War in Europe* [1943–4] *and the War in the West* [to January 45] *and East Asia 1943–1944/5* (2006); and vol. IX/1, *German Wartime Society 1939–1945* (2008). Volumes awaiting translation are vol. VIII, covering the Eastern Front in 1943–4; vol. IX/2 (aspects of German society); and vols. X/1 and X/2 (the end of the war and the series conclusion).

Richard Evans, *The Third Reich at War: How the Nazis Led Germany from Conquest to Disaster* (London: Allen Lane, 2008), provides an overview, and there is also the masterful biography by Ian Kershaw, *Hitler 1936–45: Nemesis* (London: Allen Lane, 2000). Andreas Hillgruber, *Germany and the Two World Wars* (Cambridge, MA: Harvard University Press, 1981) is an influential interpretation. Adam Tooze, *The Wages of Destruction: The Making and Breaking of the Nazi Economy* (London: Allen Lane, 2006), convincingly re-examines many commonly held misconceptions and also shows the centrality of ideology.

Max Domarus, ed., *The Chronicle of a Dictatorship*, vols. III and IV: *Hitler: Speeches and Proclamations 1932–1945* [1939–40 and 1941–5] (Mundelein, IL: Bolchazy-Carducci, 1996), was originally published in German in 1962–3.

Robert M. Citino, *The German Way of War: From the Thirty Years War to the Third Reich* (Lawrence: University Press of Kansas, 2005), provides insights into the background of German military policy and takes the story up to the end of 1941. See also Michael Geyer, 'German Strategy in the Age of Machine Warfare, 1914–1945', in Paret, *Makers of Modern Strategy*; Wilhelm Deist, 'The Road to Ideological War: Germany, 1918–1945', in Murray *et al.*, *The Making of Strategy*, and Dennis E. Showalter, 'Total War for Limited Objectives: An Interpretation of German Grand Strategy', in Kennedy, *Grand Strategies*. Geoffrey P. Megargee, *Inside Hitler's High Command* (Lawrence: University Press of Kansas, 2000), argues that the shortcomings of the German high command were not solely the fault of the Führer. See also Wolfram Wette, *The Wehrmacht: History, Myth, Reality* (Cambridge, MA: Harvard University Press, 2006), and Williamson Murray, *The Luftwaffe, 1933–1945: Strategy for Defeat* (London: Allen & Unwin, 1985).

Japan

Stephen S. Large, *Emperor Hirohito and* Shōwa *Japan: A Political Biography* (London: Routledge, 1992), and Herbert P. Bix, *Hirohito and the Making of Modern Japan* (London: Duckworth, 2000), cover the workings of the Japanese political system. Akira Iriye, *Power and Culture: The Japanese–American War, 1941–1945* (Cambridge, MA: Harvard University Press, 1981), is a thought-provoking outline of the overall relationship between the two major combatants. An unusually self-critical Japanese treatment is Saburo Ienaga, *Japan's Last War: World War II and the Japanese, 1931–1945* (Oxford: Blackwell, 1979).

A well-informed outline of the Japanese military campaigns is: Alvin D. Coox, 'The Pacific War', in *The Twentieth Century*, vol. VI of *The Cambridge History of Japan*, ed. Peter Duns (Cambridge: Cambridge University Press, 1989). For the Navy the most thoughtful source is David C. Evans and Mark R. Peattie, *Kaigun: Strategy, Tactics, and Technology in the Imperial Japanese Navy, 1887–1941* (Annapolis, MD: Naval Institute Press, 1997); despite its title the book includes a valuable analysis of 1941–5. For the Japanese Army there are Saburo Hayashi, with Alvin D. Coox, *Kōgun: Japanese Army in the Pacific War* (Westport, CT: Greenwood Press, 1978), and Edward J. Drea, *In the Service of the Emperor: Essays on the Imperial Japanese Army* (Lincoln, NE: University of Nebraska Press, 1998).

Russia

Recent general outlines of the Soviet–German War as a whole are David Glantz and Jonathan M. House, *When Titans Clashed: How the Red Army Stopped Hitler* (Lawrence: University Press of Kansas, 1995), and Evan Mawdsley, *Thunder in the East: The Nazi–Soviet War* (London: Hodder Arnold, 2005). Rolf-Dieter Müller and Gerd R. Ueberschär, eds., *Hitler's War in the East, 1941–1945: A Critical Assessment* (Oxford: Berghahn, 1997), provides in-depth coverage of the campaigns and German occupation policy. Geoffrey Roberts, *Stalin's Wars* (New Haven: Yale, 2005), is especially strong on wartime diplomacy. The details of Soviet war production are covered in Mark Harrison, *Accounting for War: Soviet Production, Employment, and the Defence Burden, 1940–1945* (Cambridge: Cambridge University Press, 1996), and Walter S. Dunn, *The Soviet Economy and the Red Army, 1930–1945* (Westport, CN: Praeger, 1995).

Alexander Werth, *Russia at War, 1941–1945* (London: Barrie & Rockliff, 1964) is a unique account, vivid and sympathetic, by a former British war correspondent. A remarkable insight into the life of the common Red Army soldier is Catherine Merridale, *Ivan's War: The Red Army 1941–1945* (London: Faber, 2005).

The United States

For an overview of the war, with an emphasis on the home front, see David M. Kennedy, *The American People in World War II* (New York: Oxford University Press, 2003), which is the second volume of the Pulitzer Prize-winning *Freedom from Fear* (1999) and vol. IX of *The Oxford History of the United States*.

Robert Dallek, *Franklin D. Roosevelt and American Foreign Policy, 1932–1945* (Oxford: Oxford University Press, 1979), is the classic biography, while James Burns, *Roosevelt: Soldier of Freedom* (London: Weidenfeld & Nicolson, 1971), focuses on the President's wartime activities. Forrest C. Pogue, *George C. Marshall*, 3 vols. (London: MacGibbon & Kee, 1964–73), is a biography of Roosevelt's closest military advisor. For a recent long-term view of American war aims see Patrick J. Hearden, *Architects of Globalism: Building a New World Order during Word War II* (Fayetteville: University of Arkansas Press, 2002).

Russell Weigley, *The American Way of War: A History of United States Military Strategy and Policy* (New York: Macmillan, 1973), is an influential treatment of the American forces, especially the Army. On naval operations and planning there are George Baer, *One Hundred Years of Sea Power: The U.S. Navy, 1890–1990* (Stanford: Stanford University Press, 1994), and Samuel Eliot Morison, *The Two-Ocean War: A Short History of the United States Navy in the Second World War* (Boston: Little, Brown, 1963).

There is a huge literature on strategic planning, going from official histories like Forrest Pogue, *The Supreme Command* (Washington: OCMH, 1954), to Mark A. Stoler, *Allies and Adversaries: The Joint Chiefs of Staff, the Grand Alliance, and U.S. Strategy in World War II* (Chapel Hill: University of North Carolina Press, 2000). See also Eliot A. Cohen, 'The Strategy of Innocence? The United States, 1920–1945', in Murray *et al.*, *The Making of Strategy.*

The American military forces maintain useful internet sources which include on-line versions of some of the official histories. See especially the US Army Center of Military History, www.history.army.mil. The detailed official history of the US Army strategic planning, the two volumes of Maurice Matloff, *Strategic Planning for Coalition Warf*are, published in 1953 and 1959, are available on line here.

Interesting museum material and links are provided by the US Navy historical site: www.history.navy.mil. For the Air Force see www.nationalmuseum.af.mil.

The National World War II Museum in New Orleans (formerly the National D-Day Museum) is located at www.nationalww2museum.org.

Chapter 1: The world in 1937

Paul Kennedy, *The Rise and Fall of the Great Powers: Economic Change and Military Conflict from 1500 to 2000* (London: Fontana, 1989), provides a useful perspective on the inter-war world, as does Charles P. Kindleberger, *The World in Depression, 1929–1939* (Berkeley: University of California Press, 1986).

Robert Boyce and Joseph A. Maiolo, eds., *The Origins of World War Two: The Debate Continues* (Basingstoke: Palgrave Macmillan, 2003), is a general discussion of the background to the war, mainly in Europe. See also *Germany and the Second World War*, vol. I.

The 1920s and 1930s saw important changes in military technology, and strategic planning was also an important background factor. See Brian McKercher and Roch Legault, eds., *Military Planning and the Origins of the Second World War in Europe*

(Westport, CN: Praeger, 2001), and Harold. R. Winton and David R. Mets, eds., *The Challenge of Change: Military Institutions and New Realities, 1918–1941* (Lincoln, NE: University of Nebraska Press, 2000).

Chapter 2: Japan and China, 1937–1940

In *The Origins of the Second World War in Asia and the Pacific* (London: Longman, 1987), Akira Iriye, an American-based Japanese scholar, brings in both Japanese and Chinese perspectives. A classic study laying out the situation from Japan's point of view, is James B. Crowley, *Japan's Quest for Autonomy: National Security and Foreign Policy 1930–1939* (Princeton: Princeton University Press, 1966). See also Ikuhiko Hata, 'Continental Expansion', in *The Twentieth Century*, vol. VI of *The Cambridge History of Japan*, ed. Peter Duns (Cambridge: Cambridge University Press, 1988), pp. 271–314.

For the terrible events at Nanjing, still a matter of controversy, see Joshua A. Fogel, ed., *The Nanjing Massacre in History and Historiography* (Berkeley: University of Califormia Press, 2000).

Jonathan Haslam, *The Soviet Union and the Threat from the East, 1933–41: Moscow, Tokyo and the Prelude to the Pacific War* (Basingstoke: Macmillan, 1992), covers Russia's relations with Japan, a neglected subject. For the Khalkin Gol border war and its context see Alvin D. Coox, *Nomonhan: Japan against Russia, 1939* (Stanford: Stanford University Press, 1985).

Chapter 3: Hitler's border wars, 1938–1939

Standard overviews of the start of the war in Europe are D. C. Watt, *How War Came: The Immediate Origins of the Second World War* (London: Heinemann, 1989), and P. M. H. Bell, *The Origins of the Second World War in Europe*, 3rd edn (Harlow: Pearson, 2007). On one great debate about Europe see A. J. P. Taylor, *The Origins of the Second World War* (London: Hamilton, 1961), and Gordon Martel, ed., *The Origins of the Second World War Reconsidered: A. J. P. Taylor and the Historians*, 2nd edn (London, Routledge, 1999). See also *Germany and the Second World War*, vol. II.

Macgregor Knox, *Mussolini Unleashed, 1939–1941: Politics and Strategy in Fascist Italy's Last War* (Cambridge: Cambridge University Press, 1982); Robert Mallett, *Mussolini and the Origins of the Second World War* (London: Palgrave Macmillan, 2003); and G. Bruce Strang, *On the Fiery March: Mussolini Prepares for War* (Westport: Praeger, 2003), are standard accounts of the Italian entry into the war.

On the 1939 conquest see Alexander B. Rossino, *Hitler Strikes Poland: Blitzkrieg, Ideology, and Atrocity* (Lawrence: University Press of Kansas, 2003). The best military account from the Polish side is Steven Zaloga and Victor Madej, *The Polish Campaign*

1939 (New York: Hippocrene Books, 1991). On later events in Poland, a useful outline is Richard C. Lukas, *The Forgotten Holocaust: The Poles under German Occupation, 1939–1944*, 2nd edn (New York: Hippocrene, 1997).

Arnold A. Offner, *The Origins of the Second World War: American Foreign Policy and World Politics, 1917–1941* (Malabar, FL: R. E. Kreiger, 1986), gives the American position in this period. For the Soviet perspective see Silvio Pons, *Stalin and the Inevitable War, 1936–1941* (London: Frank Cass, 2002).

Chapter 4: Germany re-fights World War I, 1939–1940

Talbot C. Imlay, *Facing the Second World War: Strategy, Politics, and Economics in Britain and France, 1938–1940* (Oxford: Oxford University Press, 2003), is an excellent reinterpretation of early Allied strategy. Although somewhat dated, J. L. Moulton, *A Study of Warfare in Three Dimensions: The Norwegian Campaign of 1940* (Athens, OH: Ohio University Press, 1967), is still useful for Scandinavia.

There are a number of good new books on the fall of France, the best introduction to which is Julian Jackson, *The Fall of France: The Nazi Invasion of 1940* (Oxford: Oxford University Press, 2003). See also Ernest May, *Strange Victory: Hitler's Conquest of France* (London: Tauris, 2000), and Karl-Heinz Frieser, *The Blitzkrieg Legend: The Campaign in the West, 1940* (Annapolis, MD: Naval Institute Press, 2005). An influential article, noting the decisive outcome of the fall of France, is David Reynolds, '1940: Fulcrum of the Twentieth Century', *International Affairs* 66:2 (1990), pp. 325–350. For Poland, Scandinavia, and France see *Germany and the Second World War*, vol. II.

For the Battle of Britain, a thoughtful new work is Stephen Bungay, *The Most Dangerous Enemy: A History of the Battle of Britain* (London: Aurum Press, 2000). There is also an outstanding film re-creation of the campaign, *The Battle of Britain* (1969), directed by Guy Hamilton.

Chapter 5: Wars of ideology, 1941–1942

For a discussion of Soviet foreign policy immediately before the war, based on newly available documents, see Gabriel Gorodetsky, *The Grand Delusion: Stalin and the German Invasion of Russia* (New Haven: Yale University Press, 1999). The standard work on the pre-war Red Army is David M. Glantz, *Stumbling Colossus: The Red Army on the Eve of World War* (Lawrence: University Press of Kansas, 1998).

Evan Mawdsley, 'Crossing the Rubicon: Soviet Plans for Offensive War in 1941', *International History Review* 24:4 (2003), pp. 818–865, provides an introduction to the debate about whether the German invasion was pre-emptive. The controversial work, around which much of the debate revolves, is Viktor Suvorov, *Icebreaker:*

Who Started the Second World War? (London: Hamish Hamilton, 1990); the latest incarnation is Viktor Suvorov, *The Chief Culprit: Stalin's Grand Design to Start World War II* (Annapolis, MD: Naval Institute Press, 2008).

John Erickson, *The Road to Stalingrad* (London: Weidenfeld & Nicolson, 1975), while a challenge to navigate through, is valuable and beautifully written. For a detailed narrative based on the German documents see Earl F. Ziemke and Magna Bauer, *Moscow to Stalingrad: Decisions in the East* (Washington: Center of Military History, 1987). On the German Army in 1941 there is now Geoffrey P. Megargee, *War of Annihilation: Combat and Genocide on the Eastern Front, 1941* (Lanham, MD: Rowman & Littlefield, 2005). See also *Germany and the Second World War*, vol. IV.

Klaus Reinhardt, *Moscow: The Turning Point* (Oxford: Berg, 1992), deals with the most important individual battle in this period. See also Robert M. Citino, *Death of the Wehrmacht: The German Campaigns of 1942* (Lawrence: University Press of Kansas, 2007).

Karel C. Berkhoff, *Harvest of Despair: Life and Death in Ukraine under Nazi Rule* (Cambridge, MA: Belknap Press, 2004), deals with German occupation in a key region. An influential study of German troop conduct is Omer Bartov, *The Eastern Front 1941–45: German Troops and the Barbarisation of Warfare* (London: Macmillan, 1985).

The best modern film about the Russian front is Joseph Vilsmaier's *Stalingrad* (1993), although it focuses on the sufferings of the German occupiers.

Introductions to the Holocaust are Raul Hilberg, *The Destruction of the European Jews* (1961: New Haven: Yale University Press, 2003), and Christopher R. Browning, *The Origins of the Final Solution: The Evolution of Nazi Jewish Policy, September 1939–March 1942* (London: Heinemann, 2004).

Websites about the Holocaust include Yad Vashem (The Holocaust Martyrs' and Heroes' Remembrance Authority), based in Jerusalem, www1.yadvashem.org, and the United States Holocaust Memorial Museum (which is also good on World War II in general), www.ushmm.org.

The most powerful documentary on the Holocaust is the nine-and-a-half-hour film series by the French director Claude Lanzmann, *Shoah* (1985). See also the television re-enactment of the January 1942 Wannsee Conference, *Conspiracy* (2001), directed by Frank Pierson, with Kenneth Branagh as Reinhard Heydrich.

Chapter 6: The Red Army versus the Wehrmacht, 1941–1944

On the later part of the war in the East see John Erickson, *The Road to Berlin* (London: Weidenfeld & Nicolson, 1983); Earl F. Ziemke, *Stalingrad to Berlin: German Defeat in the East* (Washington: OCMH, 1968); and David M. Glantz, *Colossus Reborn: The Red Army at War, 1941–1943* (Lawrence: University Press of Kansas, 2005). See also *Germany and the Second World War*, vol. VI and (forthcoming in translation) vol. VIII.

Anthony Beevor, *Stalingrad: The Fateful Siege: 1942–43* (New York: Viking, 1999), contains much of value and covers both sides of the battle. More straightforward are Walter S. Dunn, *Kursk: Hitler's Gamble, 1943* (Westport: Praeger, 1997), and David Glantz and Jonathan M. House, *The Battle of Kursk 1943* (Lawrence: University Press of Kansas, 1999).

Keith Sainsbury, *The Turning Point: Roosevelt, Stalin, Churchill, and Chiang Kai-Shek, 1943: The Moscow, Cairo, and Teheran Conferences* (Oxford: Oxford University Press, 1986), covers the first of the 'Big Three' conferences.

Chapter 7: Japan's lunge for empire, 1941–1942

Ronald H. Spector, *Eagle against the Sun: The American War with Japan* (New York: Free Press, 1985), remains an excellent one-volume account. For a shorter overview see D. Clayton James, 'American and Japanese Strategies in the Pacific War', in Paret, *Makers of Modern Strategy*.

John Dower, *War without Mercy: Race and Power in the Pacific War* (London: Faber, 1986), deals with the very significant cultural conflict. On the military side, a useful recent collection of articles is Daniel Marston, ed., *The Pacific War Companion: From Pearl Harbor to Hiroshima* (Oxford: Osprey Publishing, 2005). See also *Germany and the Second World War*, vol. VI.

Waldo Heinrichs, *Threshold of War: Franklin D. Roosevelt and American Entry into World War II* (New York: Oxford University Press, 1988), details the year before Pearl Harbor. The classic works on the Japanese attack, still invaluable, are Gordon Prange, *At Dawn We Slept: The Untold Story of Pearl Harbor* (Harmondsworth: Penguin, 1991), and Dorothy Borg and Okamoto Shumpei, eds., *Pearl Harbor as History: Japanese–American Relations, 1931–1941* (New York: Columbia University Press, 1973). Robert B. Stinnett, *Day of Deceit: The Truth about FDR and Pearl Harbor* (London: Constable, 2000), makes an unconvincing 'conspiracy' case but provides much newly released intelligence material. Roberta Wohlstetter, *Pearl Harbor: Warning and Decision* (Stanford: Stanford University Press, 1962), provides a more thought-through interpretation.

The complex and often difficult relationship between Britain and America is covered by Christopher Thorne, *Allies of a Kind: The United States, Britain and the War against Japan, 1941–1945* (London: Hamish Hamilton, 1978). For the 'great crescent' of British Asia there is Christopher Bayly and Tim Harper, *Forgotten Armies: Britain's Asian Empire and the War with Japan* (London: Penguin, 2004).

Louis Allen, *Singapore, 1941–1942* (London: Davis-Poynter, 1977), and Brian P. Farrell, *The Defence and Fall of Singapore* (Stroud: Tempus, 2005), cover this crucial defeat for the British Empire. The subsequent campaign is dealt with in Louis Allen, *Burma: The Longest War, 1941–1945* (London: Dent, 1986).

An important work on pre-war US naval planning, very relevant to the actual conduct of the war, is Edward S. Miller, *War Plan Orange: The U.S. Strategy to Defeat Japan, 1897–1945* (Annapolis, MD: Naval Institute Press, 1991). John Prados, *Combined Fleet Decoded* (Annapolis, MD: Naval Institute Press, 2001), covers the vital role of intelligence. The early developments in the Pacific are dealt with by H. P. Willmott, *The Barrier and the Javelin: Japanese and Allied Pacific Strategies, February to June 1942* (Annapolis, MD: Naval Institute Press, 1983). The most recent account of the decisive battle is Jonathan Parshall and Anthony Tully, *Shattered Sword: The Japanese Story of the Battle of Midway* (Dulles, VA: Potomac Books, 2005).

One of the outstanding war films is the Japanese–American co-production about Pearl Harbor, *Tora! Tora! Tora!* (1970), directed by Richard Fleischer, Fukasaku Kinji, and Masuda Toshio. For a human portrayal of the early American defeats in the Philippines, which transcends wartime propaganda, see John Ford's *They Were Expendable* (1945). Terence Malick's *The Thin Red Line* (1998) is a powerful treatment of the experience of American troops on Guadalcanal.

Chapter 8: Defending the perimeter: Japan, 1942–1944

For individual battles in the second stage of the Pacific war there are Richard Frank, *Guadalcanal: The Definitive Account of the Landmark Battle* (New York: Penguin, 1990), and H. P. Willmott, *The Battle of Leyte Gulf: The Last Fleet Action* (Bloomington: Indiana University Press, 2005).

Daniel P. Marston, *Phoenix from the Ashes: The Indian Army in the Burma Campaign* (Westport: Greenwood Press, 2003), deals with an often neglected aspect of the war in Southeast Asia. See also the highly regarded memoirs of the British commander William Slim, *Defeat into Victory* (London: Cassell, 1956). *Germany and the Second World War*, vols. VI and VII, contain some useful material.

Chapter 9: The 'world ocean' and Allied victory, 1939–1945

Brian W. Blouet, *Global Geostrategy: Mackinder and the Defence of the West* (New York: Frank Cass, 2005), and Colin S. Gray and Geoffrey Sloan, eds., *Geopolitics, Geography and Strategy* (London: Frank Cass, 1999), provide a fuller discussion of geography. On Mahan see Philip A. Crowl, 'Alfred Thayer Mahan: The Naval Historian', in Paret, *Makers of Modern Strategy*, but also the recent reinterpretation, Jon Tetsuro Sumida, *Inventing Grand Strategy and Teaching Command: The Classic Works of Alfred Thayer Mahan Reconsidered* (Baltimore: Johns Hopkins University Press, 1999).

Dan Van der Vat, *The Atlantic Campaign: World War II's Great Struggle at Sea* (New York: Harper, 1988), provides a reasonably recent account. See also Jürgen Rohwer, *Axis Submarine Successes of World War Two: German, Italian and Japanese Submarine Successes, 1939–1945* (London: Greenhill, 1999), and *Germany and the Second World War*, vol. VI. For the submarine campaign in the Pacific see Clay Blair, *Silent Victory: The U.S. Submarine War against Japan* (Philadelphia: Lippincott, 1975), and Mark P. Parillo, *The Japanese Merchant Marine in World War II* (Annapolis, MD: Naval Institute Press, 1993).

The British official history, Catherine Behrens, *Merchant Shipping and the Demands of War* (London: HMSO, 1955), deal effectively with this complex topic. Supply, from a US perspective, is outlined in Richard M. Leighton and Robert W. Coakley, *Global Logistics and Strategy*, 2 vols. (Washington: OCMH, 1955, 1968).

The best evocation of the submarine war is perhaps the West German film by Wolfgang Peterson, *Das Boot* (1981), based on the book by Lothar-Günther Buchheim; this film was also released as a television mini-series in the mid 1980s. For the escort ships there is *The Cruel Sea* (1953), directed by Charles Frend from the novel (1951) of the same name by Nicholas Monsarrat. Excellent non-official websites devoted to the German submarine force and the convoy battles are www.uboat.net, and www.convoyweb.org.uk.

Chapter 10: The European periphery, 1940–1944

Douglas Porch, *Hitler's Mediterranean Gamble: The North African and the Mediterranean Campaigns in World War II* (London: Weidenfeld & Nicolson, 2004), and Simon Ball, *Bitter Sea: The Struggle for Mastery in the Mediterranean 1935–1949* (London: HarperCollins, 2009), deal with the war in southern Europe. See also *Germany and the Second World War*, vols. III, VI, and VII. A little-known subject is covered in Davide Rodogno, *Fascism's European Empire: Italian Occupation during the Second World War* (Cambridge: Cambridge University Press, 2006).

Jon Latimer, *Alamein* (Cambridge, MA: Harvard University Press, 2002), and Neil Barr, *Pendulum of War: Three Battles of Alamein* (London: Jonathan Cape, 2004), cover the later stages of the land war in North Africa. For the Americans see Rick Atkinson, *An Army at Dawn: The War in North Africa 1942–1943* (New York: Henry Holt, 2002), which won the Pulitzer Prize. Ralph Bennett, *Ultra and Mediterranean Strategy* (London: Hutchinson, 1989), covers an essential dimension.

The next phase in the Mediterranean is covered by Carlo D'Este, *Bitter Victory: The Battle for Sicily, July–August 1943* (New York: HarperPerennial, 1988), and the second part of Rick Atkinson's 'Liberation Trilogy', *The Day of Battle: The War in Sicily and Italy, 1943–1944* (New York: Henry Holt, 2007). Philip Morgan, *The Fall of Mussolini: Italy, the Italians, and the Second World War* (Oxford: Oxford University Press, 2007), looks at the critical events of 1943 from the other perspective.

Chapter 11: Wearing down Germany, 1942–1944

David MacIsaac, 'Voices from the Central Blue: Air Power Theorists', in Paret, *Makers of Modern Strategy*, is a useful short introduction. On the American side there is Michael Sherry, *The Rise of American Air Power: The Creation of Armageddon* (New Haven: Yale University Press, 1987). See also *Germany and the Second World War*, vols. V, VII, IX, and X.

The human impact and the moral dimension are now discussed in Jorg Friedrich, *The Fire: The Bombing of Germany, 1940–1945* (New York: Columbia University Press, 2006), and A. C. Grayling, *Among the Dead Cities: Was the Allied Bombing of Civilians in WWII a Necessity or a Crime?* (London: Bloomsbury, 2006).

Two classic films dealing with the bomber crews are Henry King's *Twelve O'Clock High* (1949), and Michael Anderson's *The Dam Busters* (1955); the more recent *Memphis Belle* (1990), directed by Michael Caton-Jones, is also a powerful recreation of the air war; it is based on William Wyler's 1944 documentary about a B-17 nicknamed 'Memphis Belle'.

There is a huge literature on the Resistance. Mark Mazower, *Hitler's Empire: Nazi Rule in Occupied Europe* (London: Allen Lane, 2008), presents an overall view of the European situation. Philip W. Blood, *Hitler's Bandit Hunters: The SS and the Nazi Occupation of Europe* (Dulles, VA: Potomac, 2006), focuses on the organs of repression.

Jørgen Hæstrup, *Europe Ablaze: An Analysis of the History of the European Resistance Movements, 1939–45* (Odense: Odense University Press, 1978), and Bob Moore, ed., *Resistance in Western Europe* (Oxford: Berg, 2000), provide an overall view. For insights into the politics of the movement in France, Italy, Yugoslavia, and Greece see Tony Judt, ed., *Resistance and Revolution in Mediterranean Europe, 1939–1948* (London: Routledge, 1989). For the Partisan movement in the USSR, two recent general sources are Kenneth Slepyan, *Stalin's Guerrillas: Soviet Partisans in World War II* (Lawrence: University Press of Kansas, 2006), and Leonid D. Grenkewich, *The Soviet Partisan Movement, 1941–1944* (New York: Frank Cass, 1999).

The British role in the organisation of the Resistance is set out in David Stafford, *Britain and European Resistance, 1940–1945* (London: Macmillan, 1980); W. J. M. Mackenzie, *The Secret History of SOE* (London: St Ermin's Press, 2000), is the in-house history, completed in 1948 but kept secret for fifty years.

One of the best films about occupation is Max Ophuls's two-part documentary, *The Sorrow and the Pity (Le Chagrin et la Pitié)* (1969), which focuses on the provincial French town of Clermont-Ferrand; a powerful film about collaboration is *Lacombe Lucien* (1974), directed by Louis Malle. For the struggle in the occupied USSR there is Elem Klimov's *Come and See (Idi i smotri)* (1985).

Chapter 12: Victory in Europe, 1944–1945

Carlo D'Este, *Eisenhower: Allied Supreme Commander* (London: Cassell, 2004), is a good biography of the Allied Supreme Commander. It is supplemented by Russell F. Weigley, *Eisenhower's Lieutenants: The Campaign of France and Germany, 1944–1945* (London: Sidgwick & Jackson, 1981). Nigel Hamilton, *Monty*, 3 vols. (London: Hamish Hamilton, 1981–6), covers British Field Marshal Montgomery. See also *Germany and the Second World War*, vol. VII, and (forthcoming in translation) vol. X.

Carlo D'Este, *Decision in Normandy* (New York, HarperPerennial, 1994), and John Keegan, *Six Armies in Normandy* (London: Jonathan Cape, 1982), cover the D-Day invasion. The important intelligence background is developed in Ralph Bennett, *Ultra in the West* (London: Hutchinson, 1979).

The Caen Memorial (*Le Mémorial de Caen*) is a museum based in Normandy, but one which covers conflict broadly: see the website, www.memorial-caen.fr.

On the last-ditch defence see David K. Yelton, *Hitler's Volkssturm: The Nazi Militia and the Fall of Germany, 1944–1945* (Lawrence: University Press of Kansas, 2002), Alastair Noble, *Nazi Rule and the Soviet Offensive in Eastern Germany, 1944–1945: The Darkest Hour* (Eastbourne: Sussex Academic Press, 2008), and Anthony Beevor, *Berlin: The Downfall, 1945* (London: Penguin, 2003).

Gabriel Kolko, *The Politics of War: The World and United States Foreign Policy, 1943–1945* (New York: Random House, 1968), is a revisionist treatment of the wartime run-up to the Cold War. For a rather different and better-informed interpretation see Vojtech Mastny, *Russia's Road to the Cold War: Diplomacy, Warfare, and the Politics of Communism, 1941–1945* (New York: Columbia University Press, 1979). Wilson D. Miscamble, *From Roosevelt to Truman: Potsdam, Hiroshima, and the Cold War* (Cambridge: Cambridge University Press, 2007), is recent detailed account of the events of 1945.

Mention should be made of the gripping television ten-part mini-series 'Band of Brothers' (2001), produced by Stephen Spielberg and Tom Hanks for HBO, and based on Stephen Ambrose, *Band of Brothers, E Company, 506th Regiment, 101st Airborne: From Normandy to Hitler's Eagle's Nest* (New York: Simon & Schuster, 1992). Two of the best depictions of large-scale land warfare in Europe are *The Longest Day* (1962), a star-studded account of D-Day, and *A Bridge Too Far* (1977), which deals with the Battle of Arnhem. Both are based on books by Cornelius Ryan; *The Longest Day* was published in 1959 and *A Bridge Too Far* in 1974. A depiction of the last days in the Berlin bunker is *Downfall* (*Der Untergang*) (2004), a German/Austrian film directed by Oliver Hirschbiegel, which features a striking performance by Bruno Ganz as Hitler.

Chapter 13: End and beginning in Asia, 1945

For a recent general account see Richard B. Frank, *Downfall: The End of the Imperial Japanese Empire* (New York: Random House, 1999). Yukiko Koshiro, 'Eurasian Eclipse: Japan's End Game in World War II', *American Historical Review* 109:2 (2004), pp. 417–444, is a recent reinterpretation from a Japanese perspective.

Michael Hogan, ed., *Hiroshima in History and Memory* (Cambridge: Cambridge University Press, 1996), and J. Samuel Walker, *Prompt and Utter Destruction: Truman and the Use of Atomic Bombs against Japan* (Chapel Hill: University of North Carolina Press, 2004), provide background to the nuclear attacks. Many relevant primary sources are available on line through the site of the National Security Archive (George Washington University): 'The Atomic Bomb and the End of World War II: A Collection of Primary Sources': www.gwu.edu/~nsarchiv/NSAEBB/NSAEBB162/index.htm.

A thoughtful overview, which uses new documents to highlight Russia's involvement, is Tsuyoshi Hasegawa, *Racing the Enemy: Stalin, Truman, and the Surrender of Japan* (Cambridge, MA: Belknap Press, 2005). The best detailed study of the neglected Soviet military campaign against Japan is David M. Glantz, *Soviet Operational and Tactical Combat in Manchuria, 1945: August Storm* (London: Frank Cass, 2003).

For post-war Southeast Asia there is Christopher Bayly and Tim Harper, *Forgotten Wars: The End of Britain's Asian Empire* (London: Allen Lane, 2007).

One of the most bitter island battles of the war is sensitively depicted in two films directed by Clint Eastwood, *Flags of Our Fathers* (2006), and *Letters from Iwo Jima* (2006); the first tells the story from an American perspective, and the second from a Japanese one. The feature film *The Sun* (2005), made by the Russian director Aleksandr Sokurov, presents a remarkable portrait of the Japanese Emperor as the war ended and the occupation began.

Conclusion

For the post-war world in Europe see Istvan Deak, Jan T. Gross, and Tony Judt, *The Politics of Retribution in Europe: World War II and its Aftermath* (Princeton: Princeton University Press, 2000). Frank Biess, *Homecomings: Returning POWs and the Legacies of Defeat in Postwar Germany* (Princeton: Princeton University Press, 2006), provides an interesting perspective. On Stalin's USSR see Elena Zubkova, *Russia after the War* (Armonk, NY: M. E. Sharpe, 1998).

John W. Dower, *Embracing Defeat: Japan in the Wake of World War II* (London: Allen Lane, 1999), and Dale M. Hellegers, *We, the Japanese People: World War II and the Origins of the Japanese Constitution* (Stanford: Stanford University Press, 2001), cover post-war Japan.

There is an extensive literature on the post-war trials, including Guénaël Mettraux, ed., *Perspectives on the Nuremberg Trial* (Oxford: Oxford University Press, 2008). For the trials in the Far East see Neil Boister and Robert Cryer, *The Tokyo International Military Tribunal: A Reappraisal* (Oxford: Oxford University Press, 2008), and Richard H. Minear, *Victor's Justice: The Tokyo War Crimes Trial* (Princeton: Princeton University Press, 1971).

Notes

Introduction

1 *Akten zur deutschen auswärtigen Politik*, 1918–1945, Serie D, Band XI/1 (Bonn: Hermes, 1964), pp. 175–6.
2 John Baylis and Steve Smith, eds., *The Globalization of World Politics: An Introduction to International Relations* (Oxford: Oxford University Press, 2005), p. 8.
3 Statement of Prince Konoe, 22 December 1938, *Documents on British Foreign Policy*, Third Series, vol. VIII (London: HMS0, 1955), p. 343.
4 George McJimsey, ed., *Documentary History of the Franklin D. Roosevelt Presidency* (Bethesda, MD: University Publications of America, 2001), vol. IX, p. 11.
5 Jørgen Hæstrup, *Europe Ablaze: An Analysis of the History of the European Resistance Movements, 1939–45* (Odense: Odense University Press, 1978), p. 494.

Chapter 1: The world in 1937

1 Georgi Dimitrov, *The Diary of Georgi Dimitrov, 1933–1949*, ed. Ivo Banac (New Haven: Yale University Press, 2003), p. 65.
2 Arthur S. Link, ed., *The Papers of Woodrow Wilson* (Princeton: Princeton University Press, 1983), vol. 41, p. 525.
3 Declaration by the United Nations, 1 January 1942, *A Decade of American Foreign Policy, The Avalon Project: Documents in Law, History and Diplomacy*, at http://avalon.law.yale.edu.
4 I. V. Stalin, *Sochineniia* (Moscow: GIPL, 1951), vol. XIII, p. 39.
5 Benito Mussolini, 'What is Fascism, 1932' (*sic*), *Modern History SourceBook*, at www.fordham.edu/halsall/mod/modsbook.html.
6 Atlantic Charter, 14 August 1941, *The Avalon Project: Documents in Law, History and Diplomacy*, at http://avalon.law.yale.edu; I. V. Stalin, O Velikoi Otechestvennoi voiny Sovetskogo Soiuza, 5th edn. (Moscow: GIPL, 1951), pp. 42f.
7 Proclamation, 26 July 1945, Potsdam Conference, *The Avalon Project: Documents in Law, History and Diplomacy*, at http://avalon.law.yale.edu.
8 Joint Press Conference at Casablanca, 24 January 1942, *The American Presidency Project*, at www.presidency.ucsb.edu.

9 Quoted in Edward L. Dreyer, *China at War, 1901–1949* (London: Longman, 1995), p. 172.

10 'Mr Baldwin on Aerial Warfare', *The Times*, 11 November 1932, p. 7, at www.galeuk.com/times.

Chapter 2: Japan and China, 1937–1940

1 Quoted in Dick Wilson, *When Tigers Fight: The Story of the Sino–Japanese War, 1937–1945* (Harmondsworth: Penguin, 1983), p. 66.

2 Kellogg–Briand Pact, 27 August 1928, *The Avalon Project: Documents in Law, History and Diplomacy*, at http://avalon.law.yale.edu.

3 Fundamental Principles of National Policy, August 1936, in 'Political Strategy Prior to Outbreak of War', Japanese Monograph No. 144, Appendix 1, at www.ibiblio.org/pha/monos/144/144app01.html.

4 Anti-Comintern Pact, 25 November 1936, *The Avalon Project: Documents in Law, History and Diplomacy*, at http://avalon.law.yale.edu.

Chapter 3: Hitler's border wars, 1938–1939

1 *Time*, 25 September 1939, at www.time.com/time/magazine/article/0,9171,761969–2,00.html.

2 International Military Tribunal for Germany, Hossbach Memorandum, *The Avalon Project: Documents in Law, History and Diplomacy*, at http://avalon.law.yale.edu.

3 Minutes of a Conference on 23 May 1939, in Roderick Stackelberg and Sally A. Winkle, eds. *The Nazi Germany Sourcebook: An Anthology of Texts* (London: Routledge, 2002), p. 232.

4 The Führer's Speech, 22 August 1939, in *ibid.*, p. 245.

5 Georgi Dimitrov, *The Diary of Georgi Dimitrov, 1933–1949*, ed. Ivo Banac (New Haven: Yale University Press, 2003), p. 115.

6 *Ibid.*, p. 116.

Chapter 4: Germany re-fights World War I, 1939–1940

1 *Dokumenty vneshnei politiki 1939 goda*, 2 vols. (Moscow: Mezhdunarodnye otnosheniia, 1992), vol. II, p. 137.

2 Max Domarus, *Hitler: Speeches and Proclamations, 1932–1945*; vols. III–IV of *The Chronicle of a Dictatorship* (Mundelein, IL: Bolchazy-Carducci, 1996, vol. III, p. 1754.

3 Viscount Alanbrooke, *War Diaries 1939–1945*, ed. Alex Danchev and Daniel Todman (London: Weidenfeld & Nicolson, 2001), p. 59.

4 Walther Hubatsch, ed., *Hitlers Weisungen für die Kriegführung 1939–1945: Dokumente der Oberkommando der Wehrmacht* (Frankfurt: Bernard & Graefe, 1962), p. 61.
5 Domarus, *Hitler*, vol. III, p. 2026.

Chapter 5: Wars of ideology, 1941–1942

1 Joseph Goebbels, *Goebbels Reden 1932–1945* (Düsseldorf: Droste Verlag, 1972), p. 176.
2 Adolf Hitler, *Hitlers Politisches Testament: Die Bormann Diktate von February und April 1945* (Hamburg: Albrecht Krause, 1981), pp. 78f.
3 Walther Hubatsch, ed., *Hitlers Weisungen für die Kriegführung 1939–1945: Dokumente der Oberkommando der Wehrmacht* (Frankfurt: Bernard & Graefe, 1962), p. 84 (emphasis original).
4 F. Chuev, ed., *140 besed s Molotovym: Iz dnevnika F. Chueva* (Moscow: Terra, 1991), p. 35.
5 Jürgen Förster and Evan Mawdsley, 'Hitler and Stalin in Perspective: Secret Speeches on the Eve of Barbarossa', *War in History* 11:1 (2004), pp. 101f.
6 Franz Halder, *Kriegstagebuch* (Stuttgart: Kohlhammer), vol. III, p. 170.
7 Quoted in Earl F. Ziemke and Magna Bauer, *Moscow to Stalingrad: Decisions in the East* (Washington: Center of Military History, 1987), p. 296.
8 Förster and Mawdsley, 'Hitler and Stalin', p. 75.
9 Roderick Stackelberg and Sally A. Winkle, eds., *The Nazi Germany Sourcebook: An Anthology of Texts* (London: Routledge, 2002), p. 229.
10 Martin Gilbert, ed., *The Churchill War Papers* (London: Heinemann, 2000), vol. III, p. 1102.
11 Elke Fröhlich, ed., *Die Tagebücher von Joseph Goebbels* (Munich: Saur, 1996), Part 2, vol. II, pp. 498f.

Chapter 6: The Red Army versus the Wehrmacht, 1941–1944

1 H. Greiner and P. Schramm, eds., *Kriegstagebuch des Oberkommandos der Wehrmacht*, 4 vols. (Frankfurt: Bernard & Graefe, 1961–79), vol. I, pp. 1084f.
2 Quoted in Earl F. Ziemke and Magna Bauer, *Moscow to Stalingrad: Decisions in the East* (Washington: Center of Military History, 1987), p. 172.
3 Speech of 8 November 1942, in Max Domarus, ed., *Hitler: Speeches and Proclamations, 1932–1945* (Wauconda, IL: Bolchazy-Carducci, 1988), vol. IV, p. 2701.
4 Helmut Heiber and David M. Glantz, eds., *Hitler and His Generals: Military Conferences 1942–1945* (New York: Enigma Books, 2002), p. 28.
5 Greiner and Schramm, *Kriegstagebuch*, vol. III, part 2, pp. 1425.

Chapter 7: Japan's lunge for empire, 1941–1942

1 Nobutaka Ike, ed., *Japan's Decision for War: Records of the 1941 Policy Conference* (Stanford: Stanford University Press, 1967), p. 78.

Chapter 8: Defending the perimeter: Japan, 1942–1944

1 *Foreign Relations of the United States: The Conferences at Washington, 1941–1942, and Casablanca, 1943* (Washington: US GPO, 1968), p. 214.
2 *Reports of General MacArthur*, vol. II, Part 1, p. 32 n. 14, US Army Center of Military History, at http://www.history.army.mil.

Chapter 9: The 'world ocean' and Allied victory, 1939–1945

1 Cited in W. N. Medlicott, *The Economic Blockade* (London: HMSO, 1952), vol. I, p. 666.
2 Adam Roberts and Richard Guelff, eds., *Documents on the Laws of War*, 3rd edn (Oxford: Oxford University Press, 2000), p. 171.
3 Churchill to Roosevelt, 7 December 1940, in Warren F. Kimball, ed., *Churchill and Roosevelt: The Complete Correspondence* (Princeton: Princeton University Press, 1984), vol. I, p. 103.
4 'On Maintaining Freedom of the Seas', 11 September 1941, Franklin D. Roosevelt Library and Museum, at www.fdrlibrary.marist.edu/091141.html.
5 German Declaration of War with the United States, 11 December 1941, *The Avalon Project: Documents in Law, History and Diplomacy*, at http://avalon.law.yale.edu.

Chapter 10: The European periphery, 1940–1944

1 *Parliamentary Debates*, 5th Series, vol. 385, p. 28 (11 November 1942).

Chapter 11: Wearing down Germany, 1942–1944

1 Walther Hubatsch, ed., *Hitlers Weisungen für die Kriegführung 1939–1945: Dokumente der Oberkommando der Wehrmacht* (Frankfurt: Bernard & Graefe, 1962), p. 184.
2 Quoted in Adam Tooze, *The Wages of Destruction: The Making and Breaking of the Nazi Economy* (London: Allen Lane, 2006), p. 606.
3 I. V. Stalin, *O Velikoi Otechestvennoi voiny Sovetskogo Soiuza*, 5th edn (Moscow: GIPL, 1951), p. 33.
4 Charles Webster and Noble Frankland, *The Strategic Air Offensive against Germany, 1939–1945* (London: HMSO, 1961), vol. IV, p. 273.

5   Hugh Dalton, *The Fateful Years: Memoirs 1931–1945* (London: Frederick Muller, 1957), p. 366; M. R. D. Foot, *SOE in France: An Account of the Work of the British Special Operations Executive in France: 1940–1944* (London: Whitehall History Publishing / Frank Cass, 2004), p. 9.
6   Stalin, *O Velikoi Otechestvennoi voiny Sovetskogo Soiuza*, p. 46.

Chapter 12: Victory in Europe, 1944–1945

1   B. H. Liddell Hart, ed., *The Rommel Papers* (London: Collins, 1953), pp. 486–7.
2   Max Domarus, ed., *The Chronicle of a Dictatorship*, vols. III and IV: *Hitler: Speeches and Proclamations 1932–1945* (Mundelein, IL: Bolchazy-Carducci, 1996), vol. III, p. 1755.
3   Michael Geyer, 'Insurrectionary Warfare: The German Debate about a *Levée en Masse* in October 1918', *Journal of Modern History* 73 (2001), p. 509.

Chapter 13: End and beginning in Asia, 1945

1   Proclamation, 26 July 1945, Potsdam Conference, *The Avalon Project: Documents in Law, History and Diplomacy*, at http://avalon.law.yale.edu.
2   Statement by the President, 6 August 1945, Public Papers of the Presidents, in John T. Woolley and Gerhard Peters, *The American Presidency Project*, at www.presidency.ucsb.edu.
3   Note of 10 August 1945, in Department of State *Bulletin*, 13:320 (12 August 1945), p. 205.
4   Note of 11 August 1945, in *ibid.*, p. 206.
5   Imperial Rescript on Surrender, 15 August 1945, in David J. Lu, *Japan: A Documentary History* (Armonk, NY: M. E. Sharpe, 1997), vol. II, pp. 457f.
6   Quoted in Herbert P. Bix, *Hirohito and the Making of Modern Japan* (New York: Perennial, 2001), p. 530.
7   I. V. Stalin, *Sochineniia* (Stanford: Hoover Institution, 1967), vol. II (15), p. 214.

Chapter 14: Conclusion

1   Winston S. Churchill, 'The Hour of Our Greatest Effort is Approaching', in *Dawn of Liberation: War Speeches* (London: Cassell, 1945), p. 41.
2   Richard Overy, *Why the Allies Won* (London: Pimlico, 1995), p. 325.
3   Mark Harrison, ed., *The Economics of World War II: Six Powers in International Comparison* (Cambridge: Cambridge University Press, 1998), pp. 1f.; I. V. Stalin, *O Velikoi Otechestvennoi voiny Sovetskogo Soiuza*, 5th edn (Moscow: GIPL, 1951), pp. 42f.
4   Eric Hobsbawm, *The Age of Extremes: The Short Twentieth Century, 1914–1991* (London: Abacus, 1995), p. 176.

5 Excerpt in Richard Hofstadter, ed., *Great Issues in American History: From Reconstruction to the Present Day, 1864–1969* (New York: Vintage Books, 1969), pp. 450f.

6 'On Protracted War', in *Selected Works of Mao Tse-tung* (Peking: Foreign Languages Press, 1960), vol. II, p. 131.

Index